Connect the
Testaments

Connect the
Testaments

A 365-Day Devotional with Bible Reading Plan

John D. Barry and Rebecca Van Noord

LEXHAM PRESS

Connect the Testaments: A 365-Day Devotional with Bible Reading Plan

Copyright 2014 Lexham Press

Lexham Press, 1313 Commercial St., Bellingham, WA 98225
LexhamPress.com

Standard Paperback Edition ISBN 978-1-57-799582-1
Hardcover Gift Edition ISBN 978-1-57-799564-7

Lead Editor: Rebecca Brant
Assistant Editors: Lynnea Fraser, Jennifer Hendrix, Elliot Ritzema, Britt Rogers, Abigail Stocker, and Elizabeth Vince
Cover Design: Patrick Fore
Interior Design and Typesetting: Katherine Lloyd, The DESK

In honor of Brevard Childs
Who was dedicated to connecting the Testaments for Christ
and teaching others to do the same.
Who restored a young man's love of the Spirit
in study within a single hour.

o o ◊ o o

"Herein lies the secret of interpretation …
wherever the Spirit is not present,
there is no great explanation possible."

—BREVARD CHILDS

Introduction

Connect the Testaments originated as a small idea about making big-picture connections: We wanted to create a Bible reading plan and devotional that offered biblical theology. We wanted to engage the dialogue of the biblical writers as they discussed ideas and themes across time and across the Testaments—to show how all of Scripture connects. We desired to see how God's ideas about life have been spoken about throughout the Bible.

However, it's often difficult to see what these conversations teach us about Jesus and how they apply to daily life. The text so often seems like it was meant for another time and people. To help you engage in this dialogue, we created this resource.

This 365-day devotional accompanies a Bible reading plan that includes daily passages from the Old Testament, New Testament, and poetic biblical literature. The reading plan takes you through the entire Bible via five perspectives: "beginnings" (e.g., Genesis and Matthew), "new beginnings" (e.g., Exodus and John), "spiritual renewal" (e.g., Deuteronomy and Paul's letters), "prophets" (e.g., Isaiah and Luke), and "historians/kingdom growth" (e.g., Samuel and Mark). Each devotional also identifies one to three focus passages from the overall daily reading, which we reflect on in the devotional.

Every day, you will encounter these connections for yourself and be prompted to apply what you learn to your own life.

May God bless you as you engage the dialogue of the biblical writers. And may this conversation help you focus on Jesus and live for Him.

—Rebecca Van Noord and John D. Barry,
Bellingham, Washington

BEGINNINGS

Genesis 1–2; Matthew 1–2; Ecclesiastes 1:1–5

In the beginning, God subdues the greatest symbol of chaos in the ancient world: the waters. He also creates light—something that the ancients thought ruled everything. Even darkness, which they deeply feared, is ruled by Him.

The ancients were in the middle, asking, "God, where are you in the *midst* of this chaotic world?" He answers them with a story about beginnings. In this story, we find that God establishes order in a chaotic world. He rules other gods. He rules the light. He rules the night. It's as if God says, "Why are you afraid? I'm here. I'm working it out."

Matthew 1–2 gives us another beginning—a child born in humble circumstances. But it's through this child, Jesus, that the world itself was first created. And that's not all: In Him and through Him everything is brought together. Chaos is made orderly: "Because all things in the heavens and on earth were created by him … and he himself is before all things, and in him all things are held together" (Col 1:16–17). If we want to truly understand our origins, we need this frame of reference.

Like the ancients, we too are in the middle. We worry that evil and chaos will reign, but we must let Christ take control. He can bring order to our unruly lives. We need a new beginning. In Genesis, God wants us to see Him taking back what He created—and that includes us. —JDB

What chaos do you fear? We often feel in the middle,
but our beginnings suggest that Christ is holding
everything together. What areas of your life need God's order?
Where do you need Christ to step in and hold together?

January 2

◦ ◦ ◊ ◦ ◦

SCRIPTURE FOR WAR OR PEACE?

Genesis 3–4; **Matthew 3–4**; Ecclesiastes 1:6–11

Like many people, I use Scripture to defend my views. But so does Satan. In Matthew 4, the devil says, "If you are the Son of God, throw yourself down, for it is written, 'He will command his angels concerning you'" (Matt 4:6, citing Psa 91:11–12). In turn, Jesus responds with Scripture: "Again, it is written, 'You are not to put the Lord your God to the test'" (Matt 4:7, citing Deut 6:16, coupled with Isa 7:12).

While the devil used Scripture for his own purposes, Jesus used it for God's. This teaches us that Scripture alone isn't enough: It must be contextualized and balanced with other Scripture.

This story raises the question, "Will we use Scripture to defend our own positions, or use it to defend God's?" It's easy to quote Scripture only to defend our personal theological position. Sometimes we are too focused on being right and not necessarily on helping other believers. However, while we might believe that being right *will* ultimately help them, it's possible that we're inhibiting the gospel message instead. We might even be the one driving them away.

Many of us have some relationships that are plagued by the need to be right or to use Scripture in our personal war. But that needs to change.

When we use Scripture for our own gains or battles, we are acting like Christ's tempter—not Christ. We might think that we are defending the gospel, but if it's not about Christ's virgin birth, suffering, death, resurrection, or continued presence in our lives, it's really not about the fundamental truths. It's about our battle—about what we want. Instead, let's act more like Christ. Let's use Scripture in the proper context, balancing it with other Scripture. —JDB

How do you need to change
the way you're using Scripture?

FINDING COMFORT IN A CYNIC'S WORDS

Genesis 5; Matthew 5; **Ecclesiastes 1:12–18**

"I have seen everything that is done under the sun, and behold, all is vanity and a striving after the wind" (Eccl 1:14). These aren't exactly the words you want to hear in the morning—look who woke up on the wrong side of the bed. The intention behind them, though, is actually quite comforting.

The Preacher in Ecclesiastes goes on to prove that he doesn't need counseling, but instead should be our counselor: "What is crooked cannot be made straight, and what is lacking cannot be counted … he who increases knowledge increases sorrow" (Eccl 1:15, 18). Although we may want to deny this fact, it's a truism that haunts all great people: We may help the hurting people in our world, but we will never be able to end the pain, and knowledge alone will not get us there. Words on paper are not the solution. A manifesto, like the *Declaration of Independence*, may prompt great change, but what is it without action? It is vanity. It's a striving after the wind.

Delusions of importance have crushed many great people's efforts. In fact, I would go so far as to say that it's what keeps most people from becoming what God wants them to be. And it's not just the delusion of grandeur; it's the delusion of insignificance or the distraction of focus. You become what you do, and what you think, write, speak, or feel is meaningless if it's not what you do.

We as Christians are meant to act. As Jesus says, "You are the salt of the earth. But if salt becomes tasteless, by what will it be made salty? It is good for nothing any longer except to be thrown outside and trampled under foot by people" (Matt 5:13). If we are salt, let's be salty. If we are light, let's shine brightly (Matt 5:14). Anything other than that is vain. It's searching for knowledge for knowledge's sake. It leaves both us and the world empty.

There is comfort to be found in the Preacher of Ecclesiastes' words in that he is telling us, albeit through harshness and well-put cynicism, that we're meant for more than we usually recognize. He calls us to rise to that: to shun the unimportant and focus on God's work. What good is wisdom and knowledge if it's not for that purpose? —JDB

What are you currently delusional about?
What's vain that you're doing that God wishes for you to change?

LISTEN, BUILD, AND LISTEN AGAIN

Genesis 6–7; Matthew 6:1–7:11; Ecclesiastes 2:1–11

More often than not, what we want is not what God wants. We desire wealth, notoriety, or influence. In our ambition, we can lose sight of the very God who created us.

In the story of Noah and the flood, we see the same dichotomy: the world wants one thing and God desires another. The two aren't congruent. In this case, selfishness has led to catastrophic levels of evil: "Now the earth was corrupt in God's sight, and the earth was filled with violence … all flesh had corrupted their way on earth" (Gen 6:11–12). So God tells Noah that He is through—He's going to end it all. But Noah and his family will be spared if they're obedient to God's will.

Noah listens; he builds the ark. And God honors his work by closing the door (Gen 7:16). He's there at the end, sealing the deal. Being faithful means getting an opportunity to witness the power of God.

When our ambitions aren't guided by God's will and *His* goals, the result can mean corruption or corrupting others. We might wonder how we got there, but in reality, we know how it happened: Selfishness is to blame.

Instead of doing things our way, we must listen, build what God wants, and then listen again. We have a choice: We can seek our own ambitions— like wisdom or knowledge—or we can choose Christ's way, realizing that "in much wisdom is much vexation, and [that the one] who increases knowledge increases sorrow" (Eccl 1:18).

Ambition alone does not offer a happy ending. The only ending that results in joy is the one that focuses on God's kingdom and His desires. Rather than justify our current desires, we should acknowledge the dichotomy and the problem. Individual ambition may result in selfish desires, but a focus on Christ will result in blessings: "Blessed are the peacemakers for they will be called sons of God" (Matt 5:9). —JDB

What ambitions need to be set aside in your life?
In what ways do you need to refocus your life on Christ's goals?

∘◇∘◇∘

DECISIONS ARE VEXING, BUT THERE'S AN ANSWER

Genesis 8–9; **Matthew 7:12–8:34**; Ecclesiastes 2:12–17

Finding the right path to take in life is an ongoing challenge. It's easy to flail in the realm of possibility rather than face the realities in front of us. Waiting upon the LORD is no easy virtue.

Jesus tells us, "Enter through the narrow gate, because broad is the gate and spacious is the road that leads to destruction … narrow is the gate and constricted is the road that leads to life" (Matt 7:13–14).

Although these lines are a proclamation of how we enter God's kingdom—how we choose salvation—they're also a proclamation of how we continue to live for God's kingdom. Whatever decision we face, and whatever odds are against us, there is only one solution: following God's narrow path. He has a providential way, a primary way for us, and we are asked to follow it. When we do, we're gifted with the understanding that God is using us in the way He saw most fitting to make the most difference for others.

In Genesis 8:1–9:17, we're shown how God honored Noah because Noah decided to follow God's plans for his and his family's lives. If we're willing to follow God's calling, He will work in the same way in our lives. He has a plan for each of us, and although the blessings may come after great trial (like far too long on a boat with smelly animals), they will come—in this life or the next. —JDB

What is God calling you to? What do you need to do today
to respond accordingly? (If you don't know yet, pray.
And if you do know, continue to pray.)

I DID IT MY WAY

Genesis 10–11; Matthew 9; Ecclesiastes 2:18–26

Frank Sinatra was wrong to do things "his way." In Genesis 11, we see people uniting in building what seems like a great triumph of humanity—until we realize what their work is all about. They're tired of being distant from God, so they build a structure that will reach the heavens.

"Surely the gods will know and find us now. … Let's meet our maker," you can almost hear them say. But the true God, Yahweh, knows their plan and says, "Come, let us go down and there confuse their language, so that they may not understand one another's speech" (Gen 11:7). Because all the people spoke one language, they were dangerous to themselves. In the unity of one world, there is disunity: We choose to assault the God we should serve.

There is an alternative—a unity that God desires, where we serve Him by serving others. Jesus describes how we should act toward one another and toward Him, even teaching us how to pray. With Christ, God has resolved the reason the tower was attempted. Since the Holy Spirit came and brought us comfort (John 16:4–15), the very presence of God is always with us.

Sinatra also said that if a man doesn't have himself, "then he has naught." But God wants us to stop focusing on ourselves, building towers, and trying to do things our own way. He wants us to seek Him, and to treat others with the love, respect, and self-sacrifice that Christ gave us. He wants us to do things His way. —JDB

What towers are you building?
What type of investments should you be making instead?

A TIME FOR EVERYTHING

Genesis 12–13; Matthew 10; **Ecclesiastes 3:1–8**

"For everything there is a season, and a time for every matter under heaven" (Eccl 3:1). The Bible's most famous poem has inspired writers for generations, yet has not been improved upon. In a few short, simple lines, the Preacher ponders the whole of life: birth, death, weeping, laughing, mourning, dancing, breaking down, and building up. The buoyancy and familiarity of the text could cause us to gloss over the poetic brilliance of "the matter[s] under heaven." But when we get to "a time to hate" and "a time to kill," the romance is—well, killed. Are all these emotions and events really *ordained* by God? The strength of the poem is in contrast and repetition. By laying the seasons side by side, the Preacher effectively captures the span and cycle of human life. He isn't providing a list of experiences that we should check off our holistic life to-do list. Rather, he is emphasizing an absolute need for reliance on God.

Although evil seems to wield power in our lives and in the lives of those around us, God is present. He is there when we experience delights, and He is present when tragedy and sin overwhelm us. When we experience the death of those we love, send a soldier off to war, or experience hate, we can know that God is still making Himself known to fallen people in a fallen world.

We must pray for the Spirit to help us judge the seasons and respond appropriately to Him—with wisdom, like the Preacher advocates. We can live confidently, because "He has put eternity into man's heart" (Eccl 3:11). Nothing assures us more of this than His provision of a way out of life's seasons through His Son. —RVN

What season of life are you currently in? How are you helping friends
in difficult seasons? How are you celebrating with friends
in joyful seasons? How can you bring the good news
of Christ to bear in both situations?

JUDGING THE TIME AND SEASONS

Genesis 14–15; **Matthew 11**; **Ecclesiastes 3:9–15**

We often have difficulty judging the events in our lives and then responding appropriately. Although God has placed eternity "in our hearts," we
don't know the reason or the outcome of our life's events (Eccl 3:11).

The danger comes in being known for only one mode of operation and
one response for all seasons. In Matthew 11, Jesus speaks to a generation who
responds in one way—with skepticism and unbelief. Those who judge see John
the Baptist as a demon-possessed man rather than a prophet. They see Jesus as
a glutton, a drunkard, and a friend of tax collectors and sinners—not the one
who has come to save them from their sins.

Jesus illustrates their responses with a tale. He compares them to children
who call out to each other in the marketplaces, saying, "We played the flute for
you and you did not dance; we sang a lament and you did not mourn" (Matt
11:17). Those who hear and fail to act confuse the writer of Ecclesiastes' times
of mourning and dancing. They don't acknowledge the judgment of John the
Baptist or the joy of Jesus.

For those in His audience who refused to acknowledge His words and miracles, Jesus pronounces a judgment far worse than that against Sodom. Those
who respond with humility and faith, however, have the promise of rest. Jesus
invites them: "Take my yoke on you and learn from me, for I am gentle and
humble in heart, and you will find rest for your souls" (Matt 11:29).

This response is an act of faith. We need to rely on God's Word and His
Spirit to judge the events of our lives and to help us respond with faith. —RVN

What response are you known for?

NOTEWORTHY STORIES

Genesis 16–17; Matthew 12; Ecclesiastes 3:16–22

When God's promises are lavished on Abram in Genesis, we can't help but feel a bit surprised. It seems undeserved—mainly because we know nothing about Abram. We haven't had a chance to weigh his wisdom or foolishness, something Ecclesiastes endorses. Yet God promises to make Abram's children (a blessing in the ancient Near East) as numerous as the stars in the sky. "I will make your name great," He says. "I will make you a great nation." He also promises protection: "I am your shield." Even after the fact, God doesn't disclose why He wants to bless and protect Abram.

The greater context of the Genesis narrative shows that God's blessing is certainly not just about Abram. In Genesis 12, just before God promises to give Abram a great name, a nation, and land, He had scattered the nations over all the earth. At the Tower of Babel, God dispersed those who were grasping for a relationship with Him on their own terms.

But God doesn't leave humanity this way. He presents Abram with a promise and a gift—a plan of salvation for humanity. God re-establishes relationship on His terms.

What about Abram, then? His faith is renowned throughout Scripture (Gal 3:6; Rom 4:9; Heb 11:8–12), but it's not because he did anything particularly noteworthy—at times he even deceives others (e.g., Gen 12:10–20). It's because of his response to God's particularly noteworthy promises: "He believed the Lord, and he counted to him as righteousness" (Gen 15:6). He responded to God's promises with faith, and God counted it as righteousness.

In Christ, we have an even greater promise and a greater hope. God has lavished promise and deliverance on us. We can only stand in complete awe of His goodness and respond with trust. —RVN

Do you rest too much in your own work or failings?
In what ways can you shift the emphasis to Christ's work?

January 10

∘ ◦ ◊ ◦ ∘

WHAT KIND OF HEARER ARE YOU?

Genesis 18–19:29; **Matthew 13:1–43**; Ecclesiastes 4:1–7

While parables were often told to make truth tangible, in Matthew 13, we find that this wasn't always the case. When His disciples question why He speaks in parables, Jesus quotes the prophet Isaiah: "For the heart of this people has become dull, and with their ears they hear with difficulty, and they have shut their eyes, so that they would not see with their eyes and hear with their ears and understand with their heart and turn, and I would heal them" (Matt 13:15).

This is the case in the parable of the Sower and the Seed. The seed hits the open path, the rocky ground, the thorns, and the good soil, and Jesus describes four hearers who receive the good news in different ways. We should examine this parable and ask ourselves, "What kind of hearer am I?"

Do we seek to really understand the gospel? When we hear it told again and again, does it merely lie on the surface as commonplace? When our faith is put to the test, do we find ourselves putting hope in everything else but the good news? Or, when we become anxious about the cares of this world, do we find ourselves grasping for a firm foundation that isn't there?

The seed that falls on the good soil describes a completely different reception. This hearer receives the word and "hears it and understands it." It doesn't stop there, however. The hearer is also known for his good works, which display a heart that has been changed. These hearers bear fruit according to what they have been given: "But what was sown on the good soil—this is the one who hears the word and understands it, who indeed bears fruit and produces, this one a hundred times as much, and this one sixty, and this one thirty" (Matt 13:23).

Jesus emphasizes that the pursuit of Him isn't lethargic, or merely emotional, and it isn't cerebral. It involves pursuing Him with all of our being—in a posture of humility, with an ear that hears and a life that is changed. It involves complete surrender to His will. —RVN

What is your posture before God? Do you come
with humility—ready to hear the good news?

THE KINGDOM OF HEAVEN IS LIKE ...

Genesis 19:30–21:21; **Matthew 13:44–14:36**; Ecclesiastes 4:8–16

Few in the world have sold everything to pursue an idea. Yet Jesus claims those who discover the kingdom of heaven are willing to do so. "The kingdom of heaven is like treasure hidden in a field, that a man found and concealed, and in his joy he goes and sells everything that he has and buys that field" (Matt 13:44). It seems that hardly any of us are equally willing to give up everything for the sake of the kingdom of heaven.

The realization that Jesus has brought the kingdom of heaven to earth presents us with a choice. Will we decide that His kingdom is worth more than all things, or will we devalue it by equating it with worldly treasures?

There are many types of currency, not just money: reputation, occupational status, and social media popularity are just a few. But the kingdom is much more than material or monetary ideas. It's about giving our gifts, thoughts, and wealth. It's about being willing to sacrifice everything when God asks.

Putting aside God's priorities in our lives can be far too easy—probably because He is not standing in front of us, nagging us to do His work. But there won't be another day to get around to God's work. Instead, those who believe in Christ (the righteous) will be separated from everyone else (the wicked). In the meantime, our job is to lead the "wicked" to the ways of Christ (Matt 13:44–50). We're called to do His work, day by day. And we're called to work as if we don't have another chance—as if nothing in the world is more valuable. —JDB

Is there anything more valuable to you than God's kingdom?
How can you realign your priorities?

FEAR GOD

Genesis 21:22–23:20; Matthew 15; **Ecclesiastes 5:1–7**

In Ecclesiastes 5, the author stops to consider God's place in the heavens and our place on earth. He acknowledges that there is a great gulf between who God is and who we *think* He is. This realization should affect our entire posture before Him.

"Guard your steps when you go to the house of God," he says. "Do not be rash with your mouth, nor let your heart be hasty to utter a word before God, for God is in heaven and you are on earth." Don't attempt to offer the "sacrifice of fools" with your lips, or even your heart, he adds. Instead, we should come prepared to listen (Eccl 5:1–3).

Coming to God ready to listen doesn't mean neglecting to bring our troubles or needs before Him. He wants us to do this—but not rashly. Rather, we should offer acknowledgement that He guides our lives. Like Rachel and Leah, in Genesis 30, we may sometimes use God to justify the pursuit of our own goals, rather than seek wisdom and guidance from Him.

It's an awesome thing to think that this very God who should be approached with such humility and reverence left His place in heaven and came down to earth. This God, who is so beyond our own comprehension, has chosen to dwell in us with His Spirit. The mighty God who rules heaven, earth, and the cosmos, and who breaches all understanding, has chosen to reveal Himself to sinners like us. —RVN

What is your attitude toward God?

AVOIDING THE UNAVOIDABLE

Genesis 24; **Matthew 16–17**; Ecclesiastes 5:8–11

It's common to put people in our lives on hold—even if we love them—until something forces us to pay attention. Forgetting those who are closest to us is a frightening thought. Peter, Jesus' disciple, likely realized that people were making a similar mistake in their relationship with Jesus.

In the district of Caesarea Philippi, Jesus asks His disciples, "Who do people say that the Son of Man is?" (Matt 16:13–14). At first, they respond with the expected: John the Baptist, Elijah, Jeremiah, and the prophets—suggesting that Jesus is an esteemed and powerful prophet, but not more. Then Jesus asks the are-you-paying-attention question: "But who do *you* say that I am?" (Matt 16:15).

Simon Peter understood this, blurting out, "You are the Christ, the Son of the living God!" (Matt 16:16). Jesus asked about the Son of Man, emphasizing His humanity; Peter responds by emphasizing both His status as the anointed one of God (the Christ) and His divinity, as God's Son (which also has kingly implications).

Caesarea Philippi was a place full of altars and idols to other deities. Caesar was worshiped and celebrated as god's son there. Peter, surrounded by people worshiping the king of the known world, calls *Jesus* king.

Jesus responds by affirming that God has revealed this to Peter. And He states that following Him means completely giving up ourselves and being willing to suffer like Christ did (Matt 16:24–25).

Just like a relationship with a spouse, parent, sibling, or friend, if we think Jesus is less than He is, we will inevitably misunderstand Him. And if we understand our relationship with Him to be anything less than life altering, we treat Him like someone we have fallen out of love with. The one who died for our sins wants and deserves so much more. —JDB

Who are you not noticing in your life that you should be?
What parts of your relationship with Christ are you overlooking?

UNEXPECTED RIVALRIES

Genesis 25; Matthew 18; Ecclesiastes 5:12–20

When in survival mode, you have to compete against anything that could hinder your survival. Strong competitors, like professional athletes, often can't explain their almost inhuman acts under pressure; adrenaline takes over. The same thing that the ancients used to escape from wild animals is what makes us win. Yet, for all the good that comes from a competitive survival instinct, it can result in ostracizing others. Esau and Jacob, the twin sons of Isaac and Rebekah, remind us of this.

From the prophecy of Yahweh forward, we know that they will be rivals: "Two nations are in your womb, and two peoples from within you shall be divided; the one shall be stronger than the other, the older shall serve the younger" (Gen 25:23). Yahweh didn't necessarily desire that the two would feud. A division doesn't always mean a strained relationship, and the word "divided" in Hebrew doesn't imply derision.

Those of us with siblings know how frustrating the relationships can be, but we also know that when siblings learn to appreciate each other, they can be a great support system and a comfort in times of need.

Like many siblings, Jacob and Esau are opposites: the older, red and hairy when born—per his name (Esau); and the younger, Jacob, grabbing his brother's heel—like his name: "He who takes by the heel," or idiomatically, "an ankle biter." Indeed, the ankle biter rules his brother, but his brother makes the choice for it to be so (Gen 25:29–34). Esau, when exhausted (and likely near death), gives in to his survival instincts, allowing his competitive brother to take charge.

There is no doubt that Jacob is a swindler. But aside from the scandal, this story teaches us something about Yahweh: When given something by Him, no amount of competitiveness makes it worth forfeiting. We never know the results of the poor decisions we make in times of destitution. Esau was unaware that his impulsive, perhaps angry actions would mean forfeiting his descendants' place later in God's kingdom. And Jacob didn't know that his zeal for winning and financial certainty would plague him for the remainder of his life. He may have been rich, for a while, but he wasn't happy or joyful. —JDB

What competitions do you need to give up? How is
competitiveness impeding your relationship with God and others?

January 15

∘ ∘ ◊ ∘ ∘

I UNDERSTAND HOW THEY FELT

Genesis 26; **Matthew 19:1–20:16**; Ecclesiastes 6:1–4

"Allow the children, and do not forbid them to come to me, for to such belongs the kingdom of heaven" (Matt 19:14). This is the type of Jesus I want to know. It's easy for me to think of Jesus as a man I see in film or in Renaissance paintings—to make Him somehow distant in the process—but this Jesus is very compassionate and close. This Jesus takes the lowest members in society and promotes them to the ultimate status of equality: heirs of the kingdom of heaven.

The disciples didn't understand this yet; instead they rebuke the people bringing their children to Jesus (Matt 19:14). The people bringing their children simply wanted Jesus to lay His healing hands on them and pray for them; the disciples saw a threat to Jesus' image. The image Jesus wanted to portray was the opposite.

It seems more often than not that I find myself worrying about what others think when I should be concerned about simply doing what these children were doing: scrambling to be close to my Lord, Jesus.

And that's precisely what the young man in the next passage learns: Jesus wants him to be willing to give up everything and follow Him (Matt 19:16–30). The man knows what he needs to know, but he doesn't feel about God the way Jesus desires for him to feel. Like the disciples, and like me, he is still in the process of recognizing what it means to follow Jesus.

For this reason, I'm seeking complete surrender to God—knowing that it's not what gets me into the kingdom, but what makes me live life in a way that honors the kingdom. —JDB

In what ways is God asking you to obediently follow?

SAVE US!

Genesis 27; **Matthew 20:17–21:22**; Ecclesiastes 6:5–12

"Hosanna to the Son of David! Blessed is the one who comes in the name of the Lord! Hosanna in the highest heaven!" (Matt 21:9). Idiomatically, this means: "Save [me], I pray, the Son of David. Blessed is the one who comes in the name of Yahweh! Save [me], I pray, by the highest!"

When the people shout these words about Jesus as He enters Jerusalem, they affirm His divinely appointed role and His ability to save them. And the original psalm that this phrase comes from is about their God, Yahweh. Perhaps the people understood Jesus as one with God (Psa 118:25–26).

As He enters Jerusalem, Jesus' actions align with Zech 9:9, which foretells of a savior-king who will enter on a donkey (Matt 21:5).

For first-century Jews, everything lined up to affirm Jesus as God's way of bringing salvation, and they responded to Him as such. This prompts several questions: How often do we see the alignment between what's happening and God's plan? How many parallels or opportunities do we miss? And how often do we forget to say "save me"?

Whenever possible, and just like the whole city of Jerusalem during Passover, we should be stirred to ask, "Who is this?" (Matt 21:10). —JDB

What do you currently need Jesus to save you from?
In what areas of life could you be missing out on Jesus' presence?
How can you make Him part of those areas of your life again?

CHEER UP, PREACHER

Genesis 28–29; Matthew 21:23–22:22; **Ecclesiastes 7:1–5**

Things are getting serious for the writer of Ecclesiastes ("the Preacher"), and sometimes confusing for us, as we follow him through the labyrinth of his discourse on the meaning of life. Death is better than birth, mourning is better than feasting, and sorrow is better than laughter? What happened to his "eat and drink and find enjoyment in all the toil" statements from earlier (Eccl 5:18)?

The Preacher might sound like he's contradicting himself, but the twist in his argument is meant to show us exactly what folly we may be inadvertently embracing. It's easy to brush over these verses while thinking in terms of standard, run-of-the-mill folly or obvious sins.

But folly can even look like a daily routine: goals, successes, and our happy, fulfilling lives. It can take the form of anything that skims the surface of life, but keeps us from confronting our greatest need and the reality of eternity.

When life is good, it's tempting to gloss over our need for God. Everything is going as planned, and it's easy to rely on ourselves—not on Him. But the Preacher wants us to address this temptation. It might take death, or times of extreme pain and sadness, to help us realize the truth. Only when we attend a funeral or lose a family member does the veneer start to chip; then, we get a glimpse of the turmoil bubbling under the surface. Only when we're convicted of our great need can we admit that we truly need a Savior. —RVN

Are your successes causing you to
diminish your need for Christ?

January 18

○ ◊ ○ ◊ ○

GIVING UP CONTROL

Genesis 30; Matthew 22:23–23:36; Ecclesiastes 7:6–12

We are born bent on our own ambitions. It's in our nature to control and compete. And pride—often the source of this behavior—keenly notices the pride of others. We often want to point out the failing of the equally prideful and impose our own wills on them, even as we neglect to see these traits in ourselves.

In Genesis 30, we find a myriad of characters who are bent on obtaining favor and selfish gain—often at the expense and exasperation of others. Rachel foolishly demands a son of Jacob (Gen 30:1) and then—because the family dynamics aren't complicated enough—she has her handmaid bear that child for her. When she finally obtains a son, she is not joyful—she is triumphant: "With mighty wrestlings I have wrestled with my sister and have prevailed" (Gen 30:8). Leah uses bribery and her own handmaid to gain the attention of her neglectful husband, while Laban and Jacob continue circling, using and manipulating one another (Gen 30:16, 25–36).

Though the battle is often with the other, ultimately the battle of wills ends with God. When we are bent on our own way with others, we don't think about the one who leads and directs our lives. In Genesis 30, God is the one who is in control of events. Only when He "listened to Leah" or "remembers" Rachel do they bear children (Gen 30:17, 22–23).

Our wills are actually battling His, not others'. The Great Commandment in Matthew 22 presents another approach and mode of operation: "You shall love the Lord your God with all your heart and with all your soul and with all your mind." If we first submit to this, the second will be easier: "You shall love your neighbor as yourself."

When we are right with God and we realize how patient He is with our weaknesses, we can learn to be patient with others. —RVN

How are you fighting for control of your life and the lives of others?
How can you seek to submit your own will to God in humility?

THE MILLION DOLLAR QUESTION

Genesis 31; Matthew 23:37–24:28; **Ecclesiastes 7:13–21**

"Why do bad things happen to good people?" This is an ancient question, though it's often asked as if it's new. The Preacher in Ecclesiastes says, "There is a righteous man who perishes in his righteousness, and there is a wicked man who prolongs his life in his evildoing" (Eccl 7:15).

Answers to this age-old question do exist. The simplest is that since people gave into temptation near the beginning, havoc—caused by humans and by evil spirits—has taken hold. The time between now and when God takes full control of the world again is just grace; the moment He does is the end for all evil, including those who have not chosen Christ as their Savior.

The only way to fix the world is to rid it of all evil, but the Preacher doesn't offer this deductive explanation. Instead, he notes that life is a series of balancing acts, and he uses hyperbole to make his point (Eccl 7:16–17).

The Preacher goes on to say, "For the one who fears God shall come out from both of them"—that is, the bad and good experiences (Eccl 7:18). The real answer to that age-old question is as profound as the original: learn to respect God.

We won't ever truly understand the complexities of good and evil, or the interactions of light and darkness—just like we will never understand our ever-changing universe. But there is solace in the knowledge that in the end, it's about respecting God. And the first step toward doing that is having a relationship with Christ. —JDB

In what ways are you currently not respecting
God's role in your life? How can you change that?

WHILE YOU ARE WAITING

Genesis 32–33; **Matthew 24:29–25:13**; Ecclesiastes 7:22–29

Jesus' instructions to His disciples about His return have inspired many to incorrectly predict His second coming. But if we read His parables, we find that they're not so focused on the future. Jesus prepares His disciples for His absence, and for the end times, because He wants them to be hopeful, expecting His return. He wants them to be ready and watchful. But He wants them to do all of these things by being fully engaged in the present, readying His kingdom.

Jesus' parable of the Wise and Wicked Servants demonstrates this attitude. While the faithful and wise servant provides for the master's household during his absence, the wicked servant uses the time flippantly: carousing and beating his fellow servants. When the master returns, the faithful servant is promoted for his service, and the wicked servant is punished. The parable presses the disciples to use their time wisely during Jesus' absence by doing the work they were called to do.

The same exhortation goes out to us. Will we act like lone Christians—content to live life disconnected from God's kingdom? Instead, we should be filled with hope, expectation, and overflowing with the good news. We should be willing to build up those around us, and attract those who have no hope.

As easy as it is to forget the eternal in our everyday lives, we can just as easily forget what God's work right now means for eternity. Being actively engaged in the present means spreading the good news and being involved in His work—using our gifts to nurture His coming kingdom. —RVN

Are you busy and active in God's kingdom now?
If not, what is keeping you from becoming so?

POWER, AUTHORITY, AND ITS RESULT

Genesis 34:1–35:15; Matthew 25:14–26:13; **Ecclesiastes 8:1–9**

We all struggle with the future and the vast uncertainty it creates in our minds. It's rarely the present that keeps us awake at night; it's our concerns about what will happen if the present changes for better or worse.

But unlike other places in the Bible when we're told not to worry, the words of Ecclesiastes 8:6 are set in the context of a request to obey the king of the land. This is not because the king has a solution to the problems, although he could potentially help, but because like many other things, there is nothing that can be done about him. Why worry about that which you cannot change?

This situation is equated to life and death itself: "No man has power to retain the spirit, or power over the way of death" (Eccl 8:8). The Preacher of Ecclesiastes then goes on to reflect the cultural reality of the time: "There is no discharge from war, nor will wickedness deliver those who are given to it." Again, what can you change about it? If the king is corrupt, it will destroy him like it will destroy others—it's only a matter of time. Wickedness has no power to deliver, only to destroy.

And this is most pressing for reflection: Sin is often cast as an escape from life's pains and sometimes feelings of meaninglessness, yet it really destroys life. (If only this reasoning was present in our thinking every time we were tempted.)

The Preacher of Ecclesiastes begins to draw his thoughts to a close by telling us: People's power over one another is "hurt" (Eccl 8:9). Here in a passage about the need for people to be governed (that's likely written by one in power), we see the author admit that power will inflict pain, or more literally "evil" or "badness."

This startling reality forms another realization: In a world that was meant to have God as its king and ruler—in a world where that power only shifted after people sinned and were no longer allowed in the presence of their creator—it makes sense that power would corrupt. But we're told: what can we do about it? The only thing we can do is to be people who choose to follow the good, the good God, and work toward the overthrowing of evil and the battle against corruption. But along the way, we must realize that worry and anxiety will only paralyze, not help. —JDB

What do you need to pray about that is a worry or anxiety of yours?
In what ways can you be an agent of change in the world,
without succumbing to the pains it can bring?

○ ○○○ ○

BE VIGILANT

Genesis 35:16–36:43; **Matthew 26:14–56**; Ecclesiastes 8:10–17

Faith doesn't always come to bear until we are faced with our own fallibility. When we "enter into temptation," it often means we haven't been vigilant—that we've stopped pursuing the God who has pursued us. In the aftermath of temptation, we recognize our spiritual laziness. We become wise—but remorsefully.

Vigilance and complacency are illustrated in the garden of Gethsemane. In His last moments, Jesus requests that His closest disciples stay awake with Him (Matt 26:38). But while He repeatedly prays, they fall asleep. What seems like a request for moral support gets defined a few verses later: "Stay awake and pray that you will not enter into temptation" (Matt 26:41). Staying awake is associated with spiritual awareness. And their sleep is costly. Because of their spiritual sleepiness, they're not prepared for His end, even though He had repeatedly prepared them for His death. They abandon Him, and they even deny Him (Matt 26:56; 75).

But in this same passage, we get a picture of what vigilance looks like from the Son of God. Jesus anticipated His imminent suffering and death. "Deeply grieved, to the point of death," He turns to the Father in prayer. Jesus boldly requests relief from suffering; when it is not granted, He submits to the Father's will.

Being vigilant means seeking guidance and refuge from the God who provides it. He has provided refuge, but we must seek it out. This means asking for His Spirit to equip us for discernment. While we don't know the challenges and temptations we'll face, He does. And if we ask Him, He will provide us with all we need to face them. —RVN

Are you seeking God's guidance today?
No matter what your situation may be, pray for His Spirit
to provide you with strength and discernment.

PRIDE IN DISGUISE

Genesis 37; **Matthew 26:57–27:31**; Ecclesiastes 9:1–6

Sometimes recognizing our sin for what it is can throw us into deep shame. In Matthew, we find that two of Jesus' disciples experience this moment of remorse—Judas after he betrays Jesus, and Peter when he denies Jesus. From their responses, we learn what true repentance looks like.

Judas is remorseful when he realizes the enormity of his betrayal. But he doesn't move from remorse to repentance. He tries to absolve his guilt by returning the payment he received for betraying Jesus—an attempt to buy back his innocence. And when the "blood money" is refused and he is unable to eliminate the guilt, Judas hangs himself (Matt 27:5).

Peter, the disciple with an impulsive, childlike loyalty to Jesus, denies his Lord when questioned by a mere servant girl. When Peter remembers Jesus' prediction, he leaves, "weeping bitterly." However, the Gospel of John tells us that Peter glorified God in his death (John 21:15–19).

When sin is exposed, stopping at realization and remorse is tempting. Reveling in self-hate and self-loathing can seem fitting—we feel like inflicting punishment on ourselves will somehow absolve our guilt. But this is simply another form of relying on ourselves—it is pride in disguise. We diminish the sacrifice that Christ has completed. We deny the freedom from guilt and shame that Jesus has bought for us at a costly sacrifice.

It's only when we reach the end of our self-reliance and pride that we can look to the one who actually bore the guilt for us. —RVN

How are you holding on to guilt and shame?

∘ ◊ ◊ ∘ ∘

UNDUE FAVOR

Genesis 38–39; Matthew 27:32–28:20; Ecclesiastes 9:7–10

Genesis 38 interrupts the climax of the Joseph narrative with another tale: Judah and Tamar. Switching protagonists is surprising enough, but the tale itself shocks us. We're hardly given time to process the strange cultural practices of the ancient Near East—prostitution, deception, and the sudden death of those who displease God—before we're returned to Joseph's struggles in Egypt.

The story is additionally confusing because it seems to lack a hero. Judah uses Tamar, as his two sons did—though he at least acknowledges his actions. Tamar uses her wits and risks her life to secure a future for herself, but she does so through deplorable means.

Attempts have been made to justify the characters and put it all in perspective, but there is no neat packaging. The characters in this story face dire circumstances and a unique cultural context—one that is nearly impossible for modern readers to understand. But we don't need a lesson in ancient Near Eastern cultural studies to see that they are fallible, and that they exploit others for their own ends. And we don't need a history lesson to be able to identify with them. An honest look at ourselves reveals our own sins—subtly deplorable and respectably wrapped.

So, why is this story in the Bible? Why this tale of woe? Surprisingly, there *is* a hero. As we read, we see that God also uses people for redemption, not exploitation. Perez, the son of Judah and Tamar, is one in a long list of names that will lead to the birth of Christ. Through unlikely characters like Judah and Tamar, God prepared a way out of the sin that defined us.

Just like these characters, we are unlikely recipients of His favor. —RVN

How can you be thankful for God's faithfulness in your life?

RADIANCE

Genesis 40:1–41:37; **Hebrews 1–2**; Ecclesiastes 9:11–18

When I was a boy, my dad took me to his construction site, and told me, "Don't look directly at the welding light; it can blind you." But a welding flame is cool and dangerous. As my father was talking with the foreman, I fixated on the light. I saw spots for the rest of the evening, but didn't tell anyone. I secretly feared that the radiance had actually blinded me.

The radiance of Christ is blinding—it was for Paul (Acts 9:1–31). In an epic hymn about the work of God's Son throughout history, the author of Hebrews calls Jesus "the radiance of [God's] glory and the representation of his essence, sustaining all things by the word of power" (Heb 1:3). It's easy to wonder if sustainability is possible, if the world will one day crumble and fall. But in Christ, there is hope.

Jesus is much like the sun. You don't always notice its power, warmth, or even that it's there. That is especially the case on cloudy days. We forget that without the sun, there would be no life. It's easy to forget that it is warming us even through rain and clouds.

The same is true for Jesus in our lives. It's easy to forget Him until we desperately need Him. It's easy to overlook the daily miracles, such as life itself, when searching for something extraordinary. But the extraordinary is always present. It's here in the work of Christ, every day. His radiance shines upon us, even when we don't realize it. —JDB

What miracles can you recognize today?

A LITTLE FOLLY

Genesis 41:38–42:28; **Hebrews 3:1–5:10**; **Ecclesiastes 10:1–9**

Like dead flies in perfumer's oil, a little folly outweighs wisdom and honor according to the writer of Ecclesiastes.. Sometimes fools are elevated to positions of power, while those who are fit for the position are given no influence. The Preacher says, "I have seen slaves on horses, and princes walking on the ground like slaves" (Eccl 10:7).

It's not difficult to nod our heads and say "Amen" when we come to this example of an "evil under the sun." We probably all have a story to tell about a leader who wasn't fit for a position and about the injustices we endured under their authority. When a fool is set up as an authority figure, everyone suffers.

The Preacher gives a suggestion, though: "If the anger of the ruler rises against you, do not leave your place, for calmness will lay great offenses to rest" (Eccl 10:4). This doesn't just tell us we should have a posture of humility and obedience before bad leaders. We should also teach them by responding with love and humility—something that may calm even the worst of fools.

In Hebrews, we find the context for this. We stand naked and exposed to God, who judges our thoughts and the intentions of our hearts. On our own, sin and guilt would condemn us. But we have a high priest in Jesus Christ. He intercedes for us, just as the Old Testament high priests interceded for the people of Israel. Our confidence is not in our own wisdom and righteousness, but in Him.

We can't credit ourselves for our own wisdom. We stand before God on account of His Son's righteousness and obedience. Jesus is the one who is able to withstand our folly. We stand in His righteousness, and we can learn from His obedience. —RVN

How can you respond to authority
in a way that reflects God's righteousness?

REVENGE ISN'T SWEET

Genesis 42:29–43:34; Hebrews 5:11–7:28; Ecclesiastes 10:10–20

It's easy to revel in vigilante justice, be joyful in the irony of someone getting "what's coming to them," or feel satisfied when "bad Karma comes back around" to others. The colloquialisms alone demonstrate our infatuation with justice. Joseph is similarly impassioned; he schemes against his brothers, who sold him into slavery. At the beginning of Genesis 43, Joseph's brothers must go back to Egypt to request food from him—their younger brother, whom they do not recognize. Joseph waits for the youngest, Benjamin, to join them. What Joseph intends to do when he does, we're not told.

When Benjamin and the other brothers arrive, Joseph is either moved with empathy or chooses to act upon his original plan of revealing himself in front of *all* his brothers (Gen 43:16, 29). Joseph even helps them financially, signaling that he somehow still cares for them (Gen 44). Yet it doesn't seem that Joseph has forgiven them yet, because in Genesis 44, more evil schemes emerge.

The thought of others suffering the same kind of pain they have inflicted can cause us to feel remorse. But we're always aware of the choice; we can choose to fight our instincts. We can recognize that instead of lashing back, the best answer is turning the other cheek. This may be easy for some, but for others—especially those who have been deeply hurt—abandoning the urge to inflict injury will require spiritual strength, prayer, and self-control. —JDB

Whom do you currently desire to see hurt?
How can you let that feeling go?
How can God help you release the situation to Him?

CARPE DIEM

Genesis 44; Hebrews 8–9; **Ecclesiastes 11:1–4**

The Latin phrase *Carpe Diem* means "seize the day." Taking risks to make your life extraordinary is biblical, if done according to God's plan and principles. The idea behind this comes from Ecclesiastes: "Cast your bread upon the waters, for you will find it after many days" (Eccl 11:1).

Bread acts as the symbol for substance in the ancient world; the author of Ecclesiastes is suggesting that we should follow God's plan, even at the possible cost of our livelihood. He then suggests that what we give to God, He will return. This is opposite from a self-protection mentality. The "waters" in the proverb represent chaos, suggesting that in letting go of even the most chaotic circumstances, we learn about God's ability to give what we need.

This is further illustrated when the author says, "Give a portion to seven, or even to eight, for you know not what disaster may happen on earth. … He who observes the wind will not sow, and he who regards the clouds will not reap" (Eccl 11:2, 4). In other words, there is no real way to calculate the return on investment. Things can always go bad. But with God, that's not the case. He honors the work of those who diligently follow Him and give of themselves.

In the eyes of the world, not everything will work out perfectly for those who willingly give to God. But it will work out in the spiritual long haul. So, when God calls us to something, the answer is *Carpe Diem*. And the question we should be asking Him is, "What can I do for you and your kingdom?" —JDB

What risks are you taking for God right now?
Have you asked Him what risks He would like you to take?

THE NEW DEAL

Genesis 45–46; **Hebrews 10**; Ecclesiastes 11:5–10

"I pledge you, I pledge myself, to a new deal for the American people." These words were spoken by President Franklin D. Roosevelt in a speech that unveiled a series of economic strategies for ending the Great Depression.

We love newness because it holds hope. The same should be true when we look to the new covenant of Jesus. Although it may not feel quite as new as it did nearly 2,000 years ago—when it altered the spiritual landscape like the New Deal forced economic vitality into America—it still holds the same power today.

This covenant is first mentioned in Hebrews 8, and in Hebrews 10, we see the full implications of it: "For by *one* offering he has perfected for all time those who are made holy. … Now where there is forgiveness of [sins], there is no longer an offering for sin" (Heb 10:14, 18). Prior to Jesus, there was a need for regular sacrifices for sins to be made, but since Jesus became the ultimate sacrifice for our sins, that is no longer necessary.

I often forget just how radical this "new deal" is. In the midst of being busy, overwhelmed, or stressed, I neglect to acknowledge how much God has done for me. But every day, I live in His grace. Every day, I can be one with Him—no longer worrying about my past and future sins or shortcomings. And that is a day to be thankful for. —JDB

Have you thanked God today for the "new deal" He enacted through Jesus' death and resurrection? What are some ways this gracious act can change or add to your interactions with God?

DIFFICULT DEFINITIONS

Genesis 47–48; **Hebrews 11**; Ecclesiastes 12:1–8

As an editor, I love definitions. The field of lexicography can be complex, but when a definition is finally solidified, there's comfort to be found. It becomes something stable. This is also the reason I love the book of Hebrews: The author is keen on definitions, clarifying terminology, and using analogies to prove his points.

"Now faith is the realization of what is hoped for, the proof of things not seen" (Heb 11:1). In this succinct definition, I have perspective on the essence of faith. There is no room for doubt or error. The hope referred to is Jesus. And the proof is in an assurance that even though we cannot see Him, we have confidence in His work both presently and in the future.

The author goes on to say, "For by this [faith] the people of old were approved [by God]. By faith we understand the worlds were created by the word of God, in order that what is seen did not come into existence from what is visible. … By faith Abraham, when he was called, obeyed to go out to a place that he was going to receive for an inheritance, and he went out, not knowing where he was going" (Heb 11:2–3, 8).

Abraham, whose story is an exemplar of actions reflecting faith, shows us that belief is about hoping in God's work in Christ. And in acting on that which He has promised but we are yet to see. That's lexicography we can all depend on. —JDB

How does this definition of faith (or belief) change your
perspective on living a life that is faithful to Christ?

DISCIPLINE

Genesis 49–50; **Hebrews 12–13**; Ecclesiastes 12:9–14

I was a stubborn child. When disciplined by my parents, I would sulk for hours afterward. I didn't see discipline from my parents' perspective—as something that would mold me into a mature, loving person.

Hebrews 12 has a lesson for people like me with a history of wallowing in self-pity when disciplined. Here, the writer of Hebrews tells us that God, a Father to us through the work of Jesus, disciplines us for our good. To emphasize this, the writer of Hebrews draws on the book of Proverbs, where the father instructs his own son. "My son, do not make light of the Lord's discipline, or give up when you are corrected by him. For the Lord disciplines the one who he loves, and punishes every son whom he accepts" (Heb 12:6; compare Prov 3:11–12).

The author tells us that being disciplined is a sign of God's love. It means He is working and active in our lives (Heb 12:8). Like a chastised child, we might not always recognize God's discipline this way. When challenged by our circumstances, we might struggle against events that are meant to shape us for holiness and eternity. We might even avoid subjecting ourselves to them because we don't see God as the author of the event.

Sometimes our parents' form of discipline gives us a tainted view of its purpose. Imperfect, like us, they disciplined us "for a few days according to what seemed appropriate to them." It may have been harmful and destructive. But God disciplines us "for our benefit, in order that we can have a share in his holiness" (Heb 12:10). Because His intentions are perfect, we know that He has our ultimate good in mind. And we can approach discipline like a student, ready to learn how to better serve Him—and others—for His kingdom. —RVN

How do you respond to God's discipline in your life?
How can you change your attitude so that you view them
as teachable moments and not a means to inflict harm?

GOD'S IDEAS: MORE THAN GOOD

Exodus 1–3; **John 1:1–18**; Song of Solomon 1:1–4

It's exciting to see ideas take shape and then become reality. Even more exciting, though, is when God's ideas take form. The Bible shows us these events repeatedly. As the reader, we're given glimpses into what God is really doing—events the characters are unaware of. Sometimes we have a hint all along that God is up to something unexpected, and that He will make good out of the evil that's happening.

The story of Moses is like this. God's people are terribly oppressed, but they are many (Exod 1). And we all know there is power in numbers. When baby Moses comes along, we're ready for something amazing to happen. It will be from this unassuming moment that God will do the least expected (Exod 2:1–10): He will help those on the underside of power. Our suspicion is confirmed when Moses is willing to kill for justice (Exod 2:11–12). Moses flees, and then God hears Israel's complaints about the pain they're enduring (Exod 2:23–25). He answers their cry by calling Moses (Exod 3:1–22). Moses is hesitant because he can't speak well, but God will (as we thought) use this unexpected turn of events (Exod 4:10–17).

Like Moses' story, we see behind the veil at the beginning of John's Gospel: "In the beginning was the Word ... And the Word became flesh and took up residence among us, and we saw his glory ... For the law was given through Moses; grace and truth came through Jesus Christ" (John 1:1, 14, 17). God gave Moses His law, and He gave Moses the opportunity to guide His people from oppression to the wilderness and almost to freedom. But He gave Jesus grace *and* truth.

And that's the message of the Testaments: from cry to freedom cry, from calling upon God to salvation, and from merely men guided by God, to God *in a man* guiding men. Our love for God should be every bit as great—and far greater—than the love shown by the chorus of people in Song of Solomon. We must say about our God, like they say about people, "Let us be joyful and let us rejoice in you; let us extol your love more than wine. Rightly do they love you!" (Song 1:4).

We are called to see God's work in our everyday life. We must recognize His story. He's involved. Are we? —JDB

Are you worshiping God with your entire being—
seeing His workings in your everyday life?

THE PROBLEM WITH POWER

Exodus 4–6; **John 1:19–34**; Song of Solomon 1:5–7

Grasping for power is one of the easiest sins to fall into. At first it looks like ambition, then it looks like success, and then it quickly becomes about *your* success and *your* power. This can be costly—not just to you, but to all the people you hurt in the process. If anything is done for the purpose of power, it's not worth achieving. And don't let the snazzy word "influence" fool you; it's just a synonym for the same empty desire.

John the Baptist is an example of ambition; he is fueled by passion but constantly checked by God's calling. He is firm in his words, confident in what he must do, but humble in his understanding of his relationship to God. He is not in it for himself, but for Jesus. When asked, "Who are you?" (a leading question, since many believed him to be the Messiah the people expected), he replied, "I am not the Christ!" (John 1:19–20). When further questioned, "Then who are you? Are you Elijah?" (the supreme prophet besides the Messiah), he says, "No!" (John 1:21). When asked again about his identity, he finally responds, "I am the 'voice of one crying in the wilderness, "Make straight the way of the Lord,"' just as Isaiah the prophet said" (John 1:23).

John affirmed his identity as prophet, but he assumed nothing. He didn't even assume what ended up being the truth: that he was a type of Elijah, as Jesus would later say (Matt 17:12–13). When given the opportunity to reach for power, to be known as the Messiah, John said no. He would not claim authority that had not been given to him.

And this is where affirmation can be a scary thing. Just because other people think you're something special doesn't mean you should go along with what they say about you. Doing so is dangerous. John the Baptist's humility sets the stage for Jesus, and he ends up getting one of the greatest gifts of all: the chance to baptize Jesus.

The road between affirming God's calling and grasping for power is narrow and rocky. But when you're on the right path, you will feel it in your bones, and the Spirit of God will affirm it. —JDB

How are you grasping for power?
How is ambition throwing off the alignment of your calling?

○ ○◊○ ○

WISDOM CAN QUICKLY BECOME FOLLY

Exodus 7–8; John 1:35–51; Song of Solomon 1:8–14

What we *need* to hear and what we *want* to hear are rarely the same thing. Leaders who encourage honesty, allow for errors, and establish an environment of trust usually hear what they need to hear. Dictators, on the other hand, will never learn what they really need to know. People shield them or stay away from them; an environment of fear is only destructive. It's with this point in mind that the story of Moses, Aaron, and Pharaoh becomes even more intriguing.

Pharaoh surrounded himself with people who would tell him what he wanted to hear (Exod 7:22), not what he needed to hear: "You're oppressing the Hebrew people and they will rise up against you. And furthermore, we're afraid of their God, and we can't *really* do what He can do. We're small-time dark magic; their God is the big time." Instead of speaking this truth, Pharaoh's advisors went on pretending and conjuring up cheap tricks.

Plague after plague hit Egypt, but Pharaoh's heart remained hard. And this is where we don't really know what happened: When God hardened Pharaoh's heart, was it already too difficult for Pharaoh to give in on his own accord? We don't know the answer, but we do know that God ended up making an example of his foolishness.

Even when water turns to blood, frogs appear everywhere—followed shortly by gnats and flies (Exod 7:14–8:32)—Pharaoh didn't listen. Instead of turning to Yahweh, he turned to the same sources: his gods, his belief that he is a god (common for Egyptians), and his ill-advised counselors. And that's the lesson: If you surround yourself with "yes" people, they will say yes, and you will be ignorant. You will lose, and you will end up on the wrong side of God. —JDB

Who do you turn to for advice? Are your friends, mentors,
and church leaders more apt to tell you the truth or say something
that makes you happy? If it's the latter, who can you turn to
who will speak honestly to you about faith?

WHAT TYPE OF SAVIOR?

Exodus 9:1–10:29; **John 2:1–12**; Song of Solomon 1:15–17

It's tempting to operate life on our own terms and only call on God when we hit a crisis. If we're not busy studying how God has worked in the past and relying on the work of the Spirit in our lives, we can easily fall into the pattern of calling on Him to meet our desires rather than realizing that He is the first to deliver what we need.

In John 2, we get a sense of what this was like for Mary and the disciples at the wedding in Cana. While Mary wants Jesus to save the day—and save the bridegroom from certain ruin and humiliation—Jesus shows her that He is no magician. His soft rebuke reminds her that His plan of salvation exceeds what she can perceive: "What does your concern have to do with me, woman? My hour has not yet come" (John 2:4). (This phrase seems derogatory to our modern ears, but it actually would have been normal language between a son and mother in the first century AD.) However, after doing so, He willingly and liberally grants her request.

Those who were closest to Jesus didn't yet understand the role He came to fulfill. This miracle, the first of a series in the Gospel of John, helped Jesus' disciples believe in Him (John 2:11). But even throughout His ministry and the witnessing of other miracles, they would struggle to fully understand why He came. He constantly needed to remind and correct them.

God knows our need, and He made a plan to meet that need. His glory was displayed at Cana, but His purpose for coming—for redeeming both us and them—would be revealed at another event that would confound human understanding: the shame and glory of the cross. He fulfilled that need. And today, we can go to Him for *all* of our needs. If it is in His will, He will grant it. —RVN

How do you rely on Jesus to fulfill your deepest need?

WHY DOES GOD PUNISH PEOPLE?

Exodus 11–13; John 2:13–3:25; Song of Solomon 2:1–3

I recently heard one homeless man wisely tell another, "You wouldn't want to live in a world where God didn't punish injustices and just freely forgave sin—without any request for someone to choose the salvation He offers back. Imagine a place where injustice was never punished and people never recognized their sin and need for salvation. That would be terrible and painful."

We all want justice to reign. For a good God to be truly good, injustice must be punished. This is why it makes complete sense that Jesus had to die. There must be a payment for the evil we inflict on the world and one another. Jesus' death epitomizes God's mercy and justice—and it all happened in one act.

This also makes sense out of the Passover event (Exod 12:1–31). I usually hear this preached about as a saving act, which indeed it was, but it was also brutal: God kills firstborn sons in an act of justice against the people of Egypt for the suffering they inflicted on an innocent people. (It's important to note that the plagues that preceded Passover gave Pharaoh more than ample warning.)

Following this, evil finally loosens its grip, and God's people are freed (Exod 12:33–40). None of us truly wants to have justice fall upon us because we know that true justice would cost us our very lives. We have all done wrong against a good God, bringing evil into the world. Thus, we all deserve to be wiped out. Instead, God offers grace. But He does so only after the wages of our sin are paid with Jesus' life. Jesus makes this incredibly clear: "For God did not send his Son into the world in order that he should judge the world, but in order that the world should be saved through him" (John 3:17).

Jesus goes on to explain that salvation requires choosing God back: "The one who believes in him is not judged, but the one who does not believe has already been judged, because he has not believed in the name of the one and only Son of God" (John 3:18). Before we believe, we're judged—we are regarded to be dead in our sin. After we believe, we escape that judgment. God's faithfulness, shown in Jesus' death and resurrection, allows for that. I want to live in a world of people freed in Christ through His mercy and grace; I'm sure you want to as well. Thus, we should no longer ask, "Why judgment?" but instead, "Why not?" —JDB

In what ways are you misjudging God's motives?
How can you change that perspective?

February 6

○ ○ ○ ○ ○

STUDENT OR SCHOLAR?

Exodus 14:1–15:27; **John 3:1–21**; Song of Solomon 2:4–7

Sometimes we approach God with curiosity, but not with a spirit of humility. We enjoy participating in religious discussions, but forging the link between interpretation and application is difficult for us. We have certain expectations of who He should be for us, but we don't think about how we should align our lives with Him.

Nicodemus—a Pharisee, a leader of his fellow Jews, and a teacher of Israel—wanted answers from Jesus. He told Him, "we know that you are a teacher who has come from God, for no one is able to perform these signs that you are performing unless God were with him" (John 3:2). Was Jesus a messiah, like Moses or David, who would restore Israel?

The scholar quickly became a student. Through His answers, Jesus showed Nicodemus that he wasn't in a place to hold Jesus accountable. Rather, it was the other way around: Nicodemus needed to be challenged and transformed. He was a teacher of Israel, but he didn't really understand Jesus' teaching; his questions showed that he was hesitant to even believe Him, despite all the signs.

We might be like Nicodemus, approaching God with off-par expectations. Jesus showed Nicodemus that he had to receive the transforming work of the Holy Spirit. In order to see the kingdom of God and enter into it, we need to do the same. —RVN

Are you teachable?
Do you approach God ready to learn and apply His words?

BREAD FROM HEAVEN
AND WATER FROM A ROCK

Exodus 16–18; John 3:22–36; Song of Solomon 2:8–13

For many years, I said that I believed God would provide for me, but I'm not sure I actually did. Somewhere inside I was still convinced that I was on my own. It wasn't until recently that I felt convicted about this, and God began working in me to make the necessary changes. As I was dealing with this, I started contemplating what trust issues might've looked like for the ancients. Of nearly all biblical characters, Noah must have seemed the craziest to his friends. But I think Moses faced some of the greatest interpersonal struggles involving trust.

Over and over again, the people Moses is leading blame him for all their problems. And they rarely give him credit for his good attributes. God is faithful, though. It's Moses who sees bread come from heaven (Exod 16) and water from a rock (Exod 17:1–7).

And this really puts it in perspective: If God is capable of this kind of deliverance, what am I so afraid of? It's not my own strength that will empower me, and even if it were, what good is it? If I put my trust in my own abilities, how will I grow in my trust in God?

Like Moses, I must be willing to be audacious. If God calls me to look to the heavens for providence, I must do it. If He calls me to strike the rock, I must strike it. As the Gospel of John says, "The one who comes from above is over all. The one who is from the earth is from the earth and speaks from the earth" (John 3:31). Let's be the people who seek the one from above: Jesus. —JDB

How do you trust in yourself instead of in God for your needs?
How does this impede your relationship with Him
and the work He wants to do through you?

IT'S STANDING BETWEEN
YOU AND GOD

Exodus 19–20; John 4:1–26; Song of Solomon 2:14–17

There is nothing more frustrating than being ordered around. Few people take to a drill sergeant. Although we like to cite the Ten Commandments (Exod 20) because they're the norm, the rebellious part of our spirits has trouble with them. If we're honest with ourselves and take them the way Jesus did (Matt 5–7), we're confronted with the fact that we've all violated them at some point or another. (I don't know anyone who has always honored their father and mother.)

If everyone lived by the Ten Commandments, the world would be a peaceful place. But again, we're rebellious. The Ten Commandments reveal something about us: We're weaker than we would like to believe. They also reveal something about our place before God: It's not good—not without Jesus' saving act that redeems us from our sins.

In John 4:1–26, we see Jesus confront a woman at a well who, like us, is a commandment-breaker. And because, as a Samaritan woman, she worships in a different place and in a different way than Jewish people, she is further frowned upon by the people around her. This makes Jesus' remark to her all the more startling: "If you had known the gift of God and who it is who says to you, 'Give me water to drink,' you would have asked him, and he would have given you living water" (John 4:10). Jesus tells her that He is what she is searching for—not rules or justification for her lifestyle as a commandment-breaker.

We commandment-breakers can live as legalists or attempt to justify our own decisions. Or we can do something entirely different and admit our need for the living water: Jesus. We can recognize that our religion or inability to keep commandments is not what matters most—what really matters is what God can do for us. We must acknowledge our weakness and need for Him. We must say, like the woman, "He [being Jesus] told me everything that I have done" (John 4:39). —JDB

How is religion, self-deprivation,
or legalism standing between you and God?

SPEAKING UP

Exodus 21:1–23:33; **John 4:27–42**; Song of Solomon 3:1–2

Because we convince ourselves that people won't accept our testimony about God's work in our lives, we're not usually ready to share it. We might pre-judge their reactions or simply lack confidence. Soon, staying silent becomes a way of life. We become accustomed to the monotony and forget our calling in the world.

But we're called to action. Our words have power, and not because of our own storytelling talent or our ability to tap into others' emotions. God can and will use our words to draw people to Him through His Spirit—perhaps without our even being aware of it. In John 4:27–42, Jesus uses a Samaritan woman with a tarnished reputation to bring Samaritans (people whom the disciples and the Jews looked down upon) to faith.

Like the disciples, we have to realize the urgency of the good news. We have to show others that the kingdom of heaven is at hand.

We are called to action. Verbalizing, with humility, what God has done for us is an important part of faith. We shouldn't shy away from it or doubt that He will use it to bring others to Himself. This should bring us to a place of confidence and humility. And it should compel us to speak. —RVN

Do you speak to others about your faith?
How can you begin telling others about
the work God has done in you?

LONGING FOR THE IDEAL

Exodus 24:1–25:40; John 4:43–54; **Song of Solomon 3:3–5**

Pastors avoid or over-interpret it. We're often confused by it. But the Song of Solomon is in our Bible. Although we might stumble over the imagery (comparing a woman to a mare would hardly go over well in the modern world), we can't help but be entranced by the idealism and the tender, rather racy relationship of the joyful couple.

"'Have you seen the one whom my heart loves?' … I found him whom my heart loves. I held him and I would not let him go" (Song 3:3–4).

Their relationship appeals to what is pristine and ideal—a picture of what God created marriage to be. The lovers physically delight in each other and woo each other with affectionate words. We might brush off this poem like other romantic poetry and literature—ideal, but hardly plausible in our world, which would take pleasure over love. We further deconstruct the purity of the Song of Solomon based on the reality we experience (or at least know about): the lust, sexual abuse, and promiscuous relationships that are rampant in our world (and more rampant than we'd like to think, even in Christian circles).

Despite hesitations, we shouldn't brush aside the fact that this book is included in the biblical canon. The Song of Solomon shows us that we were created for a different life—for an ideal. We were made by a God who is perfect and intended for us to live bountifully. This realization makes us thankful that we live in the grace that Christ bought. And through the Spirit, we can put to death the sins that entangle us. It can help us look forward to a time when all that is perverted is judged, and when we ourselves are made perfect, purified from all the dross. —RVN

How does the relationship depicted in Song of Solomon help
you understand what God intended for humanity?
How does it turn you to Christ's sacrifice?

∘ ∘ ∘ ∘ ∘

GOD'S WILL: IT'S CONFUSING

Exodus 26–27; John 5:1–15; Song of Solomon 3:6–11

It's sometimes difficult to understand why God does what He does, or why He asks us to do certain things. God goes so far as to list precise materials and calculations in Exodus 26 for the tabernacle—the portable temple the Hebrew people built for God in the wilderness. You can imagine the conversation:

Nadab says, "Aaron, is it okay if I use leather for this curtain?"

Aaron responds, "No, you know the rules. If God commands it, you have to do it. I don't want another golden calf incident. I made that mistake once; I won't make it twice."

"But there is more leather," says Nadab.

"I'm not having this discussion any longer," Aaron says sternly. "Let's just get the job done." ("For an elder, you think he would know better," Aaron says under his breath.)

Aaron, in this fictional scene, is rightfully frustrated because God *does* know better. Most of us know the answer before we ask God, "Why?" But we ask Him anyway. God's will can be confusing, and it's for this reason that discerning it requires great prayer and a dedication to an ongoing relationship with Him. Trying to understand God's will without that close relationship cannot only be detrimental to us, but also to others. We see this in the golden calf incident later in the exodus narrative (Exod 32).

And isn't this often the case? God knows what we need before we do; we just don't always realize that He has already given instructions. —JDB

*Has God already given instructions for your
current situation that you may not have realized yet?*

LIAR OR LORD?

Exodus 28:1–29:46; **John 5:16–30**; Song of Solomon 4:1–3

When Jesus made a defense of His healing on the Sabbath, He was upping the ante instead of defusing the situation: "My Father is working until now, and I am working" (John 5:17). For the Jews, such a claim was blasphemous. Not only was Jesus breaking the Sabbath, He was equating Himself with the Father and thus claiming to be God. He was presenting the people with a choice.

Jesus provides compelling insight into His relationship with God. Jesus' authority stems from His relationship with the Father, which is one of complete submission. In fact, He can do nothing on His own. Whatever the Father does, He does likewise. There is complete trust and openness—the Father loves the Son and shows Him all that He is doing. Both the Father and the Son give life. But with authority, the Father has also given the Son judgment.

Jesus presents His audience with an ultimatum as He carries out God's will on earth: "The one who does not honor the Son does not honor the Father who sent him. Truly, truly I say to you that the one who hears my word and who believes the one who sent me has eternal life, and does not come into judgment" (John 5:23–24). His claims require bold acts—total faith or total rejection. He is not merely a prophet sent from God. —RVN

How do you respond to Jesus' claim?
Are you completely and solely devoted to following Him?

THE SYSTEM

Exodus 30–32; John 5:31–47; Song of Solomon 4:4–8

Religion is a tough subject. Jesus staunchly opposed religion for religion's sake, yet He was a Law-abiding Jew. He recognized the value of worship, community, and discipleship, but not the value of religious constraints: Religion can bind someone in tradition and be used for oppression. This knowledge makes it hard to understand why God set up religious systems in the first place.

In Exodus 30–31, there are full descriptions of altars, taxes, basins, oils, incense, and the Sabbath. In the middle of this, we're given a glimpse into what it's all about in a scene where God places His Spirit upon two men so that they may honor Him with a creative craft. They will depict, in art, what it means to know God. Here God is not building religion for religion's sake—He is building systems to help people understand Him.

Religion is exploited in the next chapter, where an impatient Aaron (the man meant to lead God's people to Him) promotes the worship of another god. (The golden calf was a symbol of Baal, the chief god of a neighboring people group.) Here we see what happens when people become impatient: They build their own systems, reaching out to something that can't actually help them.

And this is precisely what we do when we sin. We seek our own way, our own system, when instead we should be seeking God's way and worshiping Him the way in which He has called us.

Jesus confronts this problem with religion. "if you do not believe [Moses'] writings, how will you believe my words?" (John 5:45–47). These words would have cut to the core of a highly religious, first-century Jew. Imagine someone claiming that the very way they worshiped and their very book of teachings actually testifies against them.

Just a few lines earlier, Jesus provides His reasoning for this statement (John 5:41). Jesus does not seek glory from a religious system. He's in the business of relationships. We all have our failing systems, and they're revealed as we seek Jesus. We must let God work within us and our communities to destroy those systems. A creative act that leads to better worship, discipleship, or community is desirable, but an act that inhibits it must be destroyed. —JDB

What systems have you and your worship community built that are keeping you from fully entering into relationship with Jesus?

WHEN THINGS DON'T GO AS PLANNED

Exodus 33–34; John 6:1–14; Song of Solomon 4:9–13

I live in the world of projects. There are a few things I know for certain about them, aside from all requiring a budget and a schedule to have any hope of success. They will all take more time than I expect (at least 25 percent more), and they will all have problems. It seems that nothing ever goes according to plan. No one will complain, though, if the result, budget, and end date remain the same. There's a biblical lesson here—Moses' story is one of the best analogies for this.

Moses had likely planned for the Israelites to enter the Holy Land shortly after leaving Egypt, but mistake after mistake (on his part and the part of others) kept this from happening. In return, he spent years (about a half a lifetime) wandering in the wilderness. In Exodus 33:1, we read one of God's direct instructions, "Go, go up from here" (Exod 33:1), but Moses proceeds to argue with God, interceding for the people (Exod 33:12–23). Things aren't going according to plan—for Moses or God. Finally, God gives Moses new instructions to solve the predicament the people have gotten themselves into: "Look, I am about to make a covenant. In front of all your people I will do wonders that have not been created on all the earth and among all the nations" (Exod 34:10).

Here, in the middle of the debacle, God takes care of the problem with a promise. Over and over again, God makes promises; and unlike people, He keeps them. God performs marvels.

We see this in the events in Jesus' life as well. Jesus doesn't just feed the people, He overturns their notions about where food comes from (John 6:1–12). Jesus creates marvels like nothing anywhere in creation—other than where God Himself has worked. Of course, this shows that Jesus is indeed God. We're often waiting for a marvel, and we will truly see them when following the Spirit. But how much more often is God waiting for us to pay attention and see how He can take plan B and make it plan A—like nothing we've seen before. —JDB

What is not going as planned in your life right now?
How do you think God might use the thing that feels
out of control to show how marvelous He is?

SEARCHING FOR THE WRONG KINGDOM

Exodus 35:1–36:38; **John 6:15–24**; Song of Solomon 4:14–16

Because of the signs He performed, Jesus drew large crowds. And because of His signs, those who followed Him decided that He should be king. It seems natural and fitting, in a way, that Jesus should be revered and honored among the masses. Why shouldn't He be worshiped on earth like He is in heaven?

But Jesus wasn't interested in gaining glory and fame. He had no interest in the kingdoms of this world, as His temptation in the desert demonstrates (Matt 4:8). This scene reveals both His character and His mission—He was seeking His Father's glory and following His will.

"Now when the people saw the sign that he performed, they began to say, 'This one is truly the Prophet who is to come into the world!' Then Jesus, because he knew that they were about to come and seize him in order to make him king, withdrew again up the mountain by himself alone" (John 6:14–15).

It also reveals something about human nature. Although the crowds wanted to make Jesus king, they weren't necessarily looking to revere Him. They were looking out for themselves. They wanted to install a new kingdom—one brought on by force and political revolution. They wanted their immediate physical needs met, but they didn't necessarily consider the great spiritual revolution that needed to take place within.

Following Jesus shouldn't be something we do because it's somehow convenient for us. Following Jesus requires all of us—and it will often look like a life of sacrifice, not ease.

The Jews who followed Jesus were challenged to accept Him, not as a prophet or a Messiah, but as the Son of God. The same crowd that followed Jesus obsessively, looking for signs, was eventually confronted by teaching that shook their understanding of this Messiah and what God expected from them. —RVN

Do you follow Jesus for reasons of your own?
How can you follow Him for the right reasons?

WIT, WORDPLAY, AND EUPHEMISM

Exodus 37–38; John 6:25–51; **Song of Solomon 5:1–4**

The Bible is a passionate book. It's about a God who is impassioned for His people and who ultimately sends His Son to die for them so that they can be saved from themselves. And it also portrays the passion seen in romantic love.

Song of Solomon 5:1–4 is full of wit, wordplay, and euphemism. It's dramatic, like a play. The man is full of zeal for the woman he loves, and the woman is excited to see her man. And this isn't a Michael Bolton ballad or Kenny G song. There is haste. There is anxiety—you can almost hear the heart palpitations. This isn't the stuff for the unmarried, and it is definitely not the stuff for kids or teenagers. This is true romance as God designed it.

The woman says, "I slept, but my heart was awake" (Song 5:2). She may be asleep, but her love for the man is not. That is both the type of love we must have in marriage and the type of love we must have for our God—never sleeping, always wide awake.

Jesus makes a similar contrast between subtle love (or necessary love) and real love: "Your fathers ate the manna in the wilderness and they died. [God provided them the manna shortly after the exodus (Exod 16).] This is the bread that comes down from heaven [being Jesus and His message], so that someone may eat from it and not die" (John 6:49–50).

What fills our minds and keeps our hearts awake at night says who we really are; we will dedicate ourselves to what we care most about. Let us dedicate ourselves to love of family, others, and Christ. —JDB

What are you wrongly in love with right now?
What can you do to refocus your love?

FINDING SUSTAINMENT

Exodus 39:1–40:38; **John 6:52–71**; Song of Solomon 5:5–9

Following Jesus isn't like developing a crisis-aversion system. So often, it's tempting to treat our faith in this way—relying on Him when things get tough or when others expect us to do so. But He wants us to rely on Him continually.

After Jesus miraculously fed the crowds, He told them that He was the bread of life. But they were fickle. They wanted evidence—another sign. Instead of feeding their transient desires, Jesus delivered hard teaching: "The one who eats my flesh and drinks my blood has eternal life, and I will raise him up on the last day. For my flesh is true food, and my blood is true drink. The one who eats my flesh and drinks my blood resides in me and I in him" (John 6:54–56).

For the Jews, this teaching would have been shocking and strange—drinking blood was forbidden by Old Testament law, and He was speaking about His own body. They followed Jesus because they wanted a sign, a prophet, or a Messiah. A sacrifice was not part of their plan.

But a sacrifice was exactly what they needed. Forgiveness and eternal life were discarded by some, but not by all. Simon Peter's simple confession is actually quite stunning in the midst of all the confusion: "Lord, to whom would we go? You have the words of eternal life. And we have believed, and have come to know, that you are the Holy One of God" (John 6:68–69). The disciples didn't put hope in a transient sign—in one meal. And although they didn't always understand Jesus' teaching, they recognized that He was the true bread of life, and they relied on Him for sustenance even when His teaching seemed strange to their ears. —RVN

How are you challenging yourself to accept all the teachings of Jesus—not just the ones that are easy? How can you put your hope in Christ and look to Him for continual support?

DWELLING IN THE WILDERNESS

Leviticus 1–3; John 7:1–13; Song of Solomon 5:10–12

The book of Leviticus can feel distant, abstract, and even absurd. Its opening chapters discuss odd offerings made at the tent of meeting, where God met His people when they were wandering in the wilderness after the exodus. Yet, the book signals an appreciation for all things: animals, crops, and the general need for peace—both between people and between God and people.

In Leviticus, we also find the setup for the entire Gospel of John; Jesus' life is cast as an offering to make all people one with God again. We find the background information for Isaiah 53, where the Suffering Servant dies and is resurrected on behalf of God's people. Much of the Old and New Testaments require a general understanding of Leviticus.

Not only do these ancient rituals show the need to appreciate the entire created order, they also show how much we should appreciate a faith that doesn't require all these rituals.

Leviticus shows the distance between God and His people. The amount of work required to get near Him is enormous. And it's not because God wanted it that way, it's because a holy (set apart) God cannot come near the unholy. Holiness rituals were required for Him to interact with His people—a temporary way for people to reach Him.

Just as God camped in the middle of His people in the wilderness, today He wants to set up His tent in the middle of our lives. And this is precisely what we witness in the beginning of John's Gospel when Jesus "dwells among us," which literally translates as, "took up residence among us." God dwelled among His people in the wilderness, just as He dwells in our lives today. —JDB

Are there areas of your life you don't want God to dwell in?
What could you change to invite Him in?

ANCIENT WORDS, FUTURE HOPE

Leviticus 4:1–6:30; John 7:14–44; Song of Solomon 5:13–16

Atonement is appealing because we all have relationships we wish we could reconcile. The 12-step program involves forgiving and forging renewed relationships when possible. But the story with God is different. There's an acute awareness that *we* can't fix things with our Creator; we need someone or something else to do it for us.

Jesus is described as the atonement, the sacrifice, and the perfect offering. But what do these terms actually mean? In Leviticus 5:14–6:30, we learn what it means for Jesus to be a guilt offering: He takes the guilt of the people, incurred through their sinful acts, and places it upon Himself. He becomes the "ram without defect from the flock" (Lev 6:6).

Jesus takes the stage as the Suffering Servant in Isaiah 52:13–53:12, fulfilling the events it prophesies. Isaiah 53:10 reads, "If she places [the servant's] life a guilt offering, he will see offspring, he will prolong days. And the will of Yahweh is in his hand, it will succeed" (my translation).

When He is arrested, Jesus understands that He is on His way to die at the hands of His own people (the "she" in Isaiah is "Jerusalem" or "Zion"). Matthew notes, "But all this has happened in order that the scriptures of the prophets would be fulfilled" (Matt 26:56). Jesus acknowledges it by saying, "the Son of Man is being betrayed into the hands of sinners!" (Matt 26:45). This echoes Isaiah 53:3: "He was despised and rejected by men; a man of suffering, and acquainted with sickness, and like one from whom others hide their faces, he was despised, and we did not hold him in high regard."

Leviticus seems archaic until it is put into this perspective. The oddities of this ancient book give us a connection to Jesus. He is the fulfillment of all Israel hoped for. Isn't this the same in our lives? At first it might seem like the events are somehow disconnected or distant from God and His works. But upon a second glance—in retrospect—we see they're a foundation for hope. —JDB

In what areas of your life do you need to connect with God's work?
What does the interaction between ancient law, prophecy, and Jesus'
life teach you about God and His work in our lives?

○ ○ ○ ○ ○

DANGER IN THE
SPHERE OF INFLUENCE

Leviticus 7:1–8:36; **John 7:45–52**; Song of Solomon 6:1–5

L eadership is like a bright spotlight; when the heat intensifies, it's difficult to conceal the areas where we fail. But that's where true character is revealed.

The Pharisees didn't fare well with the pressure of authority. We can see why Jesus had such compassion for the masses by observing the Pharisees' behavior in John 7. After Jesus claimed to be the source of life and ratcheted up the conflict, the Pharisees became angry. Sensing that their authority was slipping, they judged Jesus before they had a chance to give Him a hearing. They intimidated Nicodemus, harshly rebuked the captains, and cursed the people: "This crowd who does not know the law is accursed!" (John 7:49).

Those who hold positions of authority have great influence—a reason why bad authority can be so detrimental: "Not many should become teachers, my brother, because you know that we will receive a greater judgment" (Jas 3:1). But influence isn't relegated to leaders, supervisors, or pastors. Anyone who has a measure of influence over others should carefully consider how they use that trust.

When we have earthly teachers who let us down, we can turn to God, our heavenly teacher. For those who were under the heavy hand of the Pharisees, Jesus' words must have been as refreshing and soothing as the water He spoke of: "If anyone is thirsty, let him come to me, and let him drink, the one who believes in me" (John 7:37–38). —RVN

How are you using your authority to lead others to Christ? How can you seek out forgiveness from those you may have harmed?

GRACE AMONG THE GRAPHIC

Leviticus 9–11; John 7:53–8:11; Song of Solomon 6:6–10

"Then he slaughtered the burnt offering, and Aaron's sons brought the blood to him, and he sprinkled it on the altar all around; and they brought the burnt offering to him by its pieces, as well as the head, and he burned them on the altar" (Lev 9:12–13). There are graphic scenes like this throughout the Bible, especially in Leviticus. But they act as a reminder of what sacrifice looks like and what it really means.

Even though Jesus would ultimately make the greatest sacrifice of all—laying down His life for the sins of others—He did not hold people's sins against them. Although Jesus understood that He would be brutalized like the animals sacrificed during Aaron's day, He chose to forgive people. When a woman "caught in adultery" was brought before Jesus, He did not sentence her to death, as was demanded by the Jewish authorities and laws of His time. Instead, He said, "The one of you without sin, let him throw the first stone at her!" (John 8:7). And Jesus says the same to us today. Only those without sin can throw a stone or cast judgment on others—and that's none of us.

We shouldn't use this as an excuse, though. We shouldn't say, "What happens between you and God and between you and others is up to you." Instead, we must call each other forward to follow Christ. Jesus has forgiven us, but this doesn't excuse our sins. Similarly, we can't use Jesus' graciousness as an excuse to continue sinning.

We must remember grace and offer that grace to one another. Indeed, we must not judge, but we must not excuse sin in the process. In being gracious both to ourselves and others, we must remember why we have the ability to do so: Jesus died the brutal death of a sacrifice. It was His body that was torn apart and His flesh that was flung. (It's just as harsh as it sounds.)

I don't say any of this to make us feel guilty, but to remind all of us of the price Jesus paid for our freedom.

Jesus died so that we could be one with God, not so that we could continue to sin against the God He unified us with. As Jesus says at the end of this scene, after everyone had left, "Neither do I condemn you. Go, and sin no more" (John 8:11). —JDB

In what ways are you misappropriating grace?

∘ ∘ ∘ ∘ ∘

THE LIGHT OF THE WORLD

Leviticus 12:1–13:59; **John 8:12–30**; Song of Solomon 6:11–13

"I am the light of the world! The one who follows me will never walk in darkness, but will have the light of life" (John 8:12). While some of Jesus' "I am" statements confused the Jews, the "following the light" imagery would have been familiar. God had led the Israelites out of Egypt and through the wilderness with a pillar of fire so they could walk at night (Exod 13:21). They couldn't deflect or misunderstand this claim.

Jesus used this imagery to show the Jews that He offers clarity and meaning in a dark world. He offers life, grace, and spiritual awakening to those who are lost in the darkness. But the Pharisees couldn't comprehend the light; they misinterpreted Jesus' claims and fumbled around in the darkness and the details (John 8:19, 22, 25, 27).

When we've elevated ourselves in the darkness, it's hard to humble ourselves in the light.

Even when we have inklings that tell us there is a better way, we don't want to sacrifice our own pride. We prefer to be contrary and comfortable—to dwell on the details and exert our own opinions. But if we never call out the darkness, we'll never experience the flooding of light. —RVN

Are you calling out the darkness in and around you?

FREEDOM

Leviticus 14; **John 8:31–59**; Song of Solomon 7:1–4

"Even though I know it's wrong, I sometimes think, 'If I hadn't accepted Christ, I would have so much more freedom.' And then I venture down that road and realize just how terrible it is. It takes me to a very dark place."

This deep, heart-wrenching statement by a friend made me realize there are countless people who probably feel this way about Jesus. And what if, unlike my friend, they hadn't figured out the latter part of this statement? They were probably walking a road closer to legalism than the road Christ envisions for our lives. Or they could be so far from actually experiencing grace and the empowerment of the Holy Spirit that they have yet to see how incredible a life lived for Jesus can be.

Jesus promises freedom: "Then Jesus said to those Jews who had believed him, 'If you continue in my word you are truly my disciples, and you will know the truth, and the truth will set you free'" (John 8:31–32). What we often gloss over in this passage, though, is that Jesus is speaking to *believers*. If you haven't begun to fully trust in Jesus, the thought that He gives us freedom is difficult to understand. Someone could ask, "Isn't He creating a system that forces us to live a certain way?" The answer is no: Jesus is setting up what will be a natural response to His grace.

The context of this verse also makes me wonder if someone who hasn't yet truly sacrificed for Jesus, beyond just a simple tithe, would fathom what freedom with Him looks like. The Jews Jesus is addressing would have already been experiencing some sort of social ostracism for their belief in Him—they would have understood that sacrifice brings spiritual freedom.

This concept isn't easy to grasp, but in the simplest terms possible, Jesus frees us from religious systems and gives us the Spirit to empower us to do His work. This Spirit guides us and asks us to make sacrifices for Him, but those sacrifices are minimal compared to the eternal life He gave us through the sacrifice of His life. These sacrifices don't become a system with Christ, but something we strive to do because we want to. That's the freedom of the Spirit. —JDB

Have you experienced freedom in Christ? How can you seek the Spirit's presence so you can experience more freedom?

THE DAY OF ATONEMENT

Leviticus 15–16; John 9:1–12; Song of Solomon 7:5–9

When it comes to the cost of sin, the average person probably thinks in terms of "What can I get away with?" rather than "What does this cost me and other people emotionally?" These calculations aren't made in terms of life and death, but that is literally the case when it comes to sin.

The Day of Atonement is a beautiful, though horrific, illustration of this. It takes three innocent animals to deal with the people's sin: one to purify the high priest and his family, one to be a sin offering to Yahweh that purifies the place where He symbolically dwelt (the holy of holies), and one to be sent into the wilderness to remove the people's transgressions (Lev 16:11, 15–16, 21–22).

After the blood of the first two animals is spilled on the Day of Atonement—demonstrating the purification of God's people—the final goat demonstrates God's desire to completely rid the people of their sin. "Aaron shall place his two hands on the living goat's head, and he shall confess over it all the Israelites' iniquities and all their transgressions for all their sins, and he shall put them on the goat's head, and he shall send it away into the desert" (Lev 16:21).

The Day of Atonement symbolized God's desire for His people: One day, sin would no longer stand between God and His children. Like the goat, Jesus lifts the people's iniquities (Isa 53:12). He fulfills this prophecy, becoming the ultimate ransom; no other sacrifice is ever needed.

As the author of Hebrews says, "For the law appoints men as high priests who have weakness, but the statement of the oath, after the law, appoints a Son, who is made perfect forever" (Heb 7:28). He then goes onto say, "And every priest stands every day serving and offering the same sacrifices many times, which are never able to take away sins. But this one, after he had offered one sacrifice for sins for all time, sat down at the right hand of God" (Heb 10:11–12).

The price of sin may be great, but Christ has paid that price. —JDB

In what ways do you take Jesus' sacrifice for granted?
What can you do differently?

○ ◊ ◊ ◊ ○

THE FEAR

Leviticus 17:1–19:37; **John 9:13–34**; Song of Solomon 7:10–13

We often don't realize that we're guilty of fearing others. At the time, it can feel definite and look legitimate. Fearing others can also take the form of a meticulous house, staying late at the office, or passing anxious, sleepless nights. When we hold someone else's opinions higher than God's, we suddenly find our world shaky and imbalanced.

Jesus' healing of the blind man reveals that the fear of people is not a modern concept. The Pharisees had a stranglehold on Jewish life: "for the Jews had already decided that if anyone should confess him to be Christ, he would be expelled from the synagogue" (John 9:22). The blind man's parents were victims of the Pharisees' mission, but they were willing victims. Even within the ruling ranks, though, opinions were divided, but the fear of people still ruled (John 9:16). John reports elsewhere that "many of the rulers believed in him, but because of the Pharisees they did not confess it. … For they loved the praise of men more than praise from God" (John 12:42–43).

The blind man is the antithesis of all this. Perhaps, marginalized at birth, the opinions of others didn't hold as much weight for him. Under interrogation, he is bold, quick-witted, and over-the-top incredulous. He is enraged that the Pharisees do not accept the basic facts of the story: "I told you already and you did not listen! Why do you want to hear it again? You do not want to become his disciples also, do you?" (John 9:27). While he has yet to confess in Jesus, he knows what he has experienced—he was blind, and now he sees. And as far as he can tell, only one sent by God could perform such a miracle.

Fearing people involves holding their opinions higher than God's. At its heart, though, it's an inflated opinion of our own selves—self-protection or self-esteem. But the blind man was willing to proclaim the truth about the Son of Man who healed him—physically, and then spiritually. He was willing to give up everything. —RVN

How are you guided by the opinions of others?
How can you make decisions that are aimed at
bringing glory to God?

∘ ∘ ∘ ∘ ∘

PATIENTLY WAITING

Leviticus 20:1–22:33; John 9:35–41; **Song of Solomon 8:1–5**

Delayed gratification is a foreign concept to our natural instincts. Our culture doesn't encourage patience or contentment; we would prefer to have our desires met the moment they arise.

The woman in Song of Solomon tells us that she is delighted in her beloved. She praises his attributes and tells of the wonders of their love. But throughout the poem, at seemingly random moments, she also warns the daughters of Jerusalem about love: "I adjure you … do not arouse or awaken love until it pleases!" (Song 8:4).

This is not the first time she has "adjured" them to wait and have patience: the same refrain is found elsewhere in the poem, and it acts like an oath (Song 2:7; 3:5). Although the elevated poetry glories in love, delight, and fulfillment, it also warns about immediate gratification. The woman urges us not to force love. It is something that must be anticipated and protected, not enjoyed before its time.

It doesn't feel natural to wait and anticipate, but in many ways, staying faithful and being hopeful characterizes our faith. Waiting doesn't mean we're not bold or risk-takers. It means we're faithful to God—we're waiting for things to happen in His time. We know God has something planned for us that is beyond our expectations. —RVN

How are you patiently waiting and anticipating?

∘ ◦ ◇ ◦ ∘

REALITY CAN BITE

Leviticus 23–25; **John 10:1–21**; Song of Solomon 8:6–9

Reality shows are all about people who are known or want to be known—they have celebrity syndrome. The root cause of this obsession is probably, like most things, a disconnect from our Maker. As people disconnect from the God who made us, we seek affirmation from other sources. And as wrong as this desire may be, our culture makes it feel like second nature.

The Jewish people Jesus spoke to also felt displaced. They were a people who had lost touch with their guide—their shepherd. Jesus is the answer to their call.

Echoing Ezekiel 34:11–24, He says, "I am the good shepherd, and I know my *own*, and my *own* know me, just as the Father knows me and I know the Father." But Jesus goes one step further by adding, "and I lay down my life for the sheep" (John 10:14–15). Jesus promises that He will know us, and by echoing the very words of God, He is claiming that He is the God of Israel—He is the way God will know us. He offers the affirmation we've been looking for; He essentially says, "I chose you."

But lest we understand this passage only to be about Jesus fulfilling what God had promised to the Jewish people, He remarks, "And I have other sheep which are not from this fold. I must bring these also, and they will hear my voice, and they will become one flock—one shepherd. Because of this the Father loves me, because I lay down my life so that I may take possession of it again" (John 10:16–17).

Jesus came as our good shepherd, as the one who guides us back to God. When we have the urge to obsess over those who are known to the world, or when we desire to be known ourselves, we can be assured that Jesus knows us. He knows you, and me, and He was *still* willing to die for us. —JDB

In what ways are you seeking to be known by
people or obsessing over those who are well-known?
What can you do to change that?

NEON GODS

Leviticus 26–27; John 10:22–42; Song of Solomon 8:10–14

I dolatry seems archaic. Who worships idols anymore? We all know that in other countries, traditional idol worship of gold and wooden statues still goes on, but we often forget about our own idols. What does all our furniture point toward? Why do we care who is on the cover of a magazine? How do you feel if you miss your favorite talk show? If we're really honest, what do we spend the majority of our time thinking about?

Idols are everywhere, and most of us are idol worshipers of some kind. When we put this in perspective, suddenly the words of Leviticus 26 become relevant again. The problem addressed in Leviticus is the same problem we're dealing with today.

Leviticus 26 and its harsh words against idolatry should prompt each of us to ask, "What are my idols?" and then to respond with, "I will end my idolatry." And if the temptation is too great with these things present in our lives (like the TV), we should say, "I will exile them from my home and presence."

It's not put in these terms often enough, but it should be. The "noise" of idols is keeping us away from God, and even more so, our *worship* of the noise is doing so. Likewise, our obsession with possessions and celebrities is standing between God and us.

In their song "The Sound of Silence," Simon and Garfunkel described the same situation in modern culture: "The people bowed and prayed to the neon god they made." —JDB

What neon god are you worshiping?
And what are you going to do about it?

March 1

∘ ∘ ◊ ∘ ∘

A BOLD GOD AND A BOLD PEOPLE

Numbers 1:1–46; John 11:1–27; **Psalm 1:1–6**

I magine a God so bold that He would say, "Take a census of the entire community of the children of Israel according to their clans and their ancestors' house … from twenty years old and above, everyone in Israel who is able to go to war. You and Aaron must muster them for their wars. A man from each tribe will be with you, each man the head of his family" (Num 1:2–4). It wouldn't be easy to hear God tell you that you must be ready for war.

Yet our daily decisions to follow God are not so different than the decisions and preparations Moses had to make. Every day we have opportunities to choose God—or not. It's easy to agree to this as a principle, but living it is an entirely different story. How often do distractions deter us from actually hearing God? Yet if we can't hear Him, we can't obey Him.

It's also easy to be distracted by sin, but following sinful ways will only make us like "the chaff that the wind scatters" (Psa 1:4). We must be a people constantly seeking God instead—a people that makes His law our "delight" (Psa 1:2). We must "meditate" upon it "day and night" (Psa 1:2).

We're also distracted by wicked people prospering. It's easy to think, "Why is that person moving up in the world while I seem to be falling back?" But we must remember that this world is not "the dream," and God will bring justice: "For Yahweh knows the way of the righteous, but the way of the wicked will perish" (Psa 1:6). —JDB

What's distracting you from listening to God and following Him?
What are you going to do about it?

THE POWER AND THE GLORY

Numbers 1:47–2:34; **John 11:28–57**; Psalm 2:1–12

In our day-to-day life, we acknowledge God's power and encourage others to believe in it. Yet sometimes it takes a trial for us to realize the extent and reality of our confession.

The disciples misunderstand Jesus' reference to death and resurrection (John 11:11–12), so He displays His power through a trial and a miracle—the death and raising of Lazarus. Before Jesus has raised Lazarus, Mary and Martha express, "Lord, if you had been here, my brother would not have died" (John 11:21, 32). While their statement is a confession, it reveals their limited view of Jesus' power. The crowd echoes Mary and Martha's sentiment: "Was not this man who opened the eyes of the blind able to do something so that this man also would not have died?" (John 11:37). Yet, they don't realize that Jesus has been planning for this moment to provide them with a chance to believe. (Of course, Jesus knows He could have come earlier; He chose not to so He could use this as an example.)

Jesus uses this miracle to challenge and encourage them while showing them that He is the source of life. The question He poses to Martha should be one we all consider: "I am the resurrection and the life. The one who believes in me, even if he dies, will live, and everyone who lives and believes in me will never die forever. Do you believe this?" (John 11:25–26). —RVN

What trials has God used to show you
that He is the true life?

IT MAY SEEM BLAND

Numbers 3:1-39; John 12:1-19; Psalm 3-4

Let's just admit it: genealogies and lists, like the one in Numbers 3:1–39, are the most boring elements of the Bible. But they do something for us that other formats cannot—they give us a sense of history and lineage.

With a genealogy, we can do more than just trace people; we can map their relationships to others and to the events that happen through those relationships. We can also determine who was involved in those major events.

Genealogies and lists give us a small glimpse into God's providential work, even though we may not recognize them as such. God worked among the people in those lists. He chose to use them. They didn't deserve to be used by God in mighty ways, but they were. Some of the people in Numbers 3:1–39 were given seemingly insignificant tasks: "The responsibility of the sons of Merari was the supervision of the frames of the tabernacle, its bars, pillars, bases, and all its vessels and all its service," among other things (Num 3:36). If most of us were given this assignment, we would probably think it lame and ask for another. But the sons of Merari likely understood that anything God asks of us should be followed through with honor.

The people listed in Numbers 3:1–39 were likely selected because they believed they would see God's glory.

God may ask us to do things that seem insignificant or crazy, but if we don't, we will miss out on seeing His glory. —JDB

*What is God asking of you
that seems insignificant or crazy?*

A PRAYER FOR GUIDANCE

Numbers 3:40–4:49; **John 12:20–50**; **Psalm 5:1–12**

When we feel downtrodden, it's easy to lash out at those around us. Too often, caught in the injustice of our circumstances, we might begin to feel an unhealthy amount of self-justification. It's difficult to see where the lines of right and wrong fall when anger and hurt overwhelm us.

The psalmist presents an alternative to this: turning to the God of justice for guidance, protection, and insight. Psalm 5 records a heartfelt cry. This cry is directed at the God who acts justly in a world where evil seems to win (something not always easy to comprehend). Before making a judgment, the psalmist says, "I will set forth my case to you and I will watch" (Psa 5:3). Rather than push forward with his own agenda, he calls out for God's justice because Yahweh is "not a God who desires wickedness" (Psa 5:4).

The psalmist acknowledges God's sovereignty and love, which is the basis for his confidence: "Through the abundance of your steadfast love I will enter your house. I will bow down toward your holy temple in awe of you" (Psa 5:7). Before calling out the evil actions of his enemies, he prays for direction: "Lead me in your righteousness because of my enemies; make straight before me your way" (Psa 5:8). The psalmist prays; then he acts with God's justice in view.

In John 12, Jesus states that utter and complete devotion to God and His kingdom should be the focus of our lives: "Those who love their life lose it, and those who hate their life in this world will keep it for eternal life. Whoever serves me must follow me, and where I am, there will my servant be also. Whoever serves me, the Father will honor" (John 12:25–26). —RVN

How can you pray for guidance in a world
that often seems cold and uncaring?
How can you trust God to lead you
to act in ways that please Him?

March 5

∘ ◦ ◊ ◦ ∘

ODDITIES THAT MAKE SENSE

Numbers 5:1–31; John 13:1–20; Psalm 6:1–10

Some of the Old Testament laws seem so odd they're difficult to understand. It's easy for us to see why, in a day before medicine, God would send people with "a rash … a fluid discharge, and everyone … [who had touched] a corpse" outside the tribe for a period of time to prevent infection (Num 5:2). But why would God severely punish people caught in sins not (or hardly) related to possible medical issues (Num 5:5–31)?

I think it's because God understands that a culture that allows for amoral behavior will become a culture that promotes such behavior. Considering that Jesus had not come yet and sin was not graciously atoned for, there was a need for a ritual that symbolized religious purity.

We are meant to hate the things that people in this life condone—things that may even seem right to us at the time—for the sake of loving God's work.

When evil was present among His people, God had to take drastic measures to combat it—thus, He gave specific instructions. While today we have Christ, we must still devote ourselves to following God's calling and changing our evil ways for the sake of the gospel. —JDB

In what ways are you loving evil things instead of hating them?
Be honest with yourself and God.

SIGNS AND SATIRE

Numbers 6:1–27; John 13:21–38; **Psalm 7:1–17**

The images of judgment in Psalm 7 are sometimes hard to take. We are so acquainted with a God of love that it's difficult to understand a God who blinds eyes, hardens hearts, and "has indignation every day" (Psa 7:11). While these passages paint a picture of a judging God, they also emphasize how foolish and evil people can be—specifically focusing on those who push the boundaries of God's mercy and thus eventually find themselves outside of it.

In Psalm 7, God is preparing to judge the evil man. Suddenly, the psalm switches focus to the evil man's situations: "See, he travails with evil. He is pregnant with trouble, and he gives birth to deception. He makes a pit and digs it out, then falls in the trap he has made" (Psa 7:14–15). The evil man's folly is directly correlated to God's just judgment. God is ready and willing to forgive those who repent. But the evil man dwells in evil—he conceives it and is intimately connected to it. He gives birth to it. What's more, he is willingly walking into his own punishment. His actions of digging a pit and falling into his own trap expose his foolishness—that he has effectively judged himself, as "his trouble comes back on his head, and his violence comes down on his skull" (Psa 7:16).

The same sentiment is expressed in the Gospel of John. "But as many signs as he had performed before them, they did not believe in him" (John 12:37). While they had ample opportunity to believe Jesus' words, the Jewish people depicted in the passage chose not to believe in Jesus. They had even seen miracles. But because of their unbelief, they brought about their own judgment. And although they had an opportunity to believe, they abandoned it; thus, it was "taken away."

These passages illuminate the folly of the decision to disobey. The judgment brought on those who disobey is really their own doing. It's all the more reason to believe in the just God whose sacrifice defines what love is all about. —RVN

Are you hesitant in your commitment to Jesus?
What is keeping you from devoting totally to Him?

March 7

∘ ∘ ∘ ∘ ∘

CONCERNING KNOWLEDGE AND EATING MEAT

Numbers 7:1–47; **John 14:1–31**; Psalm 8:1–9

It's easy to equate knowledge with faith and then look down on new believers. Although we might not voice it, those who are less knowledgeable in their faith can seem weak. And sometimes, instead of practicing patience, showing love, and speaking carefully about the hope within us, we enroll them in Bible boot camp for dummies.

But Jesus shows that love is what leads to growth in faith: "If anyone loves me he will keep my word, and my Father will love him, and we will come to him and will take up residence with him. The one who does not love me does not keep my words, and the word that you hear is not mine, but the Father's who sent me" (John 14:23–24).

Paul echoes this in his letter to the Corinthians: "Knowledge puffs up, but love builds up. If anyone thinks he knows anything, he has not yet known as it is necessary to know" (1 Cor 8:1–2). In reality, the opposite of what we believe is true: Anyone who lacks love actually lacks faith (1 Cor 8:3).

Love defines our relationship with God and with each other. Christ died for both the knowledgeable and the weak, and both are caught up in His sacrifice (1 Cor 8:11). God has love and patience for the people whose own search for knowledge led us away from Him. And this should give us all the more love and patience for each other. —RVN

How can you practice humility and love with
those who haven't been in the faith as long as you have?

THE VINE AND THE BRANCHES

Numbers 7:48–89; **John 15:1–16:4**; Psalm 9:1–7

Jesus isn't simply a high priority or even the highest priority of our lives. He is the source of life. In the Gospel of John, Jesus teaches the disciples that they need to depend on Him for their very lives—both in the present and for eternal life.

"I am the vine; you are the branches. The one who remains in me and I in him—this one bears much fruit, for apart from me you are not able to do anything. If anyone does not remain in me, he is thrown out as a branch, and dries up, and they gather them and throw them into the fire, and they are burned" (John 15:5–6).

We rarely think in these terms today. However, the disciples faced persecution and even death on account of their faith in Jesus. Our lives, like theirs, will be held to the same measure. They *are* being held to the same measure.

Today, when you look at your life, and the lives of those closest to you, do you see fruit and abundance? Or do you see another picture? Are you like a dried-up branch, devoid of any good works that speak of a godly source? Do your relationships suffer because you are at the center, not Jesus?

Throughout the trials you face—whether big or small—cling to Jesus as the source and giver of life. May you remain in His love. And may His love fill you with abundance and cause you to bear fruit for His kingdom. —RVN

How does your life bear fruit?

PROFOUND AND CONFOUNDING

Numbers 8–9; John 16:5–33; Psalm 9:8–20

God's provision in our lives is often hard to see. There are times when we follow His commandments, and we're able to visibly see His work. Such times are profound to the believer but can be confounding to the unbeliever.

The ancients practiced remembering these events. They built memorials (usually a stack of stones) in places where God had shown Himself to them, such as when He offered them a covenant or gave them a revelation of some kind. They also had recurring holidays for remembering God's providence in their lives. These types of traditions are nearly lost on us. Easter and Christmas were intended for this purpose, but they have become about something entirely different instead: bunnies and eggs, or a man with a red suit.

In Numbers 9:1–14, we see God's command that His people celebrate the day He saved all the firstborn of Israel while issuing a punishment against Egypt. The Passover event was profound to the Israelites, but it was confounding to those who suffered the punishment: the Egyptians. Yahweh wanted His people to remember what it was like to believe and to remember that He will rise up against those who oppress them. All the commandments about the Passover occur just prior to Yahweh visiting them again (Num 9:15–23). He intends to dwell among them.

We as believers are called to know the wisdom of Yahweh: He sent Christ to be crucified for us, and we can have new lives in the Spirit as a result. This event must be remembered among Christians, continually and daily, and we must live a life that honors God's work through Christ. We must let it be known that His work *is* confounding—until you believe. —JDB

How is Christ profoundly affecting your life,
and how should you react as a result?

March 10

○ ○ ○ ○ ○

JESUS CHRIST
(MEANT TO BE) THE SUPERSTAR

Numbers 10:1–36; **John 17:1–26**; Psalm 10:1–18

Andrew Lloyd Webber's musical, *Jesus Christ Superstar,* is certainly incorrect (and rather heretical) in its portrayal of history, but it got one thing right: Jesus is meant to be the celebrity. He—no one else—is the Savior, the Christ, the Lord.

And that's why the celebrity pastor movement is quite frightening. I don't say this as a cynic, and it's not that I'm primarily concerned with how these teachers are marketed (although that, too, can be scary at times); I'm worried about the way they're received.

Certainly there are people who can be trusted more than others, and popularity is by no means a measurement of trustworthiness. But automatically agreeing with everything a teacher says puts the disciple in a bad position with the God they worship. It also puts the teacher in a position similar to an idol. Teachers who truly follow Christ would never desire such glory for themselves.

In the Gospel of John, we see Jesus glorified by the Father. Jesus was obedient to the Father, even to death, which is why He alone is worthy of our worship. "I have glorified you on earth by completing the work that you have given me to do. And now, Father, you glorify me at your side with the glory that I had at your side before the world existed" (John 17:4–5).

Jesus prayed: "Righteous Father, although the world does not know you, yet I have known you, and these men have come to know that you sent me. And I made known to them your name, and will make it known, in order that the love with which you loved me may be in them, and I may be in them" (John 17:26). —JDB

In what parts of your life is God asking you to make a statement
similar to Paul's? What teachers are you adoring too much?

○ ○ ○ ○ ○

IN THE MOMENT OF WEAKNESS

Numbers 11–12; John 18:1–24; Psalm 11–12

All leaders have their moments of weakness. But without such times, they wouldn't stretch themselves (and that would mean they weren't really in God's will). It's not that these moments shouldn't happen, but we should turn to God when they do.

Moses dealt with more than his fair share of people getting upset with his leadership, and he felt weak as a result. He didn't always handle these situations correctly, but in Numbers 11 we see a glimpse of what an amazing leader he really was. The people were upset because they didn't have meat to eat and were (once again) wishing they were back in Egypt. They were considering going against God's will, and at least with their words, they were already doing so. Moses responded by telling God about his frustrations:

"Moses heard the people weeping according to their clans … Then Yahweh became very angry, and in the eyes of Moses it was bad. And Moses said to Yahweh, 'Why have you brought trouble to your servant? Why have I not found favor in your eyes, that the burdens of all these people have been placed on me? … If this is how you are going to treat me, please kill me immediately if I find favor in your eyes, and do not let me see my misery'" (Num 11:10–11, 15).

God uses moments of weakness to create strength. He took the burden of leading off Moses alone and divided it among the people. In doing so, He made all the people accountable together for their actions (Num 11:16–23). God may have been angry about their disobedience, but that didn't stop Him from listening to His servant, Moses, and graciously responding. God wants to interact the same way with us when we bring our burdens to Him. —JDB

In what ways are you feeling weak as a leader?
What would God have you do?

CRY OUT LIKE THE PSALMIST

Numbers 13:1–33; John 18:25–19:16; **Psalm 13:1–6**

We often read the very bold psalms of the Bible without really reading them. We're used to their cadence, their cries, and their requests. They seem appropriate in contexts where war, death, and enemies or mutinous friends were a daily reality. For that reason, these cries don't always resound off the pages and fill our own lips, even when they should.

"How long, O Yahweh? Will you forget me forever?" says the psalmist (Psa 13:1). "Consider and answer me, O Yahweh my God" (Psa 13:3).

Often, when going through the difficulties of life, these cries should be our own. Instead, we try to lean on our own strength. We rely on the bravery and wisdom that we think rests deep inside us. We try to muster courage. We engage the fear. The psalmist acknowledges that this isn't the way it's supposed to be: "How long must I take counsel in my soul, and sorrow in my heart all the day?" (Psa 13:2).

Instead, we should be crying out with the helplessness that is closer to our true reality. The next time you feel anxious, stop and pray. Turn over your cries to the one who can do something about them. When you do so, acknowledge that God is your God (Psa 13:3). Acknowledge His steadfast love (Psa 13:3). He will hear you and answer you. And, as the psalm states, He will deal bountifully with you (Psa 13:6). —RVN

How are you trying to resolve the problems of your life?
How can you turn to God in these moments?

March 13

∘ ◦ ◦ ◦ ∘

NOSTALGIA: MY OLD FRIEND

Numbers 14:1–45; John 19:17–42; Psalm 14:1–15:5

Regret and nostalgia can destroy lives. They are mirrored ideas with the same pitfalls: Neither can change the past, and both keep us from living in the present. When we live wishfully rather than interacting with the present, we're bound to miss out and hurt others. Since other people don't necessarily share our feelings about the past, they feel less important to us here and now. And indeed, we're making them less important. We're concerned instead with how things could have been or used to be.

This is precisely what happens after the Israelites flee Egypt: "Then all the community lifted up their voices, and the people wept during that night. And all the children of Israel grumbled against Moses and Aaron, and all the community said to them, 'If only we had died in the land of Egypt or in this desert!'" (Num 14:1–2).

As usual with regret and nostalgia, these words were said in frustration but born out of fear: "Why did Yahweh bring us into this land to fall by the sword? Our wives and our little children will become plunder; would it not be better for us to return to Egypt?" (Num 14:3).

And their fear even takes them to the next level of disobedience against God's will—they will overthrow Moses' leadership: "They said to each other, 'Let us appoint a leader, and we will return to Egypt'" (Num 14:4). Nostalgia is dangerous: it causes us to forget the wretchedness of the past and exchange it for fond memories. We begin to focus on the good things and drift away from obedience in the process. Regret, too, is dangerous, as we wish we had never ended the good times but kept on living the life that was never good for us to begin with.

This scene in Numbers illustrates a profound point: Collective memory enables regret and nostalgia to create mob rule instead of God rule. —JDB

What memories are you holding too dearly?
How are they holding you back from the life God has for you now?

∘ ◦ ◊ ◦ ∘

A PSALM OF CONFIDENCE

Numbers 15:1–41; John 20:1–31; **Psalm 16:1–11**

"You are my Lord," the psalmist acknowledges. "I have no good apart from you" (Psa 16:2). We know that God is everything we need, but somehow the details still get in the way. We want to alleviate our troubles through other means—that vacation, the position that will bring recognition, or the spouse who will complete us. The psalmist says that anyone who places their desire in anything other than God will only increase in sorrow (Psa 16:4).

It seems radical and difficult to live out the psalmist's simple confession. The ancient practice of idol worship is alive and well in our modern-day culture and in our own hearts. (Just look at the magazine rack or TV shows if you think I'm wrong: What is worshiped there?) We are just like the Israelites—unfaithful and prone to "hurry after another god" (Psa 16:4).

For the psalmist, however, "Yahweh is the portion which is my share and my cup" (Psa 16:5). He is all the psalmist ever needs: "I have set Yahweh before me always. Because he is at my right hand I will not be shaken" (Psa 16:8). God brings the psalmist hope, and He can do the same for us. We just need to turn to Him. —RVN

Today, pray the words of Psalm 16: "You are my Lord.
I have no good apart from you." How can we remind
ourselves that He is all we will ever need?

THE POWER STRUGGLE

Numbers 16:1–50; John 21:1–25; Psalm 17:1–15

Every leader faces power struggles. If there isn't some sort of struggle, the leader probably isn't doing his or her job well. It's simple: Those who make everyone happy probably aren't pushing people to be better, and pushing will—at times—frustrate both the leaders and the followers.

Moses regularly experienced leadership struggles. In Numbers 16, Korah—accompanied by 250 men who were leaders in Israel—calls Moses and Aaron's leadership into question: "All of the community is holy, every one of them, and Yahweh is in their midst, so why do you raise yourselves over the assembly of Yahweh?" (Num 16:3). They're using Moses' words, spoken on behalf of Yahweh, against him here: "You will belong to me as a kingdom of priests and a holy nation" (Exod 19:6). But they made one faulty assumption in doing so. Yahweh had prefaced these words by saying, "if you will carefully listen to my voice and keep my covenant, you will be a treasured possession for me out of all the peoples, for all the earth is mine, but ..." and continued with the line Korah quoted (Exod 19:5–6).

Surely Moses knows this, and he is well aware of their folly. But he responds by prostrating himself—an act of worship toward God and humility toward those he serves: the people of Israel. He then says, "Tomorrow morning Yahweh will make known who is his and who is holy, and he will bring him near to him, whomever he chooses he will bring near to him" (Num 16:5). It appears that in that moment of prostration, Moses prayed and was immediately given an answer. He insists on bringing the matter before God Himself.

Moses could have defended himself by insisting upon the special nature by which God had revealed Himself to him. He even could have noted that Korah was only in leadership at all because Moses listened to God and appointed him. But instead, he insisted on bringing it before God. He did, though, follow up by telling Korah that he had plenty of authority and shouldn't be so greedy (Num 16:8–11).

This event demonstrates the kind of faith that we should all have in what God asks us to do. —JDB

*How do you respond when people question what God has asked
you to do? How can your response in the future be more like Moses'?*

IT WILL SEEM SIMPLE IN RETROSPECT

Numbers 17:1–18:32; **1 Corinthians 1:1–31**; Psalm 18:1–12

W e're all faced with difficult tasks. When Paul wrote to the Corinthians, he was forced to confront their spiritual problems, which were slowly destroying God's work among them. Paul was thankful for them (1 Cor 1:4–8), but he was also called to a high purpose as an apostle. His calling meant saying what people didn't want to hear (1 Cor 1:1).

There were divisions among the Corinthians that were going to rip their fledgling church apart, and Paul implored them to make some difficult changes: "Now I exhort you, brothers, by the name of our Lord Jesus Christ, that … there not be divisions among you, and that you be made complete in the same mind and with the same purpose. For … there are quarrels among you" (1 Cor 1:10–11). And here's where something amazing happens that we often overlook. Paul, a confident man and a former Law-abiding Pharisee, could have stated why he was right and moved on, but he does something else:

"Each of you is saying, 'I am with Paul,' and 'I am with Apollos,' and 'I am with Cephas,' and 'I am with Christ.' Has Christ been divided? Paul was not crucified for you, was he? Or were you baptized in the name of Paul? I give thanks that I baptized none of you except Crispus and Gaius, lest anyone should say that you were baptized in my name" (1 Cor 1:12–15). Paul sticks it to them, and he reminds them that Christ deserves all the credit.

We all have moments like this, where we have the opportunity to take credit for someone else's work—or even worse, for Jesus' work. Paul had the strength and character that we should all desire. —JDB

How are you currently taking credit for
others' work or for Jesus'?

March 17

° ◊ ◊ ◊ °

LETTING EVIL BURN

Numbers 19:1–20:13; 1 Corinthians 2:1–16; Psalm 18:13–30

"And Yahweh spoke to Moses and Aaron, saying ... 'let them take to you a red heifer without a physical defect. ... And you will give it to Eleazar the priest, and it will ... be slaughtered in his presence. Then Eleazar the priest will take some of its blood on his finger and spatter it toward the mouth of the tent of assembly seven times. The heifer will be burned in his sight; its skin, its meat, and its blood, in addition to its offal, will burn'" (Num 19:1–4).

This passage is so strange and gruesome, it is clearly symbolic. The heifer represents the perfect, unblemished sacrifice—which takes care of some (not all) of the purification associated with things Yahweh deemed unclean for the purpose of teaching His people obedience, and some of the results of sin (Num 19:9).

Also, the heifer is burned because it has to be made into ashes. This beautiful creature becomes ashes. That's the cost of an impure life: Good has to become worthless. The only way to purge impurities is to burn them away. Then what has been purified through fire (and then water) can be used (Num 19:9–10). The passage goes on to describe several uses associated with this practice (e.g., Num 19:11–13).

All of our lives include things that go against God's will, and these things must burn. We must let the Spirit work in us to empower us to remove them. And there's good news for this: Jesus has already done the great work of conquering sin in the world. There is no more need for the red heifer because Jesus' sacrifice (His death) paid for our problems. He wasn't the symbol of the sacrifice, like the heifer; He was the sacrifice itself.

God calls us to the great race of running toward Him—for Him—in honor of what Christ has done among us. So let's let the evil burn. —JDB

What is God calling you to burn?

IS THIS "BAD" FROM GOD?

Numbers 20–21; 1 Corinthians 3:1–4:21; Psalm 18:31–50

God has granted us incredible grace in the salvation that Jesus' death and resurrection offers, but that very grace is often used as a theological excuse. It's dangerous to say that bad things come from God, but there are times when they actually do. What makes them good is how He uses them to help us grow. The great grace God offers doesn't mean our sins go unpunished.

We see God directly issue what seems "bad" in Numbers 21:5–7. First we're told: "The people spoke against God and against Moses, 'Why have you brought us from Egypt to die in the desert? There is no food and no water, and our hearts detest this miserable food'" (Num 21:5). Then, Yahweh sends poisonous snakes that bite the people, causing them to die (Num 21:6). Why would a good God do such a horrific thing?

In Numbers 21:1–4, the people had experienced a miraculous victory against the Canaanites living in Arad—a people they were losing to, and should have lost to, until Yahweh intervened. Yahweh showed Himself to be loyal and true; yet the people still rebelled.

When Yahweh punishes the people with the snakes, it's not because He wants to; it's because He needs to. And the result is worth it. The people say to Moses, "We have sinned because we have spoken against Yahweh and against you. Pray to Yahweh and let him remove the snakes from among us" (Num 21:7). In their response, they show faith in Yahweh and His ability to change the situation. They also show faith in the leader He appointed to them: Moses.

God sent this "bad" thing because He knew it would be a good thing (compare 1 Cor 11:30–32). This knowledge should make us boldly proclaim, as the psalmist does, "For who is God apart from Yahweh and who is a rock except our God?" (Psa 18:31). —JDB

What currently seems "bad" that is really
a result of God responding to your disobedience?

○ ○ ○ ○ ○

A MERCIFUL SMACKDOWN

Numbers 22:1–41; **1 Corinthians 5:1–6:11**; Psalm 19:1–14

Sometimes, we'd rather not be teachable. When it comes to taking advice from people in my church community, it's easier to keep an emotional distance than it is to listen. If I tread lightly on their sin, maybe they'll tread lightly on mine. If we keep our problems to ourselves, we can maintain a certain understanding. This type of tolerance has deadly results.

Unrestrained sin and pride don't just hurt the one who is sinning—their waves affect everyone (1 Cor 5:6). This is why Paul takes such a strong stance against them in 1 Corinthians 5:1–13. In Corinth, believers were using their freedom to commit all sorts of sordid sins. And instead of being broken about their sin, they were filled with pride—they were boasting about their freedom.

Paul knew he had to do something drastic to break through such thought patterns. His statement is startling for those who might practice tolerance for sin: "I have decided to hand over such a person to Satan for the destruction of the flesh, in order that his spirit may be saved in the day of the Lord" (1 Cor 5:5). This type of judging is not seen as casting someone to the depths of hell; rather, it is casting someone out of the Christian community with the purpose of helping them see their sin for what it is. (For Paul, the realm of Satan was *everything* outside of Christ; thus, everything outside of the Church was the realm of Satan.)

We aren't called to judge people who have no claim to following Jesus. Rather, we're called to hold accountable those who, like us, believe the good news (1 Cor 5:11). Within the bounds of authentic Christian community and trust, we need to be ready to call each other out when sin and pride creep in— and we need to do it with loving intolerance. —RVN

How are you reaching out to others who are struggling with sin?
How are you making yourself approachable and teachable?

○ ○ ○ ○ ○

WE DON'T (REALLY) MEAN IT

Numbers 23:1–30; 1 Corinthians 6:12–7:16; **Psalm 20:1–9**

"I'll pray for you." We say it often, but how many times do we actually remember to do it? Our biggest downfall might not be a lack of compassion—it's probably just not taking time to write down the request and not having a model of praying for others.

Some of us might feel like we've mastered the art of the task list, but it can still be difficult to keep up with praying for our friends. It's easy to think, "God knows their needs, so it's fine." But that's not the New Testament view of prayer: We're meant to pray always (Luke 18:1; 1 Thess 5:16). And Paul himself regularly asks for prayers. If they weren't important, he wouldn't ask (Col 4:3). For this reason, it would be helpful to develop a system to track what people need prayer for, like a prayer journal. But what about the model?

When I pray for God's will in my life, I've found that using the Lord's Prayer works well when I'm having trouble praying. But I haven't adopted a model for praying for others. Psalm 20 contains such a model, and the psalmist offers some beautiful words for others:

"May Yahweh answer you in the day of trouble. … May he send you help … May he remember all your offerings … May he give to you your heart's desire … May we shout for you over your victory" (Psa 20:1–5). And then the psalmist goes on to proclaim God's goodness and that He will answer (Psa 20:6). And this is the line I think I love the most: "Some boast in chariots, and others in horses, but we boast in the name of Yahweh, our God. They will collapse and fall, and we will rise and stand firm" (Psa 20:7–8).

"They will … fall … and we will rise." We must pray for our friends with this kind of confidence. And then the greatest challenge of all: We must pray for our enemies as well. —JDB

How can you hold yourself accountable to pray for others?
How can you use Psalm 20 as a model for prayer?

SINS OF OMISSION

Numbers 24–25; 1 Corinthians 7:17–40; **Psalm 21:1–13**

There's that moment when you're asked to do something you know is wrong, but you feel like you should respond. It's almost as fleeting as the decision to not stand up for what is right, even when no one asks for your opinion. Many wrongdoings occur in these moments—these chances for sins of omission. Being silent is as bad as committing the wrong action, which is why the American court system prosecutes all the people committing an armed robbery for murder when only one gunman pulls the trigger.

Balaam, the prophet from Moab, had such an opportunity. After he was asked by Yahweh to bless the people of Israel—in opposition to his own king's request (Num 22:1–6)—he could have done nothing at all. Or he could have made Yahweh like the gods of Moab—subjecting them to his will instead of their own—but he instead follows the orders of Yahweh and blesses the people of Israel (Num 24:3–9).

The psalmist addresses what can happen when things go differently: "Though they have plotted evil against you [Yahweh], though they have planned a scheme, they will not prevail. For you will turn them to flight, you will aim arrows on your bowstrings at their faces" (Psa 21:11–12).

We can hinder or help the work of God. Often this work can be done by much subtler means. Consider how you act or choose not to act in key moments, whether big or small. Today, choose to do the work that God has called you to do. —JDB

What sins of omission are currently in your life?

∘◊∘◊∘

FORSAKEN TO DELIGHT

Numbers 26:1–65; 1 Corinthians 8:1–9:27; **Psalm 22:1-13**

"My God, my God why have you forsaken me? Why are you far from help-ing me, far from the words of my groaning?" (Psa 22:1). These are some of the darkest words in Scripture. It's almost painful to speak them, to imagine a feeling of complete abandonment by God. These are also the words we hear Jesus say when He is hanging from the cross (Matt 27:46). When He utters them, He makes Himself one with this ultimate sufferer, this true lamenter, in Psalm 22. He is essentially saying, "I am He: the one who has suffered the most for God's cause and thus knows what it means to be human."

The plea in this psalm becomes even sadder, but then it is followed by a surprising affirmation of complete faithfulness in God: "O my God, I call by day and you do not answer, and by night but I have no rest. Yet you are holy, enthroned on the praises of Israel" (Psa 22:2–3). The very nature of crying out to God, even in a time of feeling like He has completely abandoned you, is an act of faith. When we cry out in His name, we affirm His presence and the real-ity that He can intercede. Even if we're not sure *how* He will intercede, crying out to Him is an act of faith. It is always the right solution; it's what Jesus did in His time of greatest need and pain.

The psalmist goes on to depict just how dire the situation is: "All who see me mock me. They open wide their lips; they shake the head, saying: 'He trusts Yahweh. Let him rescue him. Let him deliver him because he delights in him'" (Psa 22:8–9).

Jesus does precisely this: He trusts in Yahweh to be His rescuer. What the mockers—both at the cross and those depicted in this ancient psalm—don't realize is that God is delighted in the suffering for His cause. God sees the ulti-mate purpose of Jesus' suffering—the redemption of His people (compare Isa 52:13–53:12). And likewise, God sees the ultimate purpose of our suffering. He will delight in it when it is done for His purposes—His kingdom. This psalm is a model for us of what to do in those times. —JDB

What are you currently suffering through for God's purposes?
How can you use Psalm 22 as a model for your response?

○ ○ ○ ○ ○

REASON: NOT THE ULTIMATE POWER

Numbers 27:1-23; 1 Corinthians 10:1-22; Psalm 22:14-31

Reason is a gift from God, but that doesn't make it a substitute for seeking God's will through prayer.

Moses appears to have been an intelligent man. He figured out how to flee Egypt after killing an Egyptian, how to survive in the wilderness, and how to make his way back without prosecution. He also transformed non-militarized men into a military and taught them to craft the weaponry necessary to win countless battles. But Moses didn't rely on these abilities; he relied on asking God His will and waiting for His guidance.

Moses relies on God's will so often that I'm convinced that the actions that appear to come from great intelligence and reason—like his ability to escape and reenter Egypt and his ability to train people in combat—were based on God's direct guidance.

We see Moses seek God's guidance in matters that he could have used reason to discern as well. In Numbers 27, when Moses is asked if a family should receive an inheritance of land (in the promised land) even though their father died without a son to inherit it, he could have simply said, "Of course; God is gracious. He won't punish your entire family forever for your father's sins." (That was the reason they weren't granted the land automatically.) His simple reason of "God is good" probably could have answered this for him. But Moses seeks God's guidance instead. That's the right answer.

Our culture overemphasizes reason. Often, the people best at reasoning are promoted—in our workplaces, our churches, and our government—so it's easy to see reason as the ultimate power. Instead, though, we should seek God in all things. His guidance is always needed. While He gave us our minds, He also gave us the Spirit; and while the mind can fail, the Spirit, if truly sought, listened to, and waited upon, cannot. —JDB

What do you need to seek the Spirit's guidance on
that you are relying on reason for instead?

GREEN PASTURES: THEY REQUIRE ACTION

Numbers 28:1–31; **1 Corinthians 10:23–11:16**; Psalm 23

Love and complete reliance on God are interrelated concepts. When we discover what love really means, we want to praise God for it. When we learn to rely on God for all our needs, we see just how loving He is as He takes care of all aspects of our lives. And this love makes us want to show love to others.

It's those who *don't* have who are most apt to come to Jesus. They're most in need of love. For this reason, it's hard for us who *do* have—a home, a car, enough food for a week—to fully understand reliance on Christ. It takes a different type of discipline.

This is why it's still shocking to me how many people absolutely love Psalm 23. It's comforting, I suppose: "Yahweh is my shepherd; I will not lack for anything. In grassy pastures he makes me lie down; by quiet waters he leads me" (Psa 23:1–2). I think so many of us love it, though, because we're aware of how frail and vulnerable we really are. It could all be gone in a moment. Disease catches up to us, and death will eventually get us all. We often forget just how important love is in all this, and we fail to recognize why Psalm 23 has a special place in our hearts.

We are in the top percentile of wealth in the world. Many of our families own more than one car. Nonetheless, the death around us and the diseases we see show just how quickly it can be gone. And for this reason, we can recognize how crucial love is. Love carries people through hard times. It brings them to depend on God. Paul tells us we could have all sorts of incredible spiritual gifts, but if we don't have love, there's no point (1 Cor 13:1, 13).

And when Paul speaks about love, he's not talking about something we say or even feel; he's talking about something we *do*. Love requires us to give all things; or in Paul's words, it "rejoices with the truth, bears all things, believes all things, hopes all things, endures all things" (1 Cor 13:6–7). So, those of us who understand relying on Psalm 23, even in our wealth, must help those who rely on its promises but are yet to experience them. They are people all over the world, waiting for us to "bear" their burdens with them. They are the hurting, the voiceless—the people who need us to show real love. —JDB

*How can you show love to the hurting and voiceless
in the world today? God has called us all to action
—that is what love means. So how will you act?*

THOUGHTLESS ICONOCLASM

Numbers 29:1–40; **1 Corinthians 11:17–12:11**; Psalm 24:1–10

When we learn something new about life and faith, it's tempting to use our knowledge and freedom to tear down religious constructs and artifices—exposing truth in a way that's not helpful or edifying. If we're honest, pushing boundaries and living edgy and unfettered gives us a rush.

Paul warns the Corinthian Christians against this attitude: "All things are permitted, but not all things are profitable. All things are permitted, but not all things build up" (1 Cor 10:23). Paul sets up a contrast, juxtaposing the clauses to set apart what should really be the focus of the Corinthians. Paul stresses that instead of flaunting freedom, we should be focused on what is helpful and constructive for the community.

Seeking the good of the other person should be our first reflex. And it's not simply limited to the Christian community. Paul states: "Therefore, whether you eat or you drink or whatever you do, do all things for the glory of God. Give no offense both to Jews and to Greeks and to the church of God" (1 Cor 10:31–32). This is a tall order in the internet age; when we don't see someone face to face, it's much easier to tear them down.

This doesn't mean we shouldn't challenge ideas when the time is appropriate. However, it does mean we should carefully consider our audience and act in a way that will best communicate the message of the gospel. Whatever the case, we should "please all people in all things, not seeking [our] own benefit, but the benefit of the many, in order that they may be saved" (1 Cor 10:33). —RVN

How are you seeking the good of those around you?

March 26

GRACE AND FAVOR

Numbers 30:1–16; 1 Corinthians 12:12–13:13; **Psalm 25:1–22**

Usually when we seek someone's goodwill, we emphasize our own winning traits or accomplishments. Our supervisor, significant other, or family members are barraged with a list of our actions in an attempt to get the other to respond in kind. Often this results in a tug-of-war mentality, basing all we deserve on what we give.

But our relationship with God doesn't follow these rules. God's mercy isn't based on what we've done—it's based entirely on His own goodness. The psalmist, realizing this, turns all of his attention to God's mercy in Psalm 25: "Remember your compassion, O Yahweh, and your acts of loyal love, because they are from of old. Do not remember the sins of my youth or my transgressions. According to your loyal love, remember me if you will, for the sake of your goodness, O Yahweh" (Psa 25:6–7).

In this individual lament, the psalmist reaches out to Yahweh with a cry for forgiveness and guidance. Instead of justifying his actions to obtain Yahweh's favor, the psalmist turns the focus to God's works and His faithfulness in the past. What he deserves isn't what he gets—something he is altogether thankful for.

God's abundant graciousness extends far: from heaven down to earth, where Jesus paid the ultimate price for our sin. We can't be thankful enough for that great act of mercy. It's a reason for humility and thankfulness, as the psalmist expresses, and an act of faithfulness to us that we can never return. His mercy should completely transform our concept of what we deserve; it should alter us so much that we treat those around us not with expectations of who they should be for us, but with grace and love, as God treated us. —RVN

How are you extending God's grace
to the people around you?

∘ ∘∘∘ ∘

TONGUES, PROPHECY, AND THE THING WE CALL LOVE

Numbers 31:1–54; **1 Corinthians 14:1–25**; Psalm 26:1–12

Nearly anything good can become unproductive if it's abused or misused. Paul is all about embracing the side of spirituality that can seem a bit wacky to us today—gifts of tongues and prophecy, to name a few. But he is fully aware of the problems that can come from these gifts being used in a way that doesn't fit within God's will. And Paul's primary concern is that spiritual gifts are used only within the bounds of love.

Love is what it's all about. "Pursue love, and strive for spiritual gifts, but especially that you may prophesy. For the one who speaks in a tongue does not speak to people but to God, because no one understands, but by the Spirit he speaks mysteries" (1 Cor 14:1–2). By tongues, Paul is likely referencing the "tongues of angels"—some angelic language (1 Cor 13:1)—although elsewhere the term is used in reference to people speaking in a language they don't actually know for the sake of ministering to others in their native tongue (Acts 2:3–4).

Love—as manifested in Christ's death and resurrection and in our living sacrificially for Him and others—is central, and spiritual gifts should support that cause.

Paul goes on to say: "Now I want you all to speak with tongues, but even more that you may prophesy. … But now, brothers, if I come to you speaking with tongues, how do I benefit you, unless I speak to you either with a revelation or with knowledge or with a prophecy or with a teaching?" (1 Cor 14:5–6).

Spiritual gifts are meant to indwell believers. Christians are meant to be driven by God's Spirit and to do miraculous things in His name. But none of it matters if it's not for the purpose of showing Christ's love. —JDB

What gifts do you resist using?
How can you use the spiritual gifts God has given you
to show love to others, and how can you correct your use
of them if you're not currently using them for this purpose?

March 28

∘ ∘ ◊ ∘ ∘

RISK: OVERSOLD AND UNDERPLAYED

Numbers 32:1–42; 1 Corinthians 14:26–15:11; **Psalm 27:1–14**

The fears of the psalmist are not our fears today, and the fact that they aren't should bother us. The psalmist remarks, "Do not give me over to the desire of my enemies, because false witnesses have arisen against me, and each breathing out violence. Surely I believe that I will see the goodness of Yahweh in the land of the living" (Psa 27:12–13). How many of us have legitimate enemies because of our faith? And how many of us experience violence because of the way we believe?

There are many problems with Christianity today, but one of the most pervasive is the lack of willingness to take major risks for Jesus. Likewise, there is unbelief in God's incredible ability to overcome all that we face.

We may say that we affirm God's power to beat all odds, but we don't face the odds as if that were true. If we did, there would be far more world-changing Christians than there are. Instead, most Christians, at least in the Western world, are quite comfortable with a faith that generally allows for them to live a life of comfort rather than a life of being stretched for God's causes. And when I use "them," I mean that as "we." *We* struggle with this, as a people and as individuals.

I think our fear of taking risks for Jesus is directly connected to our lack of knowledge about what to do when they come along. The psalmist tells us, "Wait for Yahweh. Be strong and let your heart show strength, and wait for Yahweh" (Psa 27:14). Notice that the psalmist tells us to wait for Yahweh twice. Only something of grand importance would a poet state twice. Strength is found in Yahweh, and that strength should be shown in how we live. —JDB

How can you take more risks for God?
What are you waiting on, and how are you praying about that?

PRAYER AND HOPE FOR THE ANXIOUS

Numbers 33:1–49; 1 Corinthians 15:12–34; **Psalm 28:1–9**

Anxiety, depression, and fear aren't part of the Christian life—or the ideal Christian life, anyway. But for those who struggle with these emotions, this tidy concept isn't helpful or true. What is helpful is hope and belief in the midst of tumultuous emotion.

The writer of Psalm 28 expresses deep anxiety, but even as he does this, he expresses trust in Yahweh: "To you, O Yahweh, I call. O my rock, do not be deaf to me. Or else, if you are silent to me, then I will become like those descending to the pit" (Psa 28:1). Though he feels like God is not listening, the psalmist doesn't stop pursuing God. He worships and cries for help anyway. In contrast to the "workers of evil" who "do not regard the works of Yahweh, nor the work of his hands," the psalmist puts all of his dependence and trust in Yahweh (Psa 28:3, 5).

Halfway through the psalm, the petition turns to praise when Yahweh answers his prayer. The psalmist realizes his confidence is in the right place: "Blessed is Yahweh, because he has heard the voice of my supplications" (Psa 28:6). Even through dark times and bleak circumstances, God is faithful. He is never far from us, though emotions might dictate otherwise. He will "Shepherd them also and carry them always" (Psa 28:9). He saves, blesses, guides, and even carries us through all seasons.

We are saved not according to our own works, but the work of Christ. In the midst of struggle, we can be certain that we are experiencing salvation now, in part. And we can be "convinced of this same thing, that the one who began a good work in [us] will finish it until the day of Christ Jesus" (Phil 1:6). —RVN

How are you trusting in God in the midst of struggle?
How can you thoughtfully support someone
who is suffering through a season like this?

March 30

○ ○ ○ ○ ○

TAUNTING DEATH

Numbers 33:50–34:29; **1 Corinthians 15:35–58**; Psalm 29:1–11

My best friend's mother, a dear family friend, died of Lou Gehrig's disease (ALS). Over the span of three years, the disease attacked her nerve cells, starting with her hands and feet and moving inward to her vital organs. Every time I visited her, she would be changed—her cane became a wheelchair, and her warbled words were muffled into silence. Although she was fully alert, she slowly lost the ability to communicate her feelings and needs. In the end, only her eyes displayed the tumultuous feelings underneath.

Those who confront the reality of death or the death of a loved one don't doubt their own fallibility. They are closely acquainted with the reality that so many strangely disregard. And they cling to the hope of the resurrection that Paul eloquently relays, and that the Corinthians were slow to understand and believe: "We will all be changed, in a moment, in the blink of an eye, at the last trumpet. For the trumpet will sound, and the dead will be raised imperishable, and we will be changed" (1 Cor 15:51–52).

Christ's death and victory over sin and death bring this life to those who believe in Him. His victory is the cause for Paul's subsequent taunting of death—taunts that rip through with joy for those who realize Christ's victory: "Where, O death, is your victory? Where, O death, is your sting? Now the sting of death is sin, and the power of sin is the law. But thanks be to God, who gives us the victory through our Lord Jesus Christ!" (1 Cor 15:55–57).

Lest we think we are any different, the process of death is happening to us and to those around us. Lou Gehrig's disease is a fast-forward version of the human existence. Why, then, do we keep quiet about the hope within us? "So then … be steadfast, immovable, always abounding in the work of the Lord, because you know that your labor is not in vain in the Lord" (1 Cor 15:58). —RVN

How are you displaying and sharing the good news?

GIFTS AND GRACE

Numbers 35:1–36:13; 1 Corinthians 16:1–24; Psalm 30:1–12

"Yahweh spoke to Moses on the desert plains of Moab beyond the Jordan across Jericho, saying, 'Command the children of Israel that they give to the Levites from the inheritance of their property cities to live in; and you will give to the Levites pastureland all around the cities'" (Num 35:1–2).

The idea of giving is ancient. Before God's people even enter the promised land, they're commanded to help the Levites—who will be serving them as spiritual leaders—by giving them cities. Now that God has given to the people, He asks that they give back to His work. There is an opportunity for obedience, and this obedience will come with the blessing of continued spiritual guidance from the people to whom they are giving the land. But giving is not the only concept at play here.

Shortly after this, God asks the people to provide refuge cities for murderers (Num 35:6–8). He institutes a system of grace—a type of house arrest. The idea that synagogues and churches are places where criminals can find refuge (sanctuary) likely finds its origins in this.

This system of grace also manifests itself in types of hospitality. We see this several times in Paul's letters. For example, Paul's relationship with the Corinthians was on the rocks, yet he still requests hospitality for his fellow ministry worker: "But if Timothy comes, see that he is with you without cause to fear, for he is carrying out the Lord's work, as I also am. Therefore do not let anyone disdain him, but send him on his way in peace in order that he may come to me, for I am expecting him with the brothers" (1 Cor 16:10–11).

God is gracious, and He calls us to be the same way—even when we don't want to, and even when our sense of justice makes being gracious frustrating. —JDB

Is God calling you to be gracious to someone?
How are you going to give?

April 1

○ ○ ◉ ○ ○

MOVING ON

Deuteronomy 1:1–46; 2 Corinthians 1:1–11; Psalm 31:1–9

"You have stayed long enough at this mountain. Turn now and move on" (Deut 1:6–7). We have a terrible tendency to stay in one place or keep doing one activity longer than we should. Our meetings run long, we constantly work overtime, or we overstay a welcome. And then there's the most significant problem of all: We ignore God's command to leave a place, position, or role.

Change can be refreshing. But the countless decisions and the difficult and frustrating moments that accompany change can often keep us from moving forward. We become comfortable where we are, and we fear the unknown.

Indeed, the majority of people (including Christians) live seemingly meaningless lives. Most American Christians spend more hours per day doing comfortable things, like watching TV, than they do praying, reading their Bibles, or serving others (usually combined). Yet what do the elderly always tell us? "I wish I had taken more risks; if only I wasn't so afraid." We're all on our way to dying. But as Christians, we're also on our way to eternal life. Why should we limit God's work with our fear?

In Deuteronomy 1, God called Moses to leave the mountain—where he'd grown comfortable. Moses' new path would be far from easy. He was going to enter the land of the Amorites and Canaanites, who were feared warriors (Deut 1:7). He was about to risk the lives of everyone with him—men, women, and children—in the process of following God's will. Both young and old would once again be in danger.

But God didn't intend for Moses to remain in the wilderness; He called Moses to lead His people into the same holy land He had promised to Abraham many years before (Deut 1:8). And despite his fear, that's what Moses did: "Then we turned and set out toward the wilderness in the direction of the Red Sea, as Yahweh told me, and we went around Mount Seir for many days" (Deut 2:1).

Moses' confidence was based on one thing: what God had spoken. May your confidence be grounded in the same thing, and may you take God at His word. —JDB

What is God calling you to do now? What comforts is He calling
you to leave behind? What have you been ignoring?

April 2

○ ○○○ ○

THE FINAL SAY

Deuteronomy 2:1–3:29; **2 Corinthians 1:12–16**; Psalm 31:10–24

Having the final say in an argument is more satisfying than I'd like to admit. By default, I'd like to be right, even if I have to be pedantic. I wish I could say this was limited to petty concerns. But on more than one occasion, when discussing issues of eternal significance, I've used my trump card in a desire to win an argument.

Paul specifically addresses this type of pride and boasting throughout 2 Corinthians. However, we come across a surprising statement in 2 Corinthians 1: "For our reason for boasting is this: the testimony of our conscience that we conducted ourselves in the world, and especially toward you, in holiness and purity of motive from God, not in merely human wisdom, but by the grace of God" (2 Cor 1:12).

At first glance, Paul appears to be boasting in his own actions. Isn't this evidence of the very same pride he denounces (1 Cor 5:6)?

But the key phrases, "holiness and purity of motive from God" and "the grace of God," provide a foundation for Paul's boasting. They tell us that it's not Paul's pride that is on the line—it's the good news. Paul is claiming that the integrity of his ministry doesn't rest on his own wisdom.

Paul wasn't trying to be a star pastor. His words were motivated by a deep concern for the Corinthians. He didn't want anything he did to obstruct the message about Christ. Similarly, our actions shouldn't be an obstruction to the gospel message. We should examine our motives when we're inclined to be "right." Our words and actions should reflect God's grace in our life—evidenced by humility and a sense of purpose in our interactions with others. —RVN

How are your words and actions speaking about your own pride?
How can you be testifying about God's grace in your life?

YOUR INNER SELF

Deuteronomy 4:1–49; 2 Corinthians 1:17–24; Psalm 32:1–11

"Did I leave the burner on?" "Did I lock the door?" "I feel like I'm forgetting something."

Forgetfulness is a syndrome we all experience at one time or another. Many of our forgetful moments end up being minor inconveniences. But there is one thing we should never forget: God and His instructions.

As the Israelites prepared to enter the promised land, Moses offered them a string of commandments, including this: "Take care for yourself and watch your inner self closely, so that you do not forget the things that your eyes have seen, so that they do not slip from your mind all the days of your life" (Deut 4:9).

In watching ourselves closely, we remember what we're meant to do and who we're meant to be. And this isn't just a value added to our lives and our relationship with God. Moses went on: "And you shall make [the commandments] known to your children and to your grandchildren" (Deut 4:9).

Moses knew that God had chosen the Israelites to carry out His work in the world. He also knew that forgetting God's commandments could jeopardize that work and even their very lives. He tells them to be certain about who they are—to keep themselves in line with God.

It's precisely this point that Paul emphasizes about God's plan in 2 Corinthians 1:17–24: God is about the resounding "yes." Yes, God has affirmed us. Yes, God has chosen us. Yes, we are the receivers of His salvation. We are called—not some of us, but all of us.

And in this we should rejoice, for we can claim, as the psalmist does, "I will confess concerning my transgressions to Yahweh, and you [Yahweh] took away the guilt of my sin" (Psa 32:5).

The best way to make your "yes" be a yes and your "no" be a no is to align yourself with God's great calling upon your life. Commandments only get us so far; identity in Christ and the Spirit's work in us will take us where we need to go. —JDB

What can you do to constantly remind yourself of God's will,
your identity in Him, and His work in your life?

April 4

∘ ∘◊∘ ∘

FORGIVE, FORGET, AND COMFORT

Deuteronomy 5:1–6:25; **2 Corinthians 2:1–11**; Psalm 33

There is a subtle type of grudge that festers. When we extend forgiveness, the challenge isn't necessarily in the moment of reconciliation. It's extending that moment and letting it permeate the interactions that follow.

In 2 Corinthians, Paul doesn't just ask the Corinthians to forgive. He asks them for much more: "So then, you should rather forgive and comfort him lest somehow this person should be overwhelmed by excessive sorrow. Therefore I urge you to confirm your love for him. Because for this reason, also I wrote, in order that I could know your proven character, whether you are obedient in everything" (2 Cor 2:7–9).

Patronizing superiority suits our selfish desires, but grudging forgiveness doesn't heal a community. Paul calls the Corinthian church to much more. He wants them to live sacrificially. That's why, when Paul calls for the offender in Corinth to be reprimanded, he specifically turns to address those who were affected by the sin. The solution was intentional, ongoing forgiveness and an outpouring of love. He then reminded the Corinthians of Christ's sacrifice, which they didn't deserve (see Col 3:13). Forgiveness is undeserved—a reminder we all need. —RVN

Are you holding on to a grudge against someone—perhaps even someone you've already forgiven? How can you let go of your grudge and extend the love that has been shown to you?

TREATING THE SYMPTOM

Deuteronomy 7:1–8:20; 2 Corinthians 2:12–17; Psalm 34:1–22

I regularly predict that something will only take me an hour when it actually ends up taking two. I'm beginning to think that this is a sign of a larger issue: the tendency to underestimate the severity of a problem. In medical offices, this is called treating the symptoms and not the disease. In street ministry, it's known as getting addicts off the street rather than helping them understand their addiction.

Addicts rationalize sin. And eventually, sin becomes everything in their lives, which means they rationalize away who they are. If we're honest with ourselves, we would see that—like the addict—we like the "gray" area far too much. We want to push the boundaries in the name of freedom, rationality, or cultural appeal.

In Deuteronomy 7:1–8:20, Moses was uninterested in pushing boundaries. He even told the Israelites to stay away from foreigners who worshiped other gods because they would corrupt the fledgling worship of Yahweh (Deut 7:3–4). Paul makes a similar point in 2 Corinthians 6:14: "Do not become unevenly yoked with unbelievers, for what participation is there between righteousness and lawlessness? Or what fellowship does light have with darkness?" Paul's statement is part of a larger discussion on why the world is as black and white as God makes it out to be. In 2 Corinthians 2:15, Paul writes, "For we are the aroma of Christ to God among those who are being saved and among those who are perishing."

Christ-followers are meant to be a good smell to the world of God's work and goodness, and it's impossible for them to do this if they are not living in His "light." Corruption infects everyone affiliated with it. We are meant to *bring* the light into the darkness, not *become* part of the darkness. Interacting with culture and those who don't believe is not the same as becoming one with culture and those who don't believe.

When we see a symptom, we need to recognize there is a disease behind it. We're all metaphorical addicts. The difference between Christ-followers and the rest is that we recognize the condition and seek Christ, who can heal us and save us. —JDB

In what ways are you rationalizing your sin or problems?
What can you do to understand it the way God would like you to,
and what can you do about it?

A LETTER OF RECOMMENDATION

Deuteronomy 9:1–10:22; **2 Corinthians 3:1–8**; Psalm 35:1–11

We file letters of recommendation from pastors, past supervisors, and teachers that highlight our skills, attitude, and work ethic. They present us as ideal candidates, glossing over the things we lack and the ways in which we've failed. But Paul's letter of recommendation tells another story:

"You are our letter, inscribed on our hearts, known and read by all people, revealing that you are a letter of Christ, delivered by us, inscribed not with ink but with the Spirit of the living God, not on stone tablets but on tablets of human hearts" (2 Cor 3:2–3).

Paul saw the work God was doing in the lives of the Corinthians. Through the work of the Spirit, they were drawn together as a community. Their response to the gospel testified that Paul was fulfilling the task that he was called to do.

But Paul doesn't stay focused on himself in this passage. He switches the focus to the Spirit: "Now we possess such confidence through Christ toward God. Not that we are adequate in ourselves to consider anything as from ourselves, but our adequacy is from God" (2 Cor 3:4–5). Ultimately, Paul's confidence finds itself in Christ's work and the life-giving work of the Spirit.

Our successes and failures are put into a proper context when we read Paul's message. All the good we do attests to the Spirit's work in our lives; it is a testimony of a life redeemed by Christ. And the bad isn't glossed over by God—it is paid for. It's His letter of recommendation that really matters, for He knows who we really are. —RVN

How are you living a life that attests to God's power in you,
not your own qualities or traits?

April 7

○ ○ ◊ ○ ○

AN IRRATIONAL LIFE

Deuteronomy 11:1–12:28; 2 Corinthians 3:9–18; Psalm 35:12–28

L ove is irrational. It requires doing things that compromise every survival instinct.

Moses tells God's people to have a memory of what God has done among them and to love Him as a result: "And you shall love Yahweh your God, and you shall keep his obligations and his statutes and his regulations and his commandments always. And you shall realize today that it is not with your children who have not known and who have not seen the discipline of Yahweh your God, his greatness, his strong hand, and his outstretched arm" (Deut 11:1–2).

The Bible doesn't say, "Keep Yahweh's commandments when you *feel* like you love Him," or "Keep Yahweh's commandments when things are going your way." It says, "You shall keep [Yahweh's] … commandments *always*." God's greatest commandments are about loving Him and others (Mark 12:28–31; compare John 15:12).

We love God and keep His commandments because He first loved us; we remember what He has done whenever things get difficult. And we teach it to the next generation. That's what God has called us to.

When we sacrifice ourselves for others, we are doing what God was willing to do for us when He came as a man to die on a cross. Similarly, when we love Yahweh by doing His will, we often make decisions that seem irrational. But in actuality, they are the most rational of all decisions.

The Spirit's work within us prompts us to love, and it also opens the Scriptures for us. As Paul says, "But until today, whenever Moses is read aloud, a veil lies upon their heart, but whenever one turns to the Lord, the veil is removed. … And we all, with unveiled face, reflecting the glory of the Lord, are being transformed into the same image … glory, just as from the Lord, the Spirit" (2 Cor 3:15–18).

Yahweh has lifted the veil from Scripture and reveals His glory in the love He manifests among us through His Spirit. Living sacrificially, out of love, richly displays His love. —JDB

Which of God's commands are you breaking?
What can you do to change that behavior and show more love?

COMPELLED TO WORSHIP

Deuteronomy 12:29–14:29; **2 Corinthians 4:1–6**; **Psalm 36**

When we experience God's mercy, it shows. Our instincts change and our priorities shift from gratifying our own ego to making much of God. We stop fearing what others think of us and find our identity grounded in Christ. It's a transformation that shows God is working in our lives. Paul recognized the transformative power of the gospel, and it drove his ministry. This is evidenced in his second letter to the Corinthian church: "Just as we have been shown mercy, we do not lose heart, but we have renounced shameful hidden things, not behaving with craftiness or adulterating the word of God, but with the open proclamation of the truth commending ourselves to every person's conscience before God" (2 Cor 4:1–2).

Paul wasn't manipulating or distorting the good news for his own gain, as some were doing in the community. He preached the good news to all people with openness and sincerity. He allowed the gospel to convict people as it should, refusing to distort it to make people comfortable. He proclaimed "Christ Jesus as Lord" and he and his disciples as "slaves for the sake of Jesus" to those in Corinth (2 Cor 4:5). Bound to Christ, they lived as free slaves for His cause. They were solely dedicated to Jesus because they wanted to be, and because of the salvation He had brought them.

Psalm 36 provides an illustration of Paul's approach, highlighting the qualities of those who don't fear God. This person is characterized by "rebellion in the midst of his heart" (Psa 36:1). He is self-absorbed and rejects his need (Psa 36:2). He is deceitful (Psa 36:3).

The psalmist doesn't contrast this picture with one of the righteous man. Instead, he honors Yahweh (Psa 36:5–6). The psalmist says, "For with you is the fountain of life; in your light we see light" (Psa 36:9). Paul echoes, "For God … is the one who has shined in our hearts for the enlightenment of the knowledge of the glory of God in the face of Christ" (2 Cor 4:6). God's grace puts everything in perspective. Both passages help us assess with wisdom the message and posture of those who teach. They also challenge us to take a look at our own standing before God. —RVN

Are you transformed by the good news?
Is it apparent to others around you?

April 9

○ ○○○ ○

THE GLOBAL RESET BUTTON

Deuteronomy 15:1–17:20; 2 Corinthians 4:7–18; Psalm 37:1–22

When I was a kid, I loved playing Super Nintendo—especially Donkey Kong. Despite my love for it, it would just make me angry at times. When I couldn't handle the way the game was panning out, I would slam down the controller and hit the reset button. I would start fresh. It's more than a little sad that my entertainment made me act like a caveman. Yet those moments of resetting the entire system felt like another chance at life (albeit a virtual one).

With the state of the global economy, it often feels like the world needs a reset. It's tempting to say something as radical as, "Let's forgive all debts and start again." Though this couldn't happen—and it would be highly problematic since the statement depends on good will, free economy, and general care for one another—it doesn't stop us from hoping.

God actually created a system for this audacious idea: In the Year of Jubilee, or the Sabbatical Year, slaves were freed and debts were forgiven (Deut 15), people were celebrated as equals (Deut 16), and the land was given a rest to prevent famine. (Famine was often caused by overworking the land.) It was a reset button.

The global economy is complex. I'm not suggesting that it's time for a Year of Jubilee, but maybe it *is* time for an economic evaluation of our lives. Who is God calling you to forgive? Whose life could be better if you lifted their debts? Who needs your generosity right now? Who could you make an equal by changing something about your work or friendship? How can you celebrate with those who feel like lesser people in this world?

The economy proves the point that we are all interdependent. It also makes the case that doing something for those at the bottom of the economic ladder can have a massive impact—not just on them, but on others. Those who are forgiven are likely to forgive. —JDB

Whose life can you make better today?
Who can you bring jubilee (celebration) to?

◦ ◦ ◦ ◦ ◦

TENT-MAKING FOR ETERNITY

Deuteronomy 18:1–20:20; **2 Corinthians 5:1–10**; Psalm 37:23–40

P aul, the tentmaker, knew the temporal nature of human-made structures. For someone who made and probably repaired tents, he knew all their flaws and tendencies for wear. So it's not a stretch for him to draw the connection from tents to mortality:

"For we know that if our earthly house, the tent, is destroyed, we have a building from God, a house not made by hands, eternal in the heavens" (2 Cor 5:1).

Paul is also making a connection to the tabernacle, the tent where the Israelites first regularly experienced God. Like the tents that Paul made, these earthly homes for God would eventually break down and be destroyed. But the Spirit and the heavens, where God actually dwelled, would live on. While temporal tent worship would fall apart, eternal worship in God's heavenly "building" will remain.

Paul contrasts the art of tent-making and the beautiful worship places of Yahweh with God's work (what He actually made), which was incorruptible. Right now, we have a "building from God" waiting for us—eternity made possible by the sacrifice of Christ.

He stresses that our eternal reality transforms our "meantime." It clarifies what "we have as our ambition, whether at home in the body or absent from the body, to be acceptable to him" (2 Cor 5:9). While waiting, we don't have to live with longing. We don't need to escape. We can live for Him, spreading the news that the kingdom of God is at hand. Until then, God has given us someone who comforts us: the Holy Spirit (John 17). He reminds us of our eternal confidence and empowers us to live for God. —RVN

How would your perspective change if you looked at
your daily tasks in light of eternal significance?

○ ○ ○ ○ ○

CURSES, THE OLD TESTAMENT, AND FREEDOM

Deuteronomy 21:1–22:30; 2 Corinthians 5:11–21; Psalm 38:1–22

"And if a man commits a sin punishable by death, and so he is put to death and you hang him on a tree, his dead body shall not hang on the tree, but certainly you shall bury him on that day, for cursed by God is one that is being hung" (Deut 21:22–23).

Being hung on a tree was a sign of being cursed. Romans 5:12 tells us that the punishment of sin is death; we as sinners deserve that curse. If Christ hadn't been cursed for us by being hung on a tree (the cross), then we would still have a debt to pay and a curse to live under.

It can be difficult to find significance in the Old Testament, especially in passages that are as harsh as this one. But the Old Testament still holds meaning for us today, and that meaning often reveals our human and individual state.

The same is true for those odd laws about crimes and marrying foreigners (Deut 21:1–14). It's not that we're supposed to practice these laws; they were intended for a land and a place. But we are meant to use them to understand God's conceptual framework. God always opposes taking a life. Similarly, marrying someone who doesn't share your belief in Christ (the equivalent of an Israelite marrying a foreigner) will be detrimental to God's work: That person will lead you astray. The law may not be in force anymore, but God's framework for interpreting the moral values in the world remains the same.

There isn't always a clear connection between the Old Testament laws and our lives today since the contextual framework is often quite complex. But there is always an easy relationship between our actions and what Christ has done for us. We are free from the Old Testament laws and the curse we deserve, but that freedom is meant to prompt us to live like Christ—not for ourselves (see Rom 7). We are called to live as free people should live. We are called to live for God's kingdom. —JDB

What moral values are you learning from the Old Testament?
In what ways are you currently misusing the freedom
that Christ has given you?

COSTLY GRACE

Deuteronomy 23:1–25:19; **2 Corinthians 6:1–13**; **Psalm 39**

When we say something hurtful to a friend or a family member, we know we can't just ignore the harm we have caused (we should know, anyway). In order to repair the relationship and earn back trust, we have to acknowledge the rift we've created. But when it comes to our relationship with God, we don't always look at it the same way. Sometimes, consciously or unconsciously, we belittle the incredible love that He has shown us.

When we don't acknowledge our sin as an act of rebellion, we feel far from God. We've created this great divide because we've tarnished our relationship with Him. In Psalm 39, the psalmist is in great agony over his sin—to the point where he acknowledges that people are nothing and his life is vanity: "Surely a man walks about as a mere shadow" (Psa 39:6).

Without God, life is meaningless. The psalmist acknowledges that his transgression has done great harm. He turns to God and says: "And now, O Lord, for what do I wait?" (Psa 39:7). At the heart of that cry is a need for redemption from a God who answers. He provided a way of salvation—one that was incredibly costly—through Christ. In 2 Corinthians, Paul stresses the importance of not taking this great gift for granted: "Now because we are fellow workers, we also urge you not to receive the grace of God in vain. ... Behold, now is the acceptable time; behold, now is the day of salvation!" (2 Cor 6:1–2).

Paul's call is urgent because Jesus' coming to earth wasn't a small gesture. It was incredible. If we aren't amazed at it, if we scorn it (even by accident), we may miss out. We have a greater hope than the psalmist was ever able to realize; his broken cry would not be fully answered for centuries. So today, when you hear God's call, don't respond with silence. Respond with a thankful heart. —RVN

Are you ignoring sin in your life? How can you live with a thankful heart, since Christ has bought you with such a great sacrifice?

THE CURIOUS THING ABOUT GOD'S WORK

Deuteronomy 26:1–27:26; 2 Corinthians 6:14–7:1; **Psalm 40:1–17**

Doing God's work is a curious thing. It requires both mad rushes and patiently waiting.

Christ-followers are meant to think like the psalmist did: "I waited patiently for Yahweh, and he inclined to me and heard my cry for help" (Psa 40:1). Yet Jesus' followers are also meant to do His work at breakneck speed, as described in Deuteronomy 26:1, where the Israelites are told to take possession of the promised land and settle it.

We're meant to recognize where the answers and timeframe come from: God. Giving the first of what we make to God's work indicates this understanding: "You shall take from the firstfruit of all the fruit of the ground that you harvest from your land that Yahweh your God is giving to you … and you shall go to the priest who is in office in those days, and you shall say, 'I declare today to Yahweh your God that I have come into the land that Yahweh swore to our ancestors to give to us.' Then the priest takes the basket from your hand and places it before the altar of Yahweh your God" (Deut 26:2–4).

In ancient Israel, the firstfruits wouldn't be wasted. This sacrifice would provide the priest with a livelihood so that he could serve Yahweh by serving others.

God has asked His followers to listen and to act, but to leave the timeframe of doing both up to Him. Giving after we complete both tasks shows that we realize that God has given us all we have, and it requires us to understand the purpose of sacrifice.

Just as the Israelites were a wandering people (Deut 26:5), we were also once wandering sinners. It's for this reason, and many others, that we must trust our God in our patience, in our speed, and with our giving. —JDB

What is God asking you to be patient about,
and where should you make haste?
How are you currently neglecting to give?

April 14

○ ○ ○ ○ ○

TEARING DOWN TO BUILD UP

Deuteronomy 28:1–68; **2 Corinthians 7:2–7**; Psalm 41

It's difficult to take rebuke, especially when it's unsolicited. We feel exposed and embarrassed when our sin is brought to light. And if we don't have the humility to accept rebuke, the experience can leave us at odds with the brave soul who assumes the task.

For Paul, who rebuked the Corinthians, news of their love was a relief and comfort to him: "But God, who comforts the humble, comforted us by the coming of Titus, and not only by his coming, but also by the comfort with which he was comforted among you, because he reported to us your longing, your mourning, your zeal for me, so that I rejoiced even more" (2 Cor 7:6–7).

We form community when others challenge us and encourage us to live for God. While community can fulfill our social needs, it's this common purpose that draws us together. When we take rebuke graciously and seek forgiveness from God, it forges the bond of community. When we rebel, or when we're sensitive and prideful, it creates a rift. Because the Corinthians felt sorrow for their sin and expressed concern for Paul, it solidified their relationship. And it comforted him and brought him incredible joy during conflict and trial.

Surprisingly, the rebuked person often has to be intentional about extending love and comfort to the one who brings the rebuke. Paul tells the Corinthians to "make room for us in your hearts" (2 Cor 7:2). We should do the same for those in our community. Not all people possess Paul's zeal and boldness, so we should prepare ourselves to graciously accept correction when it comes—solicited or not. Reaching out to those around us and letting them know we appreciate their rebuke will help build up a community that is authentically following Jesus. —RVN

Do others approach you about your sin?
If you haven't been rebuked recently,
how can you make yourself more approachable?

I'LL TAKE THE ARROW

Deuteronomy 29:1–29; 2 Corinthians 7:8–16; Psalm 42:1–43:5

"Better is an arrow from a friend than a kiss from an enemy." When I first heard this saying, I was struck by what a truism it is. It wasn't until years later, though, that I began surrounding myself with wise friends who would tell me the truth even when it was difficult to hear. Paul was a true friend to the Corinthians, and it's for this reason that he rebuked them (2 Cor 7:8, 10).

I recently felt God asking me to rebuke someone. I was hesitant at first, but I followed through. Afterward, I was tempted to lighten the weight of my words by writing a follow-up explanation, but I felt that nearly all the words I had spoken were in His will to begin with. I had to be confident that the rebuke had power to lead the person to repentance and to salvation. I shouldn't regret what I had done, but embrace it.

Moses had a similar experience to Paul's. He spoke harsh words into the lives of the Israelites when renewing God's covenant with them. (e.g., Deut 29:6). When the Israelites were deprived of things they thought they deserved, it was so that they could learn about God; such deprivation would force them to be dependent upon Yahweh.

I had another experience lately where I was on the receiving end of a truthful rebuke. My typical response is defensiveness, but I sensed from my friend's voice that he was genuine. He was speaking words of experience, love, and godly wisdom. God worked in my heart and I listened. Even though they hurt, I had to be thankful for the wise words. As I've been tempted to fall into my old patterns since then, that rebuke continues to make a difference.

We often use the phrase "Judge not lest you be judged" as an excuse for not speaking the truth to someone (Matt 7:1). But Paul clearly didn't use it that way. He understood that he was the worst of sinners, and he gladly admitted it. In grace, he issued rebukes. Judging people incorrectly and out of hate or envy is a problem in our world. But so is failing to speak up when we see someone going astray. Paul didn't judge—rather, he stated that God would judge according to His plans and oracles. Paul said it like it was, based on what God led him to say. He didn't degrade people; he promoted godly behavior. —JDB

Do you have godly friends who speak honest words to you?
How can you be open to speaking the truth to others without judging them?

April 16

∘ ◊ ◊ ◊ ∘

BOLD REQUESTS

Deuteronomy 30:1–31:29; 2 Corinthians 8:1–7; **Psalm 44**

Psalm 44 is bold. Who asks the Lord to "wake up"? Who asks Him why He is sleeping? The psalmist doesn't stop with these questions. He makes claims regarding God that seem like accusations: "you have rejected and disgraced us," "you have given us as sheep for food," and "you have sold your people cheaply" (Psa 44:9, 11, 12). How do we deal with these types of psalms? Should we be as bold in our relationship with God?

But these claims aren't made without reason. The psalmist opens his lament with, "O God, we have heard with our ears; our ancestors have told us of work you worked in their days, in days of old" (Psa 44:1). He had heard stories of God's past faithfulness—how he delivered His people in battles. He also knew that God had claimed His people, that His favor to them was a testimony to the surrounding nations. But the psalmist experiences something different. Why is Israel "a taunt to our neighbors, a derision and a scorn to those around us" (Psa 44:13)?

The psalmist wrestles with his experience because he knows God's will. He appeals to God's faithfulness, love, and reputation among the nations. It's not much different from our own experience, as we wrestle with evil, sorrow, and pain, and as we wonder about God's work in the world.

But in the midst of the confusion, we still need to place trust in God. Although the psalmist questions boldly, he acknowledges, "In God, we boast all the day, and we will give thanks to your name forever" (Psa 44:8). At the end of the psalm, he still petitions God for help, on the basis of His love: "Rise up! Be a help for us, and redeem us for the sake of your loyal love" (Psa 44:26).

God *has* redeemed us for the sake of His loyal love, and He is present and active—even when it seems otherwise. Colossians 1 tells us to give thanks to the Father, "who has rescued us from the domain of darkness and transferred us to the kingdom of the Son he loves … and in him all things are held together … because he was well pleased for all the fullness to dwell in him, and through him to reconcile all things to himself, by making peace through the blood of his cross" (Col 1:12–20). —RVN

Do you trust in God's love and deliverance, even when circumstances seem grim? Do you boldly petition Him for help, acknowledging His good character in the process?

April 17

○ ◊ ◊ ○ ○

IT'S ACTUALLY QUITE SIMPLE

Deuteronomy 31:30–32:52; **2 Corinthians 8:8–15**; Psalm 45:1–17

"May my teaching trickle like the dew, my words like rain showers on tender grass ... For I will proclaim the name of Yahweh; ascribe greatness to our God!" (Deut 32:2–3).

We all teach in some way. Some of us teach at church, others teach co-workers or employees. Some teach the children in their household, and others teach simply by doing (although we don't always acknowledge these roles). If all of us lived by Moses' prayer, things would be quite different. Imagine a world where we proclaimed Yahweh's greatness in all we say and do.

Moses' words also teach us something about God. If we're looking for perfection in what we do, we should look to the one who actually manifests it. If we're looking to be faithful, we should rely on the one who is faithful in all He does. If it's right actions we desire in our lives and the world, we should seek the upright one.

There is no doubting that the problems in our lives and world are complicated. They can't be undersold, and the difficult stories can't be told too many times. But there is a place to look when we need guidance and revitalization. There is a rock to stabilize us; we have a firm foundation (compare Matt 7:24–27).

The first-century Corinthian church was tasked with carrying out Paul's work of bringing many in Corinth to Jesus and listening to the Spirit so that they could be God's hands and feet in the city. We, like the Corinthian church, have work to finish (2 Cor 8:10–12).

God has given us action steps as individuals and as communities. And if we doubt that, then it is our job to seek answers from Him. Often we are unsure because we aren't listening to Him; we aren't *really* seeking His will.

May we feel like Moses about our own teaching work—the work of proclaiming Jesus in what we do and say. May we make the same requests of God.

Then, may your words trickle down like rain showers on tender grass. May you find the words God wishes to speak through you, and may you find the people who you are meant to teach. —JDB

Who are you tasked with teaching?
What work has God given you?
How can you improve that work and make it more glorifying to Him?

OPERATING STANDARDS

Deuteronomy 33:1–34:12; **2 Corinthians 8:16–24**; Psalm 46

Sometimes I operate on the premise that if I'm honoring God and following Him, I don't have to be concerned with what other people think. But carrying this too far is just as faulty as basing my identity on the approval of others. One leads to foolish pride and independence, and the other results in idolatry.

Paul, upon receiving a generous gift from believers in Jerusalem, felt called to explain his actions to the Corinthian church. He was intentional about how he would accept the gift, "lest anyone should find fault with us in this abundant gift that is being administered by us" (2 Cor 8:20). He explains why he is so concerned: "For we are taking into consideration what is honorable not only before the Lord, but also before people" (2 Cor 8:21).

In his ministry, Paul considered how his actions would be interpreted by observers. Since he experienced opposition in the community, he wanted to communicate how he would receive the gift—to be above reproach. The gospel was primary, and he wanted to avoid accusations that would impede the message of salvation.

Daily, we face situations where we can be governed by others' opinions. We also can offend them. When are we too vigilant? How do we keep from becoming a robot, motivated by other people's desires instead of love for God? When do we challenge other people's faith, instead of tiptoeing around them? Answering these questions takes incredible wisdom.

In 2 Corinthians 8, Paul draws from Proverbs 3: "May loyal love and truth not forsake you; bind them around your neck, write them upon your heart. And you shall find favor and good sense in the eyes of God and humankind" (Prov 3:3–4). Acting out of love, with a foundation of truth, can help us learn to honor God and love people. Being human, we will not always carry this out successfully. But operating on both love and truth and seeking wisdom and guidance for every situation, we can trust God to work out those places where we fail. —RVN

When it comes to relationships,
what is your basis for operation?

HE'S DEAD, BUT YOU CAN BE ALIVE

Joshua 1:1–3:17; 2 Corinthians 9:1–5; Psalm 47:1–9

"My servant Moses is dead" (Josh 1:2). Imagine the shock of this moment for Joshua, Moses' right-hand man. He probably already knew about Moses' death before God told him (Deut 34:1–8), but it's in this moment that he really feels the tragedy. If you've experienced death, you know this feeling—the moment when someone looks you in the eyes and says, "They're gone." You can't prepare for it. It's death; there's nothing you can do to change it or handle it.

This was also the moment when Joshua was confronted with the great leadership burden that he would now carry as a result of Moses' passing—equivalent to the emotional burden a vice president carries as he's being sworn into office after the president has died.

Yahweh tells Joshua, "Get up and cross the Jordan, you and all this people, into the land that I am giving to them, to the children of Israel. Every place that the soles of your feet will tread, I have given it to you, as I promised to Moses" (Josh 1:2–3). There isn't a moment to spare; it's time to move. So Joshua leads. Of all the incredible moments in his life—the battles he won and bravery he showed in the face of danger—this moment is probably the most impressive because he simply does it (Josh 2:1).

And Joshua does so in the face of the great fear of foreign warriors: "From the wilderness and the Lebanon, up to the great river, the river Euphrates, all of the land of the Hittites, and up to the great sea in the west, will be your territory" (Josh 1:4). He will face these warriors while still overcoming grief.

We all experience moments like these that will shape who we become. We'll experience grief, pain, and difficult decisions. We may be called to lead people. What we do in these moments is what defines us; it determines what kind of Christ-followers we will be.

Joshua experienced the great comfort of God's Spirit and guidance, and Christians have the opportunity to do the same (Deut 34:9–12; John 17). That's something that no one can take away from us and no circumstance can overcome. —JDB

How are you handling grief or pain in your life?
How can you incorporate the Spirit into
everything you do at this moment?

BE GENEROUS TO CONSUME?

Joshua 4:1–6:27; **2 Corinthians 9:6–15**; Psalm 48

Our culture encourages us to absorb the latest and greatest, and then cast off our gently used devices. We are targeted to accumulate and consume. The new feature we learned about yesterday is now the one we can't live without. At first, 2 Corinthians 9 seems to appeal to our consumer lifestyle: "The one who sows sparingly will also reap sparingly, and the one who sows bountifully will also reap bountifully" (2 Cor 9:6).

This verse has often been used to encourage giving, because then God will provide us with even more. But should we give more for the sake of consuming more? Should this be our motivation for generosity?

Paul debunks this idea in the next verse: "Each one should give as he has decided in his heart, not reluctantly or from compulsion, for God loves a cheerful giver" (2 Cor 9:7). Certainly God will provide for those who give; He takes care of those who follow Him. But our willingness to give should not be out of compulsion, obligation, or giving in order to receive. Selfish giving produces selfishness, not the love and mercy God desires (Mic 6:8).

God is incredibly generous. He gives us gifts—even sending His Son to die for us. As a result of His gracious love, we should also freely give. It reflects the thankfulness in our hearts: "being made rich in every way for all generosity" (2 Cor 9:11).

God's generosity doesn't hinge on our giving. We should give out of love for Him, and not from expecting a return on our investment. —RVN

What are your motives for giving?

∘ ◊ ◊ ◊ ∘

THE MISNOMER ABOUT GOD'S WILL

Joshua 7:1–8:35; 2 Corinthians 10:1–8; Psalm 49:1–20

We often hear a great misnomer about following God's will. It usually sounds something like this: "God has commanded me to do *x*, so I'm going to go into *x* blindly without fear." A phrase like this has elements of great truth—faith *should* carry us. But it's missing a piece.

Sometimes God instructs us to follow Him quickly and blindly. When that's the case, we should certainly do it. However, His commands should almost always be combined with the abilities that He has given us, including logic and rationality. We have to find the balance. If we get too rational, it can be at the detriment of God's will; we can reason ourselves out of taking the risks God wants us to take.

Joshua, the leader of the Israelites after Moses, is a great example of proper behavior within God's will. He learned from Moses and led *out of* that strength and experience, but he was led *by* the Spirit (Deut 34:9–12). He also did the proper legwork, even though he knew that God had guaranteed success if he and the people were faithful.

We see a glimpse into this strategy in Joshua 7:2–5, the battle of Ai. Joshua sent spies into enemy territory before invading it. He then paced the troops by sending only a small regiment at first (Josh 7:3). Despite his proper behavior, Joshua was unsuccessful because of the people's disobedience (Josh 7:1).

After this, we see the pain that Joshua felt as a result of the people's spiritual failures (Josh 7:6–9). Yahweh didn't allow for this to continue, though, because He was aware of the root cause of the problem; God called Joshua to find it and change it, so he did (Josh 7:10–26).

Joshua shows us what it means to follow God's will: receive a call, be trained, act out of wisdom and preparation, accept defeat when it comes, seek Yahweh's will again to fix it, and then confront the problem head on. The result: success (Josh 8:1–29). Following their victory, Joshua rededicated himself and those he led to Yahweh (Josh 8:30–35).

If we understood how to function within God's will, we would be much more successful for God. We would see great and miraculous things happen. —JDB

What patterns of following God's will do you need to change?
How have you misunderstood what it means to live for Him?

April 22

° ° ° ° °

JUDGING GIFTS

Joshua 9:1–10:15; **2 Corinthians 10:9–18**; **Psalm 50**

Comparing our gifts to those of the person sitting in the next cubicle or pew is dangerous work. Judging ourselves by this standard denigrates or inflates the gifts we've been given, leading to either ungratefulness or pride. Because the assessment method is faulty, we will always miss the mark of success—even if we're successful.

Paul had been called by God to minister to the Gentiles (see Acts 9:15). When others in the Gentile community questioned his authority, Paul boldly defended his calling. He also pointed out the measure by which these leaders judged their gifts: each other. They were undermining Paul's authority based on his lack of verbal abilities (2 Cor 10:10). Paul was undeterred by this because he knew his calling: "But we will not boast beyond limits, but according to the measure of the assignment that God has assigned to us" (2 Cor 10:13).

If we judge our gifts and calling by comparison, we serve the idol of our own pride. But this doesn't mean we should take them for granted. Instead, we are called to live for God: "The one who boasts, let him boast in the Lord" (2 Cor 10:17).

Thankfulness is the first step to using our gifts for God's glory. In Psalm 50, the psalmist acknowledges that everything is from God—a reason to sacrifice our own pride. God says, "The world and its fullness are mine" (Psa 50:12). But He does delight in the sacrifice of a thankful heart: "Offer to God a thank offering, and pay your vows to the Most High" (Psa 50:14–15).

We'll always come up short if we judge by comparison; there will be someone who is smarter or more gifted than we are. But by thanking God for our gifts (and for others' gifts), and asking Him for guidance in developing them, we can use them appropriately—not for our own gain, but to further His kingdom. —RVN

Are you judging your gifts by comparison?
How can you judge your life in the light of God's purposes?

THE ART OF CONFESSION

Joshua 10:16–11:23; 2 Corinthians 11:1–6; **Psalm 51:1–19**

Confession is a lost art. Most Christian communities today have little outlet for doing so, and the systems for confessing that we do have are often tainted by a lack of honesty and trust.

This isn't helped by the fact that none of us like to admit wrong. Yet God calls us to confession. In revealing sin in our lives, we have an opportunity to change (Jas 5:16). When a sin is revealed, the strength of temptation wanes.

This is not to suggest that we should openly confess our sins to all people, for unsafe and abusive people certainly exist. Rather, in close friendship with other Christians, we should be honest about our failures. Most important, we must confess these things to God.

We need to overcome the fatal assumption that because we are saved by Christ's dying and rising for our sins, we no longer need to confess them. In admitting our sins to God, we move toward overcoming them and into an honest relationship with Him. God already knows who we are and what we've done, so there is no reason to fear being honest with Him. And perhaps in learning to be honest with Him we can also learn to be honest with others.

For many of us, the difficulty of praying about our sins is what prevents us from telling God what we need and what we've done. God has an answer to this, though: the psalms.

For example, in Psalm 51, the psalmist says, "Wash me thoroughly from my iniquity, and from my sin cleanse me. For I, myself, know my transgressions, and my sin is ever before me" (Psa 51:2–3). He goes on to say, "Create a clean heart for me, O God, and renew a steadfast spirit within me. Do not cast me away from your presence, and do not take your Holy Spirit from me. Restore to me the joy of your salvation, and with a willing spirit sustain me" (Psa 51:10–12).

When we confess our sins to God and to others, He is faithful to help us overcome temptations. We have been given the great gift of Christ Jesus, who purifies us from all our wrongs against Him and others. And so we must seek His presence and live in it; in doing so, we can overcome the power of sin. In light of God's power, sin is nothing; it deserves no stronghold. —JDB

Are you currently confessing your sins to God and others? How can you create a safe system to confess your sins in a way that honors God?

TONGUES, FLAMES,
AND OTHER THINGS THAT DEVOUR

Joshua 12:1–13:32; 2 Corinthians 11:7–15; **Psalm 52:1–53:6**

I'd like to skip over the description of the "mighty man" in Psalm 52. Of all of his destructive influences, the mighty man is most judged for his use of words. The psalmist's words burn because I've set more than a few forests ablaze with careless words (Jas 3:5). So how should someone like me respond to the psalmist's judgment?

"Why do you boast about evil, O mighty man? The loyal love of God endures continually. Your tongue plans destruction, like a sharp razor, working deceit. You love evil more than good, a lie more than speaking what is right. You love all devouring words, O deceitful tongue" (Psa 52:1–4).

Prideful self-reliance is at the root of the evil man's devouring, razor-sharp tongue. He boasts to make himself appear mighty. He takes "refuge in his destructiveness" (Psa 52:7). In contrast, the psalmist finds refuge in God, in the sanctuary of His loyal love: "But I am like an olive tree flourishing in the house of God. I trust in the loyal love of God forever and ever" (Psa 52:8).

On my own, I'm more like the mighty man than the stable and prosperous olive tree. I can try to manage my words, fabricating my sense of security on the basis of good behavior. But efforts born out of self-reliance—the root problem of my flippant speech—always fail me. Unless I recognize the foolishness of my pride, I cannot see my desperate need for God. Without hope in Jesus, who provided refuge through His sacrifice, I'll never resemble the psalmist's prosperous olive tree.

Oftentimes, the places where we fail so miserably, where we need the most grace, are also the places we see God's work all the more. His Spirit changes us into people who bear the fruit of thankfulness. It makes us ever more eager to say with the psalmist: "I will give thanks to you forever, because of what you have done" (Psa 52:9). —RVN

*Where do you see pride and self-reliance
taking root in your life?*

○ ◇ ○ ◇ ○

BOUND FOR THE PROMISED LAND

Joshua 14:1–15:63; 2 Corinthians 11:16–23; **Psalm 54:1–7**

Faith is not just about being faithful; it's also about trusting in God's faithfulness.

For years God dealt with the confused and waning nature of His people while they were in the wilderness. They wondered, "Will God actually do what Moses has told us?" They had seen God repeatedly act on their behalf, but they continued to grow frightened and faithless. In return, the first generation that left Egypt never saw the promises of God. Instead, a later generation witnessed His faithfulness.

In Joshua 14:1–15:63, we see God fulfilling His words. Caleb and Joshua get a chance to witness this faithfulness, but the Hebrews who doubted that God would act on their behalf did not (Josh 14:6–15; also see Num 13:25–14:45). This is an incredible moment: These two men had watched the failures of their elders and led their peers and people younger than them so that they could witness the faithfulness of God together. You can almost hear them singing, "It is well with my soul."

Faith is a two-way street. We are to be faithful, but we must also have faith in God's faithfulness. God will do what He has told us He will do. He will act upon His word like He did with Joshua and Caleb.

We will be able to look back upon the events in our lives and say, as the psalmist does, "I will freely sacrifice to you; I will give thanks to your name, O Yahweh, because it is good. Because he has delivered me from all trouble" (Psa 54:6–7).

Since we know that day will come, why should we not freely sacrifice to Him now? He will overcome our opposition. Why should we not boldly proclaim, as the old hymn says, "I am bound for the promised land," and use it as leverage to say, "God will be faithful, so there is no reason why we shouldn't be"?

God has bound us to His faithfulness; Christ's death and resurrection shows that He blesses us beyond measure. So let's be bound to God with the knowledge that we are bound for the heavens that He has promised. —JDB

In what ways has God been faithful to you?
How can these moments be a reminder to you now to be faithful?

April 26

° ◊ ◊ ◊ °

BITTER AND BETRAYED

Joshua 16:1–17:18; **2 Corinthians 11:24–33; Psalm 55**

The betrayal of a loved one can shake our world. It can make us feel vulnerable and used, and if we're not careful, it can cause us to be bitter and suspicious toward others. The psalmist in Psalm 55 experiences such a betrayal from a friend who feared God: "We would take sweet counsel together in the house of God" (Psa 55:14).

The psalmist agonizes over how he was deceived: "The buttery words of his mouth were smooth, but there was battle in his heart. His words were smoother than oil, but they were drawn swords" (Psa 55:21). How does someone move beyond a violation of trust? Instead of growing bitter, the psalmist puts his trust in Yahweh: "Cast your burden on Yahweh, and he will sustain you. He will never allow the righteous to be moved" (Psa 55:22).

Similarly, in 2 Corinthians, Paul tells the church in Corinth about his sufferings. Among Paul's lashings, stonings, shipwrecks (three of them), and robbings, he also lists "dangers because of false brothers" (2 Cor 11:26). He suffered anxiety because of the churches (2 Cor 11:28).

Paul adds to this list by discussing a force of oppression over him. He states that he prayed for his "thorn" to be taken from him (2 Cor 12:8). However, the Lord told him, "My grace is sufficient for you, because the power is perfected in weakness" (2 Cor 12:9). This reshapes Paul's perspective on suffering: "I delight in weaknesses, in insults, in calamities, in persecutions and difficulties for the sake of Christ, for whenever I am weak, then I am strong" (2 Cor 12:10). By submitting to Christ, Paul relied less on himself and more heavily on God. As a result, God's grace and power was manifested within him.

Betrayal causes bitterness that can poison our hearts. But, like Paul, we should use trials as an opportunity to submit more fully to God, and to show others His work in us. —RVN

How are you holding onto bitterness?
What would God have you do instead?

WALKING IN CIRCLES

Joshua 18:1–19:9; **2 Corinthians 12:1–10**; Psalm 56:1–13

I often wish things were more obvious. I ask God to help me understanding His timing so that I can easily act. I ask for everything to happen at the right moments. I ask Him to give me such clear directions that I can't fail in following them. I used to think this was a good thing, but I realize now that all my questions could indicate a lack of faith. It seems that my questions lead to more questions. Like a man losing his memory in old age, I end up walking in circles around the block rather than finding my way home.

Maybe it's not the lack of knowing that disturbs me, but that when I *really know* what God wants, I will have to act. In general, this seems to be the problem with faith in western Christianity. We say we don't know what God wants. However, if we're honest with ourselves, perhaps we don't really *want* to know what God wants. In our hearts, we're certain that knowing will mean uncomfortable change.

Joshua calls the Israelites on this type of faith problem: "How long will you be slack about going to take possession of the land that Yahweh, the God of your ancestors, has given you?" (Josh 18:3). The same question applies to us. *How long* will we wait? We really know what we're supposed to do? If we don't, might the reason be that we don't *want* to know?

Often we hesitate because we're afraid of our weaknesses—we don't think we have what it takes. Paul addresses this when discussing his own weaknesses: "And [God] said to me, 'My grace is sufficient for you, because the power is perfected in weakness.' Therefore rather I will boast most gladly in my weaknesses, in order that the power of Christ may reside in me'" (2 Cor 12:9).

Rather than live in fear, we should boast in our weaknesses. Christ is working in us, to use us, in spite of them. No one is perfect; only Christ has the honor of perfection. And while we are weak, He will give us strength in Him. His strength can overcome whoever we are, wherever we have been, and whatever we will do.

Rather than walking in circles looking for home, let's realize that we are already home. Our home is Christ. —JDB

In what ways are you currently walking in circles?
What should you be doing instead?

April 28

○ ○ ○ ○ ○

THE SUBTLE SINNER

Joshua 19:10–20:9; **2 Corinthians 12:11–21**; Psalm 57:1–58:11

Some sins slip through the cracks—the ones that emerge in hushed tones between like-minded Christians. Sometimes these sins seem respectable because they occur out of supposed concerns for the Church or others. But they can leave deep gashes in the life of a community because they often go unchecked. And it's these sins that Paul addresses shortly before closing his letter to the Corinthians:

"For I am afraid lest somehow when I arrive, I will not find you as I want, and I may be found by you as you do not want. I am afraid lest somehow there will be strife, jealousy, outbursts of anger, selfish ambition, slander, gossip, pride, disorder" (2 Cor 12:20).

While the Corinthians were guilty of flagrant sins like impurity, sexual immorality, and licentiousness, they were also sinning in ways that subtly undermined Paul's authority. Slander and gossip created deep divisions in the Corinthian church, just as they do in our churches today.

We often don't realize we're committing these sins until rumors reach the individual we're gossiping about. Paul had been absent from the Corinthian community for some time. During his absence, dissenters slandered him. The Corinthians should have defended Paul while he was away, but instead, he was forced to defend his own ministry (2 Cor 13:2–3). He anticipated that his return to the community would reveal the true state of the situation.

Ultimately, these subtle sins were an attack on the good news—not just Paul. Because his integrity was brought into question, the authenticity of his message was also criticized. In addition, Paul was forced to address their sin before he could reach out to other communities with the good news (2 Cor 10:15).

The decisions we make on a daily basis can lead to division or unity in our community. And choosing to be a faithful peacemaker in the midst of divisive sins might have a bigger impact than we can imagine. —RVN

What are your subtle sins that are wrongfully condoned?

ο ◊ ο ο

EXAMINE THYSELF

Joshua 21:1–22:9; **2 Corinthians 13:1–10**; **Psalm 59:1–17**

Before advising others on how they should act, self-examination is always necessary. When the Corinthians questioned the authenticity of Paul and his colleagues' ministry (which is ironic, since he had planted their church), Paul says to them, "Test yourselves to see if you are in the faith. Examine yourselves! Or do you not recognize regarding yourselves that Jesus Christ is in you, unless you are unqualified?" (2 Cor 13:5).

None of us are ready for the ministry that Jesus has for us because we're not worthy of the great gift of salvation He has offered. We are meant to find our identity and calling in Christ and to lead out of the gifts He has given us (see 1 Cor 12). For this reason, Paul makes this claim:

"For we are not able to do anything against the truth, but rather only for the truth" (2 Cor 13:8).

Paul is bound to what Christ has called him to do, which is why he often calls himself a slave for Christ (e.g., Rom 1:1). Because of His great sacrifice, Paul sees the only natural action is living fully—with his entire being—for Jesus. It is in Christ that Paul finds his strength, even in the difficulties he faces with the Corinthians: "For we rejoice whenever we are weak, but you are strong, and we pray for this: your maturity" (2 Cor 13:9).

The psalmist also has a plea for times when he faces opposition from others: "Deliver me from my enemies, O my God. Protect me from those who rise up against me. ... For look, they lie in wait for my life. The mighty attack against me, not because of my transgression or my sin, O Yahweh. Without guilt on my part they run and ready themselves. Awake to meet me and see" (Psa 59:1, 3–4).

The Bible is full of understanding and insight for moments of struggle. And we have a great Savior who can sympathize with our struggles (Heb 4:14–16). It's not a matter of *if* we as Christ-followers will experience unrighteous opposition; it's a matter of *when*. May we have the type of faithfulness that Paul and the psalmist did. May we plea to the good God who loves us. May we speak *only* His truth. —JDB

What opposition are you currently experiencing? How would
God have you to answer it? How should you be praying to Him?

THEY'RE FUTILE; THIS ISN'T

Joshua 22:10–24:33; 2 Corinthians 13:11–14; Psalm 60:1–12

I f you knew it was time to die, to say goodbye for good, what would you say? How would your final hoorah sound?

In an episode of *Northern Exposure,* Dr. Joel Fleischman is convinced that he is dying. Joel, who is usually conservative, begins risking everything: He drives a motorcycle way too fast without a helmet, gets a ticket that he rips up, and eventually crashes the bike—all feeling no remorse. He then returns to his office to learn that his doctor's initial inclination was incorrect. Almost immediately, he becomes angry that he didn't know his fate earlier. In his recklessness, he could have prematurely ended his life.

The risks you take when you think your life is over are quite different from those you're willing to take when you think you're fine. The things you say, the person you are, would be very different if you knew tomorrow were your last day.

Joshua, who led Israelites into the promised land, knew his end was coming. As an old man, he commanded the Israelites: "But *hold fast* to Yahweh your God … *One of your men put to flight a thousand*, for Yahweh your God is fighting for you, just as he promised you" (Josh 23:8–10, emphasis mine).

Paul made a similar remark: "For we rejoice whenever we are weak, but you are strong, and *we pray for this: your maturity*" (2 Cor 13:9). Paul realized that maturity in Christ will always put us in the right place in the end. He concluded his letter to the Corinthians by expanding upon this message: "Rejoice, be restored, be encouraged, be in agreement, be at peace, and *the God of love and peace will be with you*" (2 Cor 13:11).

What would you say if you were Joel, Joshua, or Paul? What would you do? As Christians, the response should be the same no matter how long we have to live; Christ could come tomorrow. Does that thought give you joy or great fear?

Whenever we experience pain, grief, or encounter enemies, the oppositions of life seem to distract us from our great purpose in Christ. They mask the brevity of our time on earth. Perhaps this is why the psalmist puts it best: "Give us help against the adversary, *for the help of humankind is futile.* Through God we will do valiantly, and it is he who will tread down our enemies" (Psa 60:11–12). —JDB

What hope are you currently placing in the futility of humankind?
What actions can you take to refocus your hope on Christ?

WHO WILL FIGHT FOR US?

Judges 1:1–2:10; **Philippians 1:1–11**; Psalm 61:1–62:12

"Who will go up first for us against the Canaanites to fight against them?" (Judg 1:1). I've felt this way before—wondering who will be my advocate in my time of need. It's ironic that we are surrounded by people, and we have constant access to communication, and yet we can still feel alone. In a world of ambient noise, we're often left feeling that no one is there to come to our aid. Most of us do have people to help us; it's just that we're not willing to ask for help. At all times, we have someone who will be our guide in times of distress.

Paul tells us that it is Christ "who began a good work in you [and He] will finish it until the day [He returns]" (Phil 1:6). In essence, the story of Paul and the Philippian believers' struggles is really the same story told in the book of Judges. God's people are at war against powers seen and unseen (Phil 3:1–4; compare Col 1:16). They feel lonely and wounded, but when they search their hearts, they see that God really is rising up to defend them. In Judges, He sends His people great advocates who go out before them in battle. In Philippians, we see Paul telling his story to a church in need of a leader so they can look to his example (e.g., Phil 1:12–25; 3:1–21). We also see Paul, time and time again, point to the greatest example: Christ (e.g., Phil 1:9–11).

In the humility of his situation, Paul sees God at work (Phil 2). When God's people found themselves in dire circumstances, being opposed by outside forces, they saw God come to their aid (e.g., Judg 4). Christ is our advocate before God the Father, and He is our guide in this life, which can often be confusing and disheartening. God's faithfulness in guiding and loving His people remains the same today as yesterday, but now we see an even greater manifestation of that love in Jesus. —JDB

What humbling situation are you going through?
How can you hand it over to God and trust in His providence?

May 2

ooooo

DON'T FOCUS ON OVERCOMING

Judges 2:11–3:31; **Philippians 1:12–18**; Psalm 63–64

When I go through difficult circumstances, I want the end. I'm so focused on escape and overcoming that I barely think about what God might be teaching me through that experience. And I'm certainly not thinking about how He might be using me to witness to others.

Paul was on a completely different wavelength. In his letter to the church at Philippi, he sets his Roman imprisonment in context: "Now I want you to know, brothers, that my circumstances have happened instead for the progress of the gospel, so that my imprisonment in Christ has become known in the whole praetorium and to all the rest" (Phil 1:12–13).

Paul wasn't just enduring or anticipating the end of his imprisonment. He was using his experience to be a witness for Christ. His captors must have wondered: what makes a person willing to suffer like this? What makes his message worth imprisonment?

Paul's circumstances didn't merely create waves with those he was testifying to. Other believers were emboldened by Paul's endurance and preached the gospel without fear (Phil 1:14).

It's not natural to be filled with joy in the midst of difficult times. It's not normal to have a sense of purpose when everything appears to be going wrong. We don't expect much from ourselves or others during these times, but God wants to refine us *and* use us. He's giving us a chance to display the "peace of God that surpasses all understanding"—as a testimony to Christ's redemptive work (Phil 4:7). Are you responding? —RVN

How can you use your difficult circumstances
to point others toward Christ?

○ ○ ◊ ○ ○

IF LIFE WERE A MUSICAL

Judges 4:1–6:10; **Philippians 1:19–30**; Psalm 65:1–13

Maybe life should be more like a musical or an oratorio—like *Les Misérables* or Handel's *Messiah*. How we feel is often expressed better in song or poetry than anything else. Literary criticism tells us that poets write verse because prose simply can't capture the emotions they're feeling. So much of the Bible is poetry, suggesting that maybe, in a way, poems and songs are the language of God.

Deborah and Barak understood this. After Yahweh claimed victory over Israel's foes through them, they "sang on that day" (Judg 5:1). The Bible records their song. It was epic—the earth trembling (Judg 5:4, 5), the people rejoicing (Judg 5:7), and everyone singing as they recounted "the righteous deeds of Yahweh" and made their way to the city gates (Judg 5:11). This is music, after all; it's expressive.

Paul breaks out in a type of song in Philippians as well (Phil 2:5–11). His song is a result of his raw excitement from reflecting on the work of the good news of Jesus in himself and others (Phil 1:12–26) and his hope that believers will be filled with "one purpose" (Phil 2:2). To truly worship God, you just have to sing. You have to feel and sound like a poet. God's too exciting for anything else to suffice.

I know someone who thinks of life as a musical. Life is joy for that person because there's a soundtrack for everything. If God is at work in everything, then we should want to worship Him constantly. We should sing His praises. We should write about our journeys, speak about them, share them, and experience God's work among us collectively.

Christianity isn't meant to be stale or dull—the early church was anything but. It was exciting, like God Himself, because His Spirit was working among believers. And His Spirit is working today. So clap, sing a little louder, and share your story. Find the soundtrack to it all. —JDB

How can you praise God more fully?

May 4

○ ○ ○ ○ ○

MORE THAN I CAN HANDLE

Judges 6:11–7:25; **Philippians 2:1–11**; **Psalm 66:1–20**

"God doesn't give us more than we can handle." This Christian maxim is a well-meaning attempt at putting our difficult times into perspective. It holds the view that God knows our weaknesses and knows when we can't measure up to a challenge. But if we're going through trials, this same saying can be debilitating when we feel that we can't possibly handle a situation.

The psalms often describe circumstances that leave the nation of Israel hopelessly struggling and helplessly in need of God: "For you have tested us, O God; you have tried us as silver is tried. You brought us into the net; you placed a heavy burden on our backs. You let men ride over our heads. We went through fire and through water, but you have brought us out to the place of abundance" (Psa 66:10–12).

Israel doesn't often "handle" situations very well. Throughout its history, the nation chosen by God repeatedly rebelled against Him. Only when God gave them over to their enemies and they suffered through trials would they cry out for deliverance. Only when they stopped relying on themselves or foreign gods to sustain them would He come to their rescue.

It may be that God does give us more than we can handle. But this is actually—perhaps strangely—a source of comfort. If we could handle every circumstance, we'd never reach the end of our self-reliance. And it's only when we get to the end of ourselves that we realize how much we desperately need Him.

Our trials give us hope. The people of Israel were "tried as silver is tried" (Psa 66:10). Just like them, we'll be purified by fire. We will go "through fire and through water," a process by which He makes us more wholly devoted to Him. And His work will bring us through "to the place of abundance" (Psa 66:12).

His faithfulness to us, even when we're unfaithful, is reason to praise Him. And this is precisely the psalmist's response: "Blessed be God, who has not turned aside my prayer, or his loyal love from me" (Psa 66:20). We see God's perfect love for us in Jesus, who was obedient when we couldn't be and suffered so we wouldn't have to (Phil 2:5–8). —RVN

Do you think you can handle the troubles in your life?
How can you see God's faithfulness to you, even when
you're going through difficult circumstances?

BELIEVING IN THE IMPOSSIBLE

Judges 8:1–9:21; Philippians 2:12–18; Psalm 67:1–7

Too often, we're cynical about circumstances. When people come to us for advice, we want to list all the reasons why they shouldn't take a certain course of action. We want to dissuade them. But what if we had a little faith instead?

In Judges, we find someone who is surprisingly idealistic. When the men of Ephraim oppose Gideon, he says, "What have I done now in comparison to you? Are not the gleanings of Ephraim better than the grape harvest of Abiezer? God has given into your hand the commanders of Midian, Oreb, and Zeeb. What have I been able to do in comparison with you?" (Judg 8:2–3).

Gideon cleverly couches his request in the middle of compliments; he places positives on either side of it. He wins back their favor: "And their anger against him subsided when he said that" (Judg 8:3).

Gideon's motives were flawed, theologically or interpersonally, but his actions do teach us something fascinating. People often want to be told that they can accomplish the impossible. Those who believe in the impossible can often accomplish things that others can't. Of course, Gideon was audacious; he and the men from Ephraim could have been crushed by these warring nations of mightier strength and military intelligence. Surprisingly, in this circumstance, he succeeded (Judg 8:15–17).

We shouldn't necessarily look to Gideon as a shining example (he makes lots of mistakes). But this incident is a reminder that we need to carefully consider our interactions with those we influence. What if we chose to be encouraging? What if we didn't default to cynic mode? When someone comes to you for advice, consider the work that God might be working in that person. If He deems that they are worthy, they will accomplish their work—even if everything looks bleak at first. —JDB

Who can you encourage?
How can you affirm people's calling?

May 6

∘ ∘ ∘ ∘ ∘

COMMUNITY DRIVEN

Judges 9:22–10:18; **Philippians 2:19–30**; Psalm 68:1–14

By default, we flag our own needs as high priority. And we often measure our church community by how well it's serving our needs. Caught up in our own spiritual growth, we tend to forget that we're meant to attend to the physical and spiritual needs of others. Paul upholds Timothy and Epaphroditus to the Philippians as examples of what this type of service should look like.

Paul was intent on sending Timothy to the Philippian church because of his discernment and his servant-like heart. In fact Timothy was the only one suited for the task. Others wouldn't "sincerely be concerned about [the Philippians'] circumstances. For they all seek their own interests, not those of Jesus Christ" (Phil 2:20–21). Likewise, Paul describes Epaphroditus as a man who suffered to the point of death in order to assist him in his ministry (Phil 2:30).

Both of these men epitomized the natural result of Paul's commands earlier in his letter: "Do nothing according to selfish ambition or according to empty conceit, but in humility considering one another better than yourselves, each of you not looking out for your own interests, but also each of you for the interests of others" (Phil 2:3–4).

"Considering another individual better" didn't mean the Philippians had to foster an exaggerated opinion of others—as if they deserved honor. Rather, Paul was instructing them to consider others' needs ahead of their own. The church in Philippi had this example in Paul, Timothy, and Epaphroditus. But the original example is found in the person of Christ, who "humbled himself by becoming obedient to the point of death, even death on a cross" (Phil 2:8).

Christ's sacrificial love was first shown undeservedly to us, and His example of humility, obedience, and service is a reminder that we should be looking for ways to serve those around us. —RVN

How can you reach out to someone who needs
guidance, love or encouragement?

MAKING GOOD OUT OF BAD

Judges 11:1–12:15; Philippians 3:1–11; Psalm 68:15–35

God is renowned for working through unlikely means with the most unlikely people. During the period of the judges, there were few candidates less likely for God's work than Jephthah, "a mighty warrior; he was the son of a prostitute, and Gilead was his father" (Judg 11:1). The man is the son of a prostitute and an adulterer, who had other sons with his wife (compare Judg 11:2). It can seem odd that details like this are included in the Bible. This one is there because God is about to do something unexpected.

When Jephthah is told that he won't inherit anything from his father, he flees and assembles a motley crew of other outlaws (Judg 11:3). If you've seen *The Magnificent Seven*, you might be tracking with this Wild West story: "After a time the Ammonites [a threatening nation of strong warriors], made war with Israel [a small nation with a reserve army at best]. When the Ammonites made war with Israel, the elders of Gilead went to bring Jephthah from the land of Tob. And they said to Jephthah, 'Come and be our commander'" (Judg 11:4–6). Just like in *The Magnificent Seven*, the fates are about to turn: The misfit rebels will rise to the defense of the people who don't understand them.

Jephthah goes to war against the Ammonites and wins, but he makes an impulsive and tragic mistake in the process (Judg 11:29–40). God had prepared him for this great work, but he fumbles—resorting to the types of vows made to foreign gods. He rebels against Yahweh and ends up killing his daughter as a result of his mistakes.

Although Jephthah was unexpectedly called to a great purpose, he didn't respond to that call with a proper understanding of God. Jephthah could have repented from his rash vow, for God would not have wanted him to do such a thing as kill his daughter, but instead, he chose to view Yahweh like every other foreign god that demanded child sacrifice. In return, the life of Jephthah's daughter was lost, and the spiritual life of Jephthah and the people he led was compromised.

What can we learn from Jephthah and his tragic mistake? Follow God's calling, even when it's unexpected. But in doing so, we must understand and embrace who He is and how He is working among us. —JDB

What does God want to do through you? How can you obey
with a proper understanding and knowledge of Him?

BEYOND REGRET

Judges 13:1–14:20; **Philippians 3:12–4:1**; Psalm 69:1–17

I've excelled at regret. When I've dwelt on the wrongs I committed against other people and my offensive rebellion against God, I lost my focus. It's difficult to be confident in our righteousness through Christ when we go through these periods.

In Philippians 3:12–14, Paul offers both hope and advice for these times based on his own experience: "But I do one thing, forgetting the things behind and straining toward the things ahead, I press on toward the goal for the prize of the upward call of God in Christ Jesus."

Paul looks forward to being with God in fullness and experiencing the fruits of his labor for the gospel, so he presses "toward the goal." He emphasizes that we need to forget the "things behind." Paul would have known the need for this. As a zealous Pharisee, he had persecuted the early church, counting himself the foremost of sinners (1 Tim 1:15).

Does forgetting imply that we act as if our failures never occurred? Not necessarily. We should seek forgiveness from others whenever possible. But it's dangerous to dwell on the failures—to live in regret. In fact, we belittle Christ's sacrifice if we purposefully or knowingly live in fear and guilt. He has paid for our sins and given us new life, and that means handing over our imperfections for Him to bear.

Paul swiftly moves from forgetting to "straining toward the things ahead, [he says,] I press on" (Phil 3:14). We are called to a new life in Christ, and this should be our focus. We will experience this, and we will know the complete fulfillment of this reality when He comes again. In the meantime, we can move forward without being crippled by our sins. —RVN

How are you caught up in your past mistakes?
How can you seek help from God during these times
while trusting in His forgiveness?

SUCCESS DECEIVES

Judges 15:1–17:13; Philippians 4:2–9; Psalm 69:18–70:5

When leaders come to power, there are always people who become insistent on stopping them. It's incredible how easy it is for people to justify envy or hatred for authority figures. Most of us have made the offhand remark, "I hate that guy." And in those words, even when they're meant in jest, we reveal the motives of the human heart. But this doesn't represent who we're meant to be—people who live for others.

Samson, an Israelite judge, endured that fate. A young warrior, he had enemies who wanted him dead and would do nearly anything to bring him down—spiritually or physically. The Philistines who opposed him went so far as to burn his wife and her father alive (Judg 15:6). Samson brought these trials on himself by disobeying God and marrying a foreign wife who would ultimately lead him to worship foreign gods. Even so, the acts of violence against him were not just his own doing.

The Philistines, like many people today, didn't like to see an enemy succeed. They were envious and frustrated, and they weren't used to being second to anyone.

There are lessons here for all of us no matter where we are in life. If we succeed, we should be thrilled when others do the same. We should try to help them succeed in the work God has called them to, designated specifically for them. If you have yet to come into that realm of success, you should be excited when others do, for the same reasons. Whatever your position in life, set aside the obstacles of envy or hatred. Set your sight on the work God has called you to and encourage those around you who are working toward theirs. —JDB

How can you help others succeed in God's work?
How can you set your sight on your own work
without becoming envious?

OLD, WISE, AND DESPERATELY
IN NEED OF GOD

Judges 18:1–19:30; Philippians 4:10–20; **Psalm 71:1–24**

Sometimes we expect that we'll naturally grow in faith as we grow older. We tend to see elderly people as those who have been molded and shaped by life—rock-solid in their faith and untapped sources of wisdom. That, or we speed around them in the grocery aisle, blissfully disengaged with the reality that our bodies, too, will slow down and endure pain.

While the psalmist seems to express a shadow of both these perspectives in Psalm 71, neither of them is complete. Adopting the point of view of an elderly person, he reflects on his life. His prayer to God shows us that maturing in faith isn't automatic.

The elderly man is respected by others, but he doesn't trust in the honor that some ascribe to him. He knows that Yahweh is the source of his strength, and he praises Him continually: "I have become a wonder to many, but you are my strong refuge. My mouth is filled with your praise, with your glory all the day" (Psa 71:7).

Perhaps forsaken or looked down on by others, he makes a request for God's presence: "Do not cast me away in the time of old age" and "even when I am old and gray, O God, do not abandon me" (Psa 71:9, 19). He continues to request God's nearness: "O God, do not be far from me. My God, hurry to help me" (Psa 71:12).

Perhaps most poignant is the intensity of the psalmist's trust in God. Even in his old age, though he has "leaned from birth" upon God, he can't place his trust in his past years of faithfulness (Psa 71:6). His "praise is of [God] continually" (Psa 71:6). He also feels a responsibility to pass on the testimony of God's works: "I will come in to tell the mighty deeds of Lord Yahweh. I will make known your righteousness, yours only" (Psa 71:16).

Maturity in faith isn't awarded like a badge after we have put in our time. It's not an achievement. The elderly man's prayer acts as a testimony of God's faithfulness—past and present. Maturity of faith is something you continue to "be" and "do" and "seek." —RVN

How do you treat the elderly people in your life?
What can you learn about God from them?

BEING GOOD AT WHAT MATTERS

Judges 20:1–21:25; Philippians 4:21-23; Psalm 72:1-20

Though prayer is important, it's an area of our faith lives that we often neglect. But people of great faith in the Bible *relied* on prayer—and not just for difficult situations. From general direction to specific details, they turned everything over to prayer. God spoke to them directly; they listened, and then they acted.

Maybe you don't believe God speaks directly to you. If that's the case, consider why you think this way. Why wouldn't He want to speak to you? He chose you by sending His own son to die for you. Jesus, that son, said that God would come and speak to you (John 17). You're important to God, and He wants to talk to you—to know you.

In Judges, we find a situation where people relied on God not just for direction, but for details. The Israelites rose up against the tribe of Benjamin because they refused to address the wickedness among them (Judg 20:12–14). But before entering battle, they inquired of God. They actually asked for the details of the plan: "'Who will go up first for the battle against the descendants of Benjamin?' And Yahweh said, 'Judah will go first.'"

We often forget how important it is to ask God about the details—to seek His guidance in all things. Neglecting prayer is a huge mistake. We need God's grace, the grace of Christ, to be with us always: "The grace of the Lord Jesus Christ be with your spirit" (Phil 4:23). Having the grace dwell upon us, and in us, in all things, requires a constant pursuit of Him. Rather than laboring over the details of your life alone, ask God. —JDB

What details in your life need to be worked out?
Have you presented them to God and sought His voice?

THE BIBLE IN THE DEVELOPED WORLD

Ruth 1:1–2:23; 1 Timothy 1:1–11; Psalm 73:1–10

In our developed world, we don't consider famines very often. If there were a famine in our lands, we could navigate it because of our importing infrastructure. This isn't the case for the developing world: Famines mean walking miles to find food and water, and often dying or suffering terrible violence just to stay alive. (Currently there are two major famines in Africa bringing these desperate situations to life.) When I used to read about famines in the Bible, I thought of hunger, but I didn't necessarily think of pain and persecution. Now that I'm more aware of what's happening in the world, stories of famine in the Bible are very vivid for me.

Consider Naomi, whose husband died during a famine, and the pain she must have felt over that loss and the loss of her two sons (Ruth 1:1–7). She was left with her daughters-in-law. As widows, they were completely desolate. Women were considered a lower class at the time; they could not own property and could not provide for themselves in an agriculturally based society. When I see photos of hurting women in the Horn of Africa, I'm reminded of Ruth and Naomi.

I think this is what the Bible is meant to do. We're called to read it historically and culturally. But we're also called to read the Bible with a sense of urgency about what's happening in our world today. We know there is no end to extreme global poverty and unnecessary pain. We can't rightfully imagine that those of us who have resources and who can help will have stepped up to eradicate these issues. But we can make the biblical story our story. We can feel their pain and think as they think. And we can act. Imagine God showing providence in your life like He did Ruth's and Naomi's, and then help those who need you. —JDB

What can you do to today make a difference in
the life of a person living in extreme poverty?

. o o o .

SHIPWRECKED

Ruth 3:1–4:22; **1 Timothy 1:12–20**; **Psalm 73:11–28**

"I am setting before you this instruction, Timothy my child, in accordance with the prophecies spoken long ago about you, in order that by them you may fight the good fight, having faith and a good conscience, which some, because they have rejected these, have suffered shipwreck concerning their faith" (1 Tim 1:18–19).

Paul had experienced being shipwrecked multiple times in his life, and in this passage, he metaphorically ascribes his experience to that of people who turn from faith in Christ. The imagery of being shipwrecked captures the spiritual state of aimlessness that results from a misguided conscience—one that isn't grounded in faith. Among those who experienced this shipwreck were Hymenaeus and Alexander, former believers who became blasphemers. They had known the truth of Jesus but were now publicly opposing it (1 Tim 1:20).

Paul admits he had once been a blasphemer himself, but he was "shown mercy because [he] acted ignorantly in unbelief" (1 Tim 1:13). In contrast, Hymenaeus and Alexander blasphemed deliberately by turning from the faith and opposing Paul, even though they knew about God's grace through Christ.

In Psalm 73, the psalmist uses similar imagery when describing those who wickedly turn from God: "abundant waters are slurped up by them." The psalmist's line captures the attitude of these wicked people. They ask mocking questions: "How does God know?" and "Does the Most High have knowledge?" (Psa 73:11). Although they acknowledge God's presence on some level, they fail to respond. They act in deliberate disobedience.

Following God isn't optional in either big or small decisions. Paul warns Timothy that this "fight" includes making daily choices that align with faith and a good conscience. Certainly we will fail in following Him—that's precisely why we need His grace so badly. But deliberately acting against what we know, when we're aware of His grace, will only result in being shipwrecked. —RVN

Are you making deliberate decisions against following God?
How has this harmed your relationship with Him?
How can you align with His expectations for your life?

A SENSE OF HISTORY

1 Chronicles 1:1–54; 1 Timothy 2:1–15; Psalm 74:1–23

When I was in sixth grade, my teacher assigned our class a family gene-alogy and history project. At first it was frustrating. It seemed like unnecessary work. But eventually I became obsessive over it as I discovered our family stories. Many of us share this same experience; we've uncovered ancestors who have done great things. Through this process, we can begin to understand not just these people of history, but also ourselves.

Although we may be especially interested in our own family history, who doesn't skip (or at least think about skipping) the genealogies of the Bible? Even if we're serious about reading biblical books front to back, we prefer to skip over the long lists of names. But that would be a mistake in the case of 1 Chronicles 1:1–54. This genealogy is about human history leading up to a monumental person: King David. The lineage also makes the book of Ruth incredibly relevant: Boaz, Ruth's husband, shows up in the line (1 Chr 2:11–12), which indicates that God had a plan to enfold non-Israelites into His people long before Christ's work brought about that result (e.g., Acts 2).

Just as our family history teaches us about the way we are, reading the Bible allows us to learn why David was the way he was. Through genealogies, we can learn about the heart and character of God and His intricate plan to save the world. —JDB

How does the sense of history conveyed in the Bible connect to your sense of history? How does it connect to the work Christ is doing in and through you today?

SMALL STARTS

1 Chronicles 2:1–55; **1 Timothy 3:1–7**; Psalm 75:1–76:12

In Paul's qualifications for overseers, he mentions a necessary trait for anyone who wants to lead in a community: "He must manage his own household well, with all dignity keeping his children submissive, for if someone does not know how to manage his own household, how will he care for God's church?" (1 Tim 3:4–5).

Though Paul speaks to overseers, his words tell us something about our own witness. Living like Christ, showing grace, and acting with wisdom toward the people who are closest to us are often more difficult than serving on a larger scale. It's more challenging to serve those who know our failings than it is to serve anyone else. By learning to be faithful in these relationships—by serving unselfishly and with dignity—we prove ourselves capable of serving others.

Paul understands that humility and love must be practiced at home before they can be adequately practiced in community. By extension, allowing ourselves to live an imbalanced or ungodly life will ultimately lessen our effectiveness elsewhere.

It's easy to take the people closest to us for granted—to see them as facets of our own lives, helping us accomplish our own goals. Guiding these relationships takes maturity. And the fruits of those relationships will prove our ability to influence the lives of others.

Paul acknowledges that the desire to be a leader is a noble one. He isn't trying to dissuade those who want to take on more responsibility; instead, he is trying to ensure that they're adequately prepared and not prone to a major public meltdown. He is preparing them to succeed at an honorable task. —RVN

Think about two or three people who are closest to you.
How can you better serve them?

DYSFUNCTIONAL PROBLEM-SOLVING

1 Chronicles 3:1–4:23; 1 Timothy 3:8–16; **Psalm 77:1–20**

When I locate a problem, I often fixate on it. I think that if I analyze it enough, I can solve it. This is a challenge when I come to difficult issues that require someone else's expertise. Stubbornly, I want to figure out the problem myself. I want to be self-sufficient. When God is the only one who can solve my problem, I've just created an impossible scenario.

When the psalmist hit troubling times and questioned the things that were accepted truths in his life, he didn't seek his answer from anyone but God. When he felt far from God and questioned all he had taken for granted, the questions he asks are close to those in our own hearts: "Why God? Have you removed your favor?" (Psa 77:7). "Has your steadfast love ceased forever?" (Psa 77:8). "Do your promises end?" (Psa 77:8).

It would have been tempting to dwell on his personal experiences to answer these questions. But instead, the psalmist turns to study God's redemptive work. This seems counter-intuitive to us, but we find this practice throughout the psalms. Why doesn't the psalmist simply address the problem at hand? He knew that to understand God's work in the present, he had to look to the past. He had to consider God's work in humanity—His wonders of old, mighty deeds, holy ways, and power among the peoples. Ultimately, though, the psalmist looks to God's work of redemption in the exodus from Egypt. He needed a backward glance—a look at God's faithfulness to His people in the past.

We have an even greater redemptive story than the exodus. When things seem to go wrong, when we question God's plan for our life, we can look back to Christ's work on the cross. We're not leaving our story for another one when we do this; instead, we're acknowledging Christ's ongoing work in our lives through the Holy Spirit. His work sets our entire life in perspective.

When life seems complicated, don't try to be self-sufficient. When your emotions dictate otherwise, take a backward glance at the cross and reckon in your mind and heart what is already true of God's love for you. There has never been such a testament of His love. Then take a faithful step forward, trusting in Him. —RVN

How are you trying to be self-sufficient? How are you
taking a backward glance at the cross and stepping forward in faith?

CONNECTING HISTORICAL DOTS

1 Chronicles 4:24–5:26; 1 Timothy 4:1–5; Psalm 78:1–12

Biblical lists can be annoying, but they're also a testament to God's faithfulness. It's a true gift when someone in a faith community records the history of the group and their work—particularly when God has answered prayers. By looking through a recorded history, like a prayer journal, faith communities can see how God used them both collectively and as individuals. They can see where He interceded and begin to see how He intends to use them in the future.

God's past faithfulness points to His future faithfulness. His specific dealings in the past point to likely dealings in the future: They show us what He has gifted us to do and thus the type of thing He is likely to call us to down the road.

First Chronicles 4:24–5:26 records God's acts among His people and points to His future faithfulness. Similarly, Psalm 78:1–12 calls God's people to hear their story told, but it's really God's story. The first account focuses on the individuals, whereas the second (Psa 78) recalls God's work among a group of people. All of God's work—among individuals and groups of people—is unique, but it is also interconnected. It is all a manifestation of His presence. Paul makes a similar remark to Timothy: "Everything created by God is good and nothing is to be rejected if it is received with thankfulness" (1 Tim 4:4).

Although God may manifest Himself in different and unique ways among individuals and groups, everything He does is for good—from the beginning until now (compare Gen 1; John 1). God desires for us to experience Him, as individuals and as members of faith communities, doing His good work. In being both, we come to understand what it means to truly follow Jesus. —JDB

How can you embark more fully into God's great work,
both in your own life and in a faith community?

A HIGHER CALLING

1 Chronicles 6:1–81; **1 Timothy 4:6–16**; Psalm 78:13–29

It's easy to get self-absorbed when we're criticized—or when we *think* others are criticizing us. Because of our real or imagined defects, we start to believe other people don't take us seriously. It's easy to get off course in an attempt to defend ourselves.

As a young leader, Timothy may have dealt with criticism in the Ephesian community because of his age. Paul gives him advice: "Let no one despise you for your youth, but set the believers an example in speech, in conduct, in love, in faith, in purity" (1 Tim 4:12).

Paul doesn't offer defensive solutions. Rather, he calls Timothy to be a living example of his teaching. He reinforces Timothy's calling by encouraging him to stay focused on his call, speech, and conduct. By *being* the contrast to the rumors about him, Timothy thwarts criticism.

But Paul isn't simply giving leadership advice. By reaffirming Timothy's purpose and calling, he is helping Timothy focus on God's work instead of his own abilities (or a defense of them). Paul doesn't want Timothy to be guided by fear of others; he wants him to think about God.

We don't have to be in a leadership position to experience this type of criticism or to respond in the way that Paul suggests. When feeling defensive or concerned about other people's opinions, we shouldn't be concerned about defending ourselves. We're not intended to reaffirm our own stellar traits or abilities. That flies in the face of the gospel. Instead, we should act in a way that points people to God's work, shifting both our focus and their focus to the one whose opinion truly matters. —RVN

Are your attempts at earning the respect or favor of others
making you self-absorbed? How can you shift your focus
to God and the work He wants you to do?

OUTLINE FOR HONOR

1 Chronicles 7:1–40; **1 Timothy 5:1–9**; Psalm 78:30–52

In most Western cultures today, we've lost our connection with the elderly. With one grandparent living halfway across the country and the others having died before I was born, I wasn't around older people until I met my wife and her family. Unlike me, my wife had the privilege of knowing her great-grandparents. She has a strong sense of tradition and respect for the elderly, as well as a deep desire to help them in all aspects of life, and she has been able to teach me to do the same. Paul is dealing with a similar experience in his first letter to Timothy.

Paul says to Timothy, "Do not rebuke an older man, but appeal to him as a father, younger men as brothers, older women as mothers, younger women as sisters, with all purity. Honor widows who are truly widows" (1 Tim 5:1–3). By "honor," Paul means showing a deep sense of concern and an earnest, regular desire to help them financially and with their daily needs. What Paul says is revolutionary for his time. It wasn't that the elderly were disrespected culturally, but they weren't sought out as teachers and people to help. Paul commanded not just equality in this scenario, but assistance and compassion. Widows, who were of the lowest rank of society, were to be loved as equals. And older men, at the higher rank, were to be respected for their understanding.

We don't make these connections as readily in Western society. Instead, we see someone's need as something to pray for, not to act on. And we see older men's perspectives as simply "old guard" rather than a legitimate opinion we should take into consideration. Paul doesn't say older people are always right, just as our fathers are not always right, but he does encourage Timothy to show them the respect they deserve "as a father." Paul's outline for honor is as powerful now as it was then. —JDB

How can you make the elderly and widowed
a part of your life and church community?

FROM CONCEPT TO CAUTION TO CAUSE

1 Chronicles 8:1–40; **1 Timothy 5:10–17**; Psalm 78:53–72

Some things in the Bible are downright surprising, including several passages in Paul's letters. Sometimes his words are so personal or they're addressed to such a specific person or group, that it's hard to understand why that particular passage is there. But God uses people to do His work, and whatever they show or teach us sets a precedent—like how to deal with difficult people, or how to best help the poor.

Some sections of Paul's letters are rarely read aloud in church; we simply can't figure out how to apply them. What application can you draw from a long list of people, or from the very specific details of how to evaluate a widow in need in your community (1 Tim 5)? What if there are no widows in your community? Do you just move on?

First Timothy 5:10–17 sets a good precedent for us as Christians, and it can serve as a standard for applying other passages. We don't know precisely why Paul told Timothy not to help widows "less than sixty years of age," but we do know that he was setting criteria for evaluating and helping the poor (1 Tim 5:9). Other than children and previously freed slaves, widows were the most impoverished members of society in biblical times.

Paul provides further criteria that would prevent a handout-based culture and that would also require a widow to have truly been transformed by Jesus' teachings (1 Tim 5:10). Helping the poor isn't enough—they need spiritual help, too. Paul also cautions against those who abuse the system (1 Tim 5:11–13), acknowledging that it can actually cause more harm than good when the church helps them.

As the Church, we want to help. But there have been times when we have done more harm than good—both locally and globally, particularly in the developing world—by failing to understand the power struggles at play in any given situation. This should not stop us from helping; instead, it should encourage us to be both fiscally wise and culturally educated before providing funds. Understanding what people are really going through and how to truly help them is nearly as important as giving. —JDB

Who is your community trying to help? How can you better educate
yourself on their real needs and how to meet them?

May 21

∘∘∘∘∘

THE POWER OF WORDS

1 Chronicles 9:1–10:14; **1 Timothy 5:18–6:2**; Psalm 79:1–13

Gossip kills churches. And gossip is always painful, especially when disguised as concern. A request to "pray for so-and-so because of this thing they did" is not asking for prayer; it's gossiping. If you know some personal detail about someone's mishap, don't share it with everyone—take it to God. Entire leadership structures have been wrongfully destroyed because of rumors starting this way.

Paul warns against rumors when he says, "Do not accept an accusation against an elder except on the evidence of two or three witnesses" (1 Tim 5:19). How often have we heard something and been so influenced by it that we accuse someone on the basis of that rumor? Hearing something may make it feel factual, but it's circumstantial at best.

Although Paul is cautious, he has no tolerance for leaders who sin repeatedly, especially those sinning directly against the community. He tells Timothy to "reprove those who sin in the presence of all, in order that the rest also may experience fear" (1 Tim 5:20). The fear Paul means is a good kind; it keeps people from sinning. It's not just a fear of getting caught, but an understanding that there are ramifications for the abuse of power or lack of godly conduct.

Paul is not creating a legalistic system here; instead, he is focusing on making people feel what God feels when they sin. They shouldn't be consumed with guilt, but they should feel enough shame in their actions to realize that they need grace—that they need to step out of a leadership position if they misuse their power. Paul doesn't demand that these people be cast out of the community. He requires that such leaders be reconciled to the faith community and be made an example so that others don't do the same.

Paul's entire framework is based on his assumption that leaders will be godly; he provided details for determining that standard earlier (e.g., 1 Tim 3:1–12). Leaders who fall short must be held accountable. And above all, leaders must be chosen wisely. If they live and conduct themselves in line with God's work, they will have no need to fear accusations against them. —JDB

*How can you help establish and support a correct
leadership structure in your faith community?
How can you help stop any false accusations or gossip?*

MOTIVE IS EVERYTHING

1 Chronicles 11:1–47; **1 Timothy 6:3–10**; Psalm 80:1–19

It's not often that we take an honest look at our motivations. But it's important to reevaluate them regularly. When our sight is not fixed on God, we might become entranced with goals that conflict with godliness. Even though we might initially be performing the right actions, our lives will start to reveal the motives of our hearts.

Paul addresses this issue within the Ephesian community, where some people were spreading conflict in order to further their own gain. And this wasn't just a problem with the perpetrators. This "constant wrangling by people of depraved mind and deprived of the truth, who consider godliness to be a means of gain" was like poison, spreading envy and strife throughout the community (1 Tim 6:5).

To counteract this, Paul states that "godliness with contentment is a great means of gain" (1 Tim 6:5–6), but the gain he talks about is not success as we traditionally define it. Rather than financial riches, Paul presents the idea of complete contentment—of being satisfied with what we have and feeling secure in the life (both eternal and physical) with which God has blessed us (1 Tim 6:8).

This is not a simple side issue. Paul states that "the love of money is a root of all evil" (1 Tim 6:10). When money becomes our guiding motivation, we're very much tempted to be self-sufficient. Our motives become muddled, and we try to find our contentment in transient things. In contrast, when we're completely satisfied in God, we won't be tempted to conflicting motives. —RVN

Are your motives conflicted?
How do you need to readjust your motives
so that you desire godliness?

FEAR: THE FIGHT AGAINST IT

1 Chronicles 12:1–13:14; 1 Timothy 6:11–21; Psalm 81:1–82:8

Fear is poisonous. When it drives our decisions, it will slowly destroy us—causing us to make moves that are against God's will and detrimental to ourselves and others. The antidote to fear is complete reliance on Yahweh, our God, and His work through the Spirit.

David is the epitome of someone who sets aside fear in favor of God's work. He surrounds himself with "feared" men, his "mighty men." The descriptions of their skills show the caliber of these warriors and thus the incredible character and skill it must have taken to lead them (1 Chr 12:1–15). It takes courage to be a leader and valor to be a leader of leaders. David was a man of valor—a man empowered by the Spirit's work.

It would have been easy for David to worry or be concerned as a leader—especially when the Spirit comes upon a smaller group of men who oppose him. People rise up around him, and they are being chosen by God in a way he had been. But David isn't concerned or resentful; instead, he affirms God's work (1 Chr 12:16–18).

The Spirit empowers David again when he seeks out the ark of the covenant, which had previously been with God's people as they went into battle and when they worshiped (1 Chr 13:1–4). In this moment, when David summons the people to undertake this task, he shows that he is not just a leader of great men, but a godly leader of great men. He understands that his own strength and skill will not carry him and his warriors. Instead, they must be guided by Yahweh. They must recover the ark that symbolized Him and His work among them, His very presence.

Rather than let fear drive him, David drives out fear in the name of His God. We should be people of the same character, showing courage and valor. —JDB

What is God doing through you?
How can you allow God to banish the fears you have?

ON A MISSION

1 Chronicles 14:1–15:29; **2 Timothy 1:1–2**; Psalm 83

"We're on a mission from God." Whenever the Blues Brothers delivered this line, they were met with a less-than-enthusiastic reception. While they had a different "mission" in mind, their famous line summarizes Paul's ministry, and their reception is strangely related to a pressing problem in our Christian communities today: We're hesitant to receive those who tell us they're on God's mission.

When we hear this line, we immediately begin to ask questions in our heads: Are they offering a critique? Making a threat? Telling us they're pursuing a ministry role in accordance with the gifts God has given them, or that they want to be directed toward such a role?

Nearly all the godly people in the Bible were appointed directly by God or His messengers to a mission, and they were given very particular (and often unique) gifts to fulfill those missions. So when someone says they're on a mission from God, we should respond with, "Tell me about it!" Consider passages like 2 Timothy 1:1, where Paul addresses Timothy and the community he leads, many of whom never met Paul:

"Paul, an apostle of Christ Jesus by the will of God according to the promise of the life that is in Christ Jesus."

Apostle means "sent one." Paul was on a mission from God, and it's because of Christ, the anointed one's promises, that he embraces this calling. God called and gifted him to do His work and share His message. Who are we to say that God doesn't commission people today? Of course, we should always be cautious and discerning; those in leadership must have proven their godly character and their ability to be used by God. They must also be confirmed by other godly leaders. Once this has been confirmed, we should encourage those called to a special mission. We, as believers, are called to work alongside them—to encourage them and help them serve what God, specifically, has appointed them to do.

We stumble when we think the Church is ours to lead; it is Christ's. He is our leader and guide, and it's by His Spirit that we will have the discernment necessary to do what He God has appointed us to do. —JDB

How can you help those who are on a mission from God?

LONGING AND BEING

1 Chronicles 16:1–17:27; 2 Timothy 1:3–18; **Psalm 84:1–12**

The general sense of what worship "is" is widely known, but the specifics of what it means are a little vague. Aside from obedience (i.e., avoiding sin and following what God asks of us), there are specific ways to show God admiration. In 1 Chronicles, during David's many great acts, we get a glimpse into ancient worship practices that are still applicable today. We know that the biblical "editors" favored these practices because they would later ascribe countless psalms to David. His way of worship was deemed "the way to worship."

After David and his comrades journey to Obed-Edom to bring back the ark of the covenant—the symbol of Yahweh's provision and advocacy for His people—David appoints "some of the Levites as ministers before the ark of Yahweh" (1 Chr 16:4). The Levites, the tribe designated as religious teachers, are first to invoke Yahweh (call upon Him). They are then to do what should be natural in all encounters with Him: thank and then praise Him. These are all acts of worship and the way to worship: Acknowledge Him by calling on Him, be thankful for His provision, and then praise Him for who He is.

David illustrates another part of worship in His song that follows this event: "Save us, O God of our salvation; gather us and rescue us from the nations, that we may give thanks to your holy name and glory in your praise. Blessed be Yahweh the God of Israel, from everlasting to everlasting!" (1 Chr 16:35–36). David petitions God, and he calls others to acknowledge His work by making their own petitions. It's not that God needs to hear how great He is—that is not why we worship. It's that we need to be reminded. In humbling ourselves before Him, we are demonstrating our rightful place in His kingdom as His servants, appointed for His great works (Eph 1:11).

Worship is really about longing for God. Our attitude toward God should be as Psalm 84:2 proclaims: "My soul longs and even fails for the courtyards of Yahweh. My heart and flesh sing for joy to the living God." —JDB

*How can you instill these worship practices
into your daily life?*

A LONGSUFFERING GOD

1 Chronicles 18:1–20:8; **2 Timothy 2:1–13**; **Psalm 85**

God is longsuffering, but sometimes we take this for granted. How often have we given into temptation, expecting to be obedient at a later date?

Psalm 85 gives a testimony of God's faithfulness in the past: "O Yahweh, you favored your land. You restored the fortunes of Jacob. You took away the guilt of your people; you covered all their sin. You withdrew all your wrath; you turned from your burning anger" (Psa 85:1–3).

As he experiences that judgment, the psalmist remembers God's past restoration, and he hopes for it once more: "I will hear what God, Yahweh, will speak, because he will speak peace to his people, even his faithful ones"; he also sets a condition: "But let them not return to folly" (Psa 85:8).

Do we wait until bad times before we realize God's amazing grace for us? God's faithfulness is also expressed in surprising moments in the New Testament, like Paul's exhortation to Timothy. Paul tells him to be strong in grace and offers comfort while presenting a challenge: "For if we died with him, we will also live with him; if we endure, we will also reign with him; if we deny him, he also will deny us; if we are unfaithful, he remains faithful—he cannot deny himself" (2 Tim 2:11–13).

These passages portray a God who is incredibly patient. But they also present a sense of urgency and demand a response. If we acknowledge our sin and seek Him, He is faithful to forgive us. But we shouldn't use His faithfulness as an excuse to delay our response. He wants our complete loyalty. —RVN

How are you responding to God's calling in your life?

○ ○◇○ ○

MATH: MAYBE NOT
A MYSTIC LANGUAGE AFTER ALL

1 Chronicles 21:1–22:19; 2 Timothy 2:14–26; Psalm 86:1–87:7

In a world of metrics, it's easy to become obsessed with statistics and start to quantify every aspect of our lives. Stats can even become a type of scorekeeping between churches or pastors: "We have more members than you do." We may never say those words out loud, but we think them; more than one person has made the mistake of measuring a ministry based on attendance. But God has His own method for measuring success.

Prompted by an adversary ("Satan" is often better translated as "adversary" or "accuser" in the Old Testament), David decides to seek metrics—to count the people of Israel. This account illustrates the harm of seeking gratification or understanding in numbers. In 1 Chronicles 21, major problems emerge from this—including placing an adversary's will above God's and predicting God's will rather than seeking it regularly.

Rather than counting our successes, we should be counting on God for success. We should also be tallying how often He is faithful rather than how many we are in number. We're more likely to see God's faithfulness when we're looking for it rather than looking for probabilities. David succeeded as a warrior and king not because he deserved it, but because God chose for him to do so. In 1 Chronicles 21, David forgets God's role, even though his (often wrong and bloodthirsty) general reminds him otherwise. In fact, God's use of Joab as His messenger demonstrates that God's providential will can come from the least likely places.

Keeping a tally isn't necessarily a bad thing, and we shouldn't avoid metrics and stats. But we need to keep information in perspective. It's not about baptizing 200 people on a Sunday—although that's a blessed thing. It's about lives being transformed and people being blessed so that they can experience transformation. —JDB

How can you count on what God is doing
instead of counting what you deem success?

THROUGH DESPAIR

1 Chronicles 23:1–32; **2 Timothy 3:1–9**; Psalm 88

Sometimes we go through dark periods in our lives where the misery feels never-ending. At times like these, we may feel forgotten by God.

In Psalm 88, we find one of the most prolonged cries of utter despair: "O Yahweh, God of my salvation, I cry out by day and through the night before you," the psalmist begins (Psa 88:1). This psalm never climaxes or hints of hope. The psalmist, feeling abandoned by God, has his loved ones taken from him. He is left to navigate the darkness alone (Psa 88:18).

How do we deal with our own misery when confronted by a tragic psalm like this? How should we respond to God? We can start with what the psalmist, despite his prolonged suffering, acknowledges about God. Although his troubles are still present, he also recognizes God as his deliverer (Psa 88:6–9). He appeals to God's reputation as a God of wonders, deserving of praise (Psa 88:10). He appeals to God's loyal love, faithfulness, and righteousness (Psa 88:11).

The psalmist never comes to a place where he expresses even a glimmer of hope. But through cries, questions, and torment, he holds on to what he knows to be true about God. In his very cry, the psalmist acknowledges that God will be present in his situation. The psalmist lives in the awareness that God cares and will eventually act. In the meantime, he places himself in God's faithfulness.

We see a parallel situation in Paul's letter to Timothy; Paul addresses the difficult days that will come. He says they will be difficult for one reason: disobedience (2 Tim 3:2–3). What's most fascinating about the parallel is that it hints at the root of what the psalmist is experiencing: disobedience may not be acknowledged in his cry (he is innocent), but the world is a disobedient place. It is full of sin and oppression. Ultimately, the sins of humanity brought pain to the world.

In this life, we'll go through dark times and struggles that may never end. We may even feel forgotten. But despite what we think or feel, we can't abandon what we know to be true of God. Even when our state or our emotions are contrary to the desire to worship Him, we are called to trust in Him and in His love.

If He was willing to abandon His only son on a cross to redeem you, then He is certainly trustworthy. If you trust in Him, He will not forsake you. —RVN

How are you trusting God through dark times?
How are you reaching out to someone who is struggling?

BLESSED STICKY NOTES

1 Chronicles 24:1–25:31; 2 Timothy 3:10–17; Psalm 89:1–22

A great friend of mine keeps sticky notes with prayer requests on a bathroom mirror. They serve as a reminder of the needs of others. This friend never seems to have an "off day" or feel sad about their particular situation. Maybe these notes play a part in that attitude, but that's not why I find the practice remarkable. What astounds me is the effort to pray for others constantly. This person reminds me of God's faithfulness in my life whenever things get tough, for me or others, and I'm grateful my name is on one of those notes. Otherwise, I think I would have lost my way several times already.

First Chronicles presents story after story of God's faithfulness. The book records how God kept His people alive in the face of powerful adversaries, and it tells how God led David in his great appointment as king. Paul's journey has several parallels with David's. Just as the chronicler watches David's narrative, as well as that of Israel in general (e.g., 1 Chr 24), Timothy watches Paul and the Christian church (2 Tim 3:10–17). Paul recounts to Timothy, "But you have faithfully followed my teaching, way of life, purpose, faith, patience, love, endurance, persecutions, and sufferings that happened to me in Antioch, in Iconium, and in Lystra, what sort of persecutions I endured, and the Lord delivered me from all of them" (2 Tim 3:10–11). Timothy is more than a colleague; he is a true friend.

What a joy it is to have someone in your life who watches "your story." Think how our lives might be different if we had more friends who faithfully prayed for us and we faithfully prayed for them. Following God is not just a matter of listening to His guidance; it's also being aware of how His faithfulness is playing out in the lives of those around us. —JDB

Who can you be praying for?
How can you commit to being a blessing to them?
How can you regularly remind yourself to do so?

○ ◌ ◌ ◌ ○

IN SEASON AND OUT OF SEASON

1 Chronicles 26:1–27:34; **2 Timothy 4:1–8**; Psalm 89:23–52

I like to operate when I feel like I'm in control. When I haven't gathered enough information or I feel uncertain of my circumstances, it's tempting to avoid making a decision or taking action.

Paul knew that this type of outlook was detrimental to Timothy's ministry. He tells Timothy that regardless of his circumstances, he was required to act: "Preach the word, be ready in season and out of season, reprove, rebuke, exhort, with all patience and instruction" (2 Tim 4:2).

Paul uses the certainty of Christ's return to motivate Timothy to stick to his task (2 Tim 4:1). Although Timothy experienced times when it was not always convenient for him to act on his calling, he had been admonished by Paul about the importance of the work they were doing together: their calling. He also knew the urgency of that calling. Christ's return and the appearance of His kingdom was their motivation (2 Tim 4:1).

We can't follow God only when the timing is right for us. We also can't rely on our own strength. When doing God's work, we can never plan well enough or anticipate all the potential kinks; our plans will never be foolproof. It's not the mark of a Christian to be certain of how everything will play out in every circumstance. The mark of a Christian is reliance on Christ as Savior, God, and guide. Through the clear and calm and through the fog, we're required to trust, act, and follow on the basis of our certainty in Jesus. Like Timothy and Paul, we must be certain of our standing in Christ and the coming of His kingdom. And that changes everything.

Whatever the task and in every circumstance, we're required to simply follow Jesus. We are charged to act for the gospel now, regardless of whether it's convenient. —RVN

How are you trusting in your own strength instead of Jesus'?
How can you be ready in the right way, in every season?

May 31

○ ○ ○ ○ ○

FIGHTING LONELINESS

1 Chronicles 28:1–29:2; **2 Timothy 4:9–22**; **Psalm 90:1–17**

Loneliness is one of the most disheartening feelings a person can know. Being alone in a time of pain is even worse. Several recent surveys suggest that lonely people—especially teenagers—subtly reach out through their social networks, desperately looking for someone who cares. In a world where anyone can get attention online, we've moved away from authentic community. We continue to crave personal interactions—perhaps more so because we have electronic witness to the interactions of others. We as Christians should see this as an opportunity to reach out to disenfranchised, lonely people and show the love of Christ to others.

Paul's second letter to Timothy illustrates how feelings of loneliness are amplified by pain. He makes one of the most candid statements in the Bible: "At my first defense, no one came to my aid, but they all deserted me; may it not be counted against them. But the Lord helped me and strengthened me, so that through me the proclamation might be fulfilled and all the Gentiles might hear, and he rescued me from the lion's mouth. The Lord will rescue me from every evil deed, and will save me for his heavenly kingdom, to whom be the glory forever and ever. Amen" (2 Tim 4:16–18).

Paul is angry and hurt, but he's well aware that God has been and will continue to be his strength. He acknowledges that he needs and craves community, but he clearly states that God is foremost in his life. He then reminds Timothy of God's work in his life and others'—ending with "Amen," meaning "So be it." Paul's reliance on God's past faithfulness bears a striking resemblance to a statement from Psalm 90: "O Lord, you have been our help in all generations. Before the mountains were born and you brought forth the earth and the world, even from everlasting to everlasting, you are God" (Psa 90:1–2).

This psalm emphasizes that God always has and always will be a "help" to His people. While we can take comfort in that, we should make every effort—as people aspiring to live like Christ—to help others. For Paul found God not only in His provision of spiritual strength, but in the kindness of others. —JDB

How can you show God's kindness
and faithfulness to people who are lonely?

WHAT WEALTH REVEALS

2 Chronicles 1:1–3:17; **Titus 1:1–4**; Psalm 91:1–16

"What would you do if you won the lottery?" This question always seems to generate the same responses: There's the person who devises an investment strategy, the dreamer who envisions ending global poverty, the individual who would travel the world, and the person who would buy the house, boat, or car they've always wanted.

These responses tell us something about each person's character and what fulfills them. The root of these desires reveals something about how they perceive their identity in relationship to their culture, family, and God.

Solomon experiences an unexpected "wish" scenario. Like winning the lottery or being granted three wishes, Solomon's response reveals what is important to him, the core of his identity, and how God responds to people who know what He desires. God says to the king, "Ask what I shall give to you" (2 Chr 1:7). Solomon replies with some of the most humble words ever spoken: "Now, give to me wisdom and knowledge that I may go out and come in before this people [an idiom for a type of leading], for who can judge this, your great people?" (2 Chr 1:10). In response, God reminds Solomon of all the great things he passed up in this moment, and how doing so showed his true character. As a result, God also blesses Solomon with "wealth, possessions, and honor" (2 Chr 1:11–12). Solomon's humility demonstrates what it looks like to have a godly identity that's focused on others rather than self.

To combat selfishness, Paul regularly reminds himself and others that he is "a slave of God, and an apostle of Jesus Christ for the faith of the chosen of God and knowledge of the truth that is according to godliness" (Titus 1:1). He grounds his statement by testifying to God's eternal work (Titus 1:2–4).

The difference between present gain and eternal gain is focus: Are we working toward the eternal good of God's work or the temporal good of our own success? When we align ourselves with who God created us to be, our desires become His desires. We, like Solomon and Paul, should understand our role in God's work and request what we need to fulfill that role, trusting that He will provide the rest. —JDB

What would you do if you came into a large sum of money?
How can you align your desires with God's?

◦ ◦◦◦◦

TRANSFORMERS

2 Chronicles 4:1–6:11; **Titus 1:5–9**; Psalm 92:1–93:5

Some people are like spectators in their faith communities—they simply watch while others interact, serve, and reach out. But Paul's instructions to Titus about overseers show us that communities need people who will do more than just show up.

"For it is necessary for the overseer to be blameless as God's steward, not self-willed, not quick-tempered, not addicted to wine, not violent, not greedy for dishonest gain, but hospitable, loving what is good, prudent, just, devout, self-controlled, holding fast to the faithful message according to the teaching" (Titus 1:7–9).

Titus was counteracting the harm false teachers had caused in the Cretan community (Titus 1:11). He needed the leaders' assistance to succeed. At first, Paul describes this type of leader as someone who *doesn't* commit certain actions—anger, desire for personal gain, drunkenness, or violence. But Paul also realized that leaders *did* need to take certain positive actions—showing hospitality, loving what is good, and holding fast to the gospel. Only by avoiding some behaviors and embracing others could they transform the community by being instruments of change.

There will be periods in our lives when we'll need to humbly accept the help of others. But there are also times for action, and our motives will be just as important as our conduct.

The believers on Crete needed to be molded and shaped for godliness. Likewise, we need God's word and His Spirit to provide us with wisdom not only to respond, but to do so with the right action—showing hospitality, loving what is good, and being committed to the good news of Jesus Christ. Then, as transformed people, we can be used to advance His kingdom. —RVN

How is God prompting you to be used in your church community?
How can you respond?

○ ○ ○ ○ ○

SEARCHING FOR JUSTICE

2 Chronicles 6:12–8:18; Titus 1:10–16; **Psalm 94:1–23**

"Do you favor justice or mercy?" Trick question. Both responses are technically incorrect: God's ways require mercy *and* justice. Mercy cannot be fully known without perfect justice, and justice without mercy is harsh and graceless.

God's mercy is a regular topic in Christian communities, but we often shy away from discussing His justice. This leaves us on our own to confront the injustices we commit against Him and others, those committed against us, and our own unjust nature. Carrying out God's justice feels scary because it requires making large-scale changes in our world. But we can't carry out His justice if we act only from the right purpose—we must also act in His way.

The psalmist cries out for justice: "O Yahweh, God of vengeance, God of vengeance, shine forth. Rise up, O Judge of the earth. … They crush your people, O Yahweh; they oppress your inheritance. They kill widow and stranger, and they murder orphans while they say, 'Yahweh does not see'" (Psa 94:1–2, 5–7).

In this plea, we see that the psalmist both understands God's nature and realizes His capabilities. The psalmist exhorts Yahweh to act. In doing so, he cites injustices against those to whom God's people were called to show mercy (e.g., Deut 14:29; 16:11–12; 24:19–20). The widow, orphan, and stranger are also those whom Yahweh cares for and advocates (e.g., Exod 22:22–24; Deut 10:18). Ultimately, the psalmist is reminding Yahweh of His role.

This request teaches us something fundamental about justice. Although the psalmist plays a role in the cause of justice, he is not the primary actor; Yahweh is. Justice is God's work. —JDB

How can you harmonize your views of justice and mercy?
How can you act more justly today?

June 4

○ ◇ ◉ ◇ ○

FAITHFUL EXAMPLES

2 Chronicles 9:1–10:19; **Titus 2:1–8**; Psalm 95:1–11

We cringe when we see other Christians exploiting the gospel, using it to advance their own personal or political agenda. Today, it doesn't take much effort to do so—it's as easy as posting a video or link online. In these situations, it's tempting to respond with anger or frustration, but if we do so, we're compounding the problem with our own behavior.

We can learn a lot from an ancient Graeco-Roman context that really isn't so different from ours. Paul had left Titus in Crete to help the Cretans learn what it looked like to live the gospel. Paul gives Titus instructions for each age and gender group to help the Cretan believers reset their old ways of being and avoid bringing the gospel message into disrepute.

Paul realized, though, that the Cretans needed real-life examples to truly change. He set up mentors within the community. The elderly women were to teach younger women so that "the word of God may not be slandered" (Titus 2:5). Titus, a young man, needed to be a model of good works. His teaching needed to show "soundness, dignity, a sound message beyond reproach" (Titus 2:7–8). His works and his teaching were intended to be a model of Christian living.

The Cretan believers had to examine their old habits and behaviors, and we're no different. All of us come from different contexts that have shaped the way we live out our faith—and sometimes we need correction. Although we're quick to look down on other Christians when they inhibit the gospel message through their faulty applications, we're often unaware when we do it ourselves.

When we see others misusing the gospel, we need to wisely and lovingly confront them about their motives. Like Titus and influential Cretan believers, though, we also have to be open to the work of Christ in our own lives. We can do this by aligning our motives with the gospel and graciously and humbly accepting correction when it's needed. Through living out the gospel, we can reflect Christ so that others are drawn to Him. —RVN

How are you being a model for other Christians?

○ ◊ ○ ◊ ○

WHEN WORDS ARE ENOUGH

2 Chronicles 11:1–13:22; Titus 2:9–2:15; Psalm 96:1–13

It's not often that words change the course of history. But Shemaiah, a little-known prophet, was given such an opportunity. We can easily pass over these life-altering moments if we're not looking for them.

Rehoboam had assembled 180,000 chosen "makers of war" to fight against Israel in hopes of restoring his kingdom. He was prepared to destroy a portion of God's people in order to gain a temporary victory. Then Shemaiah—a "man of God"—came along (2 Chr 11:2).

When Shemaiah spoke for Yahweh, Rehoboam backed down; he sent the 180,000 men home (2 Chr 11:1–4). You can imagine Rehoboam trembling in fear as he told this enormous number of warriors, "Thanks for coming out today, but Shemaiah just told me that Yahweh doesn't approve, so we can start fortifying this city instead (see 2 Chr 11:5–12), or you can just go home if you want."

Trust goes both ways in this story. Rehoboam trusted that Shemaiah spoke the true word of Yahweh, and Rehoboam had the trust of his men, who chose to listen to him instead of independently heading into battle. All of the parties decided to trust Yahweh, whether directly through His oracle or indirectly through following the words of their leaders.

When things seem out of control, we expect God to show up. But we often make that request without regard for the foundation we *should* have laid before—when things were calm. Times of rest and waiting are not times to be stagnant; instead, they are times to get to know God better so that we are prepared for what's next. Shemaiah prepared for this situation by knowing God—the best kind of preparation. —JDB

How can you establish the foundation
for your future ministry experiences now?

June 6

° ο ◊ ο °

BEING MADE NEW

2 Chronicles 14:1–16:14; **Titus 3:1–7**; Psalm 97:1–98:9

We often fall into old habits that reflect the way we once were. Although we've been made new, we haven't been made perfect, and sometimes it shows. People within our church communities might have one perception of us, but others may have experienced another side—one that can make us feel shameful about our witness (or lack thereof).

While Paul spoke to Titus about relationships within the Cretan community, he also emphasized that believers needed to think about how their actions affected those outside the community. They needed to obey authority (Titus 3:1) and show perfect courtesy to all people (Titus 3:3). Although the Cretans had been told this before, Paul wanted Titus to remind them. He would later offer another reminder as well (Titus 3:14).

We might be tempted to cultivate the impression that we're better than we really are. But we have a responsibility to interact with all people in a way that reflects Christ. Paul tells us why: "For we also were once foolish, disobedient, led astray, enslaved to various desires and pleasures, spending our lives in wickedness and envy, despicable, hating one another. But when the kindness and love for mankind of God our Savior appeared, he saved us, not by deeds of righteousness that we have done, but because of his mercy, through the washing of regeneration and renewal by the Holy Spirit" (Titus 3:3–5).

We haven't earned anything through our own goodness—and we still can't. But we have been forgiven for our old way of being. When we fail and then repent, we're reminded of our need, Christ's sacrifice, and His renewing work in us through the Holy Spirit (Titus 3:5).

When we're not honest with others—including those outside our faith communities—about our failures and our need for forgiveness, we're projecting a false righteousness that turns others off from the gospel. Instead, by being honest and transparent about our weaknesses, we're testifying to Christ's righteousness and the work of the Spirit. Knowing this, we should examine all areas of our lives and all our relationships, seeking forgiveness and restoration where it's needed. —RVN

How have you failed people in your life?
How can you reach out and seek their forgiveness?

THE FORGOTTEN CHRISTIAN VIRTUE

2 Chronicles 17:1–18:34; Titus 3:8–11; Psalm 99:1–100:5

An unfortunate effect of our emphasis on God's grace is our dwindling focus on the connection between obeying God's will and receiving His blessings. If we're not living in the primary will God designed for us, then we will not be in the right place at the right time to do His work. And if we don't show up in the right moments (as designed by God), we won't be in a position to receive the glorious blessings of the good works He intended for us.

We see the kind of obedience God requires of us in the beginning of King Jehoshaphat's life. He is quick to align himself with God's will and, as a result, God is quick to bless him (2 Chr 17:1–6). God extends blessings appropriate for a king—the right people to protect him and offer him guidance, as well as wealth and honor (2 Chr 17:12–19; 18:1).

Based on this understanding of God's desire to bless our obedience, Paul later encourages Titus to tell other believers to "be careful to engage in good deeds … [and] to avoid foolish controversies and genealogies and contentions and quarrels about the law, for they are useless and fruitless" (Titus 3:8–9).

Although the Law (Genesis–Deuteronomy) is no longer the reigning force in our lives, God still requires obedience. When we're obedient, we're in God's will, and when we're in God's will, we experience even more of His blessings. We realize what it means to be made in His image—to live as He intended us to live.

It's easy to take this connection too far, wrongly suggesting that people who seem blessed must be in God's will or that wealth is a result of following God. This is rarely the case. King Jehoshaphat is a unique example of divine blessing, and the blessings he received aligned with his needs as the leader of God's people. God's blessings are usually far less tangible—they can be things like joy in Christ, a sense of peace that comes from being in His will, or the incredible feeling that comes from being involved when someone comes to believe in Christ or know Him more deeply.

We can never be obedient enough to earn the goodness God bestows on us. But obedience puts us in the right place at the right time for experiencing God's work; it is our road map for the journey. —JDB

How can you invite God and other believers to help you with obedience?
What is one thing you can change (or work on changing) this week?

June 8

∘ ∘ ◦ ∘ ∘

BADLY ALIGNED

2 Chronicles 19:1–20:37; Titus 3:12–15; **Psalm 101:1–8**

L ike a car with bad alignment, we are prone to drift off course when we're not focused on steering our faith. Often, we use intellectual pursuits to disguise our drifting. It's easier to argue an opinion than to respond faithfully. It's stimulating to have a theoretical conversation about a complex issue because there is no hard-and-fast application. When we drift, we might even succeed in convincing ourselves that we're being faithful.

New Christians often have a zealous faith and a desire to learn that make seasoned Christians take a second look at their own faith. In Psalm 101, the psalmist expresses this type of zeal for God. While his specific actions can seem strange to our modern ears, his desire to pursue God with his entire being is one we ourselves should adopt. He follows his repeated "I will" statements with promises to sing of God's steadfast love and justice, ponder the way that is blameless, and walk with integrity of heart. He knows the danger of haughty eyes and arrogance of heart, and he determines to avoid people with these traits. Instead, he aspires to seek out faithful people who can minister to him (Psa 101:6).

Complex faith issues don't always have hard-and-fast answers. They require intelligent conversations and careful consideration. But most of all, they require humility and a committed zeal to follow God—whatever the outcome.

We need to be humble and honest about our weaknesses. If we know we need help, we need to be like the psalmist and seek out mentors who can minister to us. And if someone calls us out as arrogant and haughty, we need to address where we've drifted. —RVN

Take a look at your own heart. Where are you drifting?

WHEN GOD DOESN'T ACT

2 Chronicles 21:1–23:21; **1 John 1:1–4**; Psalm 102:1–28

"When Jehoram ascended to the kingdom of his father, he strengthened himself and murdered all his brothers with the sword, and even some of the princes of Israel. … And he did evil in the sight of Yahweh. But Yahweh was not willing to destroy the house of David on account of the covenant that he had made with David and since he had promised to give a lamp to him and to his descendants forever" (2 Chr 21:4, 6–7).

Biblical stories like this teach us not only about God's actions, but also about His decisions *not* to act. It must have been difficult for those suffering under Jehoram's ruthless reign to understand why God would allow him to stay in power over them, His people. Yet God knew there was something even larger at stake: long-term, righteous reign over His people—and salvation itself. The people's suffering could not outweigh the importance of preserving the line of David, which held the hope of God's people. Salvation comes through David's line, as Jesus, the great Savior of the world, is David's heir (Matt 1:1).

Eventually, John the evangelist was able to testify, "What was from the beginning [and thus existed even during the times of suffering we endured], what we have heard [being all that has been promised], what we have seen with our eyes, what we have looked at and our hands have touched [because John actually knew Jesus and met Him in His resurrected form], concerning the word of life [being Jesus—God as both His Word and as His personhood]. … [Now] our fellowship is with the Father and with his Son Jesus Christ" (1 John 1:1, 3). John saw the day when God would ultimately lift the suffering of His people and place it on His Son so that His Son could die as the ultimate sufferer for us (compare Isa 53:10–12; Psa 22).

God does not cause suffering, but there are moments when—as much as it hurts Him—He allows it. If He has a saving act at work among us in the midst of these moments, they're worth it. God will always make good on His promises, and He will always far exceed our expectations. —JDB

What do you think can be accomplished through
your current sufferings? Is there a hurting person in your life
you could come alongside to offer them the hope of Christ?

A GOD WHO IS PRESENT

2 Chronicles 24:1–25:28; 1 John 1:5–10; **Psalm 103:1–14**

It's sometimes difficult to grasp that the Creator of the universe cares about us—that He bothers with miniscule people like us. Because we tend to forget about others and focus on our own tasks and needs, we're prone to think that God isn't concerned with the details of His creation—that He's not intimately involved in every aspect of our lives.

Psalm 103 presents a different understanding of God. The psalmist describes a God who wants to know us and wants us to respond to Him. He illustrates a responsive love. Because of God's love for him, he declares, "Bless Yahweh … all within me, bless his holy name" (Psa 103:1). God doesn't stop at forgiving our sins and redeeming us. He "crowns [us] with loyal love and mercies" (Psa 103:4). Although we have greatly offended Him, He doesn't hold it against us: "He has not dealt with us according to our sins, nor repaid us according to our iniquities" (Psa 103:10). As a father, He knows where we fail, and He pities us: "For he knows our frame. He remembers that we are dust" (Psa 103:13–14).

We can easily forget that God is concerned about our existence and jealous for our praise. If we don't realize His work and thank Him for it, we're not bringing Him glory. Ultimately, He has shown His love through His act of reconciling us to Himself. When we forget where we stand with Him, we can look to that great testament of His love. Then we can be like the psalmist and respond with praise. —RVN

Do you doubt God's love and care for you?
Does this affect your praise for Him?

○ ○ ○ ○ ○

THE DANGER OF SUCCESS

2 Chronicles 26:1–28:27; 1 John 2:1–6; Psalm 103:15–22

Western culture is obsessed with success. Society places successful people on a pedestal, as if they're somehow smarter or better than everyone else. Christians certainly aren't immune to this trend, as is demonstrated by the growing celebrity-pastor following. The need to succeed can tilt a church out of balance when the leader or the donors with the deepest pockets become the focus and ultimate authority, instead of Christ.

Uzziah's story demonstrates the danger of success. Most of the kings of Judah prior to Uzziah—who was appointed king at the age of 16—failed God and His people. They achieved success in their own eyes, but biblical history paints them as men who were spiritually weak and sought their own gain at the sacrifice of others. Success achieved through force may look like strength, but it's actually weakness. The distinction of great leaders is their ability to rise *alongside* those they lead, not *over* them.

At the beginning of his reign, Uzziah showed every sign of becoming a great leader: "And he did what was right in the eyes of Yahweh, according to all that Amaziah his father had done. And he began to seek God in the days of Zechariah who was teaching in visions of God. And whenever he sought Yahweh God made him have success" (2 Chr 26:4–5). Uzziah rose with his people, and he was willing to be taught by those he respected.

But then King Uzziah became proud: "But on account of his strength his heart grew proud unto destruction. And he acted unfaithfully against Yahweh his God" (2 Chr 26:16). Uzziah went so far as to place himself in the role of the priests; as a result, God afflicted him with leprosy. Instead of following God's will as he always had, Uzziah let success—and the desire for ultimate authority—become his guide (2 Chr 26:16–21).

We should not judge success according to societal norms, but on our submission to God's will and reign over our lives. We should question whether we are living up to our God-given potential and using our God-given gifts for His glory. And we should be cautious of pride—both in ourselves and others—so that we can discern whether confidence comes from self or from God, as it should. —JDB

What do you feel proud of?
How can you be better at helping others rise with you?

∘ ◊ ◊ ◊ ∘

CONFLICT CREATORS AND PEACEMAKERS

2 Chronicles 29:1–30:27; **1 John 2:7-14**; Psalm 104:1–15

Conflict can be good. And in communities, it's inevitable. The ways in which we respond to it can display and develop character. But what if we are the ones responsible for creating conflict with others?

John addresses the root of chronic conflict in a letter to a church community. He tells them, "The one who says he is in the light and hates his brother is in the darkness until now. The one who loves his brother resides in the light, and there is no cause for stumbling in him. But the one who hates his brother is in the darkness, and walks in the darkness, and does not know where he is going, because the darkness has blinded his eyes" (1 John 2:9–11).

John was giving the church a way in which they could judge false teachers who created conflict and division. Those who were not walking in the light—who hated their brothers—were known by their contentious nature. Conversely, those who walked in light did *not* serve as a stumbling block for others. The light they dwelled in was shown in their love for other Christians.

Love for other Christ-followers is not optional—it's an outpouring of the love that God shows to us. The nature of our interpersonal relationships is a reflection of where we stand with Him. External conflict that has hatred at its root might point to our own internal conflict—one that can be defined by a disagreement between what we confess and how we live (1 John 1:6). —RVN

What is causing conflicts in your relationships?
If you are the one causing conflict, how can you
seek peace—with God and others?

FOR IT IS BETTER

2 Chronicles 31:1–32:33; **1 John 2:15–17**; Psalm 104:16–35

"If your right hand causes you to sin, cut it off and throw it from you! For it is better for you that one of your limbs be destroyed than your whole body go into hell" (Matt 5:30). We might struggle to relate to this outspoken Jesus; we prefer gracious Jesus, offering us a pardon from sin through His sacrifice. We like friendly, loving Jesus, who wraps His arms around us even when we act disgracefully. Jesus is all of these things, but He is also very serious about sin.

One of the most tragic trends in church history is the increasingly casual attitude toward sin. We so badly want people to receive God's grace that we've stopped expecting others—and ourselves—to fight against sin. Yet Jesus knew that fighting sin was necessary. In Matthew 5:30, He is not suggesting that we can be sinless by our own merit; salvation comes solely from the free grace He offers through His death. Jesus is telling us that we must rip sin out of our lives. Doing so is how we experience heaven on this earth that is, at times, nothing short of a hell. Jesus is building on what He knew about idolatry and the need for it to be completely abolished.

When the Israelites were confronted with their idolatry, they ripped it out of their lives: "All Israel … went out and shattered the stone pillars, cut down the Asherahs, and destroyed the high places and the altars from all Judah, Benjamin, Ephraim, and Manasseh to the very last one" (2 Chr 31:1). We must do the same. What are we idolizing? What is causing us to sin? We need to rip that idol out or rip that arm off. Otherwise our sins will continue to torment us and prevent us from knowing God.

John the evangelist perhaps put it best: "Do not love the world or the things in the world. If anyone loves the world, the love of the Father is not in him, because everything that is in the world—the desire of the flesh and the desire of the eyes and the arrogance of material possessions—is not from the Father, but is from the world. And the world is passing away, and its desire, but the one who does the will of God remains forever" (1 John 2:15–17).

Let's allow the things that are passing away to be destroyed so we can embrace what is eternal. —JDB

What sins do you need to remove from your life? How can you do away
with the things that are causing you temptation?

∘ ◊ ◊ ∘ ∘

REMEMBERING

2 Chronicles 33:1–34:33; 1 John 2:18–27; **Psalm 105:1–22**

My mom discovered scrapbooking when I was a teenager. At first, the craft seemed time consuming and burdensome; paper scraps, pictures, and double-sided tape were constantly strewn over the kitchen table. But as the books came together, I began to appreciate her new hobby. A random photo would inspire a conversation about an event I had no memory of. The way she pieced the book together showed me a timeline of my parents' sacrifice for my siblings and me. I had a deeper respect and a renewed sense of gratitude toward them.

Psalm 105 reads like a record of God's faithfulness to Israel—a scrapbook of His work in their lives. To help them remember, the psalmist details each memory, beginning with the great patriarchs with whom God initiated and renewed His covenant—Abraham, Isaac, and Jacob. God didn't choose these men because of their spotless lives. He was true to Israel, protecting, guiding, and reprimanding them when they were unfaithful and forgetful.

Although the psalmist is remembering God's work and encouraging others to do the same, he ultimately shows that *God's* act of remembering should ignite our praise. "He remembers His covenant forever, the word that he commanded for a thousand generations" (Psa 105:8).

We are wayward children who don't deserve God's love. We are forgetful and ungrateful, which often means we don't praise Him like we should. Despite this, God has remained faithful—even reconciling us to Himself through the work of His Son. We shouldn't live in ignorance of His faithfulness. Knowing that He will "remember his wonders that he has done" (Psa 105:5), we can live lives of thankfulness and praise. —RVN

How do you praise God for His faithfulness to you?

∘ ◦ ◦ ◦ ∘

ENCOURAGEMENT AND POSITIVITY

2 Chronicles 35:1–36:23; 1 John 2:28–3:4; Psalm 105:23–45

I f we were to make encouragement one of our main strategies, we'd see positive results in most situations. If we made providing for others one of our goals, the world would be a kinder place. King Josiah epitomizes both of these attributes in 2 Chronicles 35:1–19.

Josiah's actions mark not only a remarkable transition from being unfamiliar with God's Word to living it out (2 Chr 34:8–33), but also a move from religiosity to compassion. Josiah could have coldly observed the Passover out of ritual, but instead he encourages the religious leaders and empowers them to do God's work. His encouragement changes the outcome: The religious leaders embrace their task.

Josiah also provides for them, allowing them to make the necessary changes. He frees them up from their usual obligations so that they may help others (2 Chr 35:3); he takes care of their fiscal needs (2 Chr 35:7). His example inspires others to give as well (2 Chr 35:8–9).

As a result of Josiah's actions, we see God's work being done: "So all the service of Yahweh was prepared on that day to keep the Passover and to sacrifice burnt offerings on the altar of Yahweh, according to the command of King Josiah" (2 Chr 35:16).

Our actions can either inspire others or discourage them. If we're willing to develop a character of giving and encouragement—focusing on the positive rather than the negative—we're more likely to be successful in carrying out God's work. —JDB

How can you encourage someone to follow God's path
for his or her life? How can you provide for someone today?

NOT PERFECT?

Ezra 1:1–2:70; **1 John 3:5–10**; Psalm 106:1–15

Sometimes sin can discourage us to the point that we loathe ourselves. At first glance, John's letter seems to encourage this. Addressing a struggling church community, John seems to call for perfection: "And you know that that one was revealed in order that he might take away sins, and in him there is no sin. Everyone who resides in him does not sin. Everyone who sins has neither seen him nor known him" (1 John 3:5–6). Does this mean that people who struggle with sin are unable to know God?

In his letter, John is actually speaking to the false idea that was rampant in the community he addressed—that Christ's sacrifice had covered sin, and therefore it was permissible to keep sinning. This is an issue that Paul addresses in his letter to the Roman Christians: "Should we go on sinning then, that grace may increase? May it never be!" (Rom 6:2). John answers the same way. He's not saying that any sin indicates an inability to know God—he's addressing the heart of the practice of sin (1 John 3:8).

Unchecked sin is an offense against God—it's rebellion against Him and an attack on His character. Before we were brought into relationship with God, we were characterized by enslavement to sin. Through Christ's sacrifice, we're in relationship with Him, and our lives begin to reflect our new identity in Him. What should our lives look like now? John gives us an idea later in the chapter: "Everyone who does not practice righteousness is not of God, namely, the one who does not love his brother" (1 John 3:10). Instead of rampant disobedience, then, the practice of "the children of God" is righteousness and love for others.

Though sin is still present in our lives, and we may be discouraged by it, we are no longer defined by it. Rather, we desire a new type of obedience and love, which God works in us. —RVN

Does your perspective on sin need to change?
How can your actions reflect your freedom from sin?

June 17

∘ ∘ ∘ ∘ ∘

LEARNING FROM ENEMIES

Ezra 3:1–4:24; 1 John 3:11–18; Psalm 106:16–29

I f a new venture is really worth pursuing, it will probably be opposed. Some people will refuse to get on board, and others will intentionally get in the way. While these people may be trying to protect their own interests, it's more likely that they don't like change—even if it's for the better.

God's work among His people is not that different from innovation; after all, He is the Author of all good ideas since all ideas come from His creation. And just like new ventures, God's work is often rejected. The difference between new ventures and God's work, though, is that *all* people who oppose God's work are opposing Him, their Creator; they're choosing to put their own interests before His interests, which are only for good.

Jeshua and Zerubbabel faced this type of opposition in the book of Ezra. After they had restored worship in Jerusalem, they began to organize the effort to lay the foundation of the temple—the place where God's people were meant to worship. Then, the unexpected happened: Enemies arrived and began to cause trouble (Ezra 3:1–4:5). We often view such people as hateful, but in reality they were acting in their own interests. These enemies likely didn't realize the land they claimed as their own had been stolen from God's people in the first place; they probably thought they were protecting what was rightfully theirs (compare Ezra 4:6–16; see 2 Kgs 24–25).

This is often the case in our lives as well: We *think* we're doing what's legally or morally right, but we may actually be opposing God's work. Sometimes trying to act rightly can lead us to do the wrong thing. Rather than insisting on what seems or feels right, we must pause to pray about it. We must ask God what He is *really* doing. And if God is working through someone else, we need to step out of the way. He is innovating—are we willing to innovate with Him? —JDB

In what ways is God innovating around you?
How does He want to use you in this process?
In what areas should you step aside to let His work happen?

○ ○ ◊ ○ ○

WHAT IS LOVE?

Ezra 5:1–6:22; **1 John 3:19–24**; Psalm 106:30–48

I find it easy to talk about myself. I like to get to the root of why I act the way I do. Sometimes this is helpful—it helps me nail down where I struggle. But this tendency also reminds me that I'm geared inward.

The danger is that I often filter others through the sieve of my experience. Our culture encourages the mindset that other people ought to make us feel good about ourselves and help us fulfill our dreams. In this mindset, our relationships ultimately become about self-fulfillment.

John squashes this idea. He tells the recipients of his letter, "Little children, let us not love with word or with tongue, but in deed and truth" (1 John 3:18). He's not saying we should refrain from expressing love and care through words. But displaying love—putting others' needs before our own—requires much more of us.

John doesn't go on to define love. However, he does describe the ultimate example of love: "We have come to know love by this: that he laid down his life on behalf of us, and we ought to lay down our lives on behalf of the brothers" (1 John 3:16). Love is best displayed in the cross, not in poetry and with eloquent words that demonstrate more about ourselves than actual, concrete care for others.

The love displayed on the cross is a reminder that we aren't meant to lead comfortable, self-focused lives. Jesus' actions show us that love isn't merely emotion—it's sacrifice and self-denial. We live to love both God and others, and that's best done with actions that serve. —RVN

Are you really loving the people around you?
How can you love them better?

THE STORY BEHIND THE STORY

Ezra 7:1–8:36; 1 John 4:1–6; Psalm 107:1–22

The Bible is full of unexpected moments. Some events seem almost coincidental, where people are in the right place at the right time. This is exactly the case with Ezra.

In ancient times, it was unusual for a king to honor a foreigner with a decree. It was even stranger for a king to offer his own wealth to help such a foreigner. Yet that's what happened to Ezra: King Artaxerxes of Persia sent Ezra, and any Israelite willing to go with him, to his own land (and the people living there) with the blessing of silver and gold (Ezra 7:11–28).

The Bible doesn't give the reason for Artaxerxes' spontaneous generosity. He may have been motivated by politics, trying to gain the allegiance of the Israelites, govern the population in Babylonia, or inhabit a new land to control the native people there. Yet the most convincing reason for his actions seems to be that his heart was moved.

While the text doesn't explicitly say, it appears that Yahweh motivated Artaxerxes to do not only the right thing, but the selfless thing. For at least this brief moment, Artaxerxes was compassionate and empathetic. He understood that God's people needed to practice their religion freely and worship Him in their own land.

Ezra's involvement in these events wasn't a matter of chance. God intended for him to be there, in that moment, to do that work. His providential work was part of every step. —JDB

How have you been intentionally placed to do God's work?
What influence can you use for His kingdom?

○ ○ ○ ○ ○

MAN VS. NATURE

Ezra 9:1–10:44; 1 John 4:7–12; **Psalm 107:23–43**

As a teenager, I devoured stories about men and women at odds with nature. These man vs. nature struggles always told of a battle of wills. Nature was always at its most magnificent and most frightening: untamed, unwieldy, and heartless. The characters seemed to be living on the edge of human experience—they were not focused and resolute, anticipating the next turn of events like a typical Hollywood action film, but frightened and helpless before an uncaring force.

If we read Psalm 107, we'll find this genre isn't unique to contemporary novels. Biblical writers also used the man vs. nature theme to show battling wills. Psalm 107 reads like a riveting short story: "Those who went down to the sea in ships, doing business on the high seas; they saw the works of Yahweh, and his wonderful deeds in the deep. For he spoke and raised up a stormy wind, and it whipped up its waves. They rose to the heavens; they plunged to the depths. Their soul melted in their calamity. They reeled and staggered like a drunkard, and they were at their wits' end" (Psa 107:23–27).

When faced with uncontrollable forces, people make choices that mean life or death. In the stories of my youth, the characters were sometimes able to use their wits to get to safety. But most often, they died trying. The English idiom used in this psalm, "their wits' end," is actually a rendering of the Hebrew idiom, "their wisdom was swallowed up." The men in this psalm weren't just flustered; they were helpless. Their resources and smarts couldn't battle this power.

Yet the men didn't meet only a cold, deadly force when they came to the end of their own strength. "Then they cried out to Yahweh in their trouble, and he brought them out of their distresses" (Psa 107:28). Submission in the battle of wills leads to Yahweh's love and care. He is more than willing to guide us to the safe harbor (Psa 107:30). —RVN

When faced with difficult circumstances,
do you rely on your own strength, even when it's insufficient?
If you cry out to God, do you believe that He will answer?

POSITION, PRAYER, AND STRATEGY

Nehemiah 1:1–3:32; 1 John 4:13–15; Psalm 108:1–13

Trying to make a difference in the world can be disheartening; it's easy to feel like merely a drop in the bucket.

When Nehemiah first heard about the suffering of his people, he could have been discouraged. When he learned that the returned exiles were "in great trouble and shame," living in a city with no walls (Neh 1:3), he could have said, "I'd love to help, but what can I do from this far away?" Instead, he decided to take action (Neh 1:3), and he did so thoughtfully. Rather than making a rash decision, he prayed (Neh 1:4–8). He then volunteered to be the one to help God's people (Neh 1:9–11), even though doing so meant risking his life.

As the cupbearer to the king, Nehemiah recognized his unique place of influence and acted upon it (Neh 2:1–3). He chose to appear saddened before the most powerful man in the world by hanging his head. His actions could have been perceived as a sign of disrespect, which was punishable by severe beatings and even death. But God protected Nehemiah, and the king honored his request (Neh 2:4–6).

Nehemiah's initial actions show his character, but his later actions show his leadership. He moved from being a man of influence to a man of strategy. Immediately upon arriving in the city, Nehemiah inspected the city walls, found the craftsman, and began his work (Neh 2:11–3:32). He realized the urgency of his task; his people needed this wall to survive against the surrounding nations.

Nehemiah's story offers an example of identifying providence, responding to the pain of others through prayer, and acting strategically. It's a lesson in what it means to be a leader who follows *God's* leadership. Nehemiah stands as an example of one who takes action that is well-researched, strategic, and prayerful. —JDB

*What are some ways you are providentially positioned to
do God's work? How have you led while following His leadership?*

LOVE AND PEACE

Nehemiah 4:1–5:19; **1 John 4:16–21**; Psalm 109:1–15

"You have made us for yourself, and our heart is restless until it finds rest in you." Augustine's prayer, spoken so many years ago, is still poignant for us today. It appeals to our created purpose: bringing glory to God. When we're living outside of that purpose, we try to fill that void through other means.

In his first letter, John shows how the love of God and communion with Him ultimately brings a sense of peace and confidence: "We have come to know and have believed the love which God has for us. God is love and the one who abides in love abides in God and God abides in him. By this love is perfected with us, so that we may have confidence in the day of judgment, because just as that one is, so also are we in the world" (1 John 4:16–17).

God Himself has addressed the great rift we created between ourselves and Him. Through the sacrifice of His Son, He has made it possible for us to abide with Him and find peace in Him (1 John 4:15). Those who confess that Jesus is the Son of God experience this love that brings peace and confidence.

But this love isn't merely an emotion or a feeling of fulfillment; it's a growing desire to be like Christ. Because God dwells in us, we will become more like Him in love. We can be confident of His work in us when we display self-sacrificial love for our neighbor. —RVN

How are you resting in God's love?
How are you loving others?

○ ○ ◊ ○ ○

DISCERNMENT AND PRAYER

Nehemiah 6:1–7:65; 1 John 5:1–5; Psalm 109:16–31

"For all of them sought to frighten us. … And now, God, strengthen my hands" (Neh 6:9). While God calls us to "love [our] enemies and pray for those who persecute [us]" (Matt 5:44), he also calls us to act with discernment and prayer. Loving others doesn't mean we should be weak or passive. Part of loving others means discerning their hearts and motives.

"Blessed are the meek, because they will inherit the earth" (Matt 5:5). When Jesus spoke about being meek, He wasn't referring to weakness. Instead, He was teaching us to focus on others rather than ourselves. That doesn't mean we should be passive toward those who wish to harm us. Part of practicing meekness is being aware of our enemies and dealing with them cautiously. Doing so successfully takes strength and discernment—necessary components of any godly work.

Nehemiah demonstrates these traits in his interactions with his enemies. When his opponents ask him to meet with them, Nehemiah discovers that they actually wish to hurt him. He resists their attack—even calling them on their deceit (Neh 6:8).

Too often we allow ourselves to live passively. We enter into situations without thinking things through or recognizing that we're about to be hurt by others. Yet we as Christians are at war against the evil in the world—not just against people, but also the unseen forces of evil (Eph 6:12). When we feel oppression, we must resist the urge to be reactive. Instead, we must appeal to Christ, who can overcome it all. We must refuse to engage unless it's on our terms, by the power of the Spirit and completely in His will. —JDB

What battles are you engaging with that you should disengage from?
Which situations in your life need discernment?

IT'S SIMPLE

Nehemiah 7:66–8:18; **1 John 5:6–12**; Psalm 110:1–7

I tend to complicate matters. Determined to understand the nuances of a problem, I spend more time constructing a solution than I need to. Often, delaying a simple solution is my way of avoiding action that requires me to be courageous, intentional, or perhaps admit I'm wrong.

John's first letter addresses a complication of the gospel message. False teachers were causing division in the community by spreading incorrect doctrines about Christ's humanity and divinity. Without understanding that Christ is both man and God, some people in the community were in danger of diminishing Christ's saving work and confusing the gospel. John spends the greater portion of the letter guiding his readers through the murky doctrines the false teachers had introduced.

However, John's climactic point at the close of his letter is far from complex. First John 5:11–12 contains a statement about belief that is both simple and decisive: "And this is the testimony: that God has given us eternal life, and this life is in his Son. The one who has the Son has the life; the one who does not have the Son of God does not have the life." As John leads the doubting recipients of his letter back to the truth, he shows them the simplicity of the solution: Through the Son, God has provided a way out of sin. This simple truth requires a simple response: belief in the Son. —RVN

Where in your life do you complicate
an obedient response to God?

June 25

∘ ∘∘∘ ∘

FROM CONCERN TO ACTION

Nehemiah 9:1–10:27; 1 John 5:13–16; **Psalm 111:1–112:10**

When I approach God, I often try to persuade Him that I am worthy of something or that He should act on my behalf. But there is no *reason* God should act on our behalf—none is worthy of His intercession.

When we pray, we often need a change in focus. Ultimately, it's not about our rightness or goodness; it's about His. It's about what He can do, who He is, and why we *know* He can do something about the situation we're in. We should still be honest and open with God, telling Him how we really feel (even though He already knows), but instead of focusing on our own righteousness, we should focus on God and what He's already done for us.

When I shift my attention to God and His goodness, many of my previous concerns fade. Before I even begin to pray, gratitude reminds me of God's care and provision for me, allowing me to move from what *I* think matters to what matters to *God*.

Throughout the Bible, we see models of thankful prayers that emphasize God's character. In the book of Nehemiah, the priestly group descended from Pethahiah (1 Chr 24:16) proclaims: "Stand up, bless Yahweh your God from everlasting until everlasting. Blessed be your glorious name that is being exalted above all blessing and praise! 'You alone are Yahweh. You alone have made the heavens. ... '" (Neh 9:5–6).

The people go on to recite God's history of caring for them, focusing on His goodness and reminding themselves of His faithfulness when they (as a whole) had failed Him (Neh 9:7–37; compare Psa 111). They end their sermon with an agreement to honor God. They move from thankfulness, to God's story, to agreeing to be part of His work.

By focusing on God, their attention shifts from ordinary concerns (Neh 7–8) to how they will respond to God. It's this shift in focus that ultimately leads to righteousness. We also see this progression in Psalm 112: the path of the righteous is marked by blessing God and acknowledging His work (Psa 112:1–2). After all, recognizing God is the solution to most of our problems. —JDB

How can you incorporate thankfulness into your prayer life?
How can you do a better job of progressing from concerns
to being part of God's work?

A FAMOUS GOD

Nehemiah 10:28–11:36; 1 John 5:17–21; **Psalm 113:1–114:8**

Fame can have startling effects on people. Those who attain power and influence suddenly become less available: They're selective with the phone calls they take, the emails they answer, and the people they associate with. Those who receive their attention tend to feel special.

When we call on God, we expect Him to answer us and help us. Sometimes, we are so confident that He will or should help us that we forget how amazing it is that He interacts with us in the first place.

Psalm 113 reminds us that God is beyond our comprehension. The psalm praises the power and glory of God, who is "high above all nations." God isn't just ruling over the earth, though. His realm of power extends even "above the heavens" (Psa 113:4). Both earthly and heavenly powers are subject to Him.

His power is astounding, but what is most confounding is His nature and character. Psalm 113 points out that even in His power, God is still concerned with the plights of those far below: "Who is like Yahweh our God, who is enthroned on high, who condescends to look at what is in the heavens and in the earth?" (Psa 113:5–6). And He isn't just concerned with the powerful and mighty; He is concerned about the helpless and the needy. "He raises the helpless from the dust, he lifts the needy from the ash heap, to seat them with princes, with the princes of his people" (Psa 113:7–8).

God is more majestic and powerful than we can comprehend. His fame exceeds that of any celebrity. Yet He still desires to help us—to lift us "up from the ash heap." This alone should astound us, but there's more: He cares for us so much that He was willing to sacrifice His only Son to restore our relationship with Him. —RVN

How are you astounded by God's nature
and His care for you?

○ ○ ○ ○ ○

THE TRUTH ABOUT TRUTH

Nehemiah 12:1–13:31; **2 John 1–6**; Psalm 115:1–18

John the Evangelist's letter to the "elect lady" presents a picture of joy and hope, as he "rejoiced greatly to find some of [her] children walking in truth, just as we were commanded by the father" (2 John 4). One word keeps reappearing in John's letter, focusing his message: truth. John says that he loves the elect lady and her children "in truth" (2 John 1). He says that all who know the truth also love them. His reason is simple: "the truth … resides in us and will be with us forever" (2 John 2). When John speaks of truth, he's referring to Jesus (John 14:6).

After his initial greeting, John goes on to express his wishes: May "Grace, mercy, [and] peace … be with us from God the Father and from Jesus Christ the Son of the Father in truth and love" (2 John 3). In acknowledging the source of truth, John acknowledges his connection to it. All believers live in truth because they are linked to God, who is the Truth. He is the source for all they do (that is godly), all they are (that is holy), and all that they will become (that is virtuous).

In a few brief statements, John teaches us an important lesson: God is the source of all the goodness in the world. Even in acknowledging others, we must acknowledge Him. If we're to discuss truth, then we must talk about Him.

The elect lady that John addresses is not only truthful—she also leads others to the truth. When we act to encourage someone to work toward who they're meant to be, we need to follow her example. We need to first lead them to truth: God. —JDB

What is God teaching you about truth?
How can you live it?

June 28

○ ○ ◉ ○ ○

MEET AND GREET

Esther 1:1–2:23; **2 John 7–13**; Psalm 116:1–19

"If anyone comes to you and does not bring this teaching, do not receive him into your house and do not speak a greeting to him, because the one who speaks a greeting to him shares in his evil deeds" (2 John 9–11).

This passage is sometimes used as support for forming exclusive communities—ones that don't interact with people who don't believe in the gospel or who have a different faith. Based on this passage, some believe that we as Christians are not permitted to interact with nonbelievers. Is that what John is really teaching?

John issued this warning during a time when false teachers were spreading confusing doctrines about Christ. He exhorted believers to "test the spirits" to see if these teachers were actually from God (1 John 4:1). They would know if these teachers were from God if they confessed the true message of Jesus Christ—specifically that He had come in the flesh and was from God (1 John 2:1).

John wanted the community to be aware of false teachings so they wouldn't become confused or weakened in their faith. We, too, need to be intentional about the teaching we adhere to. If we are weak and troubled in our faith, we should seek out mature believers who can teach and minister to us. However, if we are confident in our faith, we should be ready and willing to share the message of salvation with those who need to hear it—both inside and outside our communities. —RVN

How are you sharing the gospel with those
who need to receive it?

BEHIND THE SCENES

Esther 3:1–7:10; 3 John 1:1–4; Psalm 117:1–118:16

Sometimes life can look so bleak that it seems as if all hope is gone. This was the situation for Esther and Mordecai: "Letters were sent by couriers to all the provinces of the king to destroy, to kill, and to annihilate all the Jews, both young and old, women and children" (Esth 3:13). Genocide was upon Esther, Mordecai, and their people, and it seemed that little could be done.

Yet God unexpectedly used Esther to do His work and made Mordecai a hero for thwarting the enemies' plan to destroy God's people (Esth 5–7). As a result, the people who wanted to kill Mordecai ended up dead (Esth 7:7–10). But these events depicted more than poetic justice; they provide an example of hope in the midst of adversity. This story shows that God is at work even when we don't realize He is there—when even prayer feels like a waste of energy.

While God is not a "character" in the book of Esther, His presence is implicit in every scene of goodness coming out of chaos. We may not see Him talking in a burning bush, but we feel His concern in the tension; we note His love and compassion through His orchestration of events. These actions aren't credited to God directly, but that, too, shows something about His character. He doesn't need the praise that we so often do, so we need to acknowledge how praiseworthy He really is. Even when we don't know how to pray, or don't pray at all, God can still answer. And that's goodness, above all else. —JDB

How is God at work in your life in ways you
may not realize—even at this very moment?

BY YOUR EXAMPLE

Esther 8:1–10:3; **3 John 5–15**; Psalm 118:17–29

By nature, we are creatures of imitation. Children mimic the traits of their parents, and even in later life we are influenced by the habits of our friends. People naturally imitate, even if they don't realize it or intend to. This is one reason why "lead by example" is such a powerful principle. It's also why leaders can change the direction of a whole community—for better or worse (Jas 3:1).

Diotrephes, an ambitious member of the early church who misused his power, was unwilling to heed the advice of John and others who reprimanded him. In his letter to Gaius, a church leader known for his faithfulness and love, John gives this advice regarding Diotrephes: "Dear friend, do not imitate what is evil, but what is good. The one who does good is of God; the one who does evil has not seen God" (3 John 11).

Throughout his letters, John emphasizes that people's actions reflect their heart. Diotrephes' actions told a dismal story. Whether he was a church leader or someone who battled for leadership, he was characterized by his selfish ambition: He wanted to be "first," and he did "not acknowledge" those in leadership roles (3 John 9). He was also known for speaking evil words that undermined other leaders (3 John 10), and he spread contention by refusing to receive missionaries and intimidating those who wanted to (3 John 10). These actions didn't reflect the work of the Spirit in his life.

We're not sure what happened to Diotrephes. Perhaps he left the Christian community. Perhaps he repented when John "call[ed] attention to the deeds he [was] doing" (3 John 10). His story, though, shows us that we shouldn't imitate blindly. Instead, we should "test the spirits to determine if they are from God" and respond wisely (1 John 4:1). —RVN

Where in your life do you need to be more careful whom you imitate?
Where do you need to set a positive example?

GOD MAKES GOOD OUT OF TROUBLE

1 Samuel 1:1–2:21; **James 1:1–8**; Psalm 119:1–16

God often shows His goodness to us through trials, making good out of human error. We see this principle in the lives of Elkanah and Hannah. Elkanah was prone to make mistakes. His first mistake was to marry two wives (1 Sam 1:1–4); his second blunder was to ignore his wives' disputes (1 Sam 1:6). On top of that, he repeatedly imposed his own form of justice by giving Hannah double what he offered Peninnah, his other wife (1 Sam 1:5). In this story, however, the goodness of God redeems the mistakes made by fallible people.

Despite Elkanah's generosity to her, Hannah was deeply disturbed: Nothing Elkanah offered could compensate for her barrenness (1 Sam 1:8–10). In this time period, women who had not borne children were often considered accursed and second rate, as demonstrated by Peninnah's persecution of Hannah. In her distress, Hannah prayed to God at the temple, seeking redemption. Eli the priest recognized the sincerity of her plea and blessed her (1 Sam 1:15–18).

God also recognized Hannah's sincerity, and He answered her call by giving her a son, Samuel, who would be a great prophet (1 Sam 1:19–28). Hannah's son offered her hope; in response, she delivered beautiful poetry to honor Yahweh's goodness (1 Sam 2:1–11). This poem was so significant that Mary would later echo it (see Luke 1:46–56). Through Hannah's story, we see that God's work among His people is so interconnected that He often chooses to answer not only our prayers, but also the prayers of others in the process.

In scenes like this—where God not only makes good out of a bad situation, but also sets up a providential event in the history of His people—we see much of the framework for the Christian life. New Testament writers including James drew on stories such as Hannah's when discussing the trials of God's people. In the first century AD, James remarks: "Consider it all joy, my brothers [and sisters], whenever you encounter various trials, because you know that the testing of your faith produces endurance. ... " (Jas 1:2–4).

Hannah's story shows us that when we pray to God, He shows up. And in the midst of our dire circumstances, He answers the call of not one, but many people. Here, in the pain, we learn what it means to know our Lord and savior. —JDB

What trials are you currently experiencing?
What do you think God is doing through them?

CONFLICT AND CERTAINTY

1 Samuel 2:22–4:22; **James 1:9–18**; Psalm 119:17–32

Conflict drives fiction and riveting movies, but if we had it our way, we'd live stable, stress-free lives. We might crave the excitement or change of a vacation, but we rarely welcome an unexpected complication. So when James says to "count it all joy … when you meet trials of various kinds" (Jas 1:2; compare Jas 1:12–14), we are tempted to dismiss his perspective as something that works on paper but should not disrupt our real lives.

James shows us how to internalize a faithful response to unwelcome conflict. He starts by describing a negative reaction: When difficult times come, we might be like the person who prays and then doubts that God will provide him with wisdom for the situation. This person complicates the conflict by internalizing it with uncertainty and doubt. He is "like the surf of the sea, driven by the wind and tossed about" (Jas 1:6).

The irony is that, although we only create more conflict when we doubt, we like to think we can trust ourselves. As long as we remain in control (we tell ourselves), we can avoid the storms of life. It's tempting to manufacture an attitude of stubborn self-sufficiency—of inner strength.

That's the opposite of how we should respond. God wants us to meet the chaos by trusting in Him. We might feel tossed about by life's events, but God provides us with wisdom for the chaos we encounter. When we ask Him and trust that He'll provide us with wisdom, He gives generously and without reproach (Jas 1:5).

Stability isn't an inner strength, but certainty in God's provision is (Jas 1:9–11). We can meet the uncertain with the certain—when we trust God to help us work through the chaos. We can also remember that, at the end of the novel, the protagonist who endures conflict is changed by the experience. In the same way, God is working through the conflict in our lives to make us more wholly devoted to Him, since "testing produces steadfastness" (Jas 1:3). And there will be an end: We'll "receive the crown of life that he has promised to those who love him" (Jas 1:12). —RVN

How are you turning to Christ
in the midst of difficult circumstances?

°○○○○

GOD'S UNSEEN WORK

1 Samuel 5:1–7:17; James 1:19–27; Psalm 119:33–48

We often fail to discern when and how it happens: God will work something out in our lives that seems virtually impossible. We get an unexpected insight into the workings of God in 1 Samuel 5.

After defeating Israel in battle, the Philistines stole the ark of the covenant, recognizing it as a powerful weapon of war. They didn't realize that it couldn't be wielded by human hands. They set it up next to the idol of their god, Dagon, unaware that the ark was the representation of Yahweh on earth. Yahweh does what He wills. In this case, He willed the ark to be returned to Israel, so He destroyed the idol and afflicted the people with disease. First Samuel notes, "The hand of the LORD was heavy against the people," (1 Sam 5:6); in fact, it was so heavy that the Philistines wanted the ark gone. After seven months, they returned it to the Israelites (1 Sam 6:10–16).

If the Philistines could recognize the work of Yahweh among them, you would think the Israelites could do the same. They should have responded to the ark's return by praising God, rejoicing, and turning back to Him. But in their failure to discern God's hand in the event, they continued to worship foreign gods until Samuel, their judge and prophet, demanded that they change their actions (1 Sam 7).

This illustrates a problem with our perception of God's work: We fail to see His work on our behalf and chalk things up to circumstance or coincidence. We stick with our idols because it's easier than admitting the truth to ourselves—for the moment we acknowledge God is at work, we must turn away from the easy path of selfish ambitions and actions.

When God's people pray, He answers—often in unexpected and miraculous ways. While we don't often see His hand at work, we do have an opportunity each day to look for God acting among us and turn away from anything we put in His place. Let's do so today. —JDB

Where have you seen God working in your life?
What idols is He asking you to turn away from?

∘ ∘∘∘ ∘

MAKING DISTINCTIONS

1 Samuel 8:1–9:27; **James 2:1–13**; Psalm 119:49–64

We're often entranced by those who have what we don't—riches, popularity, position, and power. We want to befriend cool moms, hipsters with ironic mustaches, and supervisors who can get us to the next step on the corporate ladder. We relate to them differently, even though we know we shouldn't.

Our problem is one of perception. In his letter, James reprimands members of the early church community who were displaying partiality by honoring the rich and overlooking the poor. James shows them that they need to reset their standards because making distinctions in this way doesn't reflect God's nature, and it doesn't reflect the grace He extends to us: "Did not God choose the poor of this world to be rich in faith, and heirs of the kingdom that he has promised to those who love him?" (Jas 2:5).

We shouldn't act with partiality because God didn't deal with us in that way. We don't deserve God's love, yet He, in His perfect holiness, chose to give it to the unpopular, the uncool, the dirty, and the undeserving—which is all of us. James shows us that the proper response to this grace is to love our neighbor: "If you really fulfill the royal law according to the Scripture, 'You shall love your neighbor as yourself,' you are doing well" (Jas 2:8).

Brought into a new community of faith based on grace, Christ-followers aren't meant to live by the judgment-based standards of their old way of being. The members of James' community had to reset their standards, and that's a message we still need to hear today. —RVN

Do you make distinctions?
How can you view others through the grace
that God has shown to you?

○ ○ ○ ○ ○

DISCERNMENT, KNOWLEDGE, AND ACTION

1 Samuel 10:1–11:15; James 2:14–18; Psalm 119:65–80

We often wonder whether God hears our prayers. Even when we acknowledge that God deals with each petition we send His way, we experience doubt because we don't understand how He has handled our plea. Yet instead of asking "Is God hearing me?" we should be asking God to help us grow closer to Him and gain a better understanding of His ways. We should echo the words of the psalmist, "You have dealt well with your servant, O Yahweh, according to your word. Teach me good discernment and knowledge, for I believe your commands" (Psa 119:65–66).

We often misunderstand the concepts of discernment and knowledge. Discernment allows us to know God's will and perceive the decisions He would have us make. Knowledge helps us to understand God Himself, primarily His character. Both of these concepts are grounded in our relationship with God and others, both empower us to work for Him—and we are called to cultivate both qualities in our lives.

Unless we know God, we're incapable of successfully doing His work. We must be willing to talk to God honestly about our relationships, as the psalmist does in Psalm 119:69–72. The psalmist acknowledges that he needs God's help in all matters of his relationship with God and all matters of his relationship with others. He understands that he cannot even begin to know God without the power of God helping him.

We must be empowered for action, both in the intimacy of prayer and in the reality of relationships. And we must support what we believe with our works, as the letter of James calls us to do: "For just as the body without the spirit is dead, so also faith without works is dead" (Jas 2:14–26).

Reflecting regularly on how God has worked with us and is working in us allows us to recognize that everything in our lives has a purpose. God often works in others through us, and that great calling requires us to have knowledge of Him and discernment about His workings in our world. —JDB

How are you discerning the great work of God in your life?
How are you enhancing your knowledge of God?

FAITH

1 Samuel 12:1–13:23; **James 2:19–26**; Psalm 119:81–96

Sometimes it's difficult to view our lives as a whole. We fulfill different roles as we interact with different people at school, home, work, and even church. In the natural donning and discarding of these roles, we might be tempted to compartmentalize our lives, yet we do so to the detriment of our faith. Even as we read our Bibles with intellectual vigor at home and participate in a small group at church, we might miss the mark of application. We forget to connect the dots, neglecting to treat our coworkers with kindness and our peers with love. We can know our faith intellectually but still miss out on the call to action and the response of obedience in our lives.

But James shows us that belief and action are inextricably linked. When we think about them as separate entities, we develop a deep-rooted problem: "But do you want to know … that faith apart from works is useless? Was not Abraham our father justified by works when he offered up his son Isaac on the altar? You see that his faith was working together with his works, and by the works the faith was perfected" (Jas 2:20–22).

James wasn't arguing that Abraham earned his righteousness before God; rather, Abraham was acting out of obedience as a response of faith. As people who have been redeemed by Christ, we can joyfully express our faith—we are enabled to do good works because of His work. Although we won't attain perfect obedience in this life, we will desire obedience and love. We will desire to use our lives to apply what we know in our heads and feel in our hearts. Because of our faith, we will do good works.

Real faith doesn't sit still, but it doesn't move on its own, either. We need to pray for God's Spirit to ignite this desire in us, prompting us to act with love and obedience. —RVN

In what area of your life are you missing the mark of application?
How can you pray for wisdom in that situation?
How can you act faithfully?

° ° ° ° °

RECASTING FAITH

1 Samuel 14:1–52; James 3:1–12; Psalm 119:97–120

Faith is often cast as a type of intellectual pursuit: It's something our minds rise up to, conform to, or simply agree with. But in the Bible, faith is often portrayed as rather mystical: Jonathan somehow knew that God would act on his behalf if his enemies behaved in a certain way (1 Sam 14:1–15). We don't know how Jonathan had this foreknowledge—prayer seems to be the only explanation for it—but we recognize that Jonathan had tremendous faith. Who else would take on a garrison of 20 men, armed with only one armor bearer and a hunch? Clearly God was at work.

We see God's work progress as the Philistines inadvertently turned on one another, and previous enemies of Israel joined in the charge against the Philistines (1 Sam 14:16–23). Jonathan's simple act of faith served as the catalyst for victory. If he had analyzed his inclination and pursued faith without mystery, the Israelites likely would have failed in their campaign against the Philistines.

Yet the real testimony of faith in this account belongs to the armor bearer. After hearing Jonathan's plan, the armor bearer said, "Do all that is in your heart. Do as you wish. Behold, I am with you heart and soul" (1 Sam 14:7). While the armor bearer was obligated to follow the king's son on pain of death, when faced with what appeared to be inevitable death, he could have played his odds by saying no. This scene tells us more about Jonathan: He was known for his faith in God—so much so that his armor bearer took him at his word.

I often wonder what makes a man heroic and others forever loyal to him. In Jonathan, we find the answer: a history of God working through your life and a dedication to follow the mystery of God's work among us, no matter what stands against us. —JDB

Is your faith primarily intellectual,
or is it grounded in the mystery of God?
How can you bring more of God's
mystical work into your life?

HONOR, CREDIT, AND GODLY WISDOM

1 Samuel 15:1–35; **James 3:13–18**; Psalm 119:121–136

We're primed to seek validation. Earning "likes" on our social media outlets gives us a sense of self-worth. Getting kudos for a good idea at work makes us feel important. When this is how we derive our self-worth, the opposite will also be true: Being overlooked can crush us, making us angry and jealous if others have stolen the limelight.

If we're not careful, we can easily become ruled by our need for validation. James calls this mindset and behavior "earthly," "unspiritual," and even "demonic" (Jas 3:15). When we are guided by it, chaos reigns: "For where there is jealousy and selfish ambition, there is disorder and every evil practice" (Jas 3:16).

We may be aware of how often we are tempted to follow our earthly responses, and we might try to practice restraint. We try to filter the forces at work inside us, but this won't solve the heart of the problem, as James shows us. He contrasts human ambition with godly wisdom, which "comes down from above" (Jas 3:15). He lists the virtues that display godly wisdom: "But the wisdom from above is first pure, then peaceful, gentle, obedient, full of mercy and good fruits, nonjudgmental, without hypocrisy" (Jas 3:17).

We can't attain these virtues on our own. When we're tempted to follow our gut response, to protect and promote our own image, we have to examine our hearts and confess our earthly desires to God. Then, we should seek the wisdom from above—the wisdom found in Jesus. Only He can make us new, and His Spirit can enable us to intentionally follow Him and seek godly wisdom. —RVN

*How are you seeking and praying
for godly wisdom?*

July 9

∘ ◊ ∘ ◊ ∘

MOVING FORWARD

1 Samuel 16:1–23; **James 4:1–17**; Psalm 119:137–152

Moving on after a person, a hope, or a dream has died can be one of the most difficult challenges of life. It certainly was for Samuel. The prophet Samuel believed that God had chosen Saul as king, but Saul failed God and His people (1 Sam 15:10–35). Now God was ready to select a new king, but Samuel was dragging his feet. Moving forward meant readjusting his expectations about the future and about God's work in general. God called him out on his hesitancy: "How long will you mourn about Saul? I have rejected him from king over Israel! Fill up your horn with oil and go" (1 Sam 16:1).

Samuel had to learn that things rarely play out the way we think they will. We inevitably end up on a different path than we planned—whether because of our own actions or because God's route turns in a direction we never anticipated. The key is recognizing the changes when they occur and preparing ourselves for a new reality. Clinging to misguided expectations can drive us into the ground, effectively driving God's work out of us.

Unlike Samuel, Saul's problem was *not* that God sent him in a new direction. Saul created his own situation when he chose a different route—he disobeyed, and God responded by taking away from Saul what was his to steward but not to own: a kingdom. Saul's story illustrates James' statement, "From where are conflicts and from where are quarrels among you? Is it not from this, from your pleasures that wage war among your members?" (Jas 4:1). But Saul's ultimate responsibility did not lessen Samuel's pain.

All of us must be willing to realign our expectations. More important, we must seek to be aligned with God all along. We must move on from destructive behaviors and disobedience. Along the way, we must be mindful of the things God wants to create, and we must be ready to respond when God calls us to "Fill your horn with oil and go." —JDB

What do you think God is asking you to move on from today?
What is He asking you to move toward?

OPPRESSORS, VICTIMS, AND A JUST GOD

1 Samuel 17:1–58; **James 5:1–12**; Psalm 119:153–176

Contemporary culture is often pegged as self-indulgent: We live in a have-it-now world, and we don't always think about the repercussions of our actions. But when we read James' letter to the early church, we find that self-indulgence isn't a modern phenomenon.

In his letter James addresses two groups of people. First, he reprimands the self-indulgent rich who live without thinking about the repercussions of their actions, either for others or for themselves. The day is coming when they will have to account for all their evil deeds: "Come now, you rich people, weep and cry over the miseries that are coming upon you!" (Jas 5:1). James presents them with a harsh picture of what they have been doing: "You have fattened your hearts in the day of slaughter" (Jas 5:5). They have behaved like animals; their judgment will come.

James also writes to a second group: those who are oppressed. He encourages this group to be patient "until the coming of the Lord," to exhibit the perseverance of farmers who wait for "the precious fruit of the soil" (Jas 5:7). He recognizes that often, when we're oppressed or hurt, it's difficult to avoid living in those wounds—they color our world and our interactions with others. We become bitter and selfish. James tells the oppressed, "Do not complain against one another, in order that you may not be judged" (Jas 5:9).

Both oppressors and victims put themselves in danger unless they repent and focus on God, who will set all things right. Self-indulgent, self-seeking living appears even in the smallest decisions of our lives. Or we act from a place of woundedness, and we fail to move on to forgiveness.

God loves justice, and He gives hope to those who hope in Him. Examine your life, abandon your self-indulgence and your grievances, and seek the one who makes all things right and new. —RVN

How can you leave your hurts at the cross?
How can you move from self-indulgence to trust
in God's ability to make things right?

○ ◊ ◊ ◊ ○

BEST FRIENDS FOREVER

1 Samuel 18:1–19:24; **James 5:13–20**; Psalm 120:1–7

This generation has more opportunities for communication than any before it, with email and social networking making it possible to interact with others 24/7. Yet suicide rates are higher than ever, and antidepressant medications have become almost standard fare. We have more connections than ever before, but they're not relationships. We still feel alone. People need authentic community—a sense of communing with someone—to feel whole and healthy.

The story of David and Jonathan portrays the true nature of friendship: "The soul of Jonathan became attached to the soul of David, and Jonathan loved him as his own soul" (1 Sam 18:1). Jonathan could easily have been jealous of his friend; David was a great warrior and had just been brought into the household of Jonathan's father, the king, as the king's protégé (1 Sam 17:48–58; 18:2). Instead of being jealous, Jonathan responded with love and kindness, and the two became the most steadfast friends.

Authentic relationship is built on trust, which often starts when one person sacrifices himself for the other. Jonathan made such a sacrifice: "Jonathan stripped off the robe that he was wearing and gave it to David, along with his fighting attire, and even his sword, his bow, and his belt" (1 Sam 18:3–4). Because Jonathan loved David as a friend, their relationship grew into a deep-rooted loyalty. When we share that deep trust and loyalty with a friend, we can grow in God's will together. We all need someone we can rely on; David and Jonathan demonstrate how powerful such a relationship can be.

In the early Church, authentic relationships were not just an idea—they were a way of life: "Is anyone among you sick? He should summon the elders of the church and they should pray over him, anointing him with olive oil in the name of the Lord" (Jas 5:14). The early Church didn't respond to sickness or pain by saying, "I'll pray for you." They actually prayed. Just as Jonathan, in one swift action, gave David the honor of being like the king's son, so the early Church swiftly took care of their own. They made friends by being loyal, as Christ was loyal to them. They created community by showing love and kindness without requiring that kindness to be returned. But the return on investment was great: It laid the foundation for a worldwide movement. —JDB

How can you show authentic friendship to others?

○ ○ ◊ ○ ○

ETERNAL HOPE

1 Samuel 20:1–21:15; **1 Peter 1:1–12**; **Psalm 121:1–122:9**

We don't often realize where we put our hope. We can seek sustenance, energy, or relief in the most transient, innocuous things—from our morning coffee to a vacation we've been anticipating for months. These things are not bad in themselves, but if they constantly serve as minor fixes in our daily lives, they can shift our focus. We can end up trading God's help for caffeine and a few days in the sun.

The trouble arises when we fail to see the complexity in our motives. The psalmist helps us look beyond what *seems* comforting and shielding: "I lift up my eyes to the mountains; whence will my help come? My help is from Yahweh, maker of heaven and earth" (Psa 121:1). The psalmist uses the hills and mountains to point us beyond what we can see to the true source of help and protection. These stationary shields seem to offer protection, but God is the true source of help and refuge in our often chaotic circumstances. He is constantly present—"your shade at your right hand" (Psa 121:5).

In his letter to the churches in Asia Minor, Peter addresses the "various trials" the early church faced (1 Pet 1:6). He encourages the church members to endure trials and persecution, telling them they are "protected by the power of God through faith for a salvation ready to be revealed in the last time" (1 Pet 1:5). In the midst of trial, their faith in the resurrected Christ gave them the ultimate security and strength (1 Pet 1:4). They had hope through suffering.

We think of trials on a grand scale—sickness and persecution. But we need to meet even daily trials with this same eternal hope. We need to constantly find relief, energy, and hope in God. —RVN

Where do you seek relief, energy, and hope?

July 13

∘ ◊ ◊ ∘ ∘

UNITY IN ADVERSITY

1 Samuel 22:1–23:29; **1 Peter 1:13–19**; Psalm 123:1–124:8

Distress can unite people. In difficult moments, in shared pain, we discover our true friends. When David fled from King Saul, his divided family was suddenly supportive of him, as was every man in the region who was distressed or indebted (1 Sam 22:1–2; compare 1 Sam 17:28–30). A shared sense of despair reveals the humanity in us all, helping us to get past our disputes and work together for one purpose.

For a disjointed band of brothers to be united beyond initial circumstance, they must have one purpose. That's precisely what David gave his motley crew: They would fight the Philistines (Israel's greatest enemies) together (1 Sam 23:1–5). David took a terrible situation and turned it into an opportunity to do what needed to be done. As rightful king, David was obligated to protect Israel. Yet it still took outstanding courage and raw leadership to act upon that obligation. When most people would have been paralyzed by fear, David was prepared for action—and that marked him as Israel's new leader. David's strength in adversity enabled him to unite people for a cause, and his God-centered focus made him the ideal leader of God's people.

Peter's remark in his first letter resonates with this idea: "When you have prepared your minds for action, by being self-controlled, put your hope completely in the grace that will be brought to you at the revelation of Jesus Christ. As obedient children, do not be conformed to the former desires you used to conform to in your ignorance" (1 Pet 1:13–14). The ignorance Peter addresses is sin. Although David was dealing with someone else's sin, both he and Peter identify the same solution: Focus on God and His work.

When things get difficult, we should be aware of how we are being subtly drawn away from God's work. If we can stay focused on Christ, we can stay focused on God's purposes. In return, we will find the ability to lead any motley crew toward redemption. —JDB

Where is God calling you to lead?
How can you shift your focus to be stronger in this task?

July 14

∘ ◦ ◎ ◦ ∘

SURPRISE REDEMPTION

1 Samuel 24:1–25:44; **1 Peter 1:20–25**; **Psalm 125:1–127:5**

We often fail to be amazed at redemption. Perhaps we're only dimly aware of our own failings—or (worse) we are blind to how amazing it is that God has shown us grace at all.

In Psalm 126 the psalmist describes the joy that should come as a response to God's redemption. In the past God's restorative work had cast Israel into a state of surprised shock—they "were like dreamers" (Psa 126:1). They were filled with laughter and praise. His glory was present, and His redemption was a mighty witness to both the Israelites and the surrounding nations (Psa 126:2).

But the psalmist quickly reveals that Israel is still in need of restoration. Likely taken into captivity, the people live in hope and anticipation that God will restore them once more: "Those who sow with tears shall reap with rejoicing. He who diligently goes out with weeping, carrying the seed bag, shall certainly come in with rejoicing, carrying his sheaves" (Psa 126:5–6).

In his letter to early churches, Peter speaks about the hope that the prophets had foretold and the things that angels were curious about—the grace prepared through His Son (1 Pet 1:10–12). Peter tells them that this savior "was foreknown before the foundation of the world, but has been revealed in these last times for you" (1 Pet 1:20).

This surprise redemption is unlike any other. Its hope—Christ's sure resurrection—gives us incredible security: We have been "born again, not from perishable seed but imperishable, through the living and enduring word of God" (1 Pet 1:23). We should be awed by this incredible hope and respond with obedience, praise, and love for our neighbor (1 Pet 1:22). —RVN

Are you awed by God's grace?

○ ○ ○ ○ ○

REFRAME IT

1 Samuel 26:1–27:12; 1 Peter 2:1–12; Psalm 128:1–129:8

"'Too often they have attacked me from my youth.' Let Israel say, 'Too often they have attacked me from my youth, yet they have not prevailed against me'" (Psa 129:1–2). As these verses show, sometimes problems can be solved by simply reframing the issue at hand.

Peter makes a "reframing" move in his first letter. He could have focused on the people's sin and their general need to repent, but then their attention would be on the problem, not solving it. So he shifts the focus: "Therefore, ridding yourselves of all malice and all deceit and hypocrisy and envy and all slander, like newborn infants long for the unadulterated spiritual milk, so that by it you may grow up to salvation" (1 Pet 2:1–2). Peter calls them to approach their relationship with Christ like a newborn would milk. They must make Christ such a priority that He becomes something they need and long for. And as they long, their sinful behavior will be resolved.

Similarly, Peter addresses the people's conflict with their culture as an opportunity for God to make them strong, like the stones used to build strong foundations: "And you yourselves, as living stones, are being built up as a spiritual house for a holy priesthood, to offer up spiritual sacrifices acceptable to God through Jesus Christ" (1 Pet 2:5).

We can always choose where to place our attention. Often, we turn our attention toward preventing something (sin) at the cost of actually doing something good (growing in the Lord). If we keep our focus on our relationship with Christ, we can rise above our circumstances and find victory. "The blessing of Yahweh be upon you. We bless you in the name of Yahweh" (Psa 129:8). Reframing our lives makes way for blessing—it gives God room to do transformative work. —JDB

What is God asking you to reframe?
Where is your focus?

∘ ∘ ∘ ∘ ∘

JACK-IN-THE-BOX PRIDE

1 Samuel 28:1–29:11; **1 Peter 2:13–17; Psalm 130:1–131:3**

It's dangerous to become too confident in the maturity of our own faith. Our pride is like the spring of a jack-in-the-box: Just when we think it's broken or that we've gotten the lid on tight, it springs back to life. It rears its ugly head, bobbing around like a circus fool.

It's so easy to get caught up in our own achievements—even when it comes to faith. We can grow in knowledge and then look down on others who still need to grow. The psalmist of Psalm 131 presents the solution with a sure, succinct declaration. He fully submits to God's order. He doesn't wrestle with the things that don't make sense—he is able to place these in God's hand. His inner peace comes from total trust in God: "My heart is not haughty nor my eyes arrogant, And I do not concern myself with things too great and difficult for me. Rather I have soothed and quieted my soul, like a weaned child with its mother, like the weaned child is my soul with me" (Psa 131:1–2).

Maturity of faith is found in childlike trust—trust that sees ourselves as small and God as mighty. Peter also speaks about peace that is a result of having faith that submits to God. Submission allows us to act wisely in a situation, all "for the sake of the Lord" (1 Pet 2:13). Doing good will silence the ignorant (1 Pet 2:15), and if we do good while enduring the mistreatment of others, God will show us His favor (1 Pet 2:20). Ultimately, it's Christ who serves as the example of submission. Even while suffering and enduring abuse, Jesus "did not commit sin, nor was deceit found in his mouth" (1 Pet 2:22). Instead, He "entrusted himself to the one who judges justly" (1 Pet 2:23).

Jesus' act of redemption should be the focus of all our actions. While pride is rebellion against Him, forgiveness and grace through Christ are enough to drive us to the end of ourselves and send us into the haven of God's love. His sacrifice eliminates the need to be prideful and self-seeking. It quiets our souls. —RVN

How are you turning to Christ's sacrifice
in moments of pride?

EMOTION VERSUS LOGIC

1 Samuel 30:1–31:13; 1 Peter 2:18–25; Psalm 131:1–132:18

Reacting is easy. What's difficult is overcoming emotions in a time of adversity. Although emotions are not bad, they can lead us astray. At the same time, when we stray too far in the other direction and rely entirely on reason, we risk using logic without empathy. The answer to this conundrum is not to pit emotions against reason, but instead to pray.

Throughout his life King David struggles to balance emotion and logic. Sometimes he is an emotional wreck; other times he is so calculating that he seems almost brutal. Yet in many moments in his life—especially in his early years—he seeks Yahweh when it would be more convenient not to.

In 1 Samuel 30:1–6, David returns to the town of Ziklag to find that two of his wives and many of his warriors' wives have been captured, and the city has been burned down. The text describes the emotional atmosphere of the discovery: "David and the people who were with him raised their voices and wept until there was not enough strength in them to weep." The text also states that "it was very pressed for David"—meaning that David's men are considering killing him because they view the situation as his fault (1 Sam 30:4, 6). Then we're told, "But David strengthened himself in Yahweh his God" (1 Sam 30:6). This decision changes everything.

By seeking Yahweh, David learns that he will be able to overtake the raiders of Ziklag and recover the captives (1 Sam 30:7–10). What happens next is amazing: David and his men show kindness to a stranger, who returns the kindness by showing them where the raiders are camped. David and his men then overcome the raiders and recover the captives (1 Sam 30:11–20). This is one of those "God works in mysterious ways" moments. But could God have worked in mysterious ways if David had allowed either hot emotion or cold logic to rule him? Probably not. His prayer made all the difference.

We overcome the problems we face because God works in us, through His Spirit, when we seek Him in prayer. This is also how we can overcome our weaknesses and become more like Him. —JDB

What emotions do you need to overcome through prayer?
What tensions can be resolved through God's work?

WHEN KINGS MOURN

2 Samuel 1:1–2:32; 1 Peter 3:1–7; Psalm 133:1–134:3

No one can tell you how to mourn. You have to mourn as you see fit, making sure you don't introduce sin into the grieving process.

Several people who were dear to my heart have died. Each time, I processed it differently—immersing myself in work, weeping, or getting angry. If you've lost someone close to you, your experience with death is likely similar. But you may have noticed something else in the process: When someone passes away, we become weak and vulnerable to temptation. Wanting to vent our emotions, we may fall prey to sin. But loss is no excuse for sin; there *is* no excuse.

King David, for all his strength, was always a very broken man when someone important to him died. Such brokenness is understandable, but a king must balance his behavior; he must be careful not to insult those who have loyally fought for him. David's mourning over his best friend, Jonathan, was completely understandable (e.g., 1 Sam 18:1–4; 19:1–7; 20), but his sense of loss over King Saul was overwrought. We should never celebrate anyone's death, but God had disowned Saul and anointed David (1 Sam 15:10–16:13). Saul had no right to his throne (see, e.g., 1 Sam 16:14–23). Furthermore, Saul had been trying to kill David and his men (1 Sam 19:8–24; 23:14–29). Yet while David's overly dramatic mourning of Saul may have offended his supporters, he went well beyond offense and into sin: He killed the man who put Saul to death (2 Sam 1:14–16). In this time period, it was customary for warriors to kill fallen enemies who were dying a slow and painful death, thus making David's reaction even more outlandish.

We can learn many great things from David, but in this passage, he teaches us what not to do. Don't let emotions control you in a time of pain, for those emotions could overtake you in temptation to sin. —JDB

How can you rely on God during times of mourning?
How can you ward off temptation?

∘ ∘∘∘ ∘

VENGEANCE VERSUS BLESSING

2 Samuel 3:1–4:12; **1 Peter 3:8–22**; Psalm 135:1–21

Comparing the passages of 2 Samuel 3:1–4:12 and 1 Peter 3:8–22 teaches us that all Scripture can be used for instruction: Some passages provide wisdom on how to become more like Christ, while others are best regarded as "things not to do."

Peter's first letter tells us, "be harmonious, sympathetic, showing mutual affection, compassionate, humble, not repaying evil for evil or insult for insult, but [instead] blessing others, because for this reason you were called, so that you could inherit a blessing" (1 Pet 3:8–9). We can find the same lesson, told a different way, in 2 Samuel 3:1–4:12. The violence of the war between David and Saul's houses vividly portrays how acts of vengeance rob us of harmony and blessing.

Some passages in the Bible are beautiful while others are barbaric. Both teach us we're not meant to live in vengeance, like the houses of David and Saul. While we realize these individuals often acted against God's will, we should still recognize their love for God (when it's present) and their desire to follow Him (when it appears authentic) and live in those ways. Jesus is the only leader in the Bible we can look to as a supreme example of righteousness. Every other person in the Bible is flawed in their humanity, but that gives us hope: God can use us, like He used them—despite their mistakes.

If we could live up to Peter's ideals of living in harmony and showing sympathy to others, the world would certainly be a better place, but we can't do so without depending on God. In the midst of chaos, or when we give in to ego, it's hard to live the way we should, even when we are people of faith. But when we learn to follow God in being compassionate, humble, and a blessing to people, we create opportunity for Him to bring harmony and sympathy. If David and Saul's men had put vengeance aside to seek God, their story would certainly have been less barbaric and far more beautiful. —JDB

How can you incorporate humility, compassion,
and the practice of blessing into your life?

SERVING THE GLORY OF GOD

2 Samuel 5:1–6:23; **1 Peter 4:1–11**; Psalm 136:1–26

When we avoid community, we may develop an inflated opinion of our own character. It's easy to think we're kind people when we're not held accountable to others. It's easy to think we're always right when no one disagrees with us. Conversely, it's in our relationships that our true selves are often revealed. When we're actively involved in a community, we face hundreds of instances where we need to make choices. These choices either serve others, or they serve our own desires.

When Peter states, "Above all, keep your love for one another constant, because love covers a large number of sins" (1 Pet 4:8), he's saying that choosing to love often sets all motives in the right place. It dispels our own pride and puts issues into perspective. When we are truly loving others, it's not about our pride or "being right." It's about helping others grow in faith by using our God-given gifts.

Peter goes on to show just what this looks like: "Be hospitable without complaining. Just as each one has received a gift, use it for serving one another, as good stewards of the varied grace of God. If anyone speaks, let it be as the oracles of God; if anyone serves, let it be as by the strength that God provides, so that in all things God will be glorified through Jesus Christ" (1 Pet 4:9–11). When we love others and use our gifts for their benefit, our actions do more than serve the other. Since they find their origin in Christ's love, they serve to honor and glorify Christ.

Living in community with others may often be difficult. We'll meet with challenging people and situations that will require us to continually pray to the giver of gifts for renewed strength and the ability to serve. We'll face conflict that needs to be met with wisdom and love. Through prayer and the work of God in our lives, we can love and serve others with the love of Christ. —RVN

How are you exerting your own pride in your relationships with others?
How can you serve them with your unique, God-given gifts?

TRUTH AND HONESTY
CAN BE PAINFUL

2 Samuel 7:1–8:18; **1 Peter 4:12–19**; Psalm 137:1–9

A commitment to honesty and truth often puts us in unexpected spiritual situations—something David experiences in 2 Samuel 7. David thinks he will build God a great house—a temple—but instead God plans to build a house for him—a legacy. Because David seeks God, God does great things through him. Yet, as David discovers, being part of God's work and living in His will isn't without difficulty or pain.

Consciously or subconsciously, we often cling to the notion that "If I do good works for God, He will owe me." Isn't that the assumption behind the statement, "I am loyal to God, but He has afflicted me with pain"? We frame our pain in light of God's role. Instead, we should view it in relation to the sin of our world. We sin, just as people did in the past, so why should we not expect pain?

Like David, Peter and his fellow missionaries experience a great deal of pain in doing God's work. Peter encourages them by writing, "Dear friends, do not be surprised at the fiery ordeal among you, when it takes place to test you, as if something strange were happening to you. But to the degree that you share in the sufferings of Christ, rejoice, so that also at the revelation of his glory you may rejoice and be glad" (1 Pet 4:12–13). Peter understands that the persecution they face for Christ will be used for great glory. He reminds his audience that they shouldn't be surprised. By committing themselves to following Christ, they will inevitably clash with those who are opposed to Christ.

In response to David's seeking God, God makes a covenant with David. Then as now, the central principle of covenant lies in God's loyalty to us—because of Christ's work on the cross to suffer and die for our sin—despite how much the world hates us. —JDB

Has God taught you through persecution?
In what ways is God's covenant at work among you today?

SHOWING KINDNESS TO A STRANGER

2 Samuel 9:1–10:19; **1 Peter 5:1–14**; Psalm 138:1–8

When I was a teenager, I became serious about showing unsolicited kindness while working through a 30-day intensive devotional. The devotional required me to record an act of kindness each day. My efforts included things as mundane as taking out the trash before being asked and closing schoolmates' lockers to prevent them from becoming the victims of pranks. Although the acts were simple, and mostly meaningless, the effort taught me a discipline. Kindness should be intentional, not random. But what if your kindness stems from guilt?

In 2 Samuel 9, King David shows intentional kindness to Ziba, Saul's servant, and Mephibosheth, Jonathan's son, by offering them Saul's land after Saul and Jonathan have died. It's hard to know why David does this, especially since it puts him at risk—his association with the previous regime could anger his warriors, who fought against Saul. Is David merely being a good guy? Does he feel guilty because Jonathan, who had been so loyal to him, died in battle? Is he trying to establish that he is a merciful ruler? Does he have other political motives? The question of David's motive evokes another one: Why do *we* treat others well?

Peter addressed this question of motive in his first letter, in which he exhorts ministers to "Shepherd the flock of God among you [being the people of the church], exercising oversight not by compulsion but willingly, in accordance with God" (1 Pet 5:2). He points out that if we are moved by compulsion, our motives are probably wrong.

There are times I wonder whether I treat others well because I subconsciously think that it will earn me points with them or with God. I battle this—it's something we should all fight against. The state of the heart when helping others is every bit as important as the act itself. —JDB

What motivates your acts of kindness?
What pure, kind, and intentional act can you perform today?

FINDING GOD IN SHEOL

2 Samuel 11:1–12:31; 2 Peter 1:1–8; **Psalm 139:1–24**

We've all felt distant from God. Sometimes it's sin that makes us feel separated from Him; other times it could be a lack of prayer. Either way, when we feel apart from God, God has not moved away from us. God never moves—we do. But we can find solace in the words of Psalm 139: "O Yahweh, you have searched me, and you know me. You know my sitting down and my rising up. You understand my thought from afar" (Psa 139:1–2).

We spend so much of life explaining ourselves to others. Trying to manage perceptions is a norm in our society—especially for those of us in fast-paced work environments. There's nothing wrong with this as long as our motives are pure, we're being honest, and we're not obsessed with what others think. But it's certainly comforting to know that with God, we never have to explain ourselves. He already knows. He has already searched us—and He is always present.

The psalmist writes, "You barricade me behind and in front, and set your hand upon me. … If I ascend to heaven, there you are, and if I make my bed in Sheol [the ultimate symbol of darkness in the ancient Near East], look! There you are. If I lift up the wings of the dawn, and I alight on the far side of the sea, even there your hand would lead me, and your right hand would hold me fast" (Psa 139:5, 8–10). God is in all places. We may accept these concepts intellectually, but our minds become distracted when we're feeling alone. Loneliness is heart work, as this psalm portrays.

Psalm 139 concludes with the words, "Search me, O God, and know my heart; test me and know my anxious thoughts. And see if there is in me the worship of false gods, and lead me in the way everlasting" (Psa 139:23–24). The God who created the universe is waiting for us. He is ready to find our false gods and cast them out. He is ready to help us acknowledge His work of goodness and order in the world, and to alleviate the anxiousness we feel. Only He who is all-knowing and all-present can bring us ultimate comfort. Only He can close the gap we feel. —JDB

What false gods are you fighting?
What anxiousness do you need to ask God to cast out?

SLAVES TO GOD,
EQUIPPED FOR RIGHTEOUSNESS

2 Samuel 13:1–39; **2 Peter 1:9–15**; Psalm 140:1–13

I used to think that I was powerless when it came to sin. Christ had saved me from my sinful state, but I was still wretched and helpless. Even though I knew I was no longer a slave to sin, I didn't always think about what freedom in Christ really looks like.

Peter's letter sheds light on this. After listing both virtues and vices, he encourages early Christians to examine their lives and pursue the virtues that characterize faith: "For if these things are yours and are increasing, this does not make you useless or unproductive in the knowledge of our Lord Jesus Christ. For the one for whom these things are not present is blind, being nearsighted, having forgotten the cleansing of his former sins" (2 Pet 1:8–9).

Peter shows us that Christ's sacrifice doesn't leave us helpless. We are not left alone to flounder until He returns. Earlier in his letter, Peter states that "[Christ's] divine power has bestowed on us all things that are necessary for life and godliness, through the knowledge of the one who called us by his own glory and excellence of character" (2 Pet 1:2–3).

We're not slaves to sin. Our lives are not stagnant. We're equipped and enabled to live a life pleasing to God. This isn't pride in ourselves or vanity in our own abilities; it's the opposite. It's proof of God's work in our lives that enables us to live and love as we should. As we grow in faith, praying for the work of the Spirit in our lives, we will look back and see how our lives are becoming more fully devoted to Him—all for His glory. —RVN

In what areas of your life do you feel weighed down by your sin?
How can you pray to God for help in this area of your life?

∘ ∘ ∘ ∘ ∘

THE DIFFICULT ISSUE OF THE HERETICS

2 Samuel 14:1–15:37; **2 Peter 1:16–21**; Psalm 141:1–142:7

Distinguishing between correct and false teaching has plagued nearly every church. We ask questions such as, "Are we venturing too far in that direction?" "Is this just my personal theological issue, or is this actually a big deal?" "Should I be concerned about that, or is it simply a matter of individual choice?" Thankfully, the New Testament clarifies many of these issues for us.

Throughout Peter's second letter, he addresses the challenge of warding off false teachers; he aims to defend the gospel and explain why the false teachers' claims are incorrect. To do so, Peter hinges his argument on his own experience—on what he witnessed. In his case, arguing from personal witness makes sense: Peter actually knew Jesus.

He writes, "For we did not make known to you the power and coming of our Lord Jesus Christ by following ingeniously concocted myths, but by being eyewitnesses of that one's majesty. For he received honor and glory from God the Father when a voice such as this was brought to him by the Majestic Glory, 'This is my beloved Son, in whom I am well pleased'" (2 Pet 1:16–17). For Peter, orthodoxy comes down to the foundation of the claims being made about Jesus and whether Christ is being proclaimed as Lord and as God's Son.

Peter isn't willing to put up with false prophecy, testimony, or teaching (see 2 Pet 2). To show how absurd the false teachers' claims are, Peter proclaims, "Every prophecy of scripture does not come about from one's own interpretation, for no prophecy was ever produced by the will of man, but men carried along by the Holy Spirit spoke of God" (2 Pet 1:20–21).

Correct and incorrect teaching can be distinguished based on the source of the words being spoken and whether they align with what was taught by eyewitnesses (like Peter). Although this isn't a complete guide for distinguishing between what God approves and what He doesn't, it gives us a good start to ward off basic false teachings and focus on the truth instead. Next time we come to the difficult question of "Is this heresy?" we can ask, "What would Peter think?" —JDB

What issues is your church struggling with?
How can you help investigate them in light of the claims
made by eyewitnesses like Peter?

COURTROOM DRAMA,
DAYTIME TV, AND GOOD DEITY

2 Samuel 16:1–17:29; 2 Peter 2:1–11; **Psalm 143:1–12**

I remember old television courtroom episodes where people beg for forgiveness from a cynical judge when they should seek forgiveness from the person they've wronged. Usually these shows take the irony to the next level: The judge shows less mercy to those who beg, viewing their actions as further demonstration of their weak character. Thankfully, God is not this kind of judge, though we often falsely characterize Him that way.

At the beginning of Psalm 143, the psalmist remarks, "O Yahweh, hear my prayer; listen to my supplications. In your faithfulness answer me" (Psa 143:1). He then adds, "And do not enter into judgment with your servant, because no one alive is righteous before you" (Psa 143:2). The psalmist's prayers are well spoken, but are they honest? The psalmist goes on, "Teach me to do your will, for you are my God; your Spirit is good. Lead me onto level ground" (Psa 143:10). This line demonstrates that he is not spouting rhetoric; he is living in reality.

We're often determined to convince God to see things our way. Instead, we should be determined to see things His way. God is not a judge in a courtroom drama. Furthermore, His Son has already paid the price for our sins—we have been pardoned through Jesus' intercession. The only requirement on our part is to enter into a relationship with Him.

We cannot justify our actions, for it is only by God's goodness that we are able to do good, and it's only out of severe disobedience and ungratefulness that we act poorly. We need to change our perceptions so that our conversations with God become holistic. We should not just ask; we must act. We should not just speak; we must listen. We should not just petition; we must enter into an honest relationship with God. —JDB

In what ways do you falsely characterize God?

THE TRICKS WE PLAY ON OURSELVES

2 Samuel 18:1–33; 2 Peter 2:12–22; Psalm 144:1–15

A great deal of leadership is based on consistency. King David is a prime example: He struggled most when he was inconsistent.

David's son, Absalom, committed horrific acts against David and others (2 Sam 14–17). David repeatedly responded in a manner unbefitting a king, finally sending men out to destroy Absalom's troops (2 Sam 18:1–4). He ordered his commanders—within hearing of the army—to "deal gently" with Absalom (2 Sam 18:5). With this order, David again acted beneath his role and duty as king: He asked for the leader of a rebellion to be spared—essentially using his own warriors as pawns in a game to regain his fallen son. Absalom didn't deserve to be dealt with gently; he was a ruthless, terrorizing dictator and had opposed God's chosen king. For this reason, Joab, one of David's commanders, chose to kill Absalom (2 Sam 18:14).

It's unlikely any of us will ever be in a position like David or Joab's, but their story presents some lessons in leadership. Joab demonstrates that sometimes the "right hand man" knows better than the commander-in-chief. David's repeated inability to separate his emotions from the situation (he made this same mistake with Saul) could have resulted in his untimely death and the complete destruction of the kingdom. David's actions show us that we should seek the advice of others, asking that they help us think through the full ramifications of our actions. If David would have sought advice from Joab or another of his trusted leaders, he probably would have made a wiser decision—and preserved his dignity as king.

Based on David's track record as a military leader, he would have dealt swiftly with any other uprising but ignored resistance from his own son to the point of peril. The events don't portray David as a man of love and mercy; instead, they reveal him as a man too easily swayed by conflicting feelings.

Selfishness is David's ultimate downfall. He wanted Absalom to live because it seemed best in his mind—the ideal future he envisioned. In making a move to create that future himself, David jeopardized everyone he should have protected. He even jeopardized his own reign, itself a gift from God. —JDB

What are you currently being selfish about that has,
until now, been deceiving you?

I WILL LAUD YOUR DEEDS

2 Samuel 19:1–43; 2 Peter 3:1–13; **Psalm 145:1–21**

I grew up in a family of stoics. Through example, my siblings and I were taught to keep our emotions to ourselves. Displays of excessive affection or sorrow were regarded with some suspicion, and this played out in our expressions of faith.

Psalm 145 directly challenges such a mindset. The psalmist expresses why confessing God's faithfulness is so important, especially to those we influence: "One generation will laud your works to another, and will declare your mighty deeds" (Psa 145:4). God's mighty deeds were His redemptive acts—especially the exodus from Egypt. His greatness (Psa 145:6), His righteousness (Psa 145:7), His glory, and His power (Psa 145:11, 12) were expressed.

Our praise should be centered on God's ultimate restorative work through His Son—an act that has brought us back into intimate communion with Him. We can bring our sorrows and failures to Him: "Yahweh upholds all who are falling, and raises up all who are bowed down" (Psa 145:14). He hears our desires and our cries when we call upon Him in truth (Psa 145:18–19). Calling on God in truth requires that we honestly examine our own emotions (Psa 145:18). When we bring our emotions to God, we should do so in either confession or praise.

James emphasizes that free expression isn't always a value. Since we stumble in many ways, loose talk can be dangerous and destructive in communities (Jas 3:2–6). Both speaking and silence require wisdom. When we are quick to talk about God's work of redemption and His work in us, our words bring Him honor. What better reason to be mindful of how our expressions affect those around us—especially those who look up to us. —RVN

How are you using expressions to
honor God and uplift others?

WHEN IT'S REALLY URGENT

2 Samuel 20:1–21:22; **2 Peter 3:14–18**; Psalm 146:1–10

The urgency of God's work is easily lost on us. But to the early church, Jesus' return seemed imminent. We get a sense of this urgency in Peter's second letter, where he writes that every moment between now and when Jesus returns is a moment of grace; therefore, believers must work harder than ever to bring others to Christ and grow in their relationship with Him.

Peter remarks, "Therefore, dear friends, because you are waiting for [Christ to return], make every effort to be found at peace, spotless and unblemished in him. And regard the patience of our Lord as salvation" (2 Pet 3:14–15). God wants to see more people come to Him—that is why He has not returned. When we feel like Peter's audience does, wondering why Jesus hasn't returned, Peter's explanation can help us refocus and remember that it's not really about us; it's about others.

The Christian life is marked by a focus on God and our neighbors. The more we love Him, the more we learn to love our neighbors. And the more we love our neighbors, the more we become like Christ. We get closer to God with each act of love, and each act of love brings someone else closer to Him as well.

Peter continues, "Therefore, dear friends, because you know this beforehand, guard yourselves so that you do not lose your own safe position because you have been led away by the error of lawless persons. But grow in the grace and knowledge of our Lord and Savior Jesus Christ" (2 Pet 3:17–18). For Peter, the major issue is whether his audience will stay focused on Jesus or be led astray by false teachers. If the false teachers are able to sway his audience's beliefs, then perhaps they never believed at all. By disavowing the assertions of false teachers, enduring persecution, and dedicating themselves to Christ's grace, his audience shows their true faith. The act of defying evil readies God's people for His return.

When all of our lives are focused on God's eternal work, the questions about priorities, how we show love, and what matters to God suddenly have answers. God's urgency becomes our priority. —JDB

What priorities has God given you?
Are you living as if the end could be around any corner?

DESTRUCTIVE PEOPLE

2 Samuel 22:1–51; **Jude 1:1–16**; Psalm 147:1–20

Some destructive people don't realize the carnage they leave in their wake. Others intentionally cause rifts and pain, driven by selfish motives. Jude's letter equipped early Christians to deal wisely with false teachers who had entered the church community. Today, it can provide wisdom to respond to some of the most difficult people and situations we encounter.

The community that Jude addressed contained destructive false teachers "who pervert the grace of our God into sensuality and deny our only Master and Lord, Jesus Christ" (Jude 4). They did not respect authority, but acted out of instinct rather than conviction: "But these persons blaspheme all that they do not understand, and all that they understand by instinct like the irrational animals, by these things they are being destroyed" (Jude 10).

Jude's metaphors for these false teachers give us a sense of what to look for in destructive people: "hidden reefs at your love feasts, caring for themselves, waterless clouds carried away by winds, late autumn trees without fruit, twice dead, uprooted. … " (Jude 12–13). He depicts people whose destructive, selfish behavior lacks conviction. Like wayward stars, these false teachers go off course, perhaps taking others with them.

After these descriptions, we expect Jude to warn his readers to stay away from these types of people. But he does the opposite: Jude's closing warning calls readers to interact with people of this sort—though they must do so with incredible wisdom: "Have mercy on those who doubt; save others by snatching them out of the fire; to others show mercy with fear, hating even the garment stained by the flesh" (Jude 22–23).

Interacting with people who doubt and wander requires a deep knowledge of our own weaknesses and failures. It requires maturity of faith. Jude gives three specific instructions: that we build ourselves up, pray in the Spirit, and keep ourselves in the love of God (Jude 21–22). This interaction requires the work of a God "who is able to keep you from stumbling and to present you blameless before the presence of his glory with great joy" (Jude 24). —RVN

How do destructive people in your life influence you?
Based on how they influence you, how should you
approach or end the relationship?

COSMIC, CREATION, CHAOS

2 Samuel 23:1–24:25; **Jude 1:17–25**; **Psalm 148:1–150:6**

Psalm 148 is cosmic in scope and comforting in message. It's a depiction of how Yahweh brought order to chaos in the very beginning. Yahweh put the heavens, heights, angels, hosts (His armies), sun, moon, stars, and waters in their place—each a sign of His rule over the universe (Psa 148:1–5).

The version of the creation story we typically hear tells how things came to be, which is good. But when the story is cast like in Psalm 148—where we see God as ruler and Lord over chaos—the message moves beyond intellectual knowledge. If God rules over chaos, and has since the beginning, He can bring order to the chaos in our lives. For this reason, the psalmist praises Yahweh both for His creation and His work in his own life.

The end of Psalm 148 further reveals Yahweh's intimate work with the worshiper: The psalmist declares Yahweh praiseworthy because "he has raised high a horn [the symbol of strength] for his people" (Psa 148:14). Yahweh's work in creation proves that He is the most worthy partner in adverse situations. When things get tough, Yahweh will come through.

Sadly, the message of God's provision for us has become so cliché that it's easy for us to take for granted. Perhaps that's why it's the central message of so many biblical books. For example, when Jude prays for protection for believers, he calls out to Jesus—dedicating his message to Him and His work (Jude 17–25). In doing so, Jude uses the words that would have traditionally conjured up images of God's work in either creation or war—both of which parallel psalms like Psalm 148. Jude declares that Jesus deserves "glory, power, and authority" (Jude 25) because He is the "savior" of people and the universe, both of which Yahweh created (Jude 24). Jesus is the one who came to earth to win the battle against chaos.

Next time things seem to get rough, try replacing the cliché of "God is in control" with "God is Lord over chaos." When God spoke, chaos was subdued. Likewise, when God speaks truth into our lives, the chaos in our lives is subdued. Through Christ's work, we have the opportunity for this intimate relationship with God. Through Christ's efforts in us, we can become people who act with Him to subdue chaos. —JDB

What chaos do you need God to subdue today?

CONNECTING THE STORIES

Isaiah 1:1–2:5; Luke 1:1–38; Job 1:1–12

The connections between the Testaments aren't readily apparent, but a closer reading—empowered by the Spirit—can reveal them. Such is the case with the connections among Isaiah, Luke, and Job. The authors of each of these books begin by introducing a person and then inviting us into the story.

"There was a man in the land of Uz whose name was Job. That man was blameless and upright and God-fearing and turning away from evil. And seven sons and three daughters were born to him" (Job 1:1–2).

"The vision of Isaiah son of Amoz, which he saw concerning Judah and Jerusalem in the days of Uzziah, Jotham, Ahaz, and Hezekiah, kings of Judah. Hear, heavens, and listen, earth, for Yahweh has spoken: 'I reared children and I brought them up, but they rebelled against me'" (Isa 1:1–2).

"Since many have attempted to compile an account concerning the events that have been fulfilled among us, just as those who were eyewitnesses and servants of the word from the beginning passed on to us, it seemed best to me also—because I have followed all things carefully from the beginning—to write them down in orderly sequence for you, most excellent Theophilus, so that you may know the certainty concerning the things about which you were taught" (Luke 1:1–4).

Although these three introductions represent a simple pattern repeated among the books, only later do we see the deeper parallels. Isaiah draws on the thematic framework of Job: People need an advocate—someone righteous to stand between themselves and God—because all people are unworthy (Job 9; compare Isa 49:1–3; 52:13–53:12). Luke draws upon Isaiah's framework: He identifies this advocate as a savior who will suffer on behalf of God's people (the Suffering Servant; Luke 4:22–30; compare Isa 52:14–15; 53:3).

The narratives in these books quickly lead us in directions we don't expect, and as we begin to feel the tension and disorientation of the characters, the focus of each shifts to the savior at the center of God's work in the world. In the midst of the pain these stories record, we see God working out something great—something beautiful. The world will be saved through one man: Jesus, God's Son. This Suffering Servant will pay the price for the sins of us all. God's work in the world reflects and builds on itself to accomplish His great purpose of salvation. —JDB

How does your story fit in the story of God's saving work?

August 2

∘ ∘ ⊙ ∘ ∘

SMALL PLAYERS

Isaiah 2:6–4:6; **Luke 1:39–66**; Job 1:13–22

A priest should know better. A man representing the spiritual state of God's people shouldn't be so quick to question God's promises. But for Zechariah, obedience became complicated. When the angel Gabriel told him he'd have a son, he responded with doubt: "By what will I know this? For I am an old man, and my wife is advanced in years!" (Luke 1:18). Such happy news—such unexpected goodness—deserved a glad, believing response.

While Zechariah fully expected to encounter God in the temple, Mary wasn't anticipating anything like Gabriel's appearance. Yet she readily responded to the angel's declaration with bold, simple allegiance: "Behold, the Lord's female slave! May it happen to me according to your word" (Luke 1:38). Her alignment with God echoes Job's response after he endured crippling loss: "Naked I came out from my mother's womb, and naked I will return there. Yahweh gives, and Yahweh takes. Let Yahweh's name be blessed" (Job 1:21).

It's easy to view doubting or believing responses like these in a distant way. We don't expect to experience such miraculous events or such inexplicable loss in our own lives. Because of this, we feel like small players in God's plan—small players who need only small faith.

Regardless of whether we encounter such earth-shattering events in our lives, we *did* experience the most dramatic, miraculous act of God in history when Jesus died. We have been buried with Him and will be resurrected with Him (Rom 6:3–4). Because of this, we're expected to put our hope and faith in God. Like Mary, we're expected to fully align ourselves with Him; like Job, we are to bless Him in the difficult times. And finally, we're expected to praise God when He shows us mercy we don't deserve, as He did to Zechariah (Luke 1:64). —RVN

How can you boldly and sincerely step out in faith?

○ ○ ◊ ○ ○

THE ART OF DISCIPLINE
Isaiah 5:1–6:13; Luke 1:67–2:21; Job 2:1–10

Jesus didn't die for us so that we could continue to sin—He sacrificed Himself so that we could have sinless lives. God is patient, but His patience does not last forever. We wouldn't test His patience so often if we had not lost sight of the notion of discipline, a concept that is at the forefront in the Old Testament.

In the book of Isaiah, God describes His people using the image of a vineyard (Isa 5:5–7). The vineyard described in this passage is eventually restored through Christ, who creates a new vine and new branches. Yet the vineyard still requires the same level of care and discipline (John 15:1–17).

It's tempting to justify our behaviors by arguing that it is impossible to not sin, but is this true? Jesus came to make it possible for us to live as God has always desired for us to live—this is one of the many things that makes His birth so glorious (Luke 2:14; compare Isa 6:3). While no one other than Jesus has been sinless, Christians are meant to be people who are freed from sin (Rom 6:1–14). Thus, it may be *unlikely* to live a sinless life, but it's not impossible: "All things are possible for God" (Phil 4:13).

Discipline is one way that God teaches us to become more like Him—as He intended us to be (Gen 1:26). God disciplines believers because He cares too much about His people to allow us to throw away all the grace and goodness He offers. If sin had no repercussions, we would live the lives we desire, not the lives we are meant to live. And if we don't live the lives we're meant to live, we miss out on God's blessing and lose sight of the goals He has for us, leading others astray in the process. When we openly sin (without repenting), we discourage others from wanting to live in God's likeness.

God has called us to do everything we can, with the Spirit's empowerment, to live sinless lives. We must repent daily and move closer to that goal. As we seek that goal, we have greater opportunities to live so that others may know and find Him. In the meantime, we should expect His discipline to help shape us to become more like Him. —JDB

How is God currently disciplining you?
What are you learning from it?

August 4

◦ ◊ ◊ ◊ ◦

IN GRIEF

Isaiah 7:1–8:22; Luke 2:22–52; **Job 2:11–13**

It's difficult to know how to respond to people suffering grief. Those brave enough to speak often attempt to rationalize another's grief with ill-timed theological truths. Those who feel inadequate or awkward about reaching out to grieving people sometimes avoid them altogether.

Job's friends are well known for misinterpreting Job's suffering. But they aren't often recognized for the moments when they responded to Job's anguish with wisdom. When Eliphaz, Bildad, and Zophar first heard of the tragedy, they immediately came to comfort Job:

"Thus they lifted up their eyes from afar, but they did not recognize him, so they raised their voice, and they wept, and each man tore his outer garment and threw dust on their heads toward the sky. Then they sat with him on the ground for seven days and seven nights, but no one spoke a word to him because they saw that his suffering was very great" (Job 2:12–13).

Often we try to diminish grief with clichés that seem helpful and fill the awkward silence, like "God is in control." Job's friends realized that such spoken attempts—even spoken truths—would only interrupt and add to the grieving that was necessary and appropriate. Instead, they shared his grief, offered their presence, and didn't speak a word.

Job's friends didn't keep silent for long, though, and when they did speak, Job wished they would be silent: "O that you would keep completely silent and that it would become wisdom for you" (Job 13:5). Our response to grief should be measured and prayerful. Attempts to explain events that we don't ultimately understand can bring even more pain. However, shared grief and empathy can bring comfort to someone who knows truth but is struggling to come to grips with a new reality. —RVN

How can you empathize rather than rationalize grief?

PATTERNS AND PROPHECIES

Isaiah 9:1–10:19; Luke 3:1–38; Job 3:1–16

L uke sees the events surrounding Jesus' life through the lens of Isaiah. For Luke, Jesus' life is Isaiah's prophecy made tangible and complete. Jesus is the anticipated Messiah, prophet, and savior. Even John the Baptist's role in Jesus' life is based on Isaiah's prophecy. Luke repeats the metaphor of "the wilderness" from Isaiah—used by the prophet to describe the time when the Israelites would come out from their captivity in Babylon—to cast John the Baptist as a central figure in God's work.

The wilderness metaphor doesn't originate with Isaiah. He uses it to represent the second time God's people entered the land He promised them (the term originally comes from the time when the Israelites roamed the wilderness after the exodus). Luke quotes Isaiah in casting John the Baptist as "the voice of one crying out in the wilderness, 'Prepare the way of the Lord, make his paths straight! … all flesh will see the salvation of God'" (Luke 3:4–6; quoting Isa 40:3–5). For Luke, the smoothing of the rough road represents a change in the spiritual landscape, and the flesh that sees the salvation of God means the message is not just for the Jewish people but for all people—including Luke himself.

Luke builds upon this connection by identifying Jesus as the child prophesied in Isaiah (Luke 1:26–28; Isa 9:6–7).

Luke is adept at the art of connecting the Testaments. He tells us directly that he's quoting Isaiah, and in doing so, he illustrates that God works by building current events on the foundation of past events. Those events form the basis of prophecy—God's way of telling us both what He has done and what He will do in times to come.

Although the way God works is too great for us to comprehend, He allows us to see patterns in His work; we just need to look for them and believe they are there. If we focus on God's works and the echoes and harmonies between them, our perspective on the events of our lives changes dramatically. We glimpse the reality that God is not only at work in today's matters, but He is also using them to prepare and signify the events that are to come. The patterns are as important as the events, as God uses both to reveal Himself to us. —JDB

What patterns are you noticing in your life?
How do you think God is working and will continue to work through you?

FEELING ENTITLED

Isaiah 10:20–12:6; **Luke 4:1–44**; Job 3:17–26

Familiarity breeds contempt, so the saying goes. But the line from Aesop's fable "The Fox and the Lion" wasn't meant to imply that we often take those closest to us for granted. Rather, the fox fails to properly acknowledge the lion—the king of all beasts—because he doesn't know his place. His self-perception is dangerously inflated.

The same is true for the fickle Nazarenes who heard Jesus interpret the Scriptures. When Jesus preached in the synagogue of His hometown, the Nazarenes were initially receptive. But when He interpreted the prophet Isaiah's words in a way they disliked—a way that showed Him as the one who "proclaim[s] release to the captives, and recovery of sight to the blind" (Luke 4:18; see Isa 61:1)—they belittled Him: "Is this man not the son of Joseph?" (Luke 4:22).

The Nazarenes weren't ready to admit their need (Luke 4:23). They didn't understand that they were blind and unrepentant. They may have expected Jesus to perform miracles for them—after all, He was a local. But He didn't show them physical proof of the spiritual truth that they were unwilling to grasp. Instead, He reminded them that Elijah the prophet was sent to a Sidonian woman and Elisha to a Syrian. God chose to show mercy and healing to those who were unfamiliar with Him because they were willing to believe. They were willing to humble themselves to a point where belief was possible.

The Nazarenes' response to Jesus tells a spiritual truth that we might easily overlook. When it comes to the Christian life, it's tempting to feel that we have status. When we're comfortable—when we know what to expect from preaching and have memorized the pertinent passages—we can feel a sense of entitlement that is dangerous. Entitlement breeds contempt that needs to be uprooted. Unless we see our true state—that we need to be set free—we forget that we need to humble ourselves before the Lamb of God. —RVN

Do you feel a sense of entitlement?
What would it take for you to become humble before Jesus?

○ ○ ○ ○ ○

RAISE THE SIGNAL

Isaiah 13:1–14:23; Luke 5:1–39; Job 4:1–11

The Bible echoes with great battle cries: "Raise a signal on a bare hill, lift up your voice to them; wave the hand. ... A sound of the roar of the kingdoms, of nations gathering! Yahweh of hosts is mustering an army for battle" (Isa 13:4).

In this proclamation, God declares war on Babylon for their brutal and evil deeds against His people. Yet He calls for "a signal" to be raised so that the Babylonians might repent from their great wickedness. They have an opportunity to surrender to Yahweh before it's too late—and we must do the same.

We tend to see ourselves as less evil than the infamous sinners of the past, but in a way we all carry shades of Babylon in ourselves. Just as the Babylonians did, we set up and worship idols instead of loving Yahweh with our entire being. Similarly, we attack others instead of loving them the way God has loved us. If we search our hearts, we find that painting ourselves as more righteous than past sinners doesn't work: We're *all* in need of a Savior. We've all fallen short (Rom 3:21–26). In that sense, we all come from Babylon.

Although most of us are willing to identify our private idols—such as money, power or fame—few of us realize the depth of our betrayal. When Isaiah portrays the sinner that is Babylon, he is neither tolerant nor sympathetic (Isa 13:19). Instead, he issues a harsh warning that the day of Yahweh's coming—the time of reckoning is near (Isa 13:6). It's no different for us today. When the New Testament writers depict sin, they do not underestimate how much it inhibits God's work in us and in the world (2 Pet 1:8–15). With the same urgency that Isaiah expressed, they note that now is the time to repent and do God's will (2 Pet 3).

God has called us to join Him in the battle against evil by living Spirit-filled lives in accordance with His will—lives of loving others, despite how hard that might be sometimes (Eph 4:1–6; 6:11–20). We must answer God's urgent call upon us. There is no time to waste. —JDB

How can you express love today as
a sign of God's war against evil?

DISTORTION

Isaiah 14:24–16:14; **Luke 6:1–49**; Job 4:12–21

If attending church and small group or even reading the Bible and praying become activities that we do out of obligation, then we have a bigger problem than we might realize. If our hearts are disengaged, our religious motions and listless obedience serve only as a security blanket—something that makes us feel safe and good.

The Pharisees faced this dilemma, but they took the error one step further. They took the Sabbath—a practice intended to point people toward God—and twisted it into a heavy burden. So when Jesus wanted to do good on the Sabbath, it's no surprise that they seized the opportunity to trap Him.

Jesus responded to the Pharisees' accusation by telling them He is "Lord of the Sabbath" (Luke 6:5). But He also showed them the true purpose of Sabbath while at the same time exposing their hearts: "And Jesus said to them, 'I ask you whether it is permitted on the Sabbath to do good or to do evil, to save a life or to destroy it?'" (Luke 6:9).

Caught up in their religious observance, the Pharisees misunderstood the heart of God's commands. Not only this, but they used the Sabbath to do harm—the polar opposite of Jesus' life-giving actions.

Ultimately, the actions of the Pharisees appeared holy and righteous, but underneath they were lifeless. They were like the lukewarm waters described in Revelation, for which Jesus feels utter contempt: "Thus, because you are lukewarm and neither hot nor cold, I am about to vomit you out of my mouth!" (Rev 3:16).

Nothing displeases God more than when our hearts and our actions don't match up. If this is the case for us, we need to use Scripture to examine our hearts as we pray for wisdom and the Spirit. Nothing can make us right with God unless we know why we are wrong with Him—and where our hope really lies. Our outward actions need to be infused with the desire to follow Him. —RVN

What are the motives behind your motions?

BORROWED IMAGERY

Isaiah 17:1–19:25; Luke 7:1–35; Job 5:1–7

In the Old Testament, Yahweh regularly explains Himself by using imagery familiar to the time. Sometimes Yahweh even uses images associated with other gods to emphasize that He—and not the gods of other nations—has authority over the earth. This poetic exchange would have served as an intercultural dialogue between the Israelites and their neighbors. A classic example is the image of the rider on the clouds: "Look! Yahweh is riding on a swift cloud and is coming to Egypt. And the idols of Egypt will tremble in front of him, and the heart of Egypt melts in his inner parts" (Isa 19:1).

Here, the prophet borrows a metaphor usually associated with the god Baal (from Ugaritic literature) to demonstrate Yahweh's superiority over Baal: Yahweh arrives in Egypt in greater glory than that of the god feared by Egypt's (and Israel's) Canaanite neighbor. Because Egypt has oppressed Yahweh's people, Yahweh will withhold the rains—a decision that Baal, the god of rain, was notorious for making (see Isa 19:5–8).

The writer goes on: "And I will stir up Egyptians against Egyptians, and each one will fight against his brother and each one against his neighbor, city against city, kingdom against kingdom. And the spirit of the Egyptians will be disturbed in his midst, and I will confuse his plans, and they will consult the idols and the spirits of the dead, and the ghosts and the spiritists" (Isa 19:2–3).

The threat of violence in this passage may be intimidating, but believers can find hope in it. We take comfort in seeing that Yahweh intercedes for His people. We find joy in knowing that He loves people enough to explain Himself in ways they can understand, using whatever metaphor best reveals His power and glory. On all accounts, He is God of justice. —JDB

In what situations are you currently seeking justice?
What metaphors is God using to answer your prayers?

August 10

∘ ∘∘∘ ∘

LOVE, PRAISE, FORGIVENESS

Isaiah 20:1–22:25; **Luke 7:36–8:15**; Job 5:8–16

Our praise for God is often directly connected to accepting and confessing our brokenness. Our capacity to love Him is tied to the realization of how much He has forgiven us.

The woman in Luke 7 who anointed Jesus' feet is described with one phrase: She was a sinner. We're not given clarifying detail, but we do know her sin was notorious and, as a result, she was marginalized by society. She was not only weighed down by her sin; her public identity was grounded in it, and she could not hide it. She knew that she needed to receive forgiveness from the only one who could provide it. Her necessity made her bold: She came to Simon the Pharisee's house to wash and anoint Jesus' feet.

Her behavior created quite a spectacle. Simon the Pharisee was quick to condemn her actions and question Jesus' decision to show her compassion. But Jesus turned the tables on him. While the woman was aware of her brokenness—and was all the more grateful for forgiveness—Simon ran with those who had built up a charade of holiness.

Jesus told Simon, "For this reason I tell you, her sins—which were many—have been forgiven, for she loved much. But the one to whom little is forgiven loves little" (Luke 7:47).

Our praise for Jesus—the way we speak of Him and the way we speak of our sin and forgiveness—is a reflection of the state of our hearts. Because our hearts are inclined to be prideful, it's often easier for us to defend our sin than to confess it. It's easier to go about our religious activities while rationalizing our sin. But unless we drop the charade and confess the true state of our hearts, we'll never honor Him as we should. —RVN

Do you "love little"?
What holds you back from expressing praise?

PROCLAIMING THE LIGHT

Isaiah 23:1–24:23; **Luke 8:16–56**; Job 5:17–27

M any of us wait for precisely the right moment to tell others about Christ's work in us. Yet every moment is the right moment to speak up for Christ. Every moment is the right time to fully express what Christ is doing in us and through us.

Jesus affirms this sense of immediacy when He remarks, "And no one, after lighting a lamp, covers it with a jar or puts it under a bed, but puts it on a lamp-stand, so that those who come in can see the light" (Luke 8:16).

This line becomes even more profound when we consider what happens a short time later. After Jesus heals a demon-possessed man, He says to him, "Return to your home and tell all that God has done for you" (Luke 8:39). The man doesn't wait for a better time. Instead, "he went away, proclaiming throughout the whole town all that Jesus had done for him" (Luke 8:39).

We may consider our encounter with Christ less significant than a man healed from demon-possession, but we, too, have been delivered out of the darkness and into the light. Like the demon-possessed man, we have been saved by Christ's work. We can all boldly proclaim, as the hymn "Amazing Grace" says, "I once was blind, but now I see."

In the busyness of our lives, focused on the work and worries of the day, it's too easy for us to slip the light of Christ under the bed where no one can see it—and where we cannot see ourselves in its light. Do we talk as much about Christ and His great work as we do about our jobs? If not, perhaps we should rethink our approach. If this life is merely a prologue to the eternal life to come, shouldn't the light become our main focus—both in our conversations and our actions? Why wouldn't we proudly display it for all to see? —JDB

How can you live the light today?
What needs to change in your conversation topics?

AT A GREAT PRICE

Isaiah 25:1–26:21; **Luke 9:1–27**; Job 6:1–13

It's easy to be devoted to a leader or a vision when it doesn't require much of us. In following Jesus, the disciples didn't have that option. They were called to follow Jesus in difficult circumstances—ones that required them to put their lives on the line. After Jesus told His disciples about His impending death and resurrection, He defined the true meaning of discipleship. His words required their immediate response and intense loyalty:

"And he said to them all, 'If anyone wants to come after me, he must deny himself and take up his cross every day and follow me'" (Luke 9:23).

Daily the disciples needed to commit to Him, the kingdom He was ushering in, and the possibility of facing death. We like to quote this verse, but we might not think it applies in the same way today. Because we don't face the same circumstances the disciples faced, we might not take the call to loyalty quite as seriously.

But loyalty shouldn't be dictated by circumstance. Jesus had "to suffer many things and to be rejected by the elders and chief priests and scribes, and to be killed" (Luke 9:22) to reconcile us to God. His sacrifice was incredibly costly; the grace extended to us came at a great price.

His sacrifice—not our circumstances—requires everything from us. It requires that we see our motives, our hopes, our actions—our daily lives—in the perspective of that costly grace. Jesus went on to say, "For what is a person benefited if he gains the whole world but loses or forfeits himself?" (Luke 9:25). The gospel changes everything, and it speaks into every area of our lives. It requires us to deny our own interests. It requires us to take up our cross daily and follow Him. —RVN

How are you taking up your cross daily?
What area of your life do you need to commit to Him?

HAUNTED BY LEVIATHAN

Isaiah 27:1–28:29; Luke 9:28–62; Job 6:14–30

Indiana Jones isn't afraid of anything—until a snake shows up on the scene. Then we hear him mutter, "I hate snakes!" and "Snakes, why did it have to be snakes?" Everyone is afraid of something. Even now your greatest fear is probably creeping through your mind—something completely irrational, like heights, spiders, or dolls.

Like Indy and like us, the ancients had fears as well: They hated snakes. In ancient literature the serpent Leviathan was a symbol of chaos—a great monster to be subdued. When a god subdued Leviathan in the ancient stories, it showed his supremacy.

Isaiah uses the same metaphor to proclaim that Yahweh can destroy all fears: "On that day, Yahweh will punish with his cruel, great and strong sword Leviathan, the fleeing serpent, and Leviathan, the twisting serpent, and he will kill the sea monster that is in the sea" (Isa 27:1). Yahweh Himself mentions Leviathan when He responds to Job, who had suffered the loss of all he had: "Can you draw out Leviathan with a fishhook? Or can you tie down its mouth with a cord?" (Job 41:1).

When we struggle, it's easy to focus on the Leviathans in our life, but God wants us to focus on His majesty. God can provide what we need. He can bring goodness in the midst of heartbreak (Isa 27:6). Perhaps this is why Jesus allowed Peter, James, and John to see Him in His glory (Luke 9:28–35). He knew that they needed to understand that His glory was more powerful than anything they feared. Perhaps this is also why Jesus repeatedly pushed back the powers of darkness in front of His followers (e.g., Luke 9:37–43); He showed them that He could subdue anything He encountered.

When the Lord of the universe, who crushes the head of the great Leviathan, is in our corner, we have nothing to fear. All powers of darkness should tremble, for He is creating a great vineyard for us out of the chaos (Isa 27:2). If only Indy had known. —JDB

What goodness is God making out of the fear in your life?

August 14

◦ ◦◦◦ ◦

BEING BUSY

Isaiah 29:1–30:17; **Luke 10:1–42**; Job 7:1–10

Sometimes it's difficult to deal with quiet. For most people, chaos, deadlines, managing multiple schedules, and being "so busy" are a way of life. And if we're honest with ourselves, we like it. Busyness implies we are special and valued and the work we're doing is necessary. And we have a desperate need to be valued.

When others failed to recognize Martha's work—when Mary didn't hold to the same values—she complained to Jesus. He responded by rebuking her: "Martha, Martha, you are anxious and troubled about many things! But few things are necessary, or only one thing, for Mary has chosen the better part, which will not be taken away from her" (Luke 10:41–42).

What is the "better part"? Mary "sat at the feet of Jesus and was listening to his teaching" (Luke 10:39), and Jesus praised her desire to listen and learn. Mary was captivated by the "one thing" that would change the world: Jesus and the kingdom He was ushering in. Jesus showed Martha that she should also give Him this reception—being willing to learn, not anxious about her busy schedule. He asked her to shift her perspective.

Choosing the "better part" doesn't invalidate the things we're busy with; indeed, Martha's work served the needs of others. But the things we do shouldn't shape our identity. The "one thing" that should shape our identity— the one thing we really need—is Jesus. Ultimately, it's the desire to know Him and serve Him that should shape our lives. And whatever is not dedicated to that service is not among "the few things [that] are necessary." —RVN

What things are you busy with? Why?

LETHAL PLANNING

Isaiah 30:18–32:20; Luke 11:1–36; Job 7:11–21

I'm a planner. I love schedules. The trouble is I sometimes make plans without consulting God. While I often think of this as a modern problem, I've discovered that, like many other modern issues, the Bible regularly addresses it. For example, in Isaiah 30:1 Yahweh declares, "Oh rebellious children! … to make a plan, but not from me, and pour out a libation, but not from my Spirit, so as to add sin to sin."

Apparently, God's people had been offering libations—a type of drink offering—in the ways of the Egyptians rather than in the ways of Yahweh. We make the same mistake in our lives. We seek wisdom in books or from people before consulting Yahweh. We ask our colleagues what they think before turning to our God. We look to our parents or friends instead of waiting patiently on God's resolve. We look to our own strength or influence instead of relying on the God who created us.

In our demeanor toward God, we are so much like Israel relying on Egypt—we look to others and to ourselves for salvation rather than to God. We have removed the miraculous from our faith. Instead of asserting that God will change the course of history, we determine that we will do it. Although God certainly uses us in this work, salvation doesn't come from our efforts—it comes from Yahweh. Rather than seeking to align our already formed plans with God's, we must approach Him with an open mind and a willing heart. We must find the answers we seek in Him. —JDB

How can you seek God today in all that you do?
How can you look to Him first and make Him foremost?

NO FEAR AND FULL CONFIDENCE

Isaiah 33:1–17; **Luke 11:37–12:21**; Job 8:1–10

J esus didn't exactly follow social niceties as a dinner guest. Once again while dining with a Pharisee, He exposed the hypocrisy that was rampant among those religious leaders: "Now you Pharisees cleanse the outside of the cup and of the dish, but your inside is full of greediness and wickedness" (Luke 11:39). The "woes" He followed with challenged His host and, by extension, the Pharisees in general.

His boldness is a trait He wanted to pass on to His disciples: "But nothing is concealed that will not be revealed, and secret that will not be made known" (Luke 12:2). The gospel message will not be kept secret; the new kingdom is coming into being.

Jesus wanted the disciples to be fearless among people because it is God who is in charge, not the Pharisees; they had built up a false construct of authority. And although they may have exercised authority—they could kill and spread fear—they weren't ultimately in charge.

God is in charge: "But I will show you whom you should fear: fear the one who has authority, after the killing, to throw you into hell! Yes, I tell you, fear this one! Are not five sparrows sold for two pennies? And not one of them is forgotten in the sight of God. But even the hairs of your head are all numbered! Do not be afraid; you are worth more than many sparrows" (Luke 12:5–7).

When we're overwhelmed by rampant sin and evil around us—even in us—it's comforting to maintain this sure knowledge. It is God who both judges and gives life. If we confess Jesus as God, we have nothing to fear. We can be bold in trials and have confidence in Him. —RVN

What confidence do you have in your trials?
How can you place your trust in God rather than people?

ANXIETY AND THE WILDERNESS

Isaiah 35:1–37:13; Luke 12:22–59; Job 8:11–22

Anxiety has a way of ruling over us. Although many of our concerns are legitimate—like having money to pay the rent and buy food—some of them are nonsensical. We envision future catastrophes and spend our days worrying about what might never happen, creating an emotional wilderness for ourselves.

Anxiety isn't new. The prophet Isaiah addresses the problem: "Wilderness and dry land shall be glad, and desert shall rejoice and blossom like the crocus. … Say to those who are hasty of heart, 'Be strong; you must not fear! Look! Your God will come with vengeance, with divine retribution. He is the one who will come and save you'" (Isa 35:1, 4).

Isaiah realizes that there is a time and season for everything. He proclaims that God will bring the people out of the wilderness (their exile in Babylon) and back into their land. There is an answer to the anxiety, pain, and worry that they feel about the future. His words ring with prophetic certainty because he knows them to be true—they are Yahweh's words.

Jesus also addresses anxiety when He says to His disciples, "For this reason I tell you, do not be anxious for your life, what you will eat, or for your body, what you will wear. For life is more than food, and the body more than clothing. Consider the ravens, that they neither sow nor reap; to them there is neither storeroom nor barn, and God feeds them. How much more are you worth than the birds?" (Luke 12:22–24).

Why must we worry? Why must we strive over things we cannot change? Ultimately, everything in life is a matter of depending on God. —JDB

What anxieties can you hand over to God today?

∘ ∘ ◦ ∘ ∘

CONNECTING THE DOTS

Isaiah 37:14–38:22; Luke 13:1–35; **Job 9:1–11**

When we don't have all the facts, we still like to connect the dots. Questions make us uncomfortable, so we draw lines with answers that make us feel safe and that fit our worldview. But sometimes we hold too tightly to the picture that results.

Job's friends were guilty of this error. Although they affirmed true things about God's character, they connected the dots in unhelpful ways. For example, in Job 8, Bildad pointed to God's justice and stated that Job's hardship couldn't be for nothing. Therefore, he must have sinned. Job also affirmed God's justice, wisdom, and strength, but he didn't buy into Bildad's worldview. In Job 9, he acknowledged that God was beyond his understanding. Job might have suffered, but he kept his high opinion of God.

Job wanted answers, too. He longed for God to make Himself known and settle the matter (Job 9:3). Job mourned that he had no way of defending himself before God: "There is no arbiter between us that he might lay his hand on both of us. May he remove his rod from me, and let his dread not terrify me; then I would speak and not fear him, for in myself I am not fearful" (Job 9:33–35). In the end, when Job requested an answer from God—who alone could answer his questions—God silenced him. He restored Job's prosperity, but Job still had to live without knowing why.

When we don't have the answer, we should still affirm God's love and goodness, acknowledging that "He is the one who does great things beyond understanding and marvelous things beyond number" (Job 9:10). And we do have one answer that quiets our fretful hearts—we know the arbiter and what He has done for us, which makes it easier to live with the unanswered questions. —RVN

*How are you sharing the good news of Jesus
with someone who is dealing with difficult questions?*

○ ○ ◉ ○ ○

THE COST OF COMFORT

Isaiah 39:1–40:31; Luke 14:1–35; Job 9:12–19

"'Comfort my people,' says your God. 'Speak to the heart of Jerusalem, and call to her, that her compulsory labor is fulfilled, that her sin is paid for, that she has received from the hand of Yahweh double for all her sins'" (Isa 40:1–2). God directed this command at the prophet and a group of people—possibly all those remaining in Israel. They were to speak comfort to the exiled Israelites, to call them home again.

Sometimes we feel the need for this kind of comfort. Like the prodigal son in the pig sty, we feel exiled and alone; we have paid our sentence, and we want to go home. We're not even asking for joy—just comfort. Despite their sins, God responded to the Israelites. But God did not merely restore them to their former state. He sent the Suffering Servant, prophesied later in Isaiah (Isa 52:13–53:12), to die on behalf of the people, to pay for the sins that resulted in exile in the first place. God does this so that all our sins—past, present and future—might be paid once and for all.

But God requires much from those to whom much has been given, which is all of us. The great news of the Suffering Servant, Jesus, is not only that we find comfort and peace in Him, but also that we are empowered to act—free from sin. As Jesus' disciples, we must live the way that He has called us to live, being willing to make the sacrifices that discipleship requires (e.g., Luke 14:25–35).

The grace we receive from God is free, but a great price was paid for it. We must live fully in it. We must embrace it with our entire being. For when we do, we become not just a comforted people, but a restored people, instruments of God's work in the world. —JDB

What is God calling you to sacrifice?
How can you take joy in the comfort He has
brought you, and then show others that joy?

August 20

◦ ◊ ◊ ◦ ◦

THE PURSUIT OF FAILURES

Isaiah 41:1–42:9; **Luke 15:1–32**; Job 9:20–24

Often, when we focus too much on our own failures, we don't reach the point where grace changes us. That's why the parable of the Prodigal Son is so comforting for people who are caught up and brought down by their failures. In this parable it's not the younger son's humility or the elder brother's jealousy in the limelight. It's the father's pursuit of both his sons.

After living selfishly and squandering his inheritance, the younger son realized how foolish his actions had been. He realized that even his father's hired hands received more love and attention than he had received after leaving his father's house. Deciding to plead for mercy, the younger son rehearsed his request to the father: "I will set out and go to my father and will say to him, 'Father, I have sinned against heaven and in your sight! I am no longer worthy to be called your son! Make me like one of your hired workers'" (Luke 15:18–19).

But his plan was interrupted. Before the son even finished his request, his father kissed him, put a robe around his neck, and ordered the fattened calf to be killed. And then the father repeated this action. When the elder son refused to attend the party in his brother's honor, the father again went out to meet his son, imploring him to rejoice as well (Luke 15:28, 31–32).

God pursues failures of all types. It's His grace extended to us that works in our hearts to prompt change in us. Even when we neglect Him, He pursues us. Even when we don't return His attentions, He pursues us. Instead of focusing on our failures, then, we should focus on His love. —RVN

How do you take joy in God's grace to you through His Son?
How does His love change the way you relate to Him?

August 21

∘ ◦ ◊ ◦ ∘

TRANSITIONS

Isaiah 42:10–43:28; Luke 16:1–17:10; Job 9:25–35

Life is marked by seasons—times of great difficulty and times of great joy. Usually we focus on making the transition from pain to relief as quickly as possible, but in the process, we may forget the significance of the transition itself. A transition is an opportunity to contemplate: Who is acting to move us from one season of our lives to the next? Why does winter give way to spring?

"Sing a new song to Yahweh; praise him from the end of the earth, you who go down to the sea and that which fills it, the coastlands and their inhabitants. Let the desert and its towns lift up their voice, the villages that Kedar inhabits. Let the inhabitants of Sela sing for joy; let them shout loudly from the top of the mountains. Let them give glory to Yahweh and declare his praise in the coastlands" (Isa 42:10–12).

This song of praise moves from the "end of the earth" inward, from region to region, until the whole world is involved. Yahweh is renewing everything. The world is moving from a despairing place to a place of order, which is great news. But the great news is not only the joy of renewal—it's also the way that it all comes about.

Yahweh brings war to create order (Isa 42:13). He leads the blind (Isa 42:16). He turns darkness into light (Isa 42:16). We often want healing and joy to descend on us suddenly, like a flash of lightning. But for joy to grow in our lives and in our world, great evils must first be stamped out. Like the gradual return of plants and sunlight in the spring, joy comes during and through Yahweh's patient work. We must embrace the nature of His work, and the difficulty of it, as much as we embrace the results. —JDB

What transitions are you in?
How can you depend on Yahweh in the midst of them?
What are you learning about Him in the process?

COMPLAINTS

Isaiah 44:1–45:13; Luke 17:11–18:8; **Job 10:1–10**

Complaining can be automatic. We complain about the weather, our children, our jobs. Although we might complain lightly, we still betray something about our hearts. We assume that we are owed something—that we are entitled.

We might readily admit this. We might freely say that this should not be our posture before people or before God. But Job challenges our stereotype of the complainer. In his outcries, we find someone struggling to understand his situation before God. He prays, "My inner self loathes my life; I want to give vent to my complaint; I want to speak out of the bitterness of my inner self. I will say to God, 'You should not condemn me; let me know why you contend against me'" (Job 10:1–2). He repeats and recasts his elevated and prolonged complaints in surprising similes: "Did you not pour me out like milk and curdle me like cheese?" (Job 10:10).

Although his boldness and forcefulness might be shocking to us, we also understand how someone dealing with pain and grief might wrestle with these thoughts.

The book of Job ends with God silencing Job and his friends. Job's demeanor changes when God sets everyone's perspective right. But how should we understand these passages? Should we complain like Job when we feel frustrated by the disappointments in life?

Job's complaints stemmed from a sense of loss—a realization that something was not right with the current state of affairs. This doesn't mean that all complaints are motivated by complete ingratitude. Sin, loss, injustice, hurt, and evil in the world are not reasons to dismiss our cares. Indeed, God is concerned about our cares, and He wants to know them.

But the things we wrestle with should first be brought to God. We should bring our complaints to Him, ready to have our hearts and minds examined by His Word. Not only is He very concerned about our circumstances, but He also knows our hearts and can judge our complaints rightly. He can comfort us in sorrow and provide us with all that we need. Jesus died to set right the things that are wrong with the world, so we can be completely assured of His love and care for us. —RVN

How are you responding to events in your life?
How can you bring your complaints to Him?

August 23

○ ○ ◊ ○ ○

GOD THE INNOVATOR

Isaiah 45:14–47:15; Luke 18:9–19:10; Job 10:11–22

Innovators often say they learn more from their failures than their successes. The successes come as a result of repeated failures, whether in business or in life. We must learn from our mistakes if we are to expect a different, brighter future.

God expects us to learn from our failures—the depths of which we can best understand in comparison to the glory of His successes. God speaks about Himself not only to remind people of His abilities, but also to explain where His authority begins and theirs ends.

In Isaiah 45:1–2, God gave Cyrus a lesson in these boundaries—both by what He said and by what He did not say. Like other kings of the time, Cyrus would have thought himself godlike, but God's detailed description of what He was about to do left Cyrus with no doubt about who was in charge:

"And I will give you the treasures of darkness and treasures of secret places so that you may know that I am Yahweh, the one who calls you by your name, the God of Israel, for the sake of my servant Jacob, and Israel my chosen one. And I call you by your name; I give you a name of honor, though you do not know me" (Isa 45:3–4).

From Cyrus' perspective, he had all authority and could accomplish all things. He did not yet know the Master Innovator who can reverse any situation and honor any person as an instrument in accomplishing His larger plan—to restore His people. God blessed Cyrus with wealth so that it would be easy for him to help God's people. God exercised authority over the economy to create a new spiritual economy. Cyrus may have pointed to his achievements, but God had enabled them all.

As God created the circumstances for Cyrus to succeed—and for His people to be blessed—He also showed the Israelites His perspective on failure and success. In His power and compassion, He could work in difficult and unexpected ways to bring about their redemption, despite their many failures. The Israelites may have gotten themselves into a horrible situation, but God could make a way to get them out. —JDB

What innovations is God making in your life story?
In the process, is He teaching you to completely depend on Him?

August 24

○ ○ ○ ○ ○

WHO IS TRUSTWORTHY?

Isaiah 48:1–49:26; **Luke 19:11–48**; Job 11:1–12

We might get sidetracked when reading the parable of the Ten Minas. Businessmen aren't sympathetic characters in our modern world. In movies and sometimes in life, they're often flat, miserly characters who take advantage of naïve individuals and community values.

Although there is often an element of truth to some stereotypes, it can be too easy to take sides. And we're forced to take sides in this parable. Whose view is correct—the people of the city who hate the nobleman, the fearful servant, or the nobleman and his faithful servants?

The response of the masses seems unjustified. The two servants entrusted with minas are faithful characters, but not the focus of the parable. When the final servant is summoned, we expect an interesting turn of events. Will we sympathize with him? We've already heard that the citizens hate the nobleman, and the final servant seems to confirm this: "For I was afraid of you, because you are a severe man—you withdraw what you did not deposit, and you reap what you did not sow!" (Luke 19:21).

But it's not the final servant who provides the climactic turn of events that we're looking for—it's the nobleman. Instead of punishing the servant for disobeying His commands, the nobleman holds the servant accountable to his own perceived value system: "By your own words I will judge you, wicked slave! You knew that I am a severe man, withdrawing what I did not deposit and reaping what I did not sow. And why did you not give my money to the bank, and I, when I returned, would have collected it with interest?" (Luke 19:22–23). Rather than letting him off the hook, the nobleman points out that the servant is inconsistent. He has been making excuses for his unfaithfulness all along.

Because we're imperfect characters, we need to be ready and willing to take an honest look at the lenses with which we view the world: our hearts. If we're ready to live faithfully, we need to look to the only trustworthy character—the one who sacrificed everything for us. —RVN

How do you rationalize or interpret Scripture
in a way that makes you less accountable?
Do you have someone in your life who challenges you? Why or why not?

○ ○○○ ○

RIDDLE ME THIS

Isaiah 50:1–51:23; Luke 20:1–40; Job 11:12–20

J esus' enemies regularly attempted to make Him look foolish or to disprove His authority. The absurd questions they concocted to discredit Him are rather amusing. The Sadducees posed one of the most preposterous questions about the resurrection of the dead and its relevance to divorce (Luke 20:27–33): If a woman has been married seven times, whose wife will she be when the dead are resurrected?

This scene is especially humorous in light of rabbis' habit of playing mind games to outsmart (or "outwise") one another and the Sadducees' belief that resurrection does not exist. Jesus' opponents thought they had rigged the game: Any answer to their riddle would be incorrect. It was an attempt to trap Jesus into agreeing that the resurrection of the dead is a myth. Jesus, however, offered an answer that put them in their place (Luke 20:34–40). His response made the Sadducees look even more foolish in light of larger biblical theology about marriage and divorce.

More than 500 years before this conversation, Isaiah remarked, "Thus says Yahweh: 'Where is this divorce document of your mother's divorce, with which I dismissed her? or to whom of my creditors did I sell you? Look! you were sold because of your sin, and your mother was dismissed because of your transgressions'" (Isa 50:1). The Sadducees—along with the entire nation of Israel—had already been condemned for not honoring marriage in life.

So often we are concerned with logistics or details when our energy should be spent on discerning God's will for our lives and whether we are in that will. Like the Sadducees, we tell ourselves witty lies to get around doing the will of God. We somehow believe that if we can *reason* our way forward, we can justify our inactions. But as Jesus taught the Sadducees, in any game of riddles or reason, faith will always win. —JDB

> *What are you wrongly justifying*
> *or "witting" yourself out of doing?*

August 26

∘∘∘∘∘

LIVES OF SPIRITUAL OPULENCE

Isaiah 52:1–54:17; **Luke 20:41–21:24**; Job 12:1–12

The Pharisees upheld a faulty religious system. They were supposed to be the Jews' spiritual leaders, but they were more interested in making themselves the religious elite. They loved "greetings in the marketplace and the best seats in the synagogues and the places of honor at banquets" (Luke 20:46). Their ministry was built on the backs of the poor.

In contrast, the widow depicted in Luke 21 chose to give all she had. Because she had so little, her generosity was sacrificial. Those who gave out of abundance didn't feel the loss of income like she did. But the contrast between the widow and the Pharisees shows us much more. Luke says that *spiritual* wealth can be present where we least expect it—that things aren't always as they appear.

Although Jesus is the long-anticipated Messiah, following Him is never going to bring a life of glory and fame. Jesus is ushering in a kingdom like a mustard seed (Luke 13:18–19) or yeast (Luke 13:20–21). It will grow and swell through perseverance rather than praise. It requires a life of sacrifice like the widow's, not the glory-seeking of the Pharisees.

Through these examples, Jesus warned his disciples to look beneath the shiny veneer for something more valuable. It would have been tempting simply to follow those in charge—in some ways it would have been much easier. But piety that pleases God isn't found in striving after position or place. Following Jesus means sacrifice and service. —RVN

How are you serving God with everything you have?

MY MOMMA DONE TOL' ME

Isaiah 55:1–57:21; Luke 21:25–22:23; Job 12:13–25

I went through a phase when I was obsessed with the blues. Something about the soul was at work in the music—a genre created late at night while reflecting on hard times. The music was written more for the songwriter than the audience because the audience had usually gone home by the time these songs were sung. The blues express raw, uncut emotions. The same can be said of the Old Testament prophets.

A blues singer can turn a common phrase into something profound. The idea that "I knew better, but I made the mistake anyway" becomes the blues refrain "my momma done tol' me," complete with chord structure and growling voice. And "I'm struggling—everything is falling apart" becomes "my dog done died." The prophets likewise use mundane things like water and food to describe emotional and spiritual struggles. They explain the root of the problem—the cause of our ills: "Ho! Everyone thirsty, come to the waters! And whoever has no money, come, buy and eat, and come, buy without money, wine and milk without price! Why do you weigh out money for what is not food, and your labor for what cannot satisfy? Listen carefully to me, and eat what is good, and let your soul take pleasure in rich food" (Isa 55:1–2).

Jesus did the same thing as the prophet—but on a much grander scale—when He turned the idea of bread and wine into a symbol of His sacrifice for all humanity: "'For I tell you that I will not eat it until it is fulfilled in the kingdom of God.' And he took bread, and after giving thanks, he broke it and gave it to them, saying, 'This is my body which is given for you. Do this in remembrance of me.' And in the same way the cup after they had eaten, saying, 'This cup is the new covenant in my blood which is poured out for you'" (Luke 22:16, 19–20).

But Jesus wasn't singing the blues about His broken body and His blood poured out; He was turning the phrase for a new purpose. Jesus' work turns *our* blues into beauty. —JDB

*What mundane things is God—through the redemptive act
of Christ—turning from blues to beauty in your life?*

○ ○ ○ ○ ○

MEANINGLESS MAXIMS

Isaiah 58:1–59:21; Luke 22:24–62; **Job 13:1–12**

"Your maxims are proverbs of ashes; your defenses are defenses of clay" (Job 13:12). There were bits of truth in the words spoken by Jobs' friends, Eliphaz, Bildad, and Zophar. Between their blundering interpretations were words that expressed God's majesty, justice, and sovereignty. Unfortunately, they pieced together their bits of truth and applied them incorrectly to Job's life.

Job quickly saw through their packaged solution. However, not all those struggling with loss can handle an onslaught of helpful Christians with easy answers. When people go through difficult times and ask for advice—or even if they don't— it's tempting to deliver our responses based on our own experiences. Eliphaz argued this way: "Just as I have seen, plowers of mischief and sowers of trouble will reap it" (Job 4:8).

The way we interpret and respond to events in our lives is often Scripture-based and Spirit-led. Although we should readily provide encouragement to those who struggle, we shouldn't always encourage others toward the same application. Our responses to those in need should be carefully weighed, and they should always guide others to Scripture, the good news, and the work of the Spirit. Ultimately, these are the means through which truth speaks into our experiences. We should never intend for our guidance to be the final authority in others' lives. —RVN

How are you helping others understand
their pain and sorrow?

August 29

○ ○ ◊ ○ ○

BECOMING A SAVED PEOPLE

Isaiah 60:1–62:12; Luke 22:63–23:25; Job 13:13–28

For Luke, Jesus is the fulfillment of the prophet Isaiah's message. At the beginning of Jesus' ministry, according to Luke, Jesus opened the Isaiah scroll in a synagogue and proclaimed that the words in Isaiah 61 are about Him (Luke 4:17–19): "The Spirit of the Lord Yahweh is upon me, because Yahweh has anointed me, he has sent me to bring good news to the oppressed, to bind up the brokenhearted, to proclaim release to the captives and liberation to those who are bound, to proclaim the year of Yahweh's favor, and our God's day of vengeance, to comfort all those in mourning" (Isa 61:1–2). This moment defines what Jesus' life would mean—and He was immediately persecuted for claiming the authority rightfully given to Him by God (Luke 4:20–30).

Luke's message—an extension of Isaiah's—is played out further near the end of Jesus' life. Jesus' claim to authority resulted in His being sentenced to death (Luke 23). It is easy to view the events of Jesus' life as proof that He was the figure that Isaiah prophesied—that He was exactly who He said He was. But if we stop there, we miss the larger picture. Luke has an agenda: He draws on Isaiah and uses the story of Jesus reading in the synagogue because he intends for our lives to be changed by Jesus. We are the oppressed receiving the good news. We are the captives being liberated. We are meant to be a people called out to follow Him (Isa 40:1–2; 53:10–12).

When we look upon Jesus—the Suffering Servant, Messiah, prophet, and savior—we should be confronted with the reality that we're still so far from what He has called us to be. We should be prompted to put Him at the center of our lives. We should be prompted to change. We must realize our place as the people He has saved and respond with gratitude. —JDB

How is Jesus' sacrifice changing your life?

DAWNING OF A NEW ERA

Isaiah 63:1–64:12; **Luke 23:26–24:12**; Job 14:1–10

Jesus' resurrection brings a new era. Although Jesus told His disciples and loved ones that He would suffer, die, and be raised on the third day (Luke 9:22), they didn't fully comprehend His promise. The women preparing fragrant spices and perfumes for a burial ritual fully expected to find Jesus' body in the tomb.

Instead, at the dawn of the first day of the week, they found the stone rolled away and the tomb empty. The women were perplexed by their discovery, but the angels challenged them, reminding them of Jesus' promise: "Why are you looking for the living among the dead? He is not here, but has been raised! Remember how he spoke to you while he was still in Galilee, saying that the Son of Man must be delivered into the hands of men who are sinners, and be crucified, and on the third day rise?" (Luke 24:5–7).

Jesus' resurrection presents new hope for the disciples and those who believe in Him. It also shows that He prophesied correctly about God's saving plan—presenting new hope for us. Jesus has the victory; death has no power over Him. By believing in Him, we share in His death and resurrection, giving us incredible hope as we face life, and death. Not only this, but we live knowing that our Savior is alive and acting on our behalf. We live in a new era. —RVN

How are you living in the hope of Jesus' resurrection?

○ ○ ◊ ○ ○

WALKING WITH JESUS

Isaiah 65:1–66:24; **Luke 24:13–53**; Job 14:11–22

Imagine encountering Jesus on the road to Emmaus. It would be a surreal experience. You're walking to the next town, and you start a conversation with a man beside you, only to find out later that you've been talking with the resurrected Son of God. Even more surreal, the topic of conversation up to your moment of discovery has been the death of the man walking with you (Luke 24:13–35).

I have often wondered what it would be like to meet Jesus face to face—to have Him explain to me how He exists in the biblical text from Moses, in all the prophets, and in all Scripture (Luke 24:27). How different would my life be after that experience? Would I rethink everything I had known and heard—perhaps everything I do?

Asking these questions is not only healthy, it also turns on our spiritual GPS. Are we on the path God has called us to? Have we strayed in one direction or another? Are we caught in some odd roundabout where we're explaining to Jesus what His coming means?

Many Christians—not just scholars and preachers—complicate matters of salvation. We overthink God's work or place it at a distance from our daily lives. Like the old saying, we become "too big for our britches," forgetting that, ultimately, the entire Bible points to Jesus and His redeeming work.

Jesus' work is real and surreal. In the Bible, He is present everywhere. In our lives, He is present in every aspect and every moment. We need only to acknowledge Him and act upon the truth of His message. That simple idea is what it means to walk the road with our Savior. —JDB

How can you walk more aligned with the Savior?

AN UNUSUAL PORTRAIT

Hosea 1:1–2:23; **Acts 1:1–26**; Job 15:1–9

"At the beginning when Yahweh spoke through Hosea, Yahweh said to Hosea, 'Go, take for yourself a wife and children of whoredom, because the land commits great whoredom forsaking Yahweh.' So he went and took Gomer daughter of Diblaim, and she conceived and bore him a son" (Hos 1:2–3). God's people had prostituted themselves to other nations by seeking their help instead of Yahweh's. Hosea's act, which dramatized the rebellion of God's people against Him, is one of the oddest in the Bible.

God loves His people with passion and jealousy. He has little tolerance when they seek alliances with other nations and put false gods before Him. At times, He takes shocking measures to get their attention. The act He requires of Hosea not only depicts Israel's unfaithfulness, but it also reveals God's own feelings of betrayal. Many of us can empathize.

At such moments in the Bible, it's hard to understand how God uses such behavior to further His plan. But within the view of biblical theology, desperate situations like Hosea's are transformed into redemptive scenes. Such is the case when we open the book of Acts: "I produced the former account [of the Gospel of Luke], O Theophilus, about all that Jesus began to do and to teach, until the day he was taken up, after he had given orders through the Holy Spirit to the apostles whom he had chosen, to whom he also presented himself alive after he suffered, with many convincing proofs, appearing to them over a period of forty days and speaking the things about the kingdom of God" (Acts 1:1–3). Jesus came to redeem a people who sought refuge in the arms of false gods and other nations.

When we see Hosea's story in the light of Jesus' acts and the subsequent acts of His apostles, we learn that God can indeed bring even the most wretched of people to righteousness. We also learn that sometimes it takes a vivid, if odd, real-life portrait for us to understand the truth about our false ways. —JDB

Are you seeking refuge in the wrong places or the wrong ways?
What are you placing before Yahweh and His work in your life?

○ ○ ○ ○ ○

ONLY THE VERY BEGINNING

Hosea 3:1–5:15; **Acts 2:1–41**; Job 15:10–20

Beginnings are exciting. The freshness of a new project or a new relationship sharpens our senses. When that novelty diminishes, though, it's difficult to maintain the same level of excitement.

Acts 2 is all about beginnings. In this passage we get an inside view of how God worked to gather a new community of believers to Himself. Pentecost and the arrival of the Holy Spirit signaled a new era and produced a new community, as both Jews and "devout men from every nation under heaven" converted to the Christian faith (Acts 2:5).

From where we stand, it's easy for us to see Pentecost as the pivotal moment in the history of the Church—an unparalleled event that changed the world forever. Magnificent things happened. Peter gave a moving testimony. Three thousand people came to faith.

When we celebrate the holiday of Pentecost, however, we are remembering the firstfruits of the harvest—the coming of the Holy Spirit and the original community of believers under Jesus Christ. Firstfruits are only the start of a harvest; they hint at future abundance. The wonders that began at Pentecost are still happening today. God is active and present in our lives, just as He was gathering His Church then.

We need a fresh perspective. We need the motivation and the boldness of Peter. We need to rekindle our original excitement when announcing that the kingdom of heaven is at hand, because He is at work, in us and around us. —RVN

How are you sharing this hope?

THE DISCOMFORT OF SCRIPTURE

Hosea 6:1–7:16; **Acts 2:42–3:26**; Job 15:21–35

Most of the Western world operates in the spirit of individualism. Christianity does not, though we often attempt to adapt it and make it more comfortable. It's much easier to think about "God's role in *my* life" than to reflect on "my role in *God's plan*" to help others and share the gospel.

When we attempt to shape our faith to fit our needs, we're bound to run into Scripture that makes us squirm. Some people perform interpretive backflips to wriggle out of passages such as Acts 2:42–47. Verse 44 says, "And all who believed were in the same place, and had everything in common." A fear of socialism serves as a convenient excuse to sidestep this verse, but it doesn't speak to socialism. It speaks to voluntarily joining a movement of people who care more about the betterment of the group than they do about their individual gain.

The truth is that God's Word should make us uncomfortable because we are the ones who need to conform. None of us wants to accept Acts 2:44 unless the Spirit has worked within us. Acting out our faith means we must be willing to donate what we have to help others: time, material goods, money—whatever God calls us to give. Self-sacrifice is not easy for anyone, but it becomes easier when the Spirit prompts our hearts to see the needs of others as more important than our wants.

Most people in the Western world choose the sin of selfishness over selfless service to others. Do we need to buy a coffee every morning, or could we make a cup at home? Do we need to live in a larger house, or could we downsize? Nearly all of us can find ways to give more by living with less. And we might find the motive we need when the Spirit speaks to us through the discomfort of Scripture. —JDB

How can you give what you have to help others?
What sacrifice can you make today, this week, or this month?
Who do you know who's in need?

○ ○ ◐ ○ ○

UTOPIAN TRUTH FOR TODAY

Hosea 8:1–10:15; **Acts 4:1–37**; Job 16:1–9

Wealth often tempts us to materialism, as our possessions make us feel secure, valued, and comfortable. But sometimes the lack of these assets allows this temptation to exert even more power over us, driving us to spend our lives chasing the higher salary, the bigger house, or the new car. Our pursuit of this illusion makes it easy to dismiss passages like Acts 4 as utopian fantasy—ideal for difficult times, perhaps, but hardly realistic.

"Now the group of those who believed were one heart and soul, and no one said anything of what belonged to him was his own, but all things were theirs in common. And with great power the apostles were giving testimony to the resurrection of the Lord Jesus, and great grace was on them all. For there was not even anyone needy among them, because all those who were owners of plots of land or houses were selling them and bringing the proceeds of the things that were sold" (Acts 4:32–34).

We too easily find ways to distance ourselves from the selfless acts of the early believers. Sell plots of land or houses? Give it all away? That doesn't seem reasonable. Won't people take advantage of us? Won't they grow lazy and begin to feel entitled?

The early church responded differently. They responded to the testimony of the resurrection of the Lord Jesus with concrete acts of faith. They saw Christ as Lord over all they previously regarded as their personal possessions. They were so united in purpose and prayer that the things they owned mattered little unless they could be used in service to others—in doing the work of Christ.

No matter where we stand financially, we need a new mindset. If it's difficult to imagine changing our lifestyle to help someone in need, then we need to examine our hearts. If we cling to the belief that our possessions give us security, value, and comfort, then we need to examine our faith. Either way, we have to assess our possessions, talents, and time, consider the people in our lives, and make decisions that are governed by the values of a new kingdom. —RVN

How can you better use your money, possessions,
time, and talents to serve others?

I LOVED YOU; I LOVE YOU NOW

Hosea 11:1–12:14; Acts 5:1–42; Job 16:10–22

"When Israel was a child, I loved him, and out of Egypt I called my son" (Hos 11:1). This line is beautiful if read alone, but it is sad when read in context: "When I called them, they went from my face. They sacrificed to the Baals, and they sacrificed to idols" (Hos 11:2). It's incredible how quickly we forget God's mercy and provision. All too soon we return to putting our desires before His.

When we put things in front of God's will—false gods and our own misguided ways (Baals and idols)—we thwart His will not only for our lives, but also for the lives of others. For each of us, God has a tremendous plan that also affects others, for His glory and for the betterment of the world. When we fail to seek His will, we neglect our faith and operate by our own agenda, setting His work aside.

Our missteps can have terribly painful consequences: "The sword rages in [my people's] cities; it consumes [their] false prophets and devours because of their plans. My people are bent on backsliding from me. To the Most High they call, he does not raise them at all" (Hos 11:6–7).

We endanger ourselves when we backslide. Sin tears at our very souls. Yet God is loving. Unlike us, He doesn't act out of vengeance but out of His perfect will: "I will not execute my fierce anger, I will not again destroy Ephraim; because I am God and not a mortal, the Holy One in your midst; and I will not come in wrath. They will go after Yahweh; he roars like a lion. When he roars, his children will come trembling from the sea" (Hos 11:9–10).

God's goodness is not an excuse for our poor behavior; it's the reason to run back to Him—our great lion. Let's let Him roar against the darkness that seeks to capture our desires and our hearts. Let's let Him push back. Let's call upon Yahweh. —JDB

What circumstances in your life prompt you to call on Yahweh today?
What are you battling against?

FAITH FOR EVERY MOMENT

Hosea 13:1–14:9; **Acts 6:1–15**; Job 17:1–16

Sometimes it's tempting to imagine ourselves as the hero of a dramatic scene where we're called upon to give an account of our faith. But in real life, every action and every moment of our lives is a witness—even the ordinary ones. Stephen, a leader in the early church, knew this to be true.

Stephen was appointed by the apostles to care for widows in need because he was "full of faith and of the Holy Spirit" (Acts 6:5). People recognized his witness because he was faithful when no one was watching. His devotion brought him to a place of influence and leadership in the community.

But Stephen didn't limit his witness to one area of leadership. In the next verses, we find him witnessing about Christ by performing great wonders and signs. That's when he came under fire, and his response was above reproach: "And they were not able to resist the wisdom and the Spirit with which he was speaking" (Acts 6:10). His opponents could not find a way to accuse him, so they resorted to spreading rumors (Acts 6:11). But even when Stephen stood accused before the Sanhedrin, he remained firm. Luke describes him as having "the face of an angel" (Acts 6:15), signifying that a sense of peace permeated his witness, where others might have been fearful or defensive.

It's easy to think our witness matters only for world-changing events, but we're in the spotlight all the time. Knowing this, we should be intentional about the way we interact in the small things and in the present time. Pray to be faithful, wise, and full of the Spirit for every moment. —RVN

How do you need to change your
perspective on your witness?

GOD RIDES TO BATTLE

Joel 1:1–2:21; Acts 7:1–53; Job 18:1–21

God is good, but in the words of C. S. Lewis, "He is not tame." When it comes time for evil to be purged from the world, He is not timid, and when He acts, He rarely holds back. We see such a scene prophesied concerning the Day of Yahweh—the day He will return to the earth as Christ—in Joel 2:1–11.

"Blow the trumpet in Zion, and sound the alarm on my holy mountain! Let all the inhabitants of the land tremble, for the day of Yahweh is coming—it is indeed near. A day of darkness and gloom, a day of cloud and thick darkness, like the dawn spreads on the mountains, a great and strong army! There has been nothing like it from old, and after it nothing will be again for generations to come" (Joel 2:1–2).

When God charges into battle, He seizes control of all that must be yielded so His purpose is not hindered. He then performs great and mighty deeds on behalf of His people. As Joel says, "There has been nothing like it." So why, then, has God not done this already? What is He waiting for? Why is evil allowed to continue if God can end it?

We find our answers in Joel 2:12–17. God, in His mercy, is allowing a time of repentance: "'And even now,' declares Yahweh, 'return to me with all your heart, with fasting, and weeping, and wailing. Rend your hearts and not your garments, and return to Yahweh your God, because he is gracious and compassionate, slow to anger and great in loyal love, and relenting from harm'" (Joel 2:12–13).

Indeed, God's trumpet will sound, but even with that time approaching, He is a compassionate God, and His call is simple: "Come back to me." —JDB

What do you need to turn from today?
What makes you hopeful about God's coming?

RESILIENT HOPE
AND RED HERRINGS

Joel 3:1–21; **Acts 7:54–8:25**; Job 19:1–12

The death of Stephen, the first Christian martyr, must have crushed and discouraged the early church. But in this event Luke shows us glimmers of hope. He reminds us that God is working behind the scenes.

Facing death, Stephen prayed for his persecutors, asking that God "not hold this sin against them" (Acts 7:60). God answered that cry of mercy in a generous way. As we watch Stephen being forced out of the city and stoned to death, Luke introduces us to another character present in the crowd: "The witnesses laid aside their cloaks at the feet of a young man named Saul" (Acts 7:54).

This detail seems like a red herring, but by introducing Saul (later Paul) to us before his conversion, Luke gives his readers hope in desperate circumstances. Saul was determined to squelch this dangerous new sect coming out of Nazareth, but soon Paul would become its greatest advocate. By placing Stephen's death alongside Saul's persecution, Luke shows that the church is resilient. Stephen was a source of encouragement and godly leadership for the church. Similarly, and in spite of his beginnings, Paul would expand the influence of the Church far beyond the expectations of its first followers.

In the end, Paul's presence at Stephen's stoning is not an irrelevant detail at all. God already had plans to use Paul's life to further His kingdom work beyond Jerusalem and into the nations of the world. Paul's conversion would be one of the greatest testaments of God's saving work, demonstrating that God works to gather His community in ways we might not see. Even when circumstances seem grim, He is active behind the scenes, ready to use characters in His grand narrative for His good purpose. —RVN

*How can you turn to Jesus
for hope in your hopeless circumstances?*

AS THE LION ROARS

Amos 1:1–4:5; Acts 8:26–9:19; Job 19:13–29

S urely my Lord does not do anything unless he has revealed his secret to his servants the prophets. A lion has roared! Who is not afraid? My Lord Yahweh has spoken, who will not prophesy? Proclaim to the citadel fortresses in Ashdod and the citadel fortresses in the land of Egypt and say: 'Gather on the mountains of Samaria and see the great panic in her midst and the oppression in her midst!'" (Amos 3:7–9).

It's easy to make excuses when we don't know or understand something, and it's equally hard to admit why. Amos declares that God's plan and His work in the world are known to us—if we wish to learn. If we're honest with ourselves, we have to admit that we're not trying hard enough to learn about Him and His work. God speaks through His prophets and through His Word in the Bible, so there is no reason for us to be unaware of how He is working and how He wants to use us in the process.

What was true for the Old Testament prophets was also true for the apostles. Through Philip, we see how God intimately involves people in His work. An angel tells Philip, "Get up and go toward the south on the road that goes down from Jerusalem to Gaza" (Acts 8:26). It took great faith for Philip to do as the angel instructed. The last part of verse 26 adds, "This is a desert place." Few people have encountered an angel, as Philip did, but each of us has the opportunity to experience direction from our Lord.

If we ask, God will answer. If we seek to learn how God is speaking, our path will become clear. Often we make this idea more complicated than it should be, but the work of the prophets and the early church demonstrate otherwise: Amos continued to tell of a fate that indeed came to pass, much of it in his lifetime. Philip took that desert road and led an Ethiopian man to Jesus. There is great, enduring hope for us to be part of God's work if we're willing to seek His will, listen, and act in faith. —JDB

What does God wish for you to know today?

GOD DOESN'T PROMISE EASE OR INVISIBILITY

Amos 4:6–5:27; **Acts 9:20–43**; Job 20:1–11

As Christians, we might be tempted by the lure of invisibility—the fabled cloak or ring that gives us the power to walk undetected among our friends or enemies. Although it is true that "making much of God" means making little of ourselves, we sometimes use this truth as an excuse to avoid proclaiming God's work in our lives. Living under the radar is much more comfortable.

Paul never chose the comfortable route. As a former persecutor of the Church, Paul knew the danger of preaching Christ in the open—the chief priests had once empowered him to imprison all who publically professed Christ (Acts 9:14). Yet as a new convert, Paul loudly proclaimed the name of Christ to anybody within hearing distance: "And he was going in and going out among them in Jerusalem, speaking boldly in the name of the Lord. And he was speaking and debating with the Greek-speaking Jews, but they were trying to do away with him" (Acts 9:28–29).

Most of us know that life as a Christian won't be a life of ease. But what is our image of a life of ease? Is it overstuffed chairs, butlers, and bulging bank accounts? Is it remaining silent when we should confess the name of Christ? Or is it judging from afar when we should be coming alongside people in their pain and brokenness? If we follow Paul's brazen example, we will boldly and wisely share Christ in every possible circumstance. —RVN

Are you choosing invisibility?
How can you boldly and wisely proclaim Christ?

BAD THINGS,
GOOD PEOPLE, AND GRACE

Amos 6:1–7:17; Acts 10:1–33; **Job 20:12–29**

We often wonder why God allows bad things to happen. We're not unique in this; people have asked this same question since the beginning of time. Job struggled with this question after he lost everything. Job's friends strove to answer it as they sought to prove that Job had somehow sinned against God and brought his terrible fate upon himself.

At one point, Job's friend Zophar offers up the common wisdom of the time: "Did you know this from of old, since the setting of the human being on earth, that the rejoicing of the wicked is short, and the joy of the godless lasts only a moment? … [The wicked man] will suck the poison of horned vipers; the viper's tongue will kill [the wicked man]" (Job 20:4–5, 16). Zophar is right about one thing: Eventually the wicked will be punished.

The rest of Zophar's words prove his short-sightedness. The wicked are not always punished immediately. And God does not allow evil to continue without end. Instead, He chooses to intercede at certain times to ensure that His plan stays on course. Furthermore, bad things happen because people are bad—not because God allows or causes evil to happen, and not necessarily because the afflicted people are somehow evil. Evil powers are at work in the world, seeking to thwart God's plan. We, as humanity, chose our fate when we went against God's will that first time and every time since.

God has good news for us. As Peter tells his Gentile audience in Acts, "God anointed Jesus of Nazareth with the Holy Spirit and with power. … They put him to death by hanging him on a tree, but God raised him on the third day … [and] everyone who believes in him receives forgiveness of sins through his name" (Acts 10:38–40, 42 ESV). There is redemption to be found in His Son, who will return to earth to make all things right. Every moment between now and then is a moment of grace. —JDB

How are your beliefs about evil closer to Zophar's than to the truth?
How can you find a new perspective?

DIVERSITY IN THE CHURCH

Amos 8:1–9:15; **Acts 10:34–11:18**; Job 21:1–16

In our comfortable and familiar church homes, we sometimes fail to see the Church as a community of ethnic and cultural diversity. When I returned from a year in South Korea, I was surprised when my family and friends made thoughtless generalizations about people I had come to know and love—some of them fellow believers in Christ. Most of these comments contradicted the multicultural picture of Christianity presented in the book of Acts.

Peter and the Jewish Christians in the early church underwent a shift in cultural perspective. When Peter came to Jerusalem after meeting with Gentiles, the Jews were shocked that he would eat with "men who were uncircumcised" (Acts 11:3). For so long, they had associated their religion with their identity as a nation and as a people group. Although they knew that God was extending this hope to the Gentiles, they needed to be reminded that Jesus was the Lord of all. Peter tells them, "if God gave them the same gift as also to us when we believed in the Lord Jesus Christ, who was I to be able to hinder God?" (Acts 11:17).

The hope they expected had been fulfilled in the person of Jesus Christ. Now Gentiles were being added to their number. Peter testifies, "In truth I understand that God is not one who shows partiality, but in every nation the one who fears him and who does what is right is acceptable to him" (Acts 10:34).

Strangely, Peter's speech still needs to be heard today. We tend to confine our faith within comfortable borders—cultural, regional, or racial. We need to be challenged to see people from other ethnicities and cultural backgrounds as fellow followers of Christ. If God does not show partiality, then neither should we. The reign of Jesus extends over all people; God will draw His children from all corners of the earth, and there will be no "foreigners" in His kingdom. —RVN

How does your view of the Church need to be challenged?

September 13

∘ ∘ ∘ ∘ ∘

WHO CAN BRING ME DOWN?

Obadiah 1:1–21; Acts 11:19–12:25; **Job 21:17–34**

"The pride of your heart has deceived you, you who live in the clefts of a rock, the heights of its dwelling, you who say in your heart: 'Who can bring me down to the ground?'" (Obad 3).

Pride is an especially dangerous sin because it deludes us into elevating ourselves above everyone else. It can even lead us to betray or hurt other people. In this passage Obadiah addresses the Edomites, who lived in the hills above Judah. The Edomites should have helped Judah when they were attacked, but instead they conducted raids. They believed that they were superior to and had been wronged by the Judahites and that their actions were therefore justified. This type of pride puts us in a precarious position. No wonder the Bible addresses it often.

Pride can get the best of us when we place ourselves in the "clefts" above others. It usually emerges from one of two places: Either we believe that we're as important as people tell us we are (the folly of the celebrity), or we believe that we're better than everyone else and that others just don't understand us. Either way, pride is dangerous. In the words of C. S. Lewis, "Pride always means enmity ... not only enmity between man and man, but enmity to God."

Job is also accused of pride—but unjustly. He confronts his persecutors about retribution related to pride: "How often is the lamp of the wicked put out, and their disaster comes upon them? He distributes pains in his anger" (Job 21:17). Job recognizes the ultimate source of pride: a refusal to fear Yahweh. It's difficult to maintain a superior position when we realize that everything we have comes from Him. When we fear Yahweh—when we acknowledge that He created and reigns over all things—we discover our rightful place. We can then lift Him back to the place He deserves—as ruler over us, our master. —JDB

What are you prideful about,
and what can you do to remedy the problem?

• 258 •

GOING YOUR OWN WAY

Jonah 1:1–4:11; Acts 13:1–12; Job 22:1–13

I work hard to make my disobedience socially acceptable: "I have a stubborn streak," I explain, or "I'm just like my dad." But the truth is that my weaknesses aren't cute or transitory—and they're not anyone else's fault. Instead, my disobedience is a deep-rooted, rebellious tendency to follow my own path when I should be humbling myself, seeking wisdom, or obeying leaders who know better.

The book of Jonah illustrates these opposing responses to God's will. We can easily identify with Jonah's stubborn character. When God tells Jonah to warn Nineveh of its coming judgment, Jonah not only disobeys, but he sets off in the opposite direction. As Jonah's story progresses, however, we see God orchestrate a reversal. In His incredible mercy, He breaks Jonah's stubborn streak and replaces it with humility. God also has mercy on the Ninevites—a "people who do not know right from left"—and they repent in sackcloth and ashes (Jonah 4:11).

It's easy to diminish or rationalize our persistent faults. Yet when we're faced with circumstances or people who hold up a mirror and show us who we truly are, we have the opportunity to change. God is molding us into people who want to follow His will, and He'll provide opportunities to shape us to that end. We just have to respond to His calling. —RVN

How are you stubbornly insisting on your own way?
How can you respond in a way that honors God?

○ ◇ ◇ ◇ ○

THE PAIN OF IDOLATRY

Micah 1:1–3:12; Acts 13:13–14:7; Job 22:14–30

Idolatry causes pain. If this truth were present in our minds each time we placed something before God, we would make different decisions. Micah's account of the sins of Samaria makes this fact painfully and dramatically clear:

"So I [Yahweh] will make Samaria as a heap of rubble in the field, a place for planting a vineyard. And I will pour down her stones into the valley and uncover her foundations. Then all her idols will be broken in pieces, and all her prostitution wages will be burned in the fire, and all her idols I will make a desolation. For from the wage of a prostitute she gathered them, and to the wage of a prostitute they will return. On account of this I will lament and wail. I will go about barefoot and naked. I will make a lamentation like the jackals, and a mourning ceremony like the ostriches" (Mic 1:6–8).

Throughout this section, God and the prophet's voices intermingle, a common occurrence in prophetic literature. This device creates a sense of empathy, both for God's perspective on idolatry and for the people's pain as the consequences of their idolatry bear down on them. Micah's position is one we should emulate. When we understand what God feels, we begin to see the world from His perspective. When we feel what others feel, we're able to meet their needs and learn to love them as fully and radically as God loves us.

Micah's depiction of idolatry—how God views it and what it does to us— should be a wake-up call. When God takes second place in our lives, we inflict pain on Him, ourselves, and others. We shove Him out of His rightful place and thus move ourselves out of relationship with Him. But when He is the focus of our lives, we have an opportunity to empathize with others and to love them—and our idols dissipate like smoke. —JDB

How are you combating idolatry in your life?
How are you showing love to people who love idols?

FREEDOM AND RESPONSE

Micah 4:1–6:16; Acts 14:8–15:21; Job 23:1–17

Freedom from sin gives us the power to love. But freedom from poverty or oppression or guilt sometimes makes us complacent. We forget our inclination to wander away from God's will and pursue our own, and we overlook that God will eventually call us to account. Although Micah prophesied during a time of prosperity in Israel, it was also a time of spiritual deficiency. The powerful were oppressing the weak (Mic 2:1–2; 3:2–3) politically and economically.

Micah holds Israel to account in this passage. The prophet paints a courtroom scene with God judging His people for their unfaithfulness: "He has told you, O mortal, what is good, and what does Yahweh ask from you but to do justice, and to love kindness, and to walk humbly with your God?" (Mic 6:8).

The mountains and the hills listen as Yahweh accuses Israel, and the evidence He presents is startling. God has been active and present in His people's lives, turning what was meant for evil into good. He brought Israel out of slavery in Egypt. When Balaam tried to curse Israel on behalf of Balak, the Moabite king, God turned that curse into blessing.

We know where we stand in the courtroom drama. Our sins condemn us, but God has provided new evidence that changes our fates. What prosecuting attorney becomes a defender of the accused—a mediator claiming their cause? Through His Son, God frees us from our sin. Indeed, we should say with awe and humility, "Who is a God like you?" —RVN

Our story should be a response of humility and love for God.
What story will your life tell?

September 17

∘ ∘ ∘ ∘ ∘

WHAT SHALL BE DONE?

Micah 7:1–20; Acts 15:22–16:5; Job 24:1-11

How should we respond when those around us seem to be not only falling short of the glory of God, but actually abandoning God's work? What should we do when we witness neighbors or friends tolerating or even justifying acts of injustice, oppression, greed, or idolatry? We live in such a time. So did the prophet Micah:

"Woe is me! For I have become like the gatherings of summer, like the gleanings of the grape harvest, when there is no cluster of grapes to eat or early ripened fruit that my soul desires. The faithful person has perished from the land, and there is none who is upright among humankind. All of them lie in wait; each hunts his brother with a net. Their hands are upon evil, to do it well; the official and the judge ask for the bribe, and the great man utters the evil desire of his soul; and they weave it together" (Mic 7:1–3).

Micah did what should be done—he spoke up; he told the truth. When we find ourselves in evil times among evil people, we must do the same. God may be calling us to be a voice crying in the wilderness (John 1:19–25; compare Isa 40:3). By boldly proclaiming the truth, we may make a way for others to come back to God.

Much of the world is corrupt, and it is our job as Christians to fight such corruption, to stand above it, and to help others find the better way—God's way. The brokenness of our world is not simple. How many people are led astray unconsciously? How often does money or power trump the rights of the vulnerable? Do we recognize injustice when we see it? Do we have the courage to speak up, even when it hurts?

Micah provides an example here, too. Although he spoke vividly about God's coming judgment on Samaria, he also told us where we would find the Savior who would heal our brokenness once and for all—in Bethlehem. —JDB

How are you standing against the evils of our age?

September 18

○ ○ ◊ ○ ○

ANOTHER TAKE

Nahum 1:1–3:19; Acts 16:6–40; Job 24:12–25

What do we risk when we know of God's forgiveness and then become complacent and return to our sinful ways? What happens when we turn our back on God—treating Him like an insurance agent rather than a savior?

The short, shocking book of Nahum shows what happens to those who disregard God. Where the book of Jonah displays God's mercy and Nineveh's repentance, Nahum proclaims God's judgment on the same Assyrian city. The city's deeds catch up with it, and the judgment is harsh—unrelenting.

"There is no healing for your wound; your injury is fatal. All who hear the report of you will clap their hands for joy concerning you. For who has not suffered at the hands of your endless cruelty?" (Nah 3:19). The empire responsible for conquering cities, displacing and enslaving people, and looting wealth would eventually meet its end—defeated by Babylon.

Jonah shows us that God will eagerly dispense mercy, but the book of Nahum—wholly dedicated to God's judgment of Nineveh—reminds us that His mercy cannot be taken for granted. It's a sobering but necessary reminder to respond to God's mercy with faith and trust. It's also a reminder to recognize God's full character: He delights in steadfast faithfulness, but He is also a burning fire. Don't tread on His mercy. Respond to it. —RVN

How does the idea of a God who sets all things
right bring you both awe and comfort?

HONESTLY QUESTIONING GOD

Habakkuk 1:1–2:5; Acts 17:1–34; Job 25:1–6

Many people are afraid to be honest with God—which is odd, considering that He already knows what we're thinking. The biblical authors certainly told God how they felt, and they did so eloquently and often.

The prophet Habakkuk remarked, "O Yahweh, how long shall I cry for help and you will not listen? How long will I cry out to you, 'Violence!' and you will not save?" (Hab 1:1–2). Habakkuk felt that God was not answering his prayers—that God was ignoring his petitions. He reminded God of the desperate need for His intercession. In doing so, Habakkuk reminds us that wrestling with God is a healthy and necessary component of following Him.

Habakkuk went on to make more desperate, even angry, pleas: "Why do you cause me to see evil while you look at trouble? Destruction and violence happen before me; contention and strife arise. Therefore the law is paralyzed, and justice does not go forth perpetually. For the wicked surround the righteous; therefore justice goes forth perverted" (Hab 1:3–4). Habakkuk's honest questions reveal the state of his heart. He was not afraid to tell God what he felt because he understood that God already knew. He also believed that God could be persuaded to intercede.

Yet it's not language or skillful rhetoric that causes God to intercede—after all, He is a free being who can do what He wills, and He will not be manipulated. God wants to use us for His work, and He longs for us to acknowledge what He is doing. When we pray, God listens; when God acts in response to our prayers, we know that it is His work. We must pray honestly, and we must acknowledge God's rightful place and acts. —JDB

What are you praying about?
What are you honestly confessing to God?

MEASURING OUT GOD'S GOODNESS

Habakkuk 2:6–3:19; Acts 18:1–28; Job 26:1–14

Although we don't usually question God's goodness, we do make assumptions about how He should act in the world. We expect God to use us in His work and to intercede on our behalf—and rightfully so, since those promises come from Him. But when we find ourselves in messy or uncertain situations, we sometimes run ahead of God. Frustrated with the waiting and the unknown, we risk making judgments about how well He is running the world.

As Habakkuk watches the destruction, violence, contention, and strife in Israel, he turns to Yahweh and makes bold demands: "Why do you cause me to see evil while you look at trouble?" (Hab 1:3). But by the end of the dialogue, he has changed his mind. He will rejoice in Yahweh "though the fig tree does not blossom, nor there be fruit on the vines; the yield of the olive fails, and the cultivated fields do not yield food, the flock is cut off from the animal pen, and there is no cattle in the stalls" (Hab 3:17–18).

Did Habakkuk merely give in to a hopeless situation? He didn't gain any more information about God's motives. But after his dialogue with God, his entire posture changed. The confidence in Habakkuk's final prayer hinges on his acknowledgment of Yahweh's power and His anger at the evil of those who disregard His ways. God has the situation under control; Habakkuk must simply wait.

We often associate waiting with inaction, but waiting is faith in action. Habakkuk chooses to rejoice and trust God in spite of his circumstances, and that decision shapes his new perspective: "Yet I will rejoice in the LORD; I will take joy in the God of my salvation. God, the LORD is my strength; he makes my feet like the deer's; he makes me tread on my high places" (Hab 3:18–19). Like Habakkuk, we are called to come before God in humility, waiting in faith on His timing and trusting in His goodness. —RVN

*How are faith and trust in God motivating
all your thoughts and actions?*

September 21

∘ ∘ ◦ ∘ ∘

THROWING CAUTION TO THE FLOOD

Zephaniah 1:1–3:20; Acts 19:1–41; Job 27:1–23

Words are powerful. They can restore and heal; they can also be used as deadly weapons. When we interact with one another, we know to choose our words carefully to avoid being misinterpreted or inadvertently causing harm. But Yahweh speaks words of daunting ambiguity—proclamations that can easily be misunderstood or that are frightening beyond measure.

Consider Zephaniah 1:2–3: "'I will surely destroy everything from the face of the earth'—a declaration of Yahweh. 'I will destroy humanity and beast; I will destroy the birds of the sky and the fish of the sea, and the stumbling blocks with the wicked. And I will cut off humankind from the face of the earth'—a declaration of Yahweh." Does Yahweh actually intend to destroy everything on the earth? Why is He speaking so boldly?

The phrase "face of the earth" appears twice in this passage; it encloses a miniature narrative that references the story of the flood in Genesis 6:7; 7:4. This story is used as a metaphor for why Yahweh will destroy Judah: "And I will cut off from this place the remnant of Baal, and the name of idolatrous priests with the priests, and those who bow down on the rooftops to the host of heaven, and those who bow down, swearing to Yahweh but also swearing by Milkom" (Zeph 1:4–5). Yahweh plans to destroy Judah because they have sought other gods. In other words, Judah has acted just like the evil people who caused the flood.

The startling images of destruction and death that Yahweh's proclamations evoke seem shockingly blunt. Yet these bold statements remind us that using audacious language is sometimes necessary, and evoking stories of the past can make the point more powerful. We must still take caution when choosing our words, but when we must speak an uncomfortable truth, we can turn to the example that Yahweh sets here: Live boldly for Him and speak the truth. —JDB

How can you be more bold
in your words about Yahweh?

∘ ∘ ◦ ∘ ∘

KEEP US FROM DISTRACTION

Haggai 1:1–2:23; Acts 20:1–38; Job 28:1–11

It's easy to get distracted from the good work God intends for us to do. Competing forces vie for our attention; we're sidetracked by fear or selfishness. We start living our own stories and lose sight of the greater narrative, of which our lives are just one thread.

The Jewish exiles who returned to Jerusalem had begun the work of reconstructing the temple, a symbol of God's presence among His people. In the rebuilding of the temple, they gathered up the remnants of their broken identities and together formed a collective identity as Yahweh's people. They had their priorities in order.

Then they got distracted. When they started putting their own needs and security first, Yahweh sent the prophet Haggai to remind them of their true purpose: "Is it a time for you yourselves to dwell in your houses that have been paneled while this house is desolate? … Consider your ways! You have sown much but have harvested little. You have eaten without being satisfied; you have drunk without being satiated; you have worn clothes without being warm; the one who earns wages puts it in a pouch with holes" (Hag 1:6).

The work that the Jewish exiles did outside of God's purpose for them had no lasting effect or real merit. Because they were neglecting their first calling, their frantic attempts to meet their own selfish needs were doomed to fail anyway. Outside of Yahweh, there could be no blessing. God used Haggai to speak this truth into the lives of the Jewish exiles, but He also encouraged them with His presence: "I am with you" (Hag 1:13).

Listen to the words of Haggai. Speak truth into fear and selfishness—either your own or others. Remember that you're not meant to travel through life on your own, outside of this great narrative or apart from the presence of God. —RVN

What is the priority in your life right now?
How can you shift away from priorities that aren't
part of God's grand scheme for your life?

September 23

○ ○ ○ ○ ○

BEYOND MEASURE

Zechariah 1:1–2:13; Acts 21:1–26; Job 28:12–28

When we say, "God is gracious; God is kind," do we fully comprehend the extent of God's graciousness and kindness toward us? We glimpse it in Zechariah: "You must say to them: 'Thus says Yahweh of hosts: "Return to me," declares Yahweh of hosts, "and I will return to you,"'" says Yahweh of hosts" (Zech 1:2–3).

An astounding reversal is hidden in these words, couched in a dialogue expressing how terribly God's people have treated Him (Zech 1:4–6). By relying on their ancestors' wisdom, God's people are marching toward their own destruction: "Your ancestors, where are they? And the prophets, do they live forever?" (Zech 1:5). Instead of wiping them from the face of the earth or banishing them from relationship with Him, however, God acts graciously: "Return to me … and I will return to you" (Zech 1:3). It's an incredibly generous offer, one that the people accept (Zech 1:6).

But this is not the end of the journey. Zechariah's vision goes on to illustrate painful times on the horizon before moving once again to hope (Zech 2:1–13). Ultimately, Yahweh remarks: "Many nations will join themselves to Yahweh on that day, and they will be my people, and I will dwell in your midst. And you will know that Yahweh of hosts has sent me to you. And Yahweh will inherit Judah as his portion in the holy land, and he will again choose Jerusalem" (Zech 2:11–12).

The one "that Yahweh of hosts has sent" is likely a reference to the Messiah. Here Yahweh moves from welcoming only the people of Israel to welcoming all people into His kingdom. Anyone can return to Him or come to Him— because that is what He desires. His graciousness and kindness are truly beyond measure. —JDB

What graciousness and kindness are you grateful for today?

○ ○ **○** ○ ○

SPEAKING THE TRUTH WITH LOVE

Zechariah 3:1–5:11; **Acts 21:27–22:21**; Job 29:1–12

Read today's headlines and you might conclude that Christian boldness is a thin disguise for defensiveness, anger, and demeaning behavior. Believers who feel voiceless in their society sometimes respond by becoming adamant "defenders of the faith" in ways that can be destructive. In an age of instant electronic communication, our potential for good or harm has increased exponentially. But if we lay claim to special rights as Christians, we have forgotten that we're supposed to be like Jesus.

We need wisdom and spiritual maturity to share our faith with love. Paul serves as a model for using influence in a Christ-like way. In Acts 21–22, Paul encountered an angry Jewish mob that wanted him dead. He could have responded to the crowd self-righteously, looking down on them from his enlightened position. Instead, Paul confessed that he was once a persecutor of "this Way" (Acts 22:4). He could have used his status as a Roman citizen to his own advantage. Instead, he testified about the "Righteous One" to people who vehemently opposed him.

Paul came from a place of humility. He appealed to the Jews by telling them his own story—simply, boldly, and honestly. He emphasized his transformation: He was once a persecutor of the Church, but now he shared the work of Jesus in his life.

We should be ready to do likewise, to spread the gospel by speaking the truth in love, without insisting on our rights or using our influence in self-serving ways. We should be like Paul, but mostly we should be like Jesus. We should be ready to preach wherever and whenever we can and trust that God will work out the rest. —RVN

How are you sharing the gospel with both truth and love?

VISIONS, REVELATIONS, AND QUESTIONS

Zechariah 6:1–7:14; Acts 22:22–23:22; Job 29:13–25

The prophets of old had visions and dreamed dreams. They experienced apocalyptic nightmares and witnessed breathtaking scenes of beauty. Perhaps most fascinating, though, is how they reacted. Zechariah provides us with an example of both the revelation and the proper response.

"I looked up again, and I saw, and look!—four chariots coming out from between two mountains, and the mountains were mountains of bronze. ... And I answered and said to the angel that was talking to me, 'What are these, my lord?' And the angel answered and said to me, 'These are the four winds of the heavens going out after presenting themselves before the Lord of all the earth'" (Zech 6:1–5).

Zechariah could not have understood what he was seeing, but he paid attention, and he asked questions. Although we may not experience visions as confounding as Zechariah's, we certainly have the opportunity to be perplexed by God. Our response should be modeled after Zechariah's: Ask questions and then act. Zechariah's life was marked by asking and responding, and it made a difference for his generation. People came to God because Zechariah was willing to be God's instrument.

How many people experience incredible revelations from God and then fail to respond? How many people come near enough to glimpse God's plan but never pay close enough attention to receive it from Him? How much are we losing as individuals, and as people, because we don't care enough to ask God for the answers? —JDB

What confusion or uncertainty
can you overcome by asking questions?

UNEXPECTED OPPORTUNITIES

Zechariah 8:1–9:17; **Acts 23:23–24:27**; Job 30:1–15

When we are busy doing the work of the kingdom, how do we respond to obstacles that get in our way? Do we expect God to blast a path straight through so that we can proceed? We might read the drama of Paul's life through this lens, waiting anxiously for God to open the way for Paul to continue his spectacularly successful work. Instead, God allows Paul to be imprisoned and put on trial.

But as Paul defended himself before Roman officials, he recognized that God was using him in ways he hadn't expected. The conflict and rejection Paul encountered from the Jews provided him with the opportunity to share the gospel with some of the most influential Gentiles he would ever encounter.

God used Paul's trials to expand his ministry from the Jews to the Gentiles. Through Paul's life, God displayed His power to bring about the growth of the Church and the spread of the gospel message far beyond Israel.

God is working in and among us to bring the good news to those beyond our field of vision. We should reconsider our attitude toward the conflicts and disappointments in our lives, instead seeking God's providential hand in them. —RVN

How can you pray for wisdom to see
God at work in all the circumstances of your life?

THE TRUE SOURCE OF LEADERSHIP

Zechariah 10:1–11:17; Acts 25:1–27; Job 30:16–31

When leaders latch onto power, considering it their right, it's destructive. God holds leaders to a higher standard because their words and actions cause others to rise or fall. When leaders of corporations, churches, or other organizations take their authority for granted, entire communities may end up fighting against God rather than with Him. Such was the case for the Israelites in Zechariah's lifetime.

The context suggests the people were mistakenly relying on Baal (the storm god) rather than Yahweh. Yahweh responded by reminding them and their leaders that He is the one who sends rain: "Ask rain from Yahweh in the season of the spring rain—Yahweh, who makes storm clouds, and he gives showers of rain to them, to everyone the vegetation in the field. Because the household gods speak deceit, and those who practice divination see a lie, and the dreamers of vanity speak in vain. Therefore the people wander like sheep; they are afflicted because there is no shepherd" (Zech 10:1–2). Based on what happened next, it appears that the leaders were the ones suggesting that Israel should rely on household gods.

Although Yahweh was upset with His people, He directed the main force of His anger against those in charge: "My anger burns against the shepherds, and I will punish the leaders, because Yahweh of hosts watches over his flock, the house of Judah; and he will make them like his majestic horse in war. From them the cornerstone will go out, from them the tent peg, from them the battle bow, from them every ruler, all together" (Zech 10:3–4). Israel's leaders had to change their ways first—the horrific behavior (the battle bow) came from them.

How many professing Christian leaders lean on themselves—their unearned "battle bows"—instead of being the kind of leaders Yahweh has called them to be? Even Christian leaders tend to locate the source of their power in themselves or in this world rather than in Yahweh. These misguided shepherds may achieve a temporary victory, but their work will eventually bring suffering to themselves and those in their care. —JDB

How should you lead?
What aspects of your leadership should you change?

TURNING THE TABLES

Zechariah 12:1–14:21; **Acts 26:1–32**; Job 31:1–8

W hen Paul presents the gospel before King Agrippa, we expect him to be defensive. But Paul is ready to shift the spotlight. He offers a surprisingly simple explanation of recent events and a testimony of his faith, and then he describes how the resurrection of Jesus changes everything. He deftly turns the tables and gives the king the opportunity to believe.

Paul describes the gospel as something that was intended all along—it is nothing new: "Therefore I have experienced help from God until this day, and I stand here testifying to both small and great saying nothing except what both the prophets and Moses have said were going to happen, that the Christ was to suffer and that as the first of the resurrection from the dead, he was going to proclaim light both to the people and to the Gentiles" (Acts 26:23).

Paul respectfully tells Agrippa that his testimony should come as no great surprise. Agrippa knows of the Jewish faith, and he has heard about recent events. Now Paul challenges him by presenting him with the only possible explanation—Jesus, the first of the resurrection of the dead, for whose sake Paul is now imprisoned. This faith is consistent with the Jewish belief in God. Now it is not reserved for the Jews, but also available to the Gentiles.

Paul's words put everyone else in the spotlight. He earns responses from the Roman leaders—a rebuke from Festus (Acts 26:24) and a question from Agrippa: "In a short time are you persuading me to become a Christian?" Paul responds with faith: "I pray to God, whether in a short time or in a long time, not only you but also all those who are listening to me today may become such people as I also am, except for these bonds!" (Acts 26:29).

The apostle's constant witness and his trust in God's power to turn people's hearts to Himself give Paul confidence and assurance that his words will bring about a response (Acts 26:18). If a man facing trial can present the gospel so respectfully, when he is most defensive and vulnerable, why can't we? We should have such courage. —RVN

How are you looking for opportunities
to witness to others about the hope that is in you?

∘ ◦ ◊ ◦ ∘

REBUILDING IS NOT ALWAYS WISE

Malachi 1:1–2:9; Acts 27:1–44; Job 31:9–22

W ho can rebuild what Yahweh tears down? The prophets articulate this message again and again. Yahweh tears down evil things; evil people rebuild them; the prophets insist that He will just tear them down again. God tolerates evil for a time, waiting for people to repent, but when His patience is up, it's up.

"'I have loved you,' says Yahweh, but you say, 'How have you loved us?' 'Is Esau not Jacob's brother?' declares Yahweh. 'I have loved Jacob, but Esau I have hated. I have made his mountain ranges a desolation, and given his inheritance to the jackals of the desert.' If Edom says, 'We are shattered, but we will return and rebuild the ruins,' Yahweh of hosts says this: 'They may build, but I will tear down; and they will be called a territory of wickedness, and the people with whom Yahweh is angry forever.' Your eyes will see this, and you will say, 'Yahweh is great beyond the borders of Israel'" (Mal 1:2–5).

This scene seems brutal upon first reading. If you're on Jacob's side, you're fine—Yahweh loves you even though you don't acknowledge it. But if you're on Esau's (Edom's) side, you're left wondering why God hates you so much—unless you know the backstory: Edom ravaged the lands of God's people and committed atrocities against them in their greatest time of need. When foreign nations invaded Israel, Edom preyed on its brothers instead of coming to their defense. This is the reason for Yahweh's anger—and why He will tear down whatever Edom builds.

How often do we try to excuse ourselves as Edom did—to defend our behavior as justifiable retribution for previous offenses? What does God think about the state of our hearts and the actions we take against others as a result? —JDB

How must your plan of action change, today,
in light of God's will and His standard?

○ ○○○ ○

KEY PLAYERS AND MAIN NARRATIVES

Malachi 2:10–4:6; **Acts 28:1–31**; Job 31:23–40

The book of Acts ends on a somewhat unsatisfying note. After all that Paul has been through—imprisonment, trial, shipwreck—we expect a show-down with Caesar or mass conversions of the Jews. Instead, the plot seems to sputter out.

Paul arrives in Rome and appeals to the Jews living there. He quotes Isaiah to the Jewish leaders: "You will keep on hearing, and will never understand, and you will keep on seeing and will never perceive" (Acts 28:26). When they fail to respond, Paul determines to reach out to the Gentiles. "They also will listen" (Acts 28:28) and will respond differently.

The poignant end of this book leaves Paul "proclaiming the kingdom of God and teaching the things concerning the Lord Jesus Christ with all bold-ness, without hindrance" (Acts 28:31). Facing either rejection or reception, he continues proclaiming the good news to both Jew and Gentile.

Paul is a key player in the Church that is being gathered by Jesus Christ, but the drama cannot end with Paul. Jesus is the main character in the story of humanity's redemption. The book of Acts leaves the ending open so that we can pick it up and carry it forward. The work of Jesus, through His Church, continues to the present day, and Jesus is using both you and me in His grand narrative. —RVN

How do you see your life as a story
that honors God as the key player?

October 1

° ° ° ° °

THE REAL REALITY

Ezekiel 1:1–3:15; Revelation 1:1–20; Job 32:1–10

John and Ezekiel open their prophetic books in a similar fashion—to prepare us for an unexpected view:

"The revelation of Jesus Christ, which God gave him to show to his slaves the things which must take place in a short time, and communicated it by sending it through his angel to his slave John, who testified about the word of God and the testimony of Jesus Christ, all that he saw. Blessed is the one who reads aloud and blessed are those who hear the words of the prophecy and observe the things written in it, because the time is near!" (Rev 1:1–3).

"And it was in the thirtieth year, in the fourth month, on the fifth day of the month, and I was in the midst of the exiles by the Kebar River. The heavens were opened, and I saw visions of God. On the fifth day of the month—it was the fifth year of the exile of the king Jehoiachin—the word of Yahweh came clearly to Ezekiel the son of Buzi, the priest, in the land of the Chaldeans at the Kebar River, and the hand of Yahweh was on him there" (Ezek 1:1–3).

Both authors open with heavenly visions—God testifying to His people. Both place their prophecies in a particular setting, and both articulate their ideas during tragic, despairing times. We meet John on the island of Patmos, and we meet Ezekiel on a riverbank. But more important than where the visions start is where they take us: to a scenic overlook of reality, not as it appears, but as it is. God is about to reveal what's really going on.

Prophets speak truth about what others cannot see and urge them to heed that truth. John and Ezekiel call us to something greater, something unknown. They urge us to act as if time were running out—because it is. It's only a matter of time until Jesus comes again.

The visions of both these prophets declare that God wants to use us here and now for a grand purpose—one that we may not yet comprehend but that we must nonetheless embrace. Their message is clear: Our call may be difficult, but *real* reality demonstrates God working through the pain. He is bringing goodness into the world and into our lives. All we have to do is respond. —JDB

What reality is God revealing to you today?

WHEN LOVE IS LOST, LABOR IS IN VAIN

Ezekiel 3:16–5:17; **Revelation 2:1–11**; Job 32:11–22

When zeal lacks love, faith is rendered useless. Love is the crux of faith. We can study the Bible like a scholar, pray like a warrior, evangelize like the world is ending tomorrow, but we still might miss the mark of faith. God desires our love.

The church in Ephesus, one of the most influential communities in the first century ad, patiently endured persecution and held on to their faith. But Ephesus is the first church that Jesus holds accountable in His revelation to John—and not for their lack of zeal (Rev 2:3–5).

Although the Ephesian church had remained outwardly faithful in formidable circumstances, Jesus still threatened to remove His favor. The community was doing everything right—maintaining orthodox standards, testing apostles, refusing to tolerate evil—but they no longer delighted in the grace that they first knew. They weren't motivated by the same love.

We hear the same reprimand when Paul writes to the church in Corinth: Even if we "speak with the tongues of men and angels" or "have the gift of prophecy" or have faith that "can remove mountains," we are nothing without love (1 Cor 13:1–2). Paul continues with the poetry that speaks a hard but necessary truth: Even if we "parcel out all [our] possessions" and "hand over [our] bodies] in order that [we] will be burned"—all without love—it doesn't benefit us or earn us favor with God (1 Cor 13:3–4).

These passages should shake us. If we are relying on our correct doctrines for approval, we need to take our cue from Jesus' words to the church in Ephesus. If we think our evangelizing efforts, our church involvement, or our Bible reading merit God's favor, we are mistaken. Even our suffering profits us nothing without love.

The grace God has shown us should break our hearts, drive us to Him, deepen our love—and motivate all of our labors. We must continually return to that grace. It's His love that initially motivated our love. And it's His love that sustains it. —RVN

Have your labors lost their love?
How can you dwell in His grace and love so that
all your actions are infused with meaning?

∘ ◦◦◦ ∘

IT WILL EAT YOU ALIVE

Ezekiel 6:1–8:18; Revelation 2:12–29; Job 33:1–7

I dolatry eats at our souls. And God puts up with it for only so long. "And the word of Yahweh came to me, saying, 'Son of man, set your face to the mountains of Israel and prophesy against them, and you must say, "Mountains of Israel, hear the word of the Lord Yahweh, thus says the Lord Yahweh to the mountains and to the hills, to the ravines and to the valleys: 'Look, I am bringing upon you the sword, and I will destroy your high places, and your altars will be desolate, and your incense altars will be broken, and I will throw down your slain ones before your idols, and I will place the corpses of the children of Israel before their idols, and I will scatter your bones around your altars'"'" (Ezek 6:1–6).

Ezekiel portrays God's view of the true nature of idolatry and the ramifications of living an idolatrous life. When people put wood and stone, or gadgets and entertainment, before their relationship with Yahweh, they are giving up the most valuable part of themselves.

Today, most people place entertainment above God. We value celebrity more than Jesus. We may deny this, but if we closely examine how we spend our time and money, we find that we love our idols as much as the ancients did.

How can we as Christians be instruments for the changes God wants to bring to the world if we conform ourselves to the expectations of our culture? Where we invest our time, assets, and attention reveals what we care about most. If we give ourselves over to worldly priorities instead of God's, we deserve the same fate that Yahweh prophesied for the children of Israel in Ezekiel 6:1–6.

But our good and gracious God wants to redeem us, and we should commit ourselves to seeking His blessing instead of His judgment (John 3:16–17; Rom 8). If we follow Him with our entire being—setting aside all that stands between us and Him—the world will look different. Idolatry will be revealed for what it is: a thief and a glutton, stealing the very lives God has in store for us. If we seek God with all our being, idolatry will hold no power over us. It will die from neglect while our lives take on new vitality as we boldly proclaim the glory of our life-giving God. —JDB

What idols stand between you and the life God has for you?

DEFIBRILLATORS FOR SARDIS

Ezekiel 9:1–11:25; **Revelation 3:1–13**; Job 33:8–18

We cover up the dead places in ourselves with all sorts of regalia. We fill the emptiness with fine clothing, once-in-a-lifetime experiences, or relationships in which the other is set up as god. Underneath the trappings, though, we're decaying.

Of all the churches addressed in Revelation, the church in Sardis receives the most intense critique. Sardis was a wealthy city and a military stronghold. And the church, like the city, seemed to be alive and well. But Christ, speaking truth through John's revelation, uncovers and names the decaying parts: "I know your works, that you have a name that you are alive, and you are dead. Be on the alert and strengthen the remaining things that are about to die, for I have not found your works completed before my God" (Rev 3:1–2).

The community in Sardis needed more than a stern scolding. They needed immediate resuscitation. They had so compromised their faith that many among them were spiritually dead. Those parts not already dead were dying. And the façade only perpetuated continued decay.

What was the answer? Was there hope for Sardis? Is there hope for us?

Sardis could be brought back from the edge of death, but only through repentance: "Therefore remember how you have received and heard, and observe it, and repent" (Rev 3:3). Urgency is paramount: "Be on the alert," Christ tells them. "I will come like a thief."

We have received the same instructions. Like Sardis, we might—if we try hard enough—meet others' expectations. But we shouldn't lie to ourselves. God sees our outward works, but He also knows our hidden hearts. Name your need, repent, and find hope in Christ, the only one who can fill the emptiness. —RVN

In what areas of your life do you feel empty?
How can you name your sin?

○ ◇ ◇ ◇ ○

WORDS AND ACTIONS

Ezekiel 12:1–13:23; Revelation 3:14–4:11; Job 33:19–28

Leading by example is a simple principle to understand, but it's a very diffi-cult one to live. The prophets were often called to lead by example, though doing so usually meant enduring suffering for others.

"And the word of Yahweh came to me [Ezekiel], saying, 'Son of man, you are dwelling in the midst of the house of rebellion who has eyes to see and they do not see; they have ears to hear, and they do not hear, for they are a house of rebellion. And you, son of man, prepare for yourself the baggage of an exile, and go into exile by day before their eyes. And you must go into exile from your place to another place before their eyes; perhaps they will see that they are a house of rebellion'" (Ezek 12:1–3).

By witnessing God's servant suffering, the people would be reminded of their rebellion and understand the gravity of God's displeasure. In this situation, God prescribes exile as their punishment for rebelling against His requirements and forfeiting His calling for their lives. God's prophet, Ezekiel, "pronounces" God's punishment through actions. In doing so, he becomes a type of sufferer for the people. He does not deserve their punishment, and he does not pay it for them, but he demonstrates the price of sin as he leads by example.

There is a time for words and a time for action. We all would do well to heed the words before the actions become necessary. We must also under-stand that, in our desire to emulate Christ, there are times we must go beyond warnings or advice and commit to bearing the burden for others—even suf-fering undeservedly on their behalf. We must show others what it means to follow Christ by acting as Christ would—giving unmerited grace even when it is costly. —JDB

What actions must you take today?
In what areas must you move words to deeds?
Who can you sacrifice for today?

October 6

∘ ◦ ◊ ◦ ∘

WE WANT OUT

Ezekiel 14:1–15:8; **Revelation 5:1–14**; Job 33:29–33

We've all had those moments when we just want out, when the chaos of life seems overwhelming. We want an end to the struggle with sin. We want relief from the things that are part of living in a broken world. We know Christ reigns, but we want what is "after these things" (Rev 4:1) right now.

Living in the midst of persecution, the early believers must have experienced these emotions daily. In his revelation, John himself expresses the need for hope in chaos. When he sees a scroll in the hand of "the one who is seated on the throne" (Rev 5:1)—the Father—the apostle weeps because no one has been found worthy to open it. The scroll contains the things that will happen—the judgments that will remove evil and sin and set things right. Without someone worthy enough to open the scrolls, the chaos in the world will continue forever.

But then the Lamb appears. In John's revelation the 24 elders worship the Lamb for His work of redemption: "And they were singing a new song, saying, 'You are worthy to take the scroll and to open its seals, because you were slaughtered, and bought people for God by your blood from every tribe and language and people and nation, and made them a kingdom and priests to our God'" (Rev 5:9–10).

It is Christ's work that gives Him the authority to open the seals. As the Lamb who was slaughtered, He reversed death and the fate of those who believe in Him. He is responsible for setting all things right.

This knowledge is incredibly comforting for us. God is the great chaos-fighter. Jesus has drawn us out of our own chaos with His sacrifice. He will help us live in the now—in a world that is often chaotic but will, in time, be set right. In the meantime, we can respond to His work of ordering our lives and the lives of those around us. And when we feel helpless and out of control, we can rely on the great chaos-fighter. —RVN

Are you frustrated with your life circumstances?
How can you approach difficult areas of your life
knowing God will set all things right? How can you rest
knowing Christ is at work, right now, in your life?

October 7

º ◊ º ◊ º

COURAGE AND THE TRUTH

Ezekiel 16:1–63; Revelation 6:1–7:8; Job 34:1–15

Few people are brave enough to speak the truth when it could cost them their reputation. Even fewer have the courage to speak the truth when it could cost them everything. The prophets, however, set a different example. "And the word of Yahweh came to me, saying, 'Son of man, make known to Jerusalem its detestable things'" (Ezek 16:1–2). Yahweh commands Ezekiel to confront His people about their evil behavior and demand they repent. Most people aren't happy to be criticized; charged with speaking on God's behalf, the prophet must be courageous in the face of anger.

Ezekiel declares, "Thus says the Lord Yahweh to Jerusalem: … No eye took pity on you to do to you one of these things to show compassion for you, and you were thrown into the open field in their despising of you on the day you were born" (Ezek 16:3–5).

Yahweh acknowledges the painful times His people have endured, but His description hints of disdain. The Israelites should have acted on their own to break from the Canaanites, the Amorites, and the Hittites—as they were commanded in an earlier era (e.g., Deut 1; Josh 1; compare Josh 10; Josh 24; Judg 1–2; Num 34–36). The people from these nations were leading the Israelites to follow other gods and to commit evil acts. But the children of Israel allowed the others to live among them. Instead of strengthening their borders and adhering to their worship of Yahweh, they allowed the outsiders to compromise their borders, and they adopted the religious practices of other nations time and time again (e.g., 1 Sam 10–11; 1 Kgs 13).

The same could be said of many Christians today. God commands us to walk away from temptation, yet we wander back, looking for gaps in the border between right and wrong. Such situations are even sadder when other believers excuse the sin, leading many to live lives of perpetual disobedience. God not only wants us to separate ourselves from sin, He wants us to be victorious over it. He calls us to speak against the evil of our generation rather than excuse it. Through the power of God's Spirit in us, we can fight sin inwardly, openly and courageously—despite what it may cost us. —JDB

What perpetual sin is God asking you to break from?
What should you have courage to speak up against?

ABSENCE OF PAIN, PRESENCE OF GOD

Ezekiel 17:1–18:32; **Revelation 7:9–8:13**; Job 34:16–30

When life is difficult, we often take refuge in knowing there's a life to come—one in which we'll be free from pain and the worries of this world. The thought brings us comfort. During the difficult times, the life to come might even be more appealing than the present.

Revelation shows us a picture of what new life for those redeemed by Christ will look like: "These are the ones who have come out of the great tribulation, and have washed their robes and made them white in the blood of the Lamb. Because of this, they are before the throne of God, and they serve him day and night in his temple, and the one who is seated on the throne will shelter them. They will not be hungry any longer or be thirsty any longer, nor will the sun ever beat down on them, nor any heat" (Rev 7:14–16).

In Revelation the life to come appears as a shelter from all the traumatic and stressful things afflicting the first-century church—hunger, thirst, and heat. Yet we shouldn't simply define this new life as a time when we'll be free from the stress and pain of this world.

This new life is defined by God's presence. The sacrifice of the Lamb has made life with God possible again. If we are clothed in His righteousness, we can stand before the throne of God. Revelation illustrates what our relationship with God is and is destined to be. We will serve Him day and night—as we were created to do—and He will shelter us. The Lamb will shelter and shepherd us, leading us to "springs of living waters" (Rev 7:17).

When we long for relief, we might be yearning for a renewed sense of God's presence among us. We long for His presence because it is free from difficulty and filled with His incredible love. —RVN

What are you truly longing for?

JUDGMENT: IT'S TRICKY

Ezekiel 19:1–20:49; Revelation 9:1–21; Job 34:31–37

Judgment is both a curse and a blessing. If you judge others, you might be judged yourself—especially if you judge them incorrectly. Yet if you know how to judge right from wrong, you can discern truth from fiction.

Although judgment can be a wretched thing, there is a time for it: When God has confirmed something in your heart, and the Bible verifies your view, you must stand up for it. When Jesus tells us not to judge, He is not declaring that we should be passive (see Matt 7:1–6; see also Matt 7:15–23, where He condemns false prophets and false followers). Instead, Jesus is saying that we should be careful about what we say and do, for we could be the one at fault.

Ezekiel also deals with the very fine line of judgment. Yahweh says to him, "Will you judge them? Will you judge them, son of man?" (Ezek 20:4). This question implies the very point Jesus makes: Is Ezekiel capable of dealing out judgment? Certainly not, but with the power of Yahweh, he can speak the truth. Yahweh goes on, "Make known to them the detestable things of their ancestors" (Ezek 20:4). He follows this with a commentary on "the detestable things" accompanied by a comparison to how Yahweh has treated His people despite their disobedience (Ezek 20:5–8).

Judgment is tricky, but fear of "getting it wrong" should not keep us quiet in the midst of misdeeds and misconduct. Instead, we must speak up—let's just be sure that we first pray and examine our thoughts in light of the Bible. —JDB

What have you previously been quiet about
that you should speak up against?

THE POWER BEHIND THE DRAMA

Ezekiel 21:1–22:31; **Revelation 10:1–11**; Job 35:1–8

The concerns that make up our mini-narratives can sometimes distract us from the great drama in which we have been cast. When a mighty angel appears with a scroll in John's revelation, the apostle's part in God's great redemptive drama suddenly becomes very clear. He swaps his role of scribe for that of actor, speaking God's very words:

"And I went to the angel and told him to give me the little scroll, and he said to me, 'Take and eat it up, and it will make your stomach bitter, but in your mouth it will be sweet as honey.' And I took the little scroll from the hand of the angel and ate it up, and it was sweet as honey in my mouth, and when I had eaten it, my stomach was made bitter. And they said to me, 'It is necessary for you to prophesy again about many peoples and nations and languages and kings'" (Rev 10:9–11).

John's new task parallels the prophet Ezekiel's call to speak God's words. The prophet eats a scroll to internalize and speak the words of Yahweh, which turn sweet in his mouth (Ezek 2:8–36; see Psa 119:103; Jer 15:16). The words of God are also sweet for John, but the bitterness that follows reveals that a two-fold judgment is coming. God's words are sweet and comforting for the believers, but they also bring judgment. John has seen what lies behind the curtain, and he is charged with making this drama known to all—even to those who stubbornly refuse to acknowledge the Author.

John was charged with bringing the things he had learned to the people and nations of the earth. Today we are all cast in this drama of God's redemptive work. Our individual narratives should be informed by His greater drama—they should be seamlessly intertwined so that we display His creative and redemptive work. We should, together with John, profess this truth to all those we encounter. —RVN

How are you testifying about the God who
brings both comfort and judgment?

○ ○ ○ ○ ○

GREENER GRASSES

Ezekiel 23:1–49; Revelation 11:1–14; Job 35:9–16

When God's people turn from Him, the biblical story becomes solemn, sad, and explicit.

"Now as for their names, the older was Oholah, and Oholibah was her sister. And they became mine, and they bore sons and daughters, and their names are Samaria for Oholah, and Jerusalem for Oholibah. And Oholah prostituted herself while she was still mine [being Yahweh's], and she lusted for her lovers, for Assyria who was nearby. … Therefore I gave her into the hand of her lovers, into the hand of the Assyrians after whom she lusted" (Ezek 23:4–5, 9).

There is a firm rebuke in Yahweh's words spoken through Ezekiel—the sin becomes the punishment. But this sad picture also reveals Yahweh's perspective and the pain that He feels when we walk away from Him.

Ezekiel's words should prompt us to ask questions. How often have we been blinded by our lust for "greener grasses"? How often have we sacrificed God's plan and potential for our lives at the altar of selfish desires? How often has "want" controlled us to the point of betraying the God who created us?

Our remorse should guide us into making better choices. We can walk away from the pursuit of our own desires and walk into the life that Yahweh offers us. The "two witnesses" in Revelation 11:1–14 make this very decision. Appalled by the horrifying scene of their generation (e.g., Rev 9:13–21), they find hope and power in seeking Yahweh. Rather than allowing the evil of their generation to control or change them, they seek Yahweh. For doing so, they inherit power to do His work (Rev 11:2–6).

Each sad moment in history—indeed every single moment—is an opportunity to do the will of God. Today we have an opportunity to deny the narrative of our generation (and previous ones) in favor of God. —JDB

What selfish desires is God overturning in your life?

October 12

○ ○ ◌ ◦ ○

KINGDOM POLITICS

Ezekiel 24:1–25:17; **Revelation 11:15–12:17**; Job 36:1–12

We sometimes jump on the bandwagon with politics. Yet if we put our full trust in political candidates, or believe their rise to power is an indication of our future—a common campaign platform—we're putting our hope in something transitory. No earthly person or kingdom has absolute rule. The book of Revelation portrays this in a surprising way.

In the last book of the Bible, God's judgment is loosed, and it can be overwhelming to read and interpret. Six trumpets, blown consecutively by angels, unleash God's judgment. When the seventh trumpet blows, we expect judgment to be set in motion yet again. Instead, a loud voice from heaven announces a different, glorious event: "The kingdom of the world has become the kingdom of our Lord and of his Christ, and he will reign forever and ever" (Rev 11:15).

This seems like a strange turn of events, but it's the culmination of plans and actions that have been happening all along. The initiation of God's kingdom is prophesied throughout the Bible, and it is presented in John's vision to bring hope. All of God's judgments have a purpose. They terminate an old way of life to usher in a new one—a life guided by the eternal reign of God.

In some ways, the arrival of God's kingdom is a judgment—it's a judgment on all other kingdoms. John's vision would have been a comforting reminder to the early church that the kingdoms of this age are transitory. Their flawed, corrupt rule is not forever. And while the kingdoms of the world come and go, God's kingdom will never end.

We can be hopeful, then, in hopeless situations. We need not feel morose or hopeless when the factions and kingdoms of the world struggle and disappoint. God's eternal kingdom—His exclusive, righteous rule—is our hope. —RVN

How are you living like a member of God's kingdom,
not the kingdom of this world?

October 13

◦ ◦ ◦ ◦ ◦

THE LAST PERSON YOU WOULD EXPECT

Ezekiel 26:1–27:36; Revelation 13:1–10; Job 36:13–23

Yahweh is capable of doing anything and everything He pleases. If He were not a good God, this would be deeply frightening, but considering His wonderful character, this is comforting.

In Ezekiel 26:1–6, Yahweh describes the sins of Tyre and His plans against the powerful Phoenician city-state. The people of Tyre are arrogant. They do as they please, usually to the detriment of other people. Yahweh refuses to put up with this any longer. When He finally destroys Tyre, He does it through unexpected means: Nebuchadnezzar, king of the Neo-Babylonian empire from 605–562 BC. Despite Nebuchadnezzar's cruel and ruthless nature, Yahweh uses him to enact punishment on Tyre (Ezek 26:7).

Stories like this make me wonder how written prophecy would look today. How often would we see God use people without their realizing it? How many evil-hearted people have been used for a larger and better purpose?

We're never really certain how God is acting. We learn bits of information through prayer and the Bible, but only He knows what outcome He will produce. We know the trajectory—Christ's full reign on earth and the admonishment of evil (e.g., the destruction of the beast in Rev 13:1–10)—but we don't know precisely how that will play out.

There is no easy answer to this perplexing question, but what is certain is that Yahweh will ultimately carry out His will in the world. And His will might come in unexpected ways. No one can know the mind of God but God Himself. So when we pray, let's pray for the miracle, not for the means. —JDB

How do you perceive God acting in your life and the lives of others?
What miracle should you be praying for?

∘ ∘ ◊ ∘ ∘

PERSIST, DON'T JUST EXIST

Ezekiel 28:1–29:21; **Revelation 13:11–14:13**; Job 36:24–33

The phrase "patient endurance" brings to mind the pasted-on smile of a parent regarding a misbehaving child—a parent clinging to the hope that someday this stage will pass. In Revelation the term is used in a much different way.

"Here is the patient endurance of the saints, those who keep the commandments of God and the faith in Jesus" (Rev 14:12). The statement is set in the context of judgment. Here the phrase requires more than simply sitting still and enduring persecution. It's intended to encourage first-century believers to actively abandon the sins of the day: idolatry, pride, oppression.

Encouraging patient endurance was a call for early Christians to persevere by pursuing righteousness—to follow Christ faithfully even while enduring a period of suffering (Rev 14:12). Patient endurance is active persistence, loyalty, and discernment. We get this sense as John continues: "And I heard a voice from heaven saying, 'Write: "Blessed are the dead who die in the Lord from now on!"' 'Yes,' says the Spirit, 'in order that they may rest from their labors, for their deeds follow after them'" (Rev 14:13).

Rest comes later. Right now, when we suffer trials, God asks us to live lives that reflect our loyalty to Him. This loyalty and these deeds are motivated by hope that He provides—especially through the death of Christ.

When you think about patiently enduring trials to your faith, you don't have to regard yourself as a victim. Persist because of the hope you've been given and in which God continues to uphold you. Faith doesn't sit still. —RVN

How are you patiently enduring?

October 15

○ ○○○ ○

PICTURING GOD

Ezekiel 30:1–31:18; Revelation 14:14–15:8; Job 37:1–8

If you were to ask five people at random, "How do you picture God?" you would receive five very different answers. A social network prompt to "describe God in one word" confirms this idea: It resulted in more than 50 answers. For John, that one word was *logos* or "Word." Ultimately, human languagee to capture in a painting. His intricacy of character far surpasses ours.

God is able to feel the full spectrum of emotion and able to articulate who He is using the full spectrum of vocabulary. He is able to encounter us in any way He sees fit. Where we may be able to change only our hair color, glasses, or general way of speaking, He can change anything.

Throughout the books of Ezekiel and Revelation, we see diverse descriptions of God. They are so different that they could, by analogy, range from a mannerist painting of Jesus to a surrealist or modern one. Ezekiel 30:1–8 depicts Yahweh as a warrior, whereas in Revelation 14:14–20, we see God using messengers to glean a crop and bring fire. The images vary even more when we peek into the next chapter, where a warring God sends His angels to bring plagues (Rev 15:1–8).

There is not one depiction of God in the Bible, and any attempt to create one is an ill-conceived effort. We know much about Him, but we're not capable of understanding Him fully. As we attempt to picture God, we should be aware that our words about Him and visions of Him are shortsighted compared to who He actually is. Yet one thing we do know for certain is that He, our indescribable creator, desires to enter into relationship with His creation (e.g., John 15–17). —JDB

How do you picture God?
How do you describe Him?

○ ○○○ ○

MERCY AND JUDGMENT

Ezekiel 32:1–33:33; **Revelation 16:1–21**; Job 37:9–15

"God is judge," we like to say—especially when someone is struggling with injustice. When we get to the book of Revelation, though, we might struggle to understand God's judgment. Yet even as John describes God dispensing judgment, he emphasizes God's righteousness and loving nature. He tells us we should not forget that God is a *righteous* judge.

The Bible is unapologetic and straightforward when speaking about God's judgment. This is especially true in Revelation. Here the judgment God exacts echoes the plagues that He sent on Pharaoh and Egypt in the book of Exodus—blood, darkness, fiery hail, and locusts. Although Pharaoh was given multiple opportunities to obey God's request, he still chose his own way. By turning the bodies of water into blood, God spoke what Pharaoh should have realized: "By this you will know that I am Yahweh" (Exod 7:17).

Revelation 16 pronounces God righteous not in spite of His judgment, but because of it (Rev 16:5). We might be tempted to question God's judgment, but Revelation shows us that His judgment displays His righteousness. Revelation also shows God's love for and protection of the saints—that His judgment is vengeance for their blood (Rev 16:6).

Those who receive judgment in Revelation express fierce opposition to God in their blasphemy. They rebel even to the end: "And people were burned up by the great heat, and they blasphemed the name of God who has the authority over these plagues, and they did not repent to give him glory" (Rev 16:9). When other judgments come, the responses are the same (see also Rev 16:11, 21). Nothing hints at repentance.

God's judgment is not arbitrary, and His willingness to show mercy is great. Throughout the Bible, we hear about His longsuffering nature and His mercy that extends to a thousand generations. When we speak of His judgment, we should not diminish His mercy. We should speak carefully about God as a righteous judge, but we should balance and outweigh these statements by speaking of His longsuffering nature and incredible love. —RVN

How do you carefully weigh words about God's judgment?

○ ○ ○ ○ ○

SHEPHERDING IS A TOUGH BUSINESS

Ezekiel 34:1–35:15; Revelation 17:1–18; Job 37:16–24

Leadership requires accountability, yet many leaders of the past considered themselves above rebuke. Even when their deeds failed to catch up to them in their own lifetimes, history judged them clearly. History often remembers and records people as they really are. And if history doesn't recall the truth, God does.

Ezekiel was firm in his rebuke of the leaders of his time—Yahweh commanded him to be: "And the word of Yahweh came to me, saying, 'Son of man, prophesy against the shepherds of Israel, prophesy, and you must say to them, to the shepherds, "Thus says the Lord Yahweh: 'Woe to the shepherds of Israel who were feeding themselves! Must not the shepherds feed the flock? The fat you eat, and you clothe yourself with the wool; the well-nourished animals you slaughter, but you do not feed the flock'" '" (Ezek 34:1–3).

During Ezekiel's lifetime, the leaders of God's people were not being leaders at all. They were looking out for themselves rather than the good of the people. The same is true of leaders in our own time. If absolute power corrupts absolutely, as John Dalberg-Acton remarked, then surely we are all at risk of losing our way. Rather than responding with dismay, we should determine to take right action and speak the truth.

We must be people who seek God above ourselves. We must be people who put the needs of others before our own. We must want the glory of God among all people, above all things. We are all leading in one way or another, and others are watching us. That gives each of us an opportunity to lead by example. And any leader who isn't focused on God will end up corrupt. Ezekiel's criticism presents us an opportunity to change—to accept our rebuke and choose to live above reproach. Will we take it? —JDB

How should you change your approach
to leading others in light of Ezekiel's rebuke?
What needs to change for you to live above reproach?

October 18

○ ○ ○ ○ ○

A NEW WAY OF BEING

Ezekiel 36:1–37:28; **Revelation 18:1–24**; Job 38:1–11

God calls us to live lives that are distinguished by His light, clearly separate from our old way of being. He wants to make us a new creation by separating the light from the darkness within our own hearts.

In Revelation, John describes God calling His people out of Babylon: "And I heard another voice from heaven saying, 'Come out from her, my people, so that you will not participate in her sins, and so that you will not receive her plagues, because her sins have reached up to heaven, and God has remembered her crimes'" (Rev 18:4–5).

Sometimes we can be separated from our former ways of living in the literal sense, but the light has not yet pierced our hearts. We still live in "Babylon" because it exists right where we are. While we have inflated our position, we've failed to let God's light pierce our lives. We've failed to live lives that respond to His work.

Becoming separate involves putting off the old ways of thinking, acting, and being. It involves clinging to Christ, who brings light and renewal to our lives. Christ's sacrifice has reversed death and punishment so that He can bring us new life.

We are called to be separate not for our own sake and our own reputation, but so we can proclaim Christ's work in our lives. Ultimately, it's about pointing others toward Him: "For we do not proclaim ourselves, but Christ Jesus as Lord, and ourselves as your slaves for the sake of Jesus. For God who said, 'Light will shine out of darkness,' is the one who has shined in our hearts for the enlightenment of the knowledge of the glory of God in the face of Christ" (2 Cor 4:5). —RVN

How is your life reflecting the work of Christ?

October 19

○ ○ ○ ○ ○

BIG PICTURE HOPE

Ezekiel 38:1–39:24; **Revelation 19:1–10**; Job 38:12–24

Some Bible passages are so perplexing that we're not really sure what to make of them. Such is the case with Ezekiel 38:1–39:24. As we closely examine this text, we can easily lose sight of its message. We can find ourselves so lost in the details that the big picture becomes fuzzy. So what is the big picture presented in this passage? God is on the side of His people; He will fight for them.

This message is comforting. We all experience times when we feel like an ancient Israelite, lost and wandering in the desert. We go through times when we're not sure what's next or how it will all end up. But when we realize that God is there to war on our behalf—even in the midst of supreme chaos and paradise interrupted (compare Ezek 37)—our viewpoint quickly shifts.

When we feel as though we're blindly grasping for answers in the smoke that is the future, startling realizations like the type Ezekiel envisions can provide us with the hope we need (compare Heb 11:1). The book of Revelation casts similar visions. After the lament over Babylon and all the "woes," John the Apostle experiences rejoicing in heaven—salvation has arrived: "After these things I heard something like the loud sound of a great crowd in heaven saying, 'Hallelujah! Salvation and glory and power belong to our God, because his judgments are true and righteous, because he has passed judgment on the great prostitute who corrupted the earth with her sexual immorality, and has avenged the blood of his slaves shed by her hand!'" (Rev 19:1–2).

The big picture of the confusing passages of the Bible is indeed big. God is bringing judgment against the evil in the world and ushering in His great and glorious salvation. He will war on our behalf against all we fear. He has, and will, fight for us. He is a glorious and powerful God, worthy of praise. —JDB

What is the big picture of the current situation you're dealing with?
How does it give you hope?

IT HAS BEEN GRANTED TO YOU

Ezekiel 39:25–40:49; **Revelation 19:11–20:6**; Job 38:25–33

It has been granted to her that she be dressed in bright, clean fine linen" (Rev 19:8), announces a voice from heaven in John's revelation. The voice describes the bride who waits in anticipation—representing the believers who wait in expectation of being reunited with Christ.

The text contrasts the fine linen of the bride with the purple and scarlet cloth of the harlot, Babylon, who represents all that oppose God's reign (Rev 18:16). The harlot receives criticism for her infidelity: "Fallen, fallen is Babylon the great. … For all the nations have drunk from the wine of the passion of her sexual immorality, and the kings of the earth have committed sexual immorality with her, and the merchants of the earth have become rich from the power of her sensuality" (Rev 18:2–3).

But the cry goes out in and among Babylon: "Come out from her, my people" (Rev 18:4). The bride, who is preparing herself for the wedding celebration of the Lamb (Rev 19:7), responds to the call to remain pure—to avoid the temptations of the age. She is given the opportunity to dress herself in bright, clean fine linen, representing "the righteous deeds of the saints" (Rev 19:8). These deeds do not earn the bride her righteous standing before the Lamb, but they speak of a life that is transformed.

In Revelation, John uses this imagery to entreat the early believers to live righteously while awaiting the hope promised them. Christ has won the victory for us—the final conquering of sin and evil is imminent. We are empowered to live for Him now, to prepare ourselves for the day when we will have our reward: His presence. —RVN

How does your expectation of Christ's coming
help you live for Him now?

○ ○○○ ○

VISIONS OF GRANDEUR

Ezekiel 41:1–42:20; **Revelation 20:7–21:8**; Job 38:34–41

In times of struggle, a vision of grander glory is often enough to move us beyond our current circumstances. We find encouragement in glimpsing the vastness and power of God's plan.

When Ezekiel and God's people are weary and desperate for hope, God gives His prophet an unusual vision: He shows Ezekiel the temple—not as it is, but as it should be. The temple symbolizes Yahweh's presence among His people. It points them toward proper worship and life. It reminds them not only of who He is, but who they are meant to be. As we tour the temple with Ezekiel, we see that God intends to restore not only the temple, but also proper worship (Ezek 40:1–42:20).

John the apostle's vision recorded in Revelation echoes Ezekiel's: "And I saw a new heaven and a new earth, for the first heaven and the first earth had passed away, and the sea did not exist any longer. And I saw the holy city, new Jerusalem, coming down out of heaven from God, prepared like a bride adorned for her husband" (Rev 21:1–2). This new Jerusalem, this new hope, promises restoration, revitalization, and reconciliation. It's more than just a structure—it is a way of being.

When Yahweh casts visions of this life restored, He shows His people that He cares deeply about His relationship with them. He will make it right. He will enact His plan through Jesus, the bridge and the reason why God can proclaim, "Behold, I am making all things new!" (Rev 21:5). This is our hope, now and always. —JDB

How do Ezekiel's and John's visions of the future give you hope?
How should your relationship with God change in light of this?

October 22

∘ ◦ ◇ ◦ ∘

THE NEW JERUSALEM

Ezekiel 43:1–44:31; **Revelation 21:9–27**; Job 39:1–10

We are being made new. God is working in us now, and He will one day complete His work. Scripture speaks of the ultimate hope of this renewal: our reunion with God. For the first-century Jews, the new Jerusalem signified God once again dwelling with His people.

In his revelation, John describes the relationship between God and His people when He completes His work in us: "Behold, the dwelling of God is with humanity, and he will take up residence with them, and they will be his people and God himself will be with them. And he will wipe away every tear from their eyes, and death will not exist any longer, and mourning or wailing or pain will not exist any longer. The former things have passed away" (Rev 21:3–4).

The Lamb of God has achieved this picture of new creation and dwelling in God's presence. His light is present throughout the imagery: "And the city has no need of the sun or of the moon, that they shine on it, for the glory of God illuminates it, and its lamp is the Lamb" (Rev 21:23). Because of the Lamb's sacrifice, the former things have passed away.

God will make you completely new—free from sin, suffering, and pain. You are in transformation right now; He is shining His light in your life, exposing the darkness and separating it from the light. And someday you will stand before Him without fear of sin or pain or death or sorrow—a work of new creation. —RVN

How is God making you new today?
What area of your life needs to reflect His work in you?

October 23

∘ ∘∘∘ ∘

THE TIME, SPACE, AND MONEY CONTINUUM

Ezekiel 45:1–46:24; Revelation 22:1–21; Job 39:11–23

When we think of setting things apart for God, we usually think of money first. But what about our time or even a place? Ezekiel 45:1 speaks of setting aside land for God: "And when you allocate the land as an inheritance, you shall provide a contribution for Yahweh as a holy portion from the land, its length being twenty-five thousand cubits and its width ten thousand cubits; it is holy in all its territory, all around" (Ezek 45:1).

We're comfortable with the idea of donating money; we recognize that others need our help and our churches need our support. But there are other reasons for giving. Giving itself is a righteous and perhaps sacred act. It forces us to acknowledge that all we have belongs to God—He is the provider. Giving puts us in right standing before God in a powerful way.

Similarly, allocating time and space to God helps us understand our place before Him. When we designate a particular time for God, or a particular place for meeting Him—such as a prayer room or a particular chair to sit in when we pray—we acknowledge that He deserves a special place in our lives.

Like giving, setting aside these times and places can help us glimpse what our relationship with God is meant to be. It gives us an opportunity to envision a better future fueled by a relationship with God. It gives us the energy (and the reminder) we need to follow God's will. Giving helps us see how things can and will be (e.g., Rev 22:1–3). —JDB

What should you set apart for God?

○ ○ ◊ ○ ○

CONSTANTLY IN PRAYER

Ezekiel 47:1–48:35; **1 Thessalonians 1:1–10**; Job 39:24–40:2

Desperate circumstances often dictate our prayers. We pray for others when they're in need, or we thank God for others when they fill our needs. But how often do we thank God for the faith of those around us?

When Paul writes to the believers in Thessalonica, he opens by saying, "We give thanks to God always concerning all of you, making mention constantly in our prayers" (1 Thess 1:2). Paul and his disciples thank God for their "work of faith and labor of love and steadfastness of hope in our Lord Jesus Christ in the presence of our God and Father" (1 Thess 1:3).

Those who appear to be moving along well by our standards may be struggling in their faith. Other believers, just like us, go through ebbs and flows in their journey. It shouldn't take a catastrophe for us to recognize their need for prayer.

We can learn something from Paul, a church planter and disciple maker who was no doubt keenly aware of the growth and struggles of the believers he mentored. For those of us who are less observant, these struggles may simmer underneath our radar. We should stop and take notice of the faith journeys of the people around us—people in our churches, our schools, and our workplaces. For whom can you thank God today? —RVN

Who needs your observant prayers today?

GOOD OPPORTUNITIES AND DIFFICULT DECISIONS

Daniel 1:1–2:16; 1 Thessalonians 2:1–3:5; Job 40:3–12

When Daniel is invited to dine at the king's table—a great honor reserved for the favored (Dan 1:1–4)—he turns down the offer. Instead of eating food and wine fit for a king, Daniel and the other Israelites settle on a diet of vegetables and water (Dan 1:12).

Daniel's decision seems to contradict human nature. When a good situation comes along (like being invited to eat at the royal table), we often jump at the chance. Yet in doing so, we may fail to consider the ramifications. Daniel knows that eating at the king's table means compromising Yahweh's commands against eating certain foods. So when he's offered a great opportunity, he is bold enough to say no and to offer an alternative (Dan 1:10–14). Daniel knows that God will provide for those who love Him. He also knows that being in God's will is more important than anything else, even if it means facing opposition.

Paul's statement in 1 Thessalonians 2:2 demonstrates that he understood this as well: "But after we had already suffered and been mistreated in Philippi … we had the courage in our God to speak to you the gospel of God amid much opposition." Opposition did not deter Paul from doing what was right in God's eyes, just as it didn't prevent Daniel from keeping God's commands.

When we're faced with the promises of this world, how do we react? Do we boldly pursue money, fame, or power? Or do we deny these things for the sake of following God's will? The purpose to which we've been called is too important to be set aside for things that will fade over time.

We must be willing to face opposition boldly instead of pursuing what the world has to offer. Even when we have to depend on a miracle—as Daniel depended on God to keep him healthy when others were eating better food—we must make God's will the priority. No matter how difficult it becomes, we have to seek God's will. When we consider that our relationship with God is eternal, what matters is not the opinion of one king, but the opinion of the King of the universe. —JDB

What opportunities do you have that are not God's will?

RED ROPES AND RESTRICTED ACCESS

Daniel 2:17–3:30; **1 Thessalonians 3:6–4:12**; Job 40:13–24

I often want to keep certain areas of my life roped off. God can reign over some of my relationships, but not to the extent that I need to make gut-wrenching decisions to fall in line with His will. God can move in my Bible study, but I keep the chaos of my work life outside the bounds of His sovereignty. I am in charge, I think, and I allow only restricted access.

We might not readily admit it, but subconsciously we often operate with this mindset. Paul speaks to the Thessalonians about the nature of faith. He spent time with the believers in Thessalonica, instructing them about God and life. He now sends word to encourage them to move along in faith. "We ask you and appeal to you in the Lord Jesus that, just as you have received from us how it is necessary for you to live and to please God, just as indeed you are living, that you progress even more" (1 Thess 4:1). He continues to instruct them in sanctification—the work of becoming holy by serving God, loving God, and loving others.

Even though he is grateful for the Thessalonian believers' faith, Paul doesn't want them to remain at a standstill. He doesn't want his example to be their measuring rod. He turns the believers over to Christ, entreating them to pursue Him.

God doesn't expect us to meet a faith quota. He wants to claim *all* areas of our lives fully for Himself. This is not an option; it is "necessary for you to live and to please God" (1 Thess 4:1). Nothing escapes His notice or His attention. But He doesn't expect us to go about this work on our own—that would only result in disaster. He gives us His Spirit, through whom He continues to form and shape us. Whether it's our relationships, our work life, or our time spent studying and pondering His Word, God expects our total allegiance. —RVN

Do you want to allow God only restricted access to your life?
Pray today about an area of your life that needs to be transformed.

October 27

∘ ∘ ∘ ∘ ∘

DREAMS OF REDEMPTION

Daniel 4:1–37; 1 Thessalonians 4:13–5:11; Job 41:1–9

I've known people who seemed beyond saving—who seemed to have gone too far down the wrong path to ever turn to the right one. But in the Bible we see that this is not the case. God is capable of turning anyone's heart. One of the most shocking examples is Nebuchadnezzar.

In a decree to all the nations he rules (and perhaps other nations as well), Nebuchadnezzar remarks, "It is pleasing to me to recount the signs and wonders that the Most High God worked for me. How great are his signs and wonders, how strong is his kingdom, an everlasting kingdom; and his sovereignty is from generation to generation" (Dan 4:2–3). He then goes on to recount a dream that Yahweh planted in his mind.

Before Nebuchadnezzar experiences redemption, he tastes humiliation and endures great trials (Dan 4:28–33). But Yahweh does not intend to merely humble the king—He intends to make him a righteous man who can be used for His good purposes. We don't know whether Nebuchadnezzar ever fully accepts Yahweh as his God and turns from his evil practices, but it does seem that he experiences repentance: "But at the end of that period, I, Nebuchadnezzar, lifted up my eyes to heaven, and then my reason returned to me; and I blessed the Most High and the one who lives forever I praised and I honored" (Dan 4:34). In return, God restores him.

We can never predict how God will use people, and at times we may be shocked by whom He uses. Some people we think are lost may end up being found after all. Let's dream of redemption for those who need it most. —JDB

What people in your life need redemption?
For whom are you praying?
Have you lost hope about anyone God may still redeem?

RESPECT

Daniel 5:1–6:28; **1 Thessalonians 5:12–28**; Job 41:10–20

Instead of easing the burdens of our church leaders, we often add to them. The sometimes thankless job of ministry is weighed down with our taking and not giving, our complaining, and our squirming under authority.

We can see from Paul's letters that church communities haven't changed much since the first century. In his letter to the believers in Thessalonica, Paul requests: "Now we ask you, brothers, to respect those who labor among you and rule over you in the Lord and admonish you, and to esteem them beyond all measure in love, because of their work. Be at peace among yourselves" (1 Thess 5:12).

A passage like this might convict us for our bad attitude or lack of service. We might make a greater effort to love and respect those who are in positions of authority. Or we might try to ease the load of our leaders by serving in our communities. But unless we address the disorder within our hearts, our efforts won't lead to the peace that Paul commands.

In Thessalonica, members of the community seem to have had a problem with authority. After Paul urges them to "be at peace" (1 Thess 5:12), he tells them to "admonish the disorderly" (1 Thess 5:14). He demonstrates that the problem is deeper—it rests within the natural chaos of our own hearts. It's easy to this —Yet Paul says, "see to it that no one pays back evil for evil" (1 Thess 5:15).

The disorder of our hearts and minds needs to be transformed. Only when we are presented with a true picture of ourselves and a true picture of what God has done for us can we begin to understand the chaos in our hearts. Only when God rules our chaos can we be an agent of peace in our communities. —RVN

How can you relieve the burdens of leaders in your community?
What needs to change about your attitude toward them?

October 29

° ◊ ◊ ◊ °

APOCALYPTIC AT ITS BEST

Daniel 7:1–8:27; 2 Thessalonians 1:1–12; Job 41:21–34

Daniel is full of spooky scenes. If Daniel doesn't scare you a bit, you've probably watched too many horror movies.

Apocalyptic literature in the Bible has a way of playing tricks on us. It's full of vivid imagery that can be haunting—and that's intentional. The pictures it paints are meant to stay with us. We're meant to remember what these passages are teaching. Of course, the same can be said of the entire Bible, but apocalyptic literature is especially vivid because its message requires us to choose: to follow or to turn away from God at the most important time—the end.

The dreams Daniel has, including those recorded in Daniel 7:3–14, are images of what is and is to come. The beasts in Daniel were evocative symbols for his audience. When they heard of the lion with eagles, they envisioned Babylon (Dan 7:4). When the bear appeared, they thought of Media (Dan 7:5). Likewise, the leopard with four wings and heads symbolized Persia (Dan 7:6). And the ten-horned beast with iron teeth represented Greece (see Dan 7:7; see also Dan 2). These beasts would become memory devices for Daniel's audience. Later, when Greece entered the scene, the people could say, "I won't follow the empire, for they are evil. Like a ten-horned beast with iron teeth, the empire will maul us and eat us alive."

When we misread large sections of the Bible, such as apocalyptic literature, we lose sight of what matters most about it: remembering the truth. Daniel wanted us to call it like it is. If we see evil, we need to remember that it will destroy us. We need to remember the vividness of Daniel's descriptions. Evil can, and will, capture us if we compromise. But our good God is here as our guide—let's lean on Him. —JDB

Where are you currently compromising?

October 30

∘ ∘ ◦ ◦ ∘

AN OBSTRUCTED VIEW

Daniel 9:1–10:21; 2 Thessalonians 2:1–17; **Job 42:1–9**

We need to see ourselves as we truly are, but we can't do that on our own. Our communities can help us glimpse a more accurate reflection, but we truly know ourselves only when we know God. His light brings us understanding.

After suffering incredible loss, Job tries to understand his pain. He speaks some truth, but he often misunderstands God's motives and minimizes His love. As his friends try to help him grapple with his grief, they sometimes point out truth, but more often they cause even more pain and confusion. It's only when God arrives to enlighten Job's understanding that everything changes. First God questions Job's knowledge (Job 38:19–21), power (Job 38:25–38), and ideas about justice (Job 40:10–12). Then He shows Job that He is all of these things.

The realization exposes Job's heart. "Then Job answered Yahweh and said, 'I know that you can do all things, and any scheme from you will not be thwarted. "Who is this darkening counsel without knowledge?" Therefore I uttered, but I did not understand; things too wonderful for me, but I did not know. "Hear and I will speak; I will question you, then inform me." By the ear's hearing I heard of you, but now my eye has seen you. Therefore I despise myself and repent in dust and ashes'" (Job 42:1–6).

We might struggle to understand our frailty before a God who is all-knowing and all-powerful. We might be blinded by pride and self-righteousness, which can hinder us from seeing our need for God. But it is only then that we discover how we can be redeemed from our needy state.

Although God had never stopped loving Job, He further demonstrated His love by blessing Job once again. We can be convinced of God's love for us because He sent His only Son to die for our sins. Although He is great and we are small, He was willing to die for our sins. We can be assured of His love for us. —RVN

What area of your life is filled with pride?
How can you humbly allow God to expose who you truly are?

October 31

∘ ⊚ ∘ ⊚ ∘

SPEAKING THE TRUTH

Daniel 11:1–12:12; 2 Thessalonians 3:1–18; Job 42:10–17

"And now I will reveal the truth to you" (Dan 11:2). How much better would our world be if more of us were willing to take this kind of stand—to make these kinds of statements?

The truth Daniel refers to are the prophecies foretelling what will happen in the Persian Empire. Great power and wealth are coming, and with them comes the fear of how that power and wealth may be used. If we read between the lines of the prophet's statements in Daniel 11, we can feel the trepidation. He is concerned that wickedness will once again sweep over the land.

Such was the case for Paul: "Pray for us, that the word of the Lord may progress and be honored … and that we may be delivered from evil and wicked people, for not all have the faith" (2 Thess 3:1–2). Paul was aware that unbelievers would seek his life. He wasn't sure what the future would look like. We can imagine the fear that he must have felt, wondering, "What is next? What is coming? Who is my friend? Who is my enemy?"

If you have ever been in a situation where it seems you have more enemies than friends, you know that speaking the truth becomes increasingly difficult over time. The prophecies in Daniel 11 suggest a time like this, and Paul's words tell us that life for the early Christians was uncertain. Many Christians today lead relatively safe and easy lives. For Christians in some parts of the world, though, Paul's situation is far too familiar. But no matter our present situation, we must boldly speak the truth. —JDB

What is God asking you to say?

November 1

∘ ∘ ∘ ∘ ∘

THE DANGER OF UNWARRANTED FAVOR

1 Kings 1:1–53; Mark 1:1–34; Proverbs 1:1–7

No sooner had David assumed the throne of Israel than he began to lose sight of God's way. As a young "warrior in the wilderness," he had provided a beacon of hope and an ethical example for God's people. But King David allowed emotion, rather than spiritual or even rational principles, to drive him. And David's children made the situation even worse. Although we often look to David as an example to emulate, we can also learn from the mistakes that he made, including the disaster recorded in 1 Kings 1:5–53.

As king, David was charged with protecting God's people against all outside enemies. What David didn't see coming—or so it appears from the text—was the threat from within his own family. When David's sons began to compete for power, David should have put his love for God's people and the calling God gave him above his love for his sons. The moment that Adonijah showed signs of laying claim to the throne (1 Kgs 1:5–10), David should have rebuked him—or perhaps even imprisoned or executed him, according to law of the time. Instead, David let it go.

Appointing Solomon as king was a wise political rebuttal, but David still failed to deal with the core problem—Adonijah. David may have been old and sick by this point, but he could have made better provisions for his kingdom, especially with so many loyal military leaders on his side. David's position as king made his leniency even worse: He should have treated Adonijah like any other traitor.

Why did David ignore Adonijah's rebellion? Maybe he loved his son. Maybe he was too tired or too frail to take on big problems at the end of his reign. We may never know the reason, but we do know the results. David's weakness nearly ruined all he had built for God; his mistakes nearly tore the kingdom in two.

Parents often love their children so deeply that they overlook their failings. Righteousness should maintain its proper authority over wishful thinking and ungoverned emotions—in both kingdoms and households. —JDB

Who are you unreasonably favoring?

November 2

○ ○ ○ ○ ○

WILL WE FOLLOW?

1 Kings 2:1–46; **Mark 1:35–2:28**; Proverbs 1:8–12

The Gospel of Mark opens without fanfare—certainly nothing befitting literary greatness. There is no lofty imagery like the Gospel of John, no impressive genealogies like the Gospel of Matthew, and no historical narrative like the Gospel of Luke. Instead, Mark flashes rapidly through events that build on one another. John the Baptist's prophecy is followed by short summaries of Jesus' baptism and His temptation by Satan. After calling His first disciples, Jesus begins healing and preaching both near and far—all within the first chapter. The unadorned, clipped prose communicates something urgent.

Mark's narrative captures the coming kingdom that will erupt with a power only some can see. It imparts a sense of urgency to those who know they are needy.

Mark portrays the advancing kingdom through the person and work of Jesus, who draws people. The crowds at Capernaum seek Him out (Mark 2:2), as do those marginalized by society (Mark 1:40; 2:3). Although Jesus seeks to keep His movements hidden and warns the leper to conceal the miracle of his healing, the exact opposite occurs. The leper opts to "proclaim it freely and to spread abroad the account" (Mark 1:45). When Jesus secludes Himself in deserted places because of His fame, the crowds come at Him "from all directions" (Mark 1:45). Even roofs are removed to gain access to Him (Mark 2:4).

While some question His authority, others respond with radical allegiance. Jesus' simple, direct call to Levi the tax collector, "Follow me!" requires nothing less. Jesus came for lepers and paralytics, to sinners and tax collectors—those who are sick and in need of a physician (Mark 2:16). He came for us—those who know our desperate need—and reversed our fate. With unfettered truth, Mark presents us with the opportunity for the only healing response: Will we follow? —RVN

Are you following Jesus with total allegiance?
What is holding you back?

LOVE AND COMMITMENT: NOT ALWAYS SYNONYMOUS

1 Kings 3:1–4:34; Mark 3:1–3:35; Proverbs 1:13–19

Loving God and living fully for Him are not necessarily synonymous. If I love someone, does that mean I always show untainted respect and unfailing loyalty? Love should command complete devotion and commitment—but our lives are rarely as pure as they should be.

Like his father, David, Solomon acted out of passion and love, but his commitment and respect for Yahweh faltered at the same time: "Solomon intermarried with … the daughter of Pharaoh and brought her to the city of David … Solomon loved Yahweh, by walking in the statutes of David his father; only he was sacrificing and offering incense on the high places" (1 Kgs 3:1, 3).

Solomon didn't marry Pharaoh's daughter because he needed Egypt's protection. Egypt, Israel's ancient enemy, had enslaved God's people once before, but it was not an imminent threat. Worse, Solomon committed himself to Pharaoh, an ally who viewed himself as a deity. This alliance introduced the worship of foreign gods into the chambers of the king who was supposed to steward God's kingdom.

Solomon's behavior is particularly ironic in light of his own words: "My child, do not walk in their way. Keep your foot from their paths, for their feet run to evil, and they hurry to shed blood" (Prov 1:15–16). Solomon may have avoided the wars and violence of his father's generation, but he walked into a spiritually enslaving sin. Solomon's problems epitomize Jesus' words: "And if a kingdom is divided against itself, that kingdom is not able to stand" (Mark 3:24). By bringing Pharaoh's daughter into his household, Solomon divided Yahweh's kingdom against itself.

Was it lust that drove Solomon to make this decision, or a lack of faith, or a desire for peace? We cannot know for certain, but no matter the reason, this episode shows us something about ourselves.

When we ally ourselves with God's opponents or when we lust after what God has condemned, we do more harm than we realize. We divide what God is building in us and through us against itself by tainting His pure plan. —JDB

What are you wrongly allying with or lusting after?
What are the long-term effects of doing so,
and how can this perspective help you change course?

November 4

○ ○ ○ ○ ○

CUTTING A DEAL WITH GOD

1 Kings 5:1–6:38; **Mark 4:1–24**; Proverbs 1:20–27

S ometimes we think we can make deals with God. We hear His commands, but we plan on being faithful later. Or we make light of our rebellious thoughts and actions, thinking they're only minor offenses in the grand scheme of things. Perhaps we think God will overlook them just as easily as we've rationalized them.

Jesus put special emphasis on "having ears to hear" in the Gospel of Mark. He expected much more than a captive audience, though: "'If anyone has ears to hear, let him hear!' And he said to them, 'Take care what you hear! With the measure by which you measure out, it will be measured out to you, and will be added to you'" (Mark 4:23–24).

Jesus issued this command shortly after giving His disciples special insight into the parable of the Sower and the Seed. The rocky soil, the thorns, the road, the good soil—these represented various responses to the good news. The good soil was receptive to the seeds. But more than that, such soils "receive it and bear fruit—one thirty and one sixty and one a hundred times as much" (Mark 4:20).

Jesus revealed the secret of the kingdom to His disciples, to the surrounding crowd, and to us. Now that we hear, we must take care that we respond. Bear fruit befitting His work in you (Mark 4:20), and let others know why you bear fruit (Mark 4:21–22). Because He has given to you with such abundance, He expects you to live abundantly for Him—right now. —RVN

How are you rationalizing your response to God's work?
Are you delaying responding to God?

November 5

○ ○ ○ ○ ○

OF FIELDS AND TEMPLES

1 Kings 7:1–51; **Mark 4:26–5:20**; Proverbs 1:28–33

The building of Solomon's temple and the growth of the kingdom of God are similar: Both require extensive labor. Both bring miraculous results. And in both efforts, the dredging and toil can proceed for weeks, months, or years before the fruits of the labor become apparent.

When the Bible describes the building of God's temple, it mentions features and materials that would have been incredible at the time: "He built the House of the Forest of Lebanon … It was covered with cedar above … There were three rows of specially designed windows … All of the doorways and the doorframes had four-sided casings" (1 Kgs 7:2–5). Consider the logistical, expediting, and procurement hurdles that Solomon must have faced. How could one leader build a project that required the finest materials and the most highly skilled craftsmen from all over the known world, all in his lifetime? That it was completed is nearly miraculous. Even today, major architectural feats often take longer than a lifetime (e.g., Gaudi's cathedral in Barcelona).

Like the construction of Solomon's temple, what we as Christians build into other people's lives is meant to happen miraculously. We labor for it, but the fruits are not ours—they are often unexplainable. Jesus once remarked, "The kingdom of God is like this: like a man scatters seed on the ground. And he sleeps and gets up, night and day, and the seed sprouts and grows—he does not know how. By itself the soil produces a crop: first the grass, then the head of grain, then the full grain in the head. But when the crop permits, he sends in the sickle [a tool for harvesting crops] right away, because the harvest has come" (Mark 4:26–29). We must continue to labor, knowing all the while that the results will be different than what we expect. We must rely on the Spirit for the real work. —JDB

What are you laboring at today?
How may the results be different than what you expect?

° ° ⋄ ° °

THE PURSUIT OF GOD

1 Kings 8:1–53; Mark 5:21–6:6; **Proverbs 2:1–15**

We're willing to put an incredible amount of effort into pursuing something that's really important to us. Before buying a new gadget, we'll read reviews, research the manufacturer's reputation, and consult our tech-savvy friends. Our efforts and curiosity betray the true treasures of our hearts. Other things that we say are important might not receive the same effort—often to our detriment.

In Proverbs, being curious about God's ways is vital for life. The father in Proverbs encourages his son to be curious about God's ways, representing his desire to fear God: "My child, if you will receive my sayings, and hide my commands with you, in order to incline your ear toward wisdom, then you shall apply your heart to understanding. For if you cry out for understanding, if you lift your voice for insight, if you seek her like silver and search her out like treasure, then you will understand the fear of Yahweh, and the knowledge of God you will find" (Prov 2:1–5).

The knowledge of God isn't just knowledge *about* God. It's also the desire and the process of inclining and applying your heart to understanding. The father encourages his son to cry out for understanding or lift his voice for insight—going beyond just intellectual comprehension. The son must seek understanding the same way someone might search out silver or a treasure. The father wants his son to learn about God's ways, to understand them himself so he can apply them to his life.

We might claim to hold to a life of worship, but do our actions really reflect that value? Do our efforts and decisions reflect a heart that cries out to God for His wisdom? God has redeemed us at a great price with the death of His son. He desires that we turn over our lives to Him—and that includes pursuing Him with all our being. —RVN

Are you pursuing "the knowledge of God"
and applying your heart to understanding?

November 7

○ ○ ◊ ○ ○

THE RESULTS OF
WORSHIP AND TEACHING

1 Kings 8:54–9:28; **Mark 6:7–44**; Proverbs 2:16–22

"It happened that when Solomon finished praying to Yahweh all of the prayer and this plea, he got up from before the altar of Yahweh, from kneeling down on his knees with his palms outstretched to heaven. He stood and blessed all of the assembly of Israel with a loud voice…" (1 Kgs 8:54–55).

Solomon demonstrates the natural and proper response to worship—declaring God's goodness to others and blessing them in His name. These blessings can come in simple forms, such as doing good for others, or they may look more elaborate, as Solomon's prayer continues in 1 Kings 8.

Worship can become stilted when we focus on our place before Yahweh instead of His natural and rightful place. We're meant to view Yahweh for who He is and what He has done, and to respond to His work by helping others.

Jesus demonstrated a similar point in His own ministry. He could have kept His disciples with Him day and night, but instead He sent them on their way to do God's will (Mark 6:6–13). For Jesus, teaching was a means to an end. Everything the disciples had learned up to that point would carry them in the ministry work they were about to do. They weren't meant to hoard their knowledge or focus on learning for learning's sake. Instead, teaching led to action.

We, too, must follow worship with actions. When we learn, we must act upon what we have learned. Anything that stays in a vacuum is useless. It's only when we apply what God is doing in our lives that we live up to our calling in Him. —JDB

What is God asking you to live out?

TRADITIONS AND
A PRIORITY PROBLEM

1 Kings 10:1–11:8; **Mark 6:45–7:13**; Proverbs 3:1–5

Traditions make us feel secure. They give us a sense of camaraderie with those who came before us, and they can build a sense of community with those around us. But traditions handed down unexamined can be dangerous. We can apply them in contexts that differ from those in which they were born—often leading to disastrous results, offenses, and misunderstanding. More dangerously, we might consider these human traditions to be the commands of God—or above His commands. In doing so, we hold the opinions of people to be higher than God's. We commit the same type of idolatry we find rampant in the Old Testament.

In many communities, traditions can carry the heavy weight of religiosity, as if God were the very author of the tradition. Many of the Pharisees in Jesus' time were known to "tie up heavy burdens and put them on people's shoulders" (Matt 23:4). When the Pharisees confront Jesus because His disciples did not wash before eating, Jesus quotes from Isaiah: "This people honors me with their lips, but their heart is far from me; in vain do they worship me, teaching as doctrines the commandments of men" (Mark 7:6–7).

To us, hand-washing seems like a smart, valuable tradition. For these Pharisees, it is a cleansing ritual meant to protect against defilement. Jesus shows how the practice sharply conflicts with the state of their hearts, which are far from God. The Pharisees often excuse some of God's commands if it means following their traditions—like offering sacrifices while neglecting to provide for the material needs of parents (Mark 7:11–13).

Are there areas in your life in which you hold others' opinions above those of God? Do you have nagging guilt because you're not living up to others' expectations? Why? Examine your life, seek biblical wisdom, and ask God to show you how best to serve Him. —RVN

How are you holding the values
of people higher than those of God?

November 9

○ ○ ◊ ○ ○

FEAR NOT WHAT'S
OUTSIDE BUT INSIDE

1 Kings 11:9–12:33; **Mark 7:14–8:10**; Proverbs 3:6–3:12

How should we respond to a miraculous experience? Worshiping God for His goodness is the right place to start, but our ongoing response is every bit as important as our initial reaction. We see this play out in Solomon's life.

"Yahweh was angry with Solomon, for he had turned his heart from Yahweh, the God of Israel who had appeared to him twice. And [Yahweh] commanded [Solomon] concerning this matter not to go after other gods, but he did not keep that which Yahweh commanded" (1 Kgs 11:9–10).

Despite Solomon's experience with Yahweh, he chose to deny Him. This angered Yahweh—not just because of the general disobedience, but also because, after Solomon's miraculous experience, he had more reason than anyone to stay devoted. Solomon's refusal of the opportunity to turn back to Yahweh only aggravated the situation.

We don't know exactly what led Solomon to disobey, although selfish desire, lust, and power seem to dominate his poor decisions. We can be certain that his inner thoughts drove him to act in the way he did. Solomon's situation is reminiscent of Jesus' remark about what defiles a person: "For from within, from the heart of people, come evil plans, sexual immoralities, thefts, murders, adulteries, acts of greed, malicious deeds, deceit, licentiousness, envy, abusive speech, pride, foolishness. All these evil things come from within and defile a person" (Mark 7:21–23).

How many of us have at some point walked off God's path and excused our actions in the name of grace? Solomon had ample opportunity to return to God, yet he continued to aggravate Him. How many of us react the same way to the goodness God has offered us? —JDB

What is happening "in" you that leads to the evil in your life?
How can you allow the Spirit to resolve that?

∘ ◊ ◊ ◊ ∘

TAKE UP YOUR CROSS

1 Kings 13:1–34; **Mark 8:11–9:1**; Proverbs 3:13–22

The way we respond to desperate circumstances often clarifies what gives us hope. Jesus' followers faced the very real threat of death by choosing to follow Him—something He warns them about: "And summoning the crowd together with his disciples, he said to them, 'If anyone wants to come after me, let him deny himself and take up his cross and follow me. For whoever wants to save his life will lose it, but whoever loses his life on account of me and of the gospel will save it'" (Mark 8:34–35).

In Jesus' time, "taking up the cross" would have been associated with a shameful death at the hands of the ruling Roman powers. To risk suffering this type of shameful death required more than lukewarm commitment.

Jesus doesn't limit this calling to His disciples; anyone who "wants to come after" faces this uncertainty and must hold a faith that displays this loyalty. Yet

Many of our lives reflect a lax neutrality—a purposeless ease that avoids conflict and commitment. We might shy away from bold claims. We might fade into the wallpaper in an attempt to fit in. We might show reluctance to declare Christ's name.

What does commitment look like for you? Are you following Jesus with this type of devotion? Or do you hesitate to share the good news? —RVN

How are you taking up your cross?

November 11

∘ ∘ ◊ ∘ ∘

TRADITIONS AND MIRACLES

1 Kings 14:1–15:24; **Mark 9:2–37**; Proverbs 3:23–35

In the face of perplexing situations, we naturally respond with what we know and understand—we even take refuge in familiar traditions. This is precisely how Jesus' disciples respond when Jesus is transfigured before them.

After Jesus is transformed and Moses and Elijah appear, Peter says, "Rabbi, it is good that we are here! And let us make three shelters, one for you and one for Moses and one for Elijah" (Mark 9:5). Peter is drawing on the Festival of Tabernacles (or Booths), which celebrated God's dwelling among His people (Lev 23:42–43). Peter isn't certain how to respond, so he evokes a tradition. At least Peter understands that this confusing event shows God at work among His people.

But is Peter's response the correct one? Mark gives us a hint in an aside: "For [Peter] did not know what he should answer, because they [Peter, James, and John] were terrified" (Mark 9:6). It's not surprising that Peter has trouble understanding this situation—who could? But his response, underscored by the editorial aside in Mark, suggests something larger about how we, as the audience of this Gospel, should understand Jesus.

When Jesus reveals Himself to us—really inaugurates His reign in our lives—it may be terrifying, but we do not need to resort to our traditions to understand it. By going back to our old ways, we might lose sight of the point of God's work altogether. Instead, we must be ready to accept what is new. We must realize that when God acts, the results will be unexpected and perhaps unexplainable. When God intercedes in our lives, when He lets us experience Him, our lives—our very view of the world—will change. —JDB

What traditions is Jesus radically altering in your life?

○ ○ ○ ○ ○

EXCLUSIVITY

1 Kings 15:25–17:24; **Mark 9:38–10:16**; Proverbs 4:1–7

We often think that God needs *us*—that we are His arms rather than His agents. When we see our work as integral to God's kingdom—thinking that God needs us, our vision, our doctrines, or our ideas in order to further His kingdom—we might be guilty of something else entirely. These feelings are often motivated by our own feelings of inadequacy. We can sometimes be more concerned with proving ourselves than honoring God.

When the disciples learned that others were casting out demons in Jesus' name, they tried to prevent them. "We saw … and we tried to prevent him because he was not following us," they told Jesus (Mark 9:38). But Jesus only rebuked them: "There is no one who does a miracle in my name and will be able soon afterward to speak evil of me. For whoever is not against us is for us. For whoever gives you a cup of water to drink in my name because you are Christ's, truly I say to you that he will never lose his reward" (Mark 9:38–41).

The disciples needed to be reminded that they had been chosen, but they were not exclusive agents. Having had difficulty casting out demons themselves, the disciples may have been jealous of this man's ability. But Jesus reminded them that even the smallest task completed in His name—even giving someone a drink of water—is work done for His kingdom that will be rewarded.

Although He doesn't need our help, Jesus invites each of us to be part of His plan. He desires our involvement if we do so obediently and willingly, with no thought to how great our actions will be weighed. When we accept that offer and join in His work, we are following Him and making much of Him. We won't be distracted by ourselves. —RVN

How open are you to the idea that God
can work in ways that don't depend on us?

THE SPIRITUAL BATTLE

1 Kings 18:1–46; Mark 10:17–52; Proverbs 4:8–17

Sometimes our work for God requires severe actions. In these times—ones that we can't possibly prepare for—we need to rely on the Spirit and its work to empower us.

I have always admired Elijah the prophet because he goes into firestorms with little, if any, preparation. The Spirit of God is his leader, sword, and shield. One of the most frightening moments in Elijah's life is his encounter with the prophets of Baal at Mount Carmel. How could Elijah prepare to face 450 prophets from the enemy nation who are endorsed by Elijah's own king? He faced certain death. Perhaps he had even reconciled himself to the idea that his life would end on that mountain.

Elijah's supreme confidence in Yahweh is inspiring. He instructs the prophets of Baal, "Choose for yourselves one bull and prepare it first, for you are the majority, and call on the name of your god, but don't set fire under it" (1 Kgs 18:25). After the other prophets fail to bring down fire from heaven, Elijah does what must be done: He calls down fire, and then he kills the evil prophets (1 Kgs 18:30–40).

Although Elijah's particular actions do not apply directly today, his boldness certainly does. We should never fear walking into a fight against evil; instead, we should be ready to engage those who lead others astray. We must be certain that God will give us His words. He will act through us.

Whenever we're in need, no matter how severe the situation, God can deliver us. We cannot prepare for the battle against the great evil that lurks in the world, but we can be certain that God will be with us. —JDB

What evil must you face? What do you need?
Have you asked God for it?

STAYING THE COURSE

1 Kings 19:1–20:25; Mark 11:1–33; **Proverbs 4:18–27**

"May your eyes look forward and your gaze be straight before you. May the path of your foot be balanced and all your ways be sure. Do not swerve right or left; remove your foot from evil" (Prov 4:25–27).

These verses reflect someone who has incredible purpose. I imagine an acrobat walking a tightrope—knees bent, one foot carefully placed in front of the other, and nothing but a slender rope keeping him from plummeting to the ground. Such efforts would require incredible calm, effort, and focus—especially focus. The body naturally follows the path of our eyes, which is detrimental if we're focused on the wrong thing.

The idea of staying the course illustrates God's path and purpose for us. When we act, speak, and follow that path, we are carrying out His will for our lives. But there's a problem: We can't. All of our efforts are tainted. Our knees are bound to buckle, we're sure to misstep, and it's just a matter of time before we swerve to our own disadvantage.

Before we lose hope, though, we can remember God's sacrifice. Jesus' work of redeeming us has reversed our fate. The threat is gone—and that changes everything. Our lives are infused with the incredible purpose of His costly death. We have a renewed sense of hope because of His resurrection.

The cross puts everything in perspective. It is the new focus of our gaze. From His sacrifice to the time when redemption is complete, we are meant to live intentional lives that reflect His purpose. Keeping our eyes on Him helps us to stay on the path. —RVN

How are you staying the course?

ECONOMICS, CURRENCY, AND CAESAR

1 Kings 20:26–21:29; **Mark 12:1–34**; Proverbs 5:1–10

Jesus' command to pay taxes is one of the trickier passages in the New Testament. The actual line isn't tricky—"Give to Caesar the things of Caesar, and to God the things of God" (Mark 12:17)—but its origins and Jesus' exact reasoning aren't as clear.

People have taken this passage to suggest that Jesus was in favor of government or taxes. But this interpretation misses the point. We're meant to learn from Jesus here, not take away some regulation. Certainly Jesus condones paying taxes and charity work, but those points touch only on the basics of His statement.

First, Jesus is annoyed. The Pharisees and Herodians are testing Him with this question, and He doesn't approve. His reaction suggests that simply taking away a "law" here would sadden Him, for that's all the Pharisees and Herodians cared about (Mark 12:15). The "law" would address only the political question.

Jesus goes on to ask for a denarius, signaling that He doesn't have one—He is poor (Mark 12:15–16). This coin had Caesar's image on it and claimed divinity for Caesar. Jesus' remark acknowledges the claim: "Give to Caesar the currency of his kingdom's economy." He also addresses the larger issue of the "image of God" (Gen 1:27): "Give to God the things of God" (Mark 12:17). What belongs to God? The entire world and everything in it—our very selves. We are meant, as members of God's work, to act as people who operate within His currency of sacrificial living.

The Pharisees and Herodians' question and Jesus' answer are political, but the politics are eternal. The economics have ramifications for all people, for all time. They change the way we as Christians act and operate. They change what we value. The economic shift is an "image-bearing" shift.

Whom do you serve? Give to God what He deserves. Give to the kingdoms of this world what they have created (their currency). Give to God what is God's—your very life. Operate under God's currency as one who bears His image. —JDB

What is God asking you to give?

I (DON'T) WANT TO HEAR IT

1 Kings 22:1–53; Mark 12:35–13:23; Proverbs 5:11–23

My attempts to find guidance are often flawed. I long for honest appraisal of my actions, but I can sometimes be sneaky about choosing my appraiser. When those who know me present a real, raw look at my life and offer hard, helping words, I can become defensive and angry. I might pick a fresh voice instead—someone who doesn't know my weaknesses and tendencies. "They're not biased," I tell myself.

When Ahab and Jehoshaphat combine forces to recapture Ramoth-gilead from the Syrians, they want divine assurance. However, they aren't necessarily willing to receive divine direction. Ahab, king of Israel, inquires of his 400 prophets, and they assure him of victory. Jehoshaphat isn't convinced, so he asks for "a prophet of Yahweh."

Ahab's response isn't so far from my own: "Then the king of Israel said to Jehoshaphat, 'There is still one man to inquire from Yahweh, but I despise him, for he never prophesies anything good concerning me, but only bad: Micaiah the son of Imlah'" (1 Kgs 22:8).

Micaiah can't really win when it comes to Ahab. When he responds sarcastically to Ahab's request—telling him he'll conquer and win—Ahab demands he tell the truth. When Micaiah reveals what Ahab doesn't want to hear—imminent defeat—Ahab complains that Micaiah never prophesies anything good about him.

When we hear hard words, we often take our aggression out on the messengers. We regard them as the one at fault. "You always respond this way," we'll say. "You don't really understand me." Soon, we avoid these truth-tellers because their words of truth expose our sin. And if our sin remains concealed, we won't have to admit it exists. If we don't admit it, we won't have to confess it. And if we don't confess it, we won't have to turn from it.

It's all too easy to avoid necessary reform. But if we truly seek to follow God, we can't avoid the hard truth. When we truly need guidance, we must be willing to face the truth-tellers—even when it hurts. —RVN

Who are the people you go to for guidance? Why?
Whose guidance are you really rebelling against?

November 17

○ ◌ ◈ ◌ ○

WHEN IN NEED

2 Kings 1:1–2:5; Mark 13:24–14:21; Proverbs 6:1–5

When we encounter trouble, we tend to look wherever we can for help: We turn in whatever direction seems most promising at the moment. In doing so, we may unwittingly walk away from Yahweh. Should practicality or convenience stand between God and us?

When King Ahaziah falls through a lattice and is injured, he seeks help from a foreign god rather than Yahweh—likely because it *seems* natural or right. He thinks the god of Ekron, Baal-Zebub, can provide the healing he needs. But what Ahaziah sees as a desperate situation is actually an opportunity for Yahweh to act; Yahweh plans to use this situation for His glory.

When Ahaziah sends messengers to Ekron, Yahweh intercedes. Elijah approaches them bearing a word from Yahweh that had been spoken to him by an angel: "Is it because there is no God in Israel that you are going to inquire of Baal-Zebub, the god of Ekron?" (2 Kgs 1:3).

When we experience physical or spiritual pain, do we first recognize Yahweh's power and seek Him, or do we turn to other sources? Does our turning to other places demonstrate a lack of faith? What do we really believe in when we seek people, ideas, or things rather than God in our time of need?

The consequences of turning away from Yahweh can be tragic. Elijah goes on to declare: "The bed upon which you have gone, you will not come down from it, but you shall surely die" (2 Kgs 1:4). Let us turn to God before it comes to this. Let us choose Yahweh. —JDB

Whom are you turning to right now
in your time of need?

∘ ◊ ◊ ◊ ∘

WARRING TENDENCIES
AND SPIRITUAL AIRS

2 Kings 3:1–4:17; **Mark 14:22–50**; Proverbs 6:6–11

"I will do this!" I declare as I resolve to get in shape, eat better, save money, study and meditate on the Word more, journal more, read more. My plans escalate, growing grander in scale and depth. Although I succeed in them for a while, I easily become overwhelmed when I can't live up to the inflated vision I've projected for myself.

It's especially easy to do this spiritually. It's simple to hand out godly advice with a spiritual air, to speak wise words about past failings (read subtext: "Look how far I've come!"), and to talk about personal growth. But when we mess up on a colossal scale, it's humiliating and surprising to all—especially ourselves. "What happened?" we might ask. "I was doing so well!"

Simon Peter had a tendency to make grand plans: "Even if they all fall away, certainly I will not!" he declared, proclaiming his loyalty to the Savior (Mark 14:29). They're words to fall flat on your face by. When Jesus found the disciples sleeping, He knew who needed the reprimand and the warning: "And he came and found them sleeping, and he said to Peter, 'Simon, are you sleeping? Were you not able to stay awake one hour? Stay awake and pray that you will not enter into temptation. The spirit is willing, but the flesh is weak!'" (Mark 14:37–38).

Jesus' reprimand should have exposed Simon Peter's pride, which was parading as loyalty. For all his exuberant claims, Simon Peter lacked true understanding of his nature. When he considered his spiritual state, he was optimistic about his own efforts. No one was more humiliated and more surprised than he when he later betrayed Jesus around a charcoal fire to curious strangers.

Our desire to follow Jesus is not the problem. Instead, it is our competitive nature, our pride, that needs to be repeatedly humbled. We need real understanding of our spiritual state—a picture we shouldn't try to project in any other way—coupled with a total dependency on Him. A war is being waged inside of us. We can only win because of what Christ has done and because of the Spirit's work in us. To God belongs all the glory. —RVN

Are you spinning your sin,
making it seem less dire than it really is?

PAIN, ANGUISH, AND RESURRECTION

2 Kings 4:18–5:27; Mark 14:51–15:15; Proverbs 6:12–19

Pain and anguish resound in the narrative of the Shunammite's son and Elisha (2 Kgs 4:18–37). Reading the story, we can't help but feel empathy for the Shunammite woman whose son has died. Yet Elisha seems so cavalier. What would prompt him to act this way? What is Elisha teaching us in this series of events?

Even those who have experienced miracles struggle to accept that God can handle anything. The Shunammite woman remarks to Elisha, "Did I ask for a son from my lord? Did I not say that you must not mislead me?" (2 Kgs 4:28). Elisha seems to recognize God's capability, however, even when his colleague, Gehazi, and the Shunammite woman fail to see it. Elisha is so confident in God's work that he remarks to Gehazi, "Gird up your loins [meaning 'get ready'] and take my staff in your hand and go. ... You must put my staff on the face of the boy" (2 Kgs 4:29). Elisha doesn't even feel the need to visit the child himself.

In the events that follow, we see complete empathy from Elisha, as well as total trust in God's ability to intercede. After learning that his staff didn't work, Elisha shows up himself. He lies on top of the dead boy's body and breathes into his mouth (2 Kgs 4:32–34). After the boy's body becomes warm again, Elisha paces for a while; then he bends over the boy, and the boy is resurrected (2 Kgs 4:35–36). The boy's mother recognizes the miracle and praises God for it (2 Kgs 4:37).

So why is Elisha so cavalier? He understands that whatever God gives is also God's to take away or to look after (2 Kgs 4:13–17). He knows that God is in the resurrection business. This is the same kind of situation we see with Lazarus and Jesus (compare John 11). Through Elisha's story, we learn of God's ability to bring back to life those whom He brought into the world in the first place; through Jesus, we learn that God will bring all back to life.

Sometimes difficult things have to happen for us to see what God can do. Elisha uses a moment of weakness to show God's strength over flesh itself. Jesus allows Himself a moment of pain ("he wept"—John 11:35) to show God's strength over all flesh. He has the ability to resurrect our broken bodies and our broken lives. —JDB

What part of your life needs redemption?
How does the hope of resurrection change your
feelings about current circumstances?

REJECTED AND DESPISED BY MEN

2 Kings 6:1–7:20; **Mark 15:16–47**; Proverbs 6:20–27

In Mark's Gospel, Jesus' crucifixion and death occur in stages of mockery and humiliation. The story is propelled by those who scorn—the soldiers, the chief priests and scribes, and even those who pass by. Jesus is spat on, stripped of His clothing, and mockingly forced to wear a purple robe with a crown of thorns. Throughout, He silently receives His undue punishment.

It's not until Jesus nears death that Mark slows the narrative: "And at the ninth hour Jesus cried out with a loud voice, 'Eloi, Eloi, lema sabachthani?' (which is translated, 'My God, my God, why have you forsaken me?')" (Mark 15:34).

These words have been spoken before, and this pain and humiliation has previously been told. In Psalm 22, the psalmist cries out to God in the midst of being mocked and scorned by his enemies. The song of lament relates the bitter anguish the psalmist experiences at the hands of enemies. "He trusts Yahweh," the psalmist's enemies jeer, "Let him deliver him because he delights in him" (Psa 22:8). The psalmist says he is "poured out like water" in his weakened state (Psa 22:14). His clothing is divided and given out by casting lots (Psa 22:18).

The psalm doesn't end here, though. It ends with the psalmist proclaiming God's deliverance to all the nations and to future generations: "Descendants will serve him. Regarding the Lord, it will be told to the next generation. They will come and tell his saving deeds to a people yet to be born, that he has done it" (Psa 22:30–31).

Jesus' words reveal Him to be the ultimate sufferer. It wasn't until His death that He was acknowledged for who He was. The Roman centurion proclaims it: "Truly this man was God's Son!" (Mark 15:39). The Servant who obediently came to die has delivered us. He has done it. —RVN

In what ways do you feel forsaken by God?
What difference does it make to know that Jesus
also cried out in His godforsakenness?

WALK LIKE THE SHUNAMMITE

2 Kings 8:1–9:29; **Mark 16:1–20**; Proverbs 6:28–35

Trust is a fickle matter. What does it take for us to trust another person—especially with our livelihood? Our decision to trust someone can usually be determined by whether we see God in that person.

When the Shunammite woman must decide whether to trust Elisha, it is a simple choice. God has already worked in her life through Elisha—giving her a son and then resurrecting him—so she understands that what he says is from Yahweh. When Elisha says to her, "Get up and go, you and your household, and dwell as an alien wherever you can, for Yahweh has called for a famine, and it will come to the land for seven years," she trusts him (2 Kgs 8:1). She goes to Philistia (2 Kgs 8:2).

Would we do the same—leave everything and go to a foreign land at one godly person's word? What does it take for us to trust someone with our lives? What does it take for us to trust God with our lives?

We will probably never encounter the decision the Shunammite woman had to make, but contemplating our answer reveals where we stand with God and others. It's tempting to answer with a quick, "Of course," but that would be to ignore the magnitude of her decision, and thus deny the seriousness of what God really asks of us—complete obedience, no matter what, to any degree necessary. Think about that for a moment: any degree necessary (compare Mark 8:34–38).

Are we really willing to acknowledge the gravity of what Jesus did in His death and resurrection (Mark 16:1–10)? Are we willing to live our lives as He intends? Are we willing to go to any place, to trust the word of God completely, to allow God to speak to us directly and through others, and to live passionately for Christ despite the cost? —JDB

Are you willing to go wherever God calls you?

∘ ◌ ◌ ◌ ∘

COUNTERFEIT GOSPELS

2 Kings 9:30–10:36; **Galatians 1:1–2:21**; Proverbs 7:1–9

We're fine with the idea of God being our savior, but we're not always keen on the notion of letting Him transform every area of our lives. We often emphasize sharing the gospel, but do we consider the reality of the outcome?

It's a question Paul poses to the church in Galatia. Typically, when Paul opens a letter to a church, he follows his greeting with a prayer of thanksgiving for the members of the community. But in his correspondence with the Galatians, he skips the niceties and opts for a biting remark, signaling that something is drastically wrong: "

I am astonished that you are turning away so quickly from the one who called you by the grace of Christ to a different gospel, not that there is a different gospel, except there are some who are disturbing you and wanting to distort the gospel of Christ" (Gal 1:6–9).

Paul's message is especially cutting because the Galatians knew better. Paul himself had preached the gospel to them. After he left and false teachers infiltrated the community, the Galatians veered off course. Instead of holding to the true teaching or even testing these teachers' claims against the gospel message, the Galatians adopted a new, counterfeit gospel.

Paul interrogates the Galatians, who may have been affected by the teaching of people who wanted them to adopt Jewish legal requirements, asking, "Did you receive the Spirit by works of the law or by hearing with faith? Are you so foolish? Having begun by the Spirit, are you now being perfected by the flesh?" (Gal 3:2–3). The simple gospel had been cluttered by attempts to remain obedient to the law. The believers were no longer living in the Spirit.

We are prone to push aside the lesson in this passage by claiming that it's specific to that context, but we might be guilty of this very fault. Do we think of becoming a Christian—getting saved—as the end of the journey? The reality of the gospel should affect all areas of our lives, which can now be used to give God the glory. Our entire lives—our thought processes, our ideals and theologies, our relationships—should reflect Christ and be shaped by the Spirit. The gospel isn't for one moment. It's going to transform everything. —RVN

Have you, without realizing it, turned from the gospel?
What area of your life needs to be transformed?

○ ◇ ◇ ◇ ○

THE GAMES WE PLAY

2 Kings 11:1–12:21; **Galatians 3:1–29**; Proverbs 7:10–20

We live in the age of online résumés, with pages dedicated to us and our faces. We can broadcast our thoughts in seconds and republish ideas that make us look smart by association. And we do it all in an effort to earn recognition or acceptance. We want to be heard in the midst of the noise—to earn a spot in the spotlight. The works of the law that drove Judaism in the first century AD weren't much different; they were pitched as a way to obtain God's favor as well as the favor of others.

Paul responds to the ideals of his age: "Who has bewitched you, before whose eyes Jesus Christ was publicly portrayed as having been crucified? I want only to learn this from you: Did you receive the Spirit by the works of the law, or by the hearing of faith?" (Gal 3:1–2). Paul's questions are rhetorical. We're not saved by works, but by the graciousness of God. It is not through works that the Spirit dwells among us, but through God's goodness shown in sending His Son to earth to die for humanity and then rise again.

We struggle to admit that we're looking for recognition—both from God and others. We know we can't earn our way into heaven, but that doesn't stop us from trying. We still think that if we can be good enough, smart enough, or successful enough, God and others will accept us. It's a game we play that is for naught—we cannot earn what God offers. —JDB

What are you fooling yourself
into thinking is important?

THE TIES THAT BIND

2 Kings 13:1–14:29; **Galatians 4:1–31**; Proverbs 7:21–27

We don't often consider our former lives as enslavement. We characterize our lives before Christ by bad decisions and sinful patterns, but not bondage. We like to think of ourselves as neutral beings. But Paul paints another picture. The things or people we once put our trust in were the things that enslaved us. Paul asks the Galatians why they would ever want to return to bondage.

"But at that time when you did not know God, you were enslaved to the things which by nature are not gods. But now, because you have come to know God, or rather have come to be known by God, how can you turn back again to the weak and miserable elemental spirits? Do you want to be enslaved to them all over again?" (Gal 4:8–9).

Paul tells the Galatians that turning back to the things they trusted formerly—whether the law for the Jews or spiritual beings for the Gentiles—is choosing enslavement. For us, it could be anything from thought patterns, greed, habits, people—anything we used to find value, comfort, or worth that is not God.

Before, we were subject to these things, which ruthlessly dictated our fate. Yet God didn't leave us in this state. Paul says we "have come to know God, or rather have come to be known by God" (Gal 4:9). While we were still sinners, He broke into our spiritual bondage and broke the chains, giving us freedom and life in Christ.

We are no longer slaves with no freedom to make decisions; we are adopted as sons and daughters—we are heirs (Gal 4:7). By making this association, Paul shows the Galatians that Christ has paid the price. He also pushes them to grow up. They can't just continue on in spiritual immaturity. Rather than trusting in the former things, they must continue in faith by being transformed by the Spirit. —RVN

What things from your life before Christ
tempt you to return to spiritual bondage?

YOU HAVE TO MEAN IT

2 Kings 15:1–17:5; Galatians 5:1–6:18; **Proverbs 8:1–8**

W isdom really isn't all that difficult to find. We think of this attribute as hidden or fleeting, but the book of Proverbs portrays Wisdom calling out to us: "Does not wisdom call, and understanding raise its voice? Atop the heights beside the road, at the crossroads she stands. Beside gates, before towns, at the entrance of doors" (Prov 8:1–3). When we seek Wisdom, she shows up. She's everywhere. She's waiting—not to be found, but to be embraced.

The intelligence of Wisdom, the prudence she teaches, is at our fingertips. In Proverbs 8:3–5, Wisdom cries out, "To you, O people, I call, and my cry is to the children of humankind. Learn prudence, O simple ones; fools, learn intelligence." Maybe the real problem is that few of us are wise enough to *be* what Wisdom requires us to be. The folly of humankind may not be in a lack of seeking, but a lack of doing. If we really want something, we work for it. Wisdom requires sacrificing what we want for what she desires.

And the key to knowing what Wisdom desires—identifying the wise decision—is right in front of us as well. As Wisdom says in Proverbs, "My mouth will utter truth, and wickedness is an abomination to my lips. All sayings of my mouth are in righteousness; none of them are twisted and crooked" (Prov 8:7–8). The wise decision is the opposite of what's "twisted" and "crooked." If it feels wrong, it is wrong. If our conscience is aligned with God's, we will know what's right. The rest will seem like an "abomination." If we want Wisdom, she's ours for the having—ours for the living (Jas 1:5–8). —JDB

For what decision do you need wisdom?
How should you be seeking it?

November 26

○ ◊ ◊ ◊ ○

A MOMENT TO REFLECT

2 Kings 17:6–18:12; **Ephesians 1:1–23**; **Proverbs 8:9–18**

Anyone will admit that wisdom is more than just knowledge. We think of wisdom as thoughtful insight acquired with life experience. However, Paul and the author of Proverbs tell us that it is not something we gain with a little age and some good direction. Wisdom is inseparable from the fear of God.

The author of Proverbs tells us wisdom is "knowledge and discretion"; it's associated with the desire to fear God, and it is a *reward* to those who seek it out. "I love those who love me," says Wisdom personified. "Those who seek me diligently shall find me" (Prov 8:17). Paul speaks of wisdom in light of understanding the grand story of salvation we're part of. When writing to the Ephesians, Paul prays that they will receive a certain type of spirit so they can grow in faith—"that the God of our Lord Jesus Christ, the glorious Father, may give you a spirit of wisdom and revelation in the knowledge of him (the eyes of your hearts having been enlightened), so that you may know what is the hope of his calling, what are the riches of the glory of his inheritance among the saints, and what is the surpassing greatness of his power toward us who believe" (Eph 1:17–19).

The Ephesian believers were brought into this family of faith through the work of Christ as part of God's plan (Eph 1:3–14). Paul prays for them to understand what it means for them to live as a hope-filled community that has been adopted—a treasured inheritance in God's great plan of salvation. The Ephesians will receive this type of wisdom and revelation as it is given by God, not on their own accord. Understanding their place in this story will, in turn, shape their entire existence.

Both Paul and the author of Proverbs note this need to seek out wisdom, which God will give if we ask. Stop to consider your place in God's redemptive work on your behalf. Pray for a spirit of wisdom to understand His work in your life. —RVN

Do you pray for wisdom?
What type of response do you offer because of
God's work on your behalf?

November 27

○ ○◊○ ○

WHEN HEZEKIAH
GAVE AWAY THE FARM

2 Kings 18:13–19:37; Ephesians 2:1–3:21; Proverbs 8:19–26

After the announcement that Hezekiah "did right in the eyes of Yahweh," the next description comes as a surprise: "At that time, Hezekiah cut off the doors of the temple of Yahweh and the doorposts which Hezekiah king of Judah had overlaid, and he gave them to the king of Assyria" (2 Kgs 18:3, 16).

For a moment Hezekiah was a strong king over Israel—he abolished idolatry and refused to obey the king of Assyria (2 Kgs 18:4, 7). As 2 Kings 18:6 describes, "He held on to Yahweh; he did not depart from following him, and he kept his commands that Yahweh had commanded Moses." But Hezekiah did not possess fortitude (see 2 Kgs 18:13–18). In an attempt to gain peace, he gave away not only treasures, but even pieces of Yahweh's temple itself (2 Kgs 18:15–16).

We've all been in situations where it's tempting to do anything for peace. Perhaps we've even compromised our ethics or values in these moments. But no matter the situation, giving away the farm like Hezekiah did is never the answer. Politicians often talk about "peace at all costs," but our world is full of dilemmas that don't allow for that option.

When desperate situations arise, we must have fortitude. We must seek solace in God and His will instead of giving in. If we make a decision based on the circumstances, it will be the wrong one. If we make our decisions based on prayer, we will make the correct moves.

Hezekiah could have relied on God when Sennacherib came knocking on his door and knocking down the cities of Judah, but he didn't. He paid a high price for his decision; the cost was his relationship with Yahweh. Even death is preferable to that.

Sometimes our decisions are more important than we realize because they may involve our relationship with God. We must let that relationship drive our decision making. Rather than being distracted by fear, anxiety, pressure, or even concern for anyone else, we must focus on God and His will; He alone will look out for us and others. We must give Him the opportunity to act. —JDB

What decisions do you need
God's intercession for?

THE UNITY OF BELIEVERS

2 Kings 20:1–21:26; **Ephesians 4:1–32**; Proverbs 8:27–36

It's easy to sort believers in a community based on the quantity of their service. Most of us could roll out the masking tape and divide those who contribute their time and efforts from those who don't. If we're honest, the topic itself easily divides us—it makes us feel used, overtasked, and resentful. But that's not the picture of unity of purpose that Paul presents in Ephesians. He describes the church as a body—one in which "each single part" is needed for the growth of the whole.

"But speaking the truth in love, we are to grow into him with reference to all things, who is the head, Christ, from whom the whole body, joined together and held together by every supporting ligament, according to the working by measure of each single part, the growth of the body makes for the building up of itself in love" (Eph 4:15–16).

We are each given unique abilities for the growth of the body, and "each single part" is necessary to grow the body of Christ. God gives gifts to each supporting ligament—each person—in order to build up the community. But it is Christ who joins and holds the church together.

Because of Christ's unifying role, a key aspect of growth as a community and as individuals includes speaking the truth in love—helping others grow to spiritual maturity in the truth of the gospel. Instead of chiding, we can remind others of God's goodness to them through Christ. Instead of further ostracizing them, we can invite them in by speaking the truth with love, realizing that God has blessed them with special abilities that will soon be realized. —RVN

How can you use your gifts to serve your community?
How can you lovingly help others recognize theirs?

REVITALIZATION:
MOVING BEYOND THE CATCH WORD

2 Kings 22:1–23:27; Ephesians 5:1–33; Proverbs 9:1–12

Ideally, spiritual renewal wouldn't be necessary—we would continually grow closer to God. But that's not the case. There are ups and downs in our walk with Yahweh. We experience times of intimacy and times of distance. We lose focus, energy, or the desire to obey. These highs and lows could be the result of our fallen world or our taking God for granted, but whatever the reason, we need renewal. essential. We can *always* grow closer to God.

During his reign, King Josiah launches a reformation—a revitalization of the way God's people think and act. He even changes the people's understanding of God Himself. After finding a scroll (likely of Deuteronomy), Josiah tears his clothes in remorse and repentance and instructs the priests to inquire of Yahweh on behalf of the people (2 Kgs 22:8–13). Yahweh is aware of their misdeeds. Then Josiah immediately does what needs to be done: He reforms the land (2 Kgs 23:1–20).

Josiah makes the difficult choice to do what God requires. He ignites God's work among His people again. He restores obedience. The work is challenging and exhausting—it means changing the way people live.

If we were faced with an opportunity like this, would we have the strength and dedication to take it? Would we be willing to change what must be changed? Would we be willing to proclaim the word of Yahweh to people who are not ready to hear it—who may resist the change? Would we carry out Yahweh's work despite its unpopularity? These are issues we face every day.

The time of hypothetical speculation must end, and the time of igniting real renewal and real reform must begin. It starts with us, and it doesn't end until all the lives around us are renewed, changed, and transformed. —JDB

In what area is God asking you to lead change?

◦ ◊ ◦ ◊ ◦

DO NOT TURN TO FOLLY

2 Kings 23:28–25:30; **Ephesians 6:1–24**; **Proverbs 9:13–18**

I have a problem with criticism. Being one of the youngest in a large, opinionated family, I quickly learned how to stand up for myself and get my way as a young child. I learned to deflect teasing. I also learned I had a knack for ignoring reprimands—punishment free (there are certain, inalienable rights that shouldn't be bestowed on the youngest). The louder I projected my voice, the better; the more stubborn my stance, the more respect I earned. I wish I could say it was a phase that I quickly grew out of.

When we're challenged by others, we often interpret the wisdom offered as criticism. We defensively deflect feedback like beams of light, hoping they'll land in their rightful place (our neighbor's darkness, not our own). This type of reaction can become second nature. Soon, even messages in church are meant for others: "I wish [insert person currently annoying us] was here. He or she really needs to hear this."

Proverbs tells us that we don't just deflect criticism to the detriment of others. Although we might shock people with our strong reactions, or scandalize them with our biting comments, we ignore their advice to our own detriment: "If you are wise, you are wise for yourself, and if you scoff, alone you shall bear it" (Prov 9:12).

Wisdom offered and received is part of God's intention for community. It's a means through which God builds us up—a theme found throughout the book of Ephesians. We don't grow as individuals—the helpful conflict provided by community (the truth in love) helps us know ourselves better. But when we deflect criticism, we rush headlong into the peril we've created for ourselves. Proverbs has startling words for this type of peril. When the young man chooses to listen to the words of Folly personified, his fate is sealed: "Whoever is simple, may he turn here!" (Prov 9:16) she cries. "But he does not know that the dead are there, in the depths of Sheol are her guests" (Prov 9:18).

The next time someone offers you criticism and you're tempted to react, choose to examine your heart and motives. Ask God for the wisdom you need to respond to criticism offered in love. —RVN

Think back to the last time you received criticism.
How did you react? How should you react?

⚬ ◇◇◇ ⚬

THE CALLING OF JEREMIAH, COLOSSAE, AND US

Jeremiah 1:1–2:37; **Colossians 1:1–14**; Proverbs 10:1–32

We all have trouble accepting our calling. When God asks us to do His work, we tend to wonder whether we're able to execute His will. We are not alone in this—the prophet Jeremiah felt the same way: "And the word of Yahweh came to me, saying, 'Before I formed you in the womb I knew you, and before you came out from the womb I consecrated you; I appointed you as a prophet to the nations.' Then I said, 'Ah, Lord Yahweh! Look, I do not know how to speak, for I am a youth'" (Jer 1:4–6).

Jeremiah had been chosen by God *before his birth*, and yet he struggles. The issue at the heart of Jeremiah's hesitancy is doubt about how it will all play out. A simple reframing of his call creates the reassurance he needs: "'Do not be afraid of them, for I am with you to deliver you,' declares Yahweh. Then Yahweh stretched out his hand and he touched my mouth, and Yahweh said to me, 'Look, I have put my words in your mouth. ... '" (Jer 1:8–10). After God reassures Jeremiah that He will be with him—that He will deal with all of his fears—Jeremiah is ready to be the man he's been called to be. He goes on to become one of the greatest prophets who ever lived.

Paul takes on a similar role as God's mouthpiece to the Colossians, reassuring them of their calling: "We give thanks always to God the Father of our Lord Jesus Christ when we pray for you, since we heard about your faith in Christ Jesus and the love that you have for all the saints, because of the hope reserved for you in heaven, which you have heard about beforehand in the word of truth, the gospel" (Col 1:3–5). God has called the church at Colossae, and He is now moving them toward something greater—something more like what Jesus wants for their lives.

Like Jeremiah and the church at Colossae, we must take hope in the calling God has given us. We must reconcile ourselves to His work in our life. We must realize that He will give us what we are lacking, whether resources, confidence, or skill. —JDB

What do you fear? What do you need God to provide
o you can better do His work? How should you go about acquiring this?

December 2

° ◦ ◊ ◦ °

THE MYSTERY OF GOD

Jeremiah 3:1–4:18; **Colossians 1:15–2:5**; Proverbs 11:1–12

"God wanted to make known what is the glorious wealth of this mystery among the Gentiles, which is Christ in you, the hope of glory" (Col 1:27).

Paul's use of the word "mystery" in this passage may strike us as a bit strange. How is the person and work of Christ shrouded in secrecy? And why would Paul present Christ as a mystery if his point is that God wanted to make Christ known?

The answer is found in the culture of early Colossae, a city known for its infatuation with magic and the occult. Among the Gentile cults, "mystery" was often associated with a secret ritual that people must perform to create a relationship with a god. False teachers in the community at Colossae were promoting alternative ways to get to God—secret rituals that would lead to special knowledge for a select few.

Paul contextualizes the gospel for the Colossians. He adopts this "mystery" language to show that Christ is the only way to God. The mystical path presented to the Colossians was a farce—a shell of what the Colossian believers had in Christ. It's in Him that "all the treasures of wisdom and knowledge are hidden" (Col 2:3).

Paul wisely draws on language and tradition familiar to his audience to make the "mystery" of Christ known to all—not just a select few. Paul says he proclaims Christ so that "by admonishing every person and teaching every person with all wisdom … we may present every person mature in Christ" (Col 1:28).

Because he was familiar with the culture of Colossae, Paul was able to acknowledge the challenges the believers faced, and then present the gospel as they needed to hear it: Christ is the only way. How are you resting in Christ as the only way to God? How are you thoughtfully revealing this "mystery" to those in your church and community? —RVN

Do you look for other ways to get to God,
like your own goodness or your own ability to earn favor?

December 3

∘ ∘ ⋄ ∘ ∘

FACING THE STORMS
ON THE HORIZON

Jeremiah 4:19–5:31; Colossians 2:6–23; Proverbs 11:13–31

Having knowledge or insight into a situation and feeling helpless to act upon that information is one of the most frightening feelings we can experience. It makes us anxious, even pained.

Jeremiah 4 describes an experience like this: "My heart is restless within me, I cannot keep silent, for I hear in my inner self the sound of a horn, the alarm of war. Destruction on destruction is proclaimed, for all of the land is devastated. … 'For my people are foolish, they have not known me. They are foolish children, and they do not have insight. They are skillful at doing evil, and they do not know how to do good'" (Jer 4:19–22).

How should we react in moments like these? How should we operate? There are no simple answers to these questions. But what *is* certain is that we must depend on God and His provision over our lives. We must look at the coming storms in our lives and the lives of others and recognize that Yahweh will be at work—regardless of the difficulties we encounter in the process.

Like Jeremiah, we must speak up, but we must root ourselves in Christ as we do so. As Paul writes, "As you have received Christ Jesus the Lord, live in him, firmly rooted and built up in him and established in the faith, just as you were taught, abounding with thankfulness" (Col 2:6–7). We must thank Christ for His work in us and live as He has asked us to live. If we are called to tell others about the ramifications of their actions, we must always be motivated by Christ's love. For as the book of Proverbs tell us, "A gossip walks about telling a secret, but the trustworthy in spirit keeps the matter. Where there is no guidance, a nation shall fall, but there is safety in an abundance of counsel" (Prov 11:13–14).

Let our counsel be godly counsel. Let our words be truthful. Let us see that God will guide us in the events we can change and those that we can't. And let our actions proceed from thankfulness and love. —JDB

What storm are you anxious about?
How can you depend on God in that storm?

PUT OFF, PUT ON

Jeremiah 6:1–7:29; **Colossians 3:1–17**; Proverbs 12:1–28

We often hear that being a good Christian means not doing bad stuff. This statement is true—but not exhaustive. In Colossians 3, Paul says, "Therefore put to death what is earthly in you: sexual immorality, uncleanness, lustful passion, evil desire, and greediness, which is idolatry" (Col 3:5). He then lists other inappropriate behaviors: "anger, rage, wickedness, slander, abusive language" (Col 3:8). And he also lists new behaviors we need to "put on," like "affection, compassion, kindness, humility, gentleness, patience" (Col 3:12).

From this we can gather that, as Christians, our lives should look different. But is there more to this command than certain behaviors?

We're not supposed to put on new behaviors simply so that we can have polished, admirable lives. Colossians 3 opens with a statement: "Therefore, if you have been raised together with Christ, seek the things above, where Christ is" (Col 3:1). Believers identify with Christ—just like we've died with Him, we've also been raised with Him. He is life for us. And one day, we will be reunited with Him, and we'll reflect Him perfectly.

All of Paul's teaching rests on this truth. And all of our actions should reflect this new life we have in Christ. We shouldn't continue in the old behaviors that used to be common to us (Col 3:7). We are changing into His likeness. "You have taken off the old man together with his deeds, and have put on the new man that is being renewed in knowledge according to the image of the one who created him" (Col 3:9–10).

Avoiding certain behaviors is part of being a Christian, but it's hardly just that. It's about a new life built completely on the foundation of Christ's life-giving work. We should forgive one another because He forgave us (Col 3:13). We should love each other and strive for unity because He loved us and united us to Him (Col 3:14). We should strive for peace with one another because Christ has conquered chaos (Col 3:15). The message of Christ and our new life in Him should help us encourage and challenge each other as believers (Col 3:16). —RVN

Does your life reflect this new life? How can you turn from simply avoiding bad behavior to seeking new life in Him?

December 5

∘ ◊ ◊ ◊ ∘

DO NO HARM

Jeremiah 7:30–9:26; **Colossians 3:18–4:18**; Proverbs 13:1–25

L ove can hurt. Many well-intentioned people have done more harm than good while attempting to care for others. This is especially the case in cross-cultural situations, as well-meaning people attempt to introduce change without understanding the local culture. But it can even be true in our homes. Paul's words in Colossians 3:18–4:1 have been misused countless times by those seeking to gain or maintain power. Yet Paul's main goal is to teach the church in Colossae to help without hurting as he works toward seeing cultural norms in the light of the gospel.

When Paul talks about wives "submitting" to their husbands, he frames it in light of the phrase, "husbands love your wives" (Col 3:18–19). The submission he speaks of is not about giving up will or freedom; Paul is acknowledging the cultural and economic realities of the time and encouraging the Church to operate within those norms. In Graeco-Roman culture, married women having their own livelihoods—and thus holding complete autonomy in decision making—was incomprehensible. Women couldn't own property or vote. Paul acknowledges that Christ's work in making all people equal will radically reframe culture (Gal 3:23–4:7), yet in Colossians 3:18–4:1, he's concerned that if the Church introduces radical changes, it will gain a negative reputation. He wants the Christian work in culture to help, not harm.

It's for this same reason that Paul includes a provision for masters and slaves; however, as with men and women, he reframes the cultural norms: Masters are to grant their slaves "justice and fairness" (Col 4:1). As his decision to subtly ask Philemon to free Onesimus shows, Paul likely wished to completely overturn slavery, but he also understood that doing so would take time (see especially Phlm 15–16). Paul's charges to slaves and masters in Colossians 3:22–4:1 are meant to help until a more complete reform could take place.

Paul sees the Church as first setting basic examples, then progressing to a more radical framework as culture itself is changed by Christianity. Therefore, Paul creates provisions to help people during the process of the change.

Love must work to change things that need to change. But ultimately, love must always avoid harm. —JDB

What is God calling you to change?

THE EASY WAY

Jeremiah 10:1–11:23; Philemon 1:1–7; **Proverbs 14:1–14**

There is a certain amount of freedom in being foolish. Foolish people don't stop to reflect on their actions. Characteristically unimaginative, foolish people don't stop to consider how their words and actions affect others. The scary effect of foolishness is that it's contagious: "Leave the presence of a foolish man, for you will not come to know words of knowledge. The wisdom of the clever is understanding his ways, but the folly of fools is deceit" (Prov 14:7).

There is an ease in self-deception because it's our natural state. "There is a way that seems upright to a man, but its end is the way of death" (Prov 14:12). But the right way is not simply a more reflective, thoughtful life. We need a new way of life that can only be brought about in Christ—the one who reversed the power of death. Following the right way doesn't mean relying on our own ability to be righteous through thoughtful actions. Rather, it means understanding our need for His righteousness. It's God's work in us, recreating us. It's His Spirit, directing our ways and making us new in Him.

The fool does have influence, but a life transformed has far-reaching influence because it's not our own work—it's God's. This is the calling of which Paul reminds Philemon. Paul tells Philemon that he has "great joy and encouragement" because of Philemon's love. Because of his love, "the hearts of the saints have been refreshed through you, brother" (Phlm 7). For this reason, Paul also holds Philemon to a high standard. Because of his great influence, he needs to be intentional about how he treats Onesimus, the redeemed slave who had wronged him.

Pray for a transformed life, and pray for the work of the Spirit in your life, dividing the light from the darkness and the foolish, deceitful parts from the wise. He will help you understand His ways if you ask Him. He will make the darkness evident, and He will show you the way of wisdom—a life that reflects Christ. —RVN

How are you praying for the Spirit's ongoing
work in your life, dividing the foolish ways from the wise?

RELATIONSHIP WILL CHANGE US

Jeremiah 12:1–13:27; Philemon 1:8–25; Proverbs 14:15–35

Although God has granted us complete access to Him through Christ, we struggle at times to live this reality (John 17:15–17). The stale or frightening depictions of God in stained glass and Renaissance paintings have convinced us that He is distant, quick to anger, or disinterested. Nothing could be further from the truth; the Psalms remind us that He is caring, close, and listening (e.g., Pss 22; 23; 26), and He yearns for a relationship with us.

Sometimes it helps to hear the words of others who have struggled with the same thing. Jeremiah provides us with such an example. He remarks, "You will be in the right, O Yahweh, when I complain to you. Even so, let me speak my claims with you. Why does the way of the wicked succeed? All those who deal treacherously with treachery are at ease" (Jer 12:1). Jeremiah knows that Yahweh is right in all He does, but this does not prevent him from freely expressing his concerns.

If we really look into our hearts, we may find that fear is preventing us from entering into an intimate relationship with Him. We're afraid of what He will say; we're concerned that He may rebuke us. Indeed, this is what He does when Jeremiah speaks to Him: "If you have fallen in a peaceful land, then how will you do in the thickets of the Jordan? For even your relatives, and the house of your father, even they have dealt treacherously with you, even they call loudly after you. You must not trust in them, though they speak kindly to you" (Jer 12:5–6). Yet within this rebuke, we also find advice—and the advice is comforting. By openly communicating his concerns to God, Jeremiah now knows how he must act.

There is joy to be found in knowing that we have a God who listens—a God who is not offended when we speak to Him but is eager for our company. What are we afraid of? After all, He already knows what's on our minds. We need to grasp the idea that God is all about relationship. —JDB

*What would change about your life if you went
deeper into your relationship with Christ?
What should you be asking God right now?*

THE GOSPEL FOR BARBARIANS AND FOOLS

Jeremiah 14:1–15:21; **Romans 1:1–17**; Proverbs 15:1–33

It's dangerous when we feel entitled. We may come to believe *our* communities are righteous while all those outside are not. This can even take place inside our faith communities—popularity or various achievements can create subtle feelings of superiority. We begin to believe it's something we've *done* that brings us favor.

As he writes to the church in Rome, Paul explains that it's not anything we do, anything we are, or anything we obtain that makes us right with God. His calling verifies this: "I am under obligation both to Greeks and to barbarians, both to the wise and to the foolish. Thus I am eager to proclaim the gospel also to you who are in Rome" (Rom 1:14).

Ethnicity was a big obstacle for the early church to overcome, as the church was now made up of both Jewish and Gentile believers. God promised Abraham that through him "all the peoples on earth will be blessed" (Gen 12:3). Christ's redemptive work had finally made this blessing a reality. God's favor was no longer reserved for those who might be educated or wise. Paul emphasizes that God can redeem those who—to us—might seem unlikely recipients of redemption.

But most important, our standing before God is not based on our goodness. Paul is eager to proclaim the gospel in Rome because it is belief in Jesus, the fulfillment of the promise, that makes believers righteous before God—"the gospel … is the power of God for salvation to everyone who believes" (Rom 1:16). Christ's righteousness has become our righteousness.

If anything, this fact should eliminate any sense of entitlement we might harbor and prompt us to walk in humility with believers and non-believers alike. Our relationship with God is intimately tied to how deeply we understand our need for God. The gospel frees us of any need to attain or achieve. For this, we should be incredibly thankful to God and live with humility for Him. —RVN

Do you put stock in the things
you think make you a "favored" Christian?

SELF-EVIDENT HOPE

Jeremiah 16:1–17:27; **Romans 1:18–2:11**; Proverbs 16:1–11

"For the wrath of God is revealed from heaven against all impiety and unrighteousness of people, who suppress the truth in unrighteousness, because what can be known about God is evident among them, for God made it clear to them" (Rom 1:18–19). A statement like this could easily be taken out of context if we leave off everything after "people." But when we contextualize this message, we find hope instead of hopelessness.

Paul goes on to tell us that creation itself reveals God and His goodness to humanity, so there is no excuse for failing to understand God and the salvation He offers: "For from the creation of the world, his invisible attributes, both his eternal power and deity, are discerned clearly, being understood in the things created, so that they are without excuse" (Rom 1:20).

We have all heard people who are concerned that salvation seems unfair: What about the people who won't ever hear about Jesus? Yet Paul argues that everyone has an opportunity to witness Christ at work in creation itself. In Colossians he remarks that it's in the "Son [Jesus] … whom we have the redemption, the forgiveness of sins, who is the image of the invisible God, the firstborn over all creation, because all things in the heavens and on the earth were created by him, things visible and things invisible, whether thrones or dominions or rulers or powers, all things were created through him and for him" (Col 1:13–16).

All people have an opportunity to know God. No one has an excuse. God's justice reigns in creation; it reigns in Christ; and it reigns in the lives of those who choose Christ. Christ is everywhere, in all things. The world is not condemned unfairly by a God of unreasonable wrath; instead, it's ruled by a God of joy and empathy who is love. —JDB

What misperceptions do you have of God?
How can you correct them and work in the lives
of others to do the same? How can you spread
the empathy God wants you to display?

∘ ◊ ◊ ◊ ∘

CONSTRUCTING LIVES BY THE LAW

Jeremiah 18:1–18; **Romans 2:12–29**; Proverbs 16:12–33

Dispensing good, helpful advice gets the benevolent juices flowing. As easy as it is to give advice, though, it often hits me with the irony of a cartoon anvil when I end up tripping over my own counsel. When this happens, I'm convicted to examine my motives for advice-giving.

In his letter to the Romans, Paul challenges the superior mindset that was common among some Jewish people at the time: "But if you call yourself a Jew and rely on the law … and are confident that you yourself are a guide of the blind, a light to those in darkness, and instructor of the foolish, a teacher of the imma-ture, having the embodiment of knowledge and of the truth in the law. Therefore, the one who teaches someone else, do you not teach yourself?" (Rom 2:17–21).

Paul is explaining why looking to the Old Testament law for righteousness is futile. No person could perfectly keep the law. By holding to it, they were in fact condemning themselves. Paul even points out that some Jews thought they had attained a higher moral standing because of their knowledge of the law—and believed they were in a position to teach others. Yet they were still breaking the law.

It's easy for us to discard this as an early church issue. Yet we still some-times take comfort in "keeping the law" today. If we cling to our own good behavior rather than the righteousness we have in Christ, we commit the same sin. We can attempt to live like a saint—we can cultivate a reputation for good-ness and dishing out wisdom—but we'll set ourselves up for imminent failure because we can never keep up the pretense of godly behavior on our own.

However, if our "circumcision is of the heart"—if we trust in Christ's sacri-fice for our righteousness and the Spirit is working in us—then our hearts will be in the right place. That place is where we know we are great sinners, and where we are receptive to His transforming work to bring us into complete loyalty to Him. Then we will seek God's favor, not the favor and superiority we crave from others.

If our lives are truly changed, we will be motivated to love others out of the love God shows us. That will give us the right perspective for seeing the transformation that God is working in their hearts. And it will free us to give the best advice of all: Seek God in everything. —RVN

What are your motives for giving advice?

FAITHFUL DECISION MAKING

Jeremiah 21:1–22:30; Romans 3:1–20; Proverbs 17:1–28

"I asked God, and He didn't answer me." When I hear people say this, I'm often tempted to reply, "Haven't you read the prophets?" Because sometimes what people are really saying is, "I asked God to do something for me, and He didn't answer in the way I expected, so He must not be listening or He must not care." Yet the prophets repeatedly tell us the opposite. God is not human, so He does not make decisions like a human. Instead, He sees all possible outcomes and knows the best route. We simply struggle to understand the wisdom of His decisions.

One particular event in the book of Jeremiah illustrates this point. When King Zedekiah (the last king of Judah) asks Jeremiah to intercede with Yahweh on behalf of Jerusalem against King Nebuchadnezzar of Babylon, Jeremiah gives an unexpected reply: Yahweh has refused to do so. He will not intercede for His own people. Rather, He will make Nebuchadnezzar's task easier (Jer 21:1–7).

Before we view Yahweh as harsh and unforgiving, let's recall that this occurs after God's people have been rebelling against Him for hundreds of years. Even so, in Jeremiah 21:8–10, God's people are given a choice: They can remain in Jerusalem and die—for Yahweh has deemed that the city must fall— or they can enter what appears to be death but is actually life. Yahweh sets up a faith choice for them: "He who goes out and goes over to the Chaldeans who are laying siege to you will live, and his life will be to him as booty" (Jer 21:9).

Even in the midst of unbearable circumstances, Yahweh offers a way of grace. Even when everything seems to fail, we can decide to choose faith. This story mirrors what we experience on our deathbed. It also mirrors the decision we face every day of our lives: Will we listen to the voices of the world, or will we listen to the prophets who proclaim honest indignation and faithful decision making? Will we stay in the city, or will we go where God calls us—no matter how difficult it may seem or how improbable? —JDB

Where is God calling you?
What must you walk away from?
What faith decision is before you?

○ ○○○ ○

FORGIVEN AND FORGIVING

Jeremiah 23:1–24:10; Romans 3:21–31; **Proverbs 18:1–24**

I dioms are often unhelpful because their overuse has robbed them of meaning. But the idiom "putting up walls" has a twist in Proverbs: "A brother who is offended is worse than a city of strength, and quarrels are like the bars of a fortification" (Prov 18:19).

The writer of this proverb gives us imagery that helps us understand how people react to offenses. Regardless of whether we intend to, we can raise a great structure, like a "city of strength," in the gulf between ourselves and others. Such barriers make it difficult to reach those we have offended, which may suit us perfectly. But we're called to live differently.

None of us can live perfectly in this life, so conflict is inevitable. If we have the insight to see that "we all fall short of the glory of God"—and more specifically, *how* we have fallen—we'll see we have no right to hold a grudge (Rom 3:23). When rifts develop in relationships, we need to own our sin and bring it to God. His forgiveness and His reconciling work make it possible for us to be vulnerable with others and seek their forgiveness—even if they have also offended us.

When we choose to humbly admit our failings, we break down "the bars of a fortification" and create space for reconciliation. We might be spurned, or we might be forgiven. The other person may take responsibility for their fault, or they may not. But either way, we rest secure in God's forgiveness.

Have you offended someone? Have you neglected to confess your sin and seek forgiveness? Reconciliation is a picture of what God has done for us—He has returned us to Himself. Be like the peacemaker: Seek and offer forgiveness. —RVN

Have you offended someone without asking forgiveness?
If so, how can you step forward to confess your
offense to God and the offended person?

SAGE ADVICE

Jeremiah 25:1–26:24; Romans 4:1–24; **Proverbs 19:1–29**

Proverbs is full of sage advice, and some examples deserve special attention. No words could better describe the concept expressed here: "Better a poor person walking in integrity than one who is perverse in his speech and is a fool" (Prov 19:1).

When times get tough—especially when money runs out—integrity is often the first thing we sacrifice. Yet only those who have truly lived in poverty understand the trials it brings. We can't begin to know how we would act if we had nothing. For this reason, we should mentally prepare for times of want. In doing so, we might better gauge whether we're conducting ourselves appropriately in times of plenty.

I heard of a man who chose to live as a homeless person so that he could understand their plight. It's easy for the rich person to call such an act foolish, but how much did that man learn as he was challenged to maintain his integrity during hard times? Does the rich person own that wisdom?

Proverbs 19:2 seems to hint at this idea: "A life without knowledge is not good, and he who moves quickly with his feet misses the mark." Some people move so quickly in and out of circumstances that they don't learn from their experiences. It's better to move a little slower than normal and pay attention to our actions and their ramifications than to make a mistake and not learn from it. Likewise, we must have knowledge about our work and what we're doing, or we inevitably fail.

Let's learn from people with integrity. And let's learn from our mistakes, both in hypothetical situations and real ones. Let's take the time to notice what went wrong and what went right. —JDB

What situation is God using to teach you?
Where should you slow down?

December 14

○ ○ ◇ ○ ○

PATIENT ENDURANCE

Jeremiah 27:1–28:17; **Romans 5:1–21**; Proverbs 20:1–12

In theory, it's easy to provide answers to difficult faith questions. But when we face real trials, everything changes. We gain a new perspective on the Bible passages we've memorized; the Christian maxims we've passed on to others reverse and hit us full force. We don't have the option to talk in hypotheticals. Trials require heartfelt faith and total reliance on God.

Suffering and trials are not punishment or neglect on God's part. In fact, they're quite the opposite. Paul describes how God works through trials to build us up in faith. And His work is not a quick fix or an easy answer. It's a process, as Paul describes in his letter to the Roman church: "And not only this, but we also boast in our afflictions, because we know that affliction produces patient endurance, and patient endurance, proven character, and proven character, hope, and hope does not disappoint, because the love of God has been poured out in our hearts through the Holy Spirit who was given to us" (Rom 5:3–5).

In times of suffering, we aren't meant to abandon mourning or put up an artifice of strength. We're not supposed to conquer and overcome and become the next Christian success story. God uses these trials to work in us—a slow, evolving work that begins with endurance, creates character, and culminates with a hope that won't disappoint. We don't embark on such a process by ourselves. Throughout our suffering, "the love of God has been poured out in our hearts through the Holy Spirit who was given to us" (Rom 5:5).

We will face trials and suffering in our lifetime—whether everyday difficulties or life-altering events. But affliction doesn't separate us from God's love (Rom 8:35). Indeed, God uses it to confirm His love for us. May Paul's words give us comfort and perspective for the work God is or will be doing in us. —RVN

What trials or suffering are you enduring?
How do Paul's words shed light on your trials?

AFTER THE STORM

Jeremiah 29:1–30:24; **Romans 6:1–14**; Proverbs 20:13–30

A s we blink and squint in the light that emerges after a storm, we marvel that the sun was there all along and we just couldn't see it. The same is true during times of difficulty. When we're in pain or worried, it seems impossible to find God, but in retrospect, it always seems obvious: God was there all along. Jeremiah prophesied to God's people about their unraveling. The people heard words from Jeremiah's mouth that must have seemed hopeless and full of despair. But in Jeremiah 29, we catch a glimpse of the light that comes after: "Build houses and live in them, and plant gardens and eat their fruit. Take wives and father sons and daughters … and multiply there, and you must not be few" (Jer 29:5–6).

Even in exile, God will continue to guide His people. Because of their sins, they have endured (and lost) war and have been driven away from the land that God gave them; but God remains with them nonetheless. They may need to experience the pain of exile to understand the consequences of turning away from God, but God still plans to be good to them. He will provide for them.

We witness a parallel picture in Romans 6. After describing the death that sin brings into the world and the current sad state of humanity, Paul presents a full vision of living without sin—of conquering the very problem that drove God's people into exile: "What therefore shall we say? Shall we continue in sin, in order that grace may increase? May it never be! How can we who died to sin still live in it?" (Rom 6:1–2).

Even with the grace God has offered us, Paul encourages us to live the vision God has created through Jesus—one that strives to be sinless. Likewise, Jeremiah does not offer empty words without the command that God's people follow Him with their entire beings (Jer 29:8–14).

We have all made mistakes. We've all lost ourselves in the storms—in storms we caused and storms that came upon us for no apparent reason. But what's certain in both instances is that God is with us and desires for us to be one with Him. —JDB

> *What storm are you currently in, coming out of, or anticipating?*
> *What is God teaching you through it? What is He asking of you?*

FREEDOM

Jeremiah 31:1–40; **Romans 6:15–7:6**; Proverbs 21:1–12

We like to think of ourselves as autonomous. Our modern culture champions freedom and the right to pursue happiness. But if we apply the concept of rights when we think about faith, following Christ can feel like religion, dogma, rules—a type of bondage that requires us to think and behave in ways that make our autonomous selves bridle.

Paul looks at the issue differently: "Do you not know that to whomever you present yourselves as slaves for obedience, you are slaves to whomever you obey, whether sin, leading to death, or obedience, leading to righteousness?" (Rom 6:16). He uses another analogy in his letter to the church in Rome—one that draws on the practice of the slavery within his own culture—to highlight the opposite view. If we live without God, he says, we have a debt that binds us. We are slaves to sin, and it's the type of bondage that leads to death.

Yet, there is hope. Although we were slaves to sin, we can be redeemed from that slavery. Christ has paid the debt we incurred. He has set us free and brought us into a new bondage—not one that binds to death, but one that binds us to Him in life. If we believe this is true and put our trust in Him, we are no longer slaves.

As redeemed people, we're called to a new life. While we once charted our own independent path—one that led to death—we can turn and follow a path that leads to sanctification and eternal life, a path that God charts just for us. While our path required a toll—death—Christ has paid that toll so we can walk in new life: "The gift of God is eternal life in Christ Jesus our Lord" (Rom 6:23). —RVN

How have your old habits and patterns
of behavior changed now that you've been set free?
What still needs to change to reflect your new loyalty to Christ?

LAND AND DEEDS

Jeremiah 32:1–44; Romans 7:7–25; Proverbs 21:13–31

Those of us who have purchased a home know the frightening feeling of closing day—"Am I signing my life away? Am I binding myself to this building forever?" Imagine, on top of those feelings, knowing that the place you're buying is about to be overrun by a foreign nation and may no longer belong to you. That's what the prophet Jeremiah experienced.

Yahweh tells Jeremiah that his cousin will arrive with an offer to purchase a field. So when Jeremiah's cousin shows up, Jeremiah views it as Yahweh's will that he purchase the land, and he does (Jer 32:1–12). Meanwhile, Jeremiah knows that the Babylonians are coming and that they will overrun the land of God's people, including the land that he has just purchased. This is not a reckless act; this is a moment of faith. Jeremiah seizes the opportunity to proclaim Yahweh's faithfulness.

Turning to his assistant, Baruch, Jeremiah remarks in front of everyone witnessing the purchase, "Thus says Yahweh of hosts, the God of Israel, 'Take these deeds, this deed of the purchase, the sealed one, and this opened deed, and you must put them in an earthenware jar so that they may be kept preserved many days.' For thus says Yahweh of hosts, the God of Israel: 'Houses and fields and vineyards will again be bought in this land'" (Jer 32:14–15).

Each of us has moments when we must do what no one else will do—and that includes saying what others are not willing to say. What "land" is God asking you to buy, and what is He asking you to proclaim about it? —JDB

What deed is God asking you to do today?
What are you to say about Yahweh's faithfulness,
and how are you to act upon it?

∘ ∘ ∘ ∘ ∘

INTO THE FAMILY

Jeremiah 33:1–34:22; **Romans 8:1–17**; Proverbs 22:1–16

As people once bound to sin and destined for death, our ability to approach God personally—to call Him our Father—should astound us. Yet we sometimes forget to pray. We can take it for granted that He looks out for our every need.

The concept of approaching God as Father would have been a radical concept for the Roman community. In his letter to the church there, Paul discusses how our former lives without God were nothing but slavery to sin and death, the wages of sin. Christ's work has set us free from this trajectory: "For you have not received a spirit of slavery leading to fear again, but you have received the Spirit of adoption, by whom we cry out, 'Abba! Father!' The Spirit himself confirms to our spirit that we are children of God, and if children, also heirs— heirs of God and fellow heirs with Christ, if indeed we suffer together with him so that we may also be glorified together with him" (Rom 8:15–17).

Paul's audience would have used the term "Abba! Father!" only within immediate family relationships. To call God "our Father" would have been a shocking paradigm shift—especially for Jewish believers. However, Christ's sacrifice made this relationship possible. He paid our debt and repaired the rift. Because of His work, and because we share in His Spirit, we also share in His relationship with the Father. We can call out to God, just as Jesus did. And the Father cares for us, just as He cares for His Son.

We may forget our intimate relationship with God, yet the Spirit continues to work within us to bring our lives into accordance with this relationship with the Father. Pray for insight and gratitude for your new position because of Christ. When you call on God, relate to Him as a child would to a loving father—bringing all to Him and knowing He understands you and knows what is best for you. —RVN

Do you neglect prayer?
Pray that the Spirit would work to bring you
a childlike faith and trust in God.

THE RECHABITE SAGA

Jeremiah 35:1–36:32; Romans 8:18–39; Proverbs 22:17–23:18

We're often slow to learn and quick to speak. We think we know God's ways, but He can easily prove us wrong. Many of us have made this mistake: We think we're living righteously, and then God slams us for our actions. He quickly deconstructs our worldview, calling into question our ethics, our way of being, our lifestyles. Why? Because even if we don't think we're breaking any rules, we might be living by our own choices rather than Yahweh's will—and that is disobedience. The story of the Rechabites demonstrates this point.

Yahweh had requested that the Rechabites shun alcohol and live in tents, so they did. They obeyed this request until Nebuchadnezzar invaded Judah, which they inhabited with the rest of God's people. Then Yahweh sent them one final test: He asked His prophet, Jeremiah, to prompt them to drink wine. They resisted—and passed the test (Jer 35:1–11).

The Rechabites' obedience stands as a model that shows the actions of the rest of God's people reprehensible by comparison. Yahweh remarks to Jeremiah, "Go and say to the people of Judah and to the inhabitants of Jerusalem, 'Can you not learn a lesson to listen to my words?' declares Yahweh. 'The words of Jonadab, the son of Rechab, that he commanded his descendants to not drink, have been carried out, and they have not drunk until this day, for they have obeyed the command of their ancestor. But I have spoken to you over and over again, and you have not listened to me'" (Jer 35:13–14). God's people had disobeyed Him by seeking other gods and committing other sins, but this line hints at the deeper problem: They had not carried out Yahweh's basic commandment to listen to His will.

God's people thought they were in the right. They believed they were behaving correctly. But in reality, they had disobeyed His basic commandments and then disobeyed His very will. Are you, like God's people, living in disillusionment, failing to acknowledge that you're living outside of God's will? —JDB

Ask yourself: "Am I really on the right track?
Is this really God's will, or is it the manifestation of
a false belief about my obedience that I'm creating?"

LOOKING TO GOD AND OTHERS

Jeremiah 37:1–38:28; **Romans 9:1–12**; Proverbs 23:19–35

We have a natural tendency to be concerned with our own condition. As redeemed people, God is transforming us from being self-centered people—concerned with our own ambitions—to other-centered people who want to see God's work done in and around us. Sometimes even our spiritual concerns point us inward. But God's work in us shouldn't be just about us.

Paul sets a startling example in his concern for those who hadn't come to know Christ: "I am telling the truth in Christ—I am not lying; my conscience bears witness to me in the Holy Spirit—that my grief is great and there is constant distress in my heart. For I could wish myself to be accursed from Christ for the sake of my brothers, my fellow countrymen according to the flesh" (Rom 9:1–3).

Although he was called especially to be an apostle to the Gentiles, Paul was deeply concerned about the spiritual state of the Jewish people—his own people. The promise of the Messiah was given to them, yet many refused to believe the fulfillment of this promise, the redeeming work of Christ. They weren't aware of the fulfillment of that promise given especially to them. Paul was so grieved by their rejection of their salvation that he was willing to be accursed for their sakes.

God is at work in us—transforming us for His purpose. We should be keenly aware of His work. But our gaze shouldn't be fixed inward. We should be looking to God, amazed by His grace and His concern for people like us. As we are changed into His likeness, we should be caught up in caring for the things that deeply concern Him. We should care about the people He wants to be transformed to His likeness. He is molding and shaping us into His likeness so that we can be His instruments, His agents on earth. The people we meet and the situations we encounter are all opportunities to reflect Christ—not because we want to be holy examples, but because we have a task to do. —RVN

How is God's work transforming you to
be deeply concerned about the spiritual state of others?
Who can you pray for? Who can you reach out to?

EXPENSES

Jeremiah 39:1–41:18; Romans 9:13–29; Proverbs 24:1–22

I t's important to pause occasionally to reflect on the cost of sin. If we don't, we can find ourselves living in it without thought of the ramifications. Few passages illustrate the cost of sin more vividly than the fall of Jerusalem recorded in Jeremiah 39. The fall of Jerusalem is brutal, depressing, and sadistic, but we can learn from Jeremiah's account of the event.

We could view Jeremiah's depictions as merely historical, or we could recognize the theological lessons they offer: Sin is expensive. Sin will destroy you. Sin will bring a nation to its knees. Sin will leave you begging for mercy. Sin is death. That's what God's people learned from this event: Disobeying Yahweh is a costly action. It's not that God wants His people to endure this pain, but pain is a natural consequence of their decisions. He cannot defend people who refuse to live as beacons of light—of goodness, beauty, and blessing—to the world. If they aren't willing to live in His image, then He is not willing to be their defender. If Yahweh did not allow for Nebuchadnezzar to destroy Jerusalem, the people would never learn. And the exile that comes in this moment is also a natural result of their sin.

When we're faced with the horror of the destruction of Jerusalem, we're given a choice: Will we listen to the prophets of our age and respond accordingly? Will we hear God when He calls us back to obedience? Or will we continue to live in sin and suffer the consequences?

As a side effect of the grace that God has given us in Jesus, many people assume that sin is somehow okay—that it's okay to allow it to exist. God's response is the opposite. The grace is unmerited, and we must respond with the only merited response: complete dedication and obedience to Him. We must see the death of sin and deny it. —JDB

What sin is currently present in your life?
What do you need to repent from?
Have you asked God to direct you in this?

A FALSE FORM OF RIGHTEOUSNESS

Jeremiah 42:1–43:13; **Romans 9:30–10:21**; Proverbs 24:23–34

Zeal can be treacherous if it's misplaced. It may lead us to set and strictly follow standards that have nothing to do with God's work—standards that make us feel like good people but that can devastate our lives and the lives of others.

Paul addresses the misplaced zeal of many Jewish people in his letter to the Roman church: "Brothers, the desire of my heart and my prayer to God on behalf of them is for their salvation. For I testify about them that they have a zeal for God, but not according to knowledge. For ignoring the righteousness of God, and seeking to establish their own, they did not subject themselves to the righteousness of God. For Christ is the end of the law for righteousness to everyone who believes" (Rom 10:1–4).

Many Jewish people who had rejected the Messiah were attempting to make themselves right with God by keeping the Old Testament law. In doing so, they missed God by seeking their own righteousness. Paul tells the Romans that these Jewish people ignored the "righteousness of God"—God's work of salvation in Jesus Christ. It's only by submitting to God that they could be "right with God" through Jesus Christ.

This lesson isn't applicable only to the Jewish people and their relationship to the law. Jesus restored relationship with God when we couldn't. We only have to believe in Him. Yet a dangerous zeal can still trip us up. If we rest in anything except Christ's work and try to reach God by being good people, we are sure to miss Him. And in the process, we can become stumbling blocks in the lives of others.

Are you trying to attain righteousness through your own effort? How does your life reflect humility because of Christ's work in you? How can you lovingly point others toward the righteousness of God, found only through His son, Jesus Christ? —RVN

What are you trying to attain?
How can you focus your hope and the hope of others
on Christ and the righteousness He has attained for you?

THE RISE TO POWER

Jeremiah 44:1–46:28; Romans 11:1–10; **Proverbs 25:1–28**

If you're driven, you've probably worked very hard to get to where you are. Being driven is a good thing, but being driven at a cost to others or by elevating yourself by your own accord is detrimental. Proverbs 25 offers this warning from the perspective of King Solomon: "Do not promote yourself before the king, and in the place of the great ones do not stand. For it is better that he say to you, 'Ascend here,' than he humble you before a noble" (Prov 25:6–7).

People tend to get nasty when power or money is involved. It's uncomfortable to wait for that promotion, but God asks us to remain patient. At the end of the day, attaining leadership because you're worthy is a much greater honor than obtaining it because you were louder than someone else or placed yourself in front of them. We should always take initiative and strive to succeed, but we need to remember that it's not our place to decide our fates. We must place that in God's hands, and we must wait to be asked to take the reins rather than snatch them ourselves.

Many people would put themselves before others when given the opportunity; they would promote themselves at the cost of someone else. As Christians, we have to ward off such temptations. We must maintain our integrity. Proverbs speaks about this as well: "What your eyes have seen [in a king's court], do not hastily bring out to court, for what will you do at its end, when your neighbor puts you to shame? Argue your argument with your neighbor himself, the secret of another do not disclose, lest he who hears shame you and your ill repute will not end" (Prov 25:8–10).

Abuse of power is one of the most common leadership problems. People seeking and obtaining power when they're not ready can be equally disastrous. As we seek to advance ourselves, we must be cautious with how we earn power—and with how we handle power when we've earned it. —JDB

What "power" situations are you currently handling well?
What must change in your current "power" struggles?

YOU SHOULD DO THIS,
BUT MAYBE YOU SHOULDN'T

Jeremiah 47:1–48:47; Romans 11:11–24; **Proverbs 26:1–11**

We all know the feeling. When someone belittles us in front of others, we want to rail against them or make their lives miserable by filtering our rage through our best passive-aggressive behavior. When a friend continuously doles out inflammatory remarks, it's easy to snap and say (or tweet) something inspired by the white-hot rage sweeping through us.

We'd be better off turning to the book of Proverbs, which can offer wisdom for dealing with these situations. The book seems to deliver hard-and-fast rules for life we can easily apply—do this; don't do that. Do this and you'll prosper; do that and you'll suffer for your foolishness. However, Proverbs 26 delivers statements that confuse those who live by the rules: "Do not answer a fool according to his folly lest you become like him—even you. Answer a fool according to his folly, or else he will be wise in his own eyes" (Prov 26:4–5). Do we answer the fool or leave him alone?

The entire trajectory of Proverbs is the attainment of wisdom. The author of this proverb isn't offering a simple rule. He's giving guidance. Although it's sometimes better to keep silent—when speaking would inspire us to be equally foolish—other times the situation might call for us to reprimand the fool. If the fool is misleading others, we need to gently correct them for their good and everyone else's. The fool may be teachable, just lacking in instruction and discipline.

We need discernment to know which response the situation requires. Pray for guidance in your interactions with others. Pray for wisdom from the Spirit, who can provide you with the discernment you need to answer in the right way. Just don't be the fool and set the conversation ablaze with inflammatory words (Jas 3:5). —RVN

How do you respond to foolish people?
How can you, guided by the Holy Spirit, answer
(or choose to remain silent) in ways that
build up or challenge the fool?

LAZINESS AND LIONS

Jeremiah 49:1–39; Romans 11:25–12:8; **Proverbs 26:12–28**

When we consider ourselves wise, we're in danger of losing perspective on the truth and making others feel small. The Proverbs often discuss this problem, remarking, "Do you see a man wise in his own eyes? There is more hope for a fool than for him" (Prov 26:12). This foolishness doesn't just appear when we elevate ourselves or fail to consider others; it also shows up when we fail to consider our own needs.

When we're lazy or do less than we can, we're actually sinning—we're ignoring what God meant us to be and thus holding back His plan, not just our own productivity. One of the Proverbs says, "A lazy person says 'A lion is in the road! A lion among the streets!' … A lazy person buries his hands in the dish; he is too tired to return it to his mouth. A lazy person is wiser in his eyes than seven who answer discreetly" (Prov 26:13, 15–16). The Bible's condemnation of laziness makes sense for hyperbolic situations like lions showing up or someone being too lazy to eat, but it is even more practical when applied to regular situations.

If you consider many of the problems in our world—hunger, water, sanitation, or medical issues—it becomes clear that laziness and funds are often the obstacles preventing us from resolving them. If we stopped ignoring the lions and considering ourselves so wise, we would be able to help many people in need. We would also stop hurting those around us with our arrogance.

God wants to intercede in our world. He wants to use us to do so—we just have to step up. —JDB

What type of laziness are you excusing?

December 26

∘ ◊ ◊ ◊ ∘

COMMUNITY

Jeremiah 50:1-46; **Romans 12:9-13:7**; Proverbs 27:1-27

She might be the one we tend to avoid—the member of a small group who always states the obvious or brings up topics unrelated to the discussion at hand. I'm always a bit impatient for her to finish speaking so that others can offer more insightful comments, but generally her comments are followed by only awkward pauses. Or, he's the person we're attempting to avoid after church and small group because he always repeats the story about his grand-kids that we've heard more than just a few times. I hope someone else will be there for him. If I'm feeling extra congenial, I might chat with him—good to earn some kindness points.

Reading Romans 12:9–16 convicts me. The list of instructions on build-ing up the community quickly reveals the selfish bent of my motives. Paul, who has just finished explaining that each member has specific spiritual gifts, shows what living in loving community is supposed to look like: "Love must be without hypocrisy. Abhor what is evil; be attached to what is good, being devoted to one another in brotherly love, esteeming one another more highly in honor, … do not think arrogantly, but associate with the lowly. Do not be wise in your own sight" (Rom 12:9–16).

I'm not meant to approach my small group study as a support group to help me work out my problems. Faith communities are familial settings where the gifts I have are meant to be developed and worked out for the good of others. It's where I'm called to serve people around me—even, and especially, people who are lonely or a little different than me. I can only do that with a heart that is devoted to others, highly esteems them, and looks out for their needs. It's when I humbly serve that I learn things I didn't know in passing—the death of her husband and her difficulty in finding the right words to convey her ideas and experiences. It's there where I learn that his kids barely call, and he's reciting the same information from the yearly Christmas card. It's where I help when I can, and pray when I can't. And along the way, through my service, I may learn a thing or two from people who have gifts I have yet to discover. —RVN

Are you involved in a community? If you are, are you actually involved?
How can you use your gifts to build up the people around you?

December 27

° ° ◊ ° °

LOVE IS GOOD NEWS

Jeremiah 51:1–64; Romans 13:8–14:12; Proverbs 28:1–28

Love is good news for those seeking guidance. Love is the guide we need. Many first-century Jewish Christians faced the question of what to do with the Law (the first five books of the Bible), by which they had lived previously. Now that they had Jesus, what would they do with their traditions? Paul's answer is based on love: "Owe nothing to anyone, except to love one another, for the one who loves someone else has fulfilled the law" (Rom 13:8). He goes on: "For the commandments, 'You shall not commit adultery, you shall not commit murder, you shall not steal, you shall not covet,' and if there is any other commandment, are summed up in this statement: 'You shall love your neighbor as yourself.' Love does not commit evil against a neighbor. Therefore love is the fulfillment of the law" (Rom 13:9–10). These are beautiful words, and I'm not saying that because they let me off the hook for keeping the law; they also answer the problem that the Old Testament prophets addressed.

The prophet Jeremiah, commenting on the sin of Babylon, notes: "All humankind turns out to be stupid, without knowledge. Every goldsmith is put to shame by the divine image. For his cast image is a lie, and there is no breath in them. They are worthless, a work of mockery. At the time of their punishment, they will perish. The portion of Jacob is not like these, for he is the creator of everything, and the tribe of his inheritance. Yahweh of hosts is his name" (Jer 51:17–19).

Jeremiah's words teach us that we are lost without Yahweh as our guide. Without Him, we will, like Babylon, seek things as dumb as golden images. Yahweh, in His great love for us, guides us to Himself. In Him, we see love; in Jesus, we see His loving image made visible. In Yahweh, we see the way we should go; in Jesus, we see the way back to Yahweh. —JDB

Are you seeking love or golden images?
What law do you need to be free from?
Are you fully living the good news?

December 28

○ ◇ ◇ ○ ○

UNITY

Jeremiah 52:1–34; **Romans 14:13–15:7**; Proverbs 29:1–27

Paul calls us to refrain from judging others (Rom 14:3). That's easy enough to do when the people in our communities are the people we'd *want* to have over for dinner. What happens when those in our community don't value (or disvalue) the things we value (or disvalue)?

"Now may the God of patient endurance and of encouragement grant you to be in agreement with one another, in accordance with Christ Jesus, so that with one mind you may glorify with one mouth the God and Father of our Lord Jesus Christ. Therefore accept one another, just as Christ also has accepted you, to the glory of God" (Rom 15:5–7).

In this portion of his letter, Paul asks the Roman believers to stretch themselves. For the Roman believers, judgment might have centered on the issue of eating the meat of unclean animals or the observance of Jewish holidays. Paul asks them to withhold judgment of one another because only God has that right (Rom 14:10). He also asks them not to "be a cause for stumbling or a temptation" for people who genuinely struggle with things from which others feel free.

It's easy to be in agreement when we're in community with people of similar personalities, hobbies, and backgrounds. But when we need to be in agreement with someone who disagrees with the way we work out our faith, we feel inconvenienced. Here, Paul states that we not only need to be mindful; we need to be accepting. We can do so for one reason: "Christ also has accepted you" (Rom 15:7). We were reconciled to God while we were still His enemies (Rom 5:10). The great Peacemaker calls us to seek relationship with others because of His work. And His love puts our inconvenience in a whole new light. —RVN

How are you seeking unity in Christ with those
who don't reflect the things you do (or don't) value?

○ ○ ◊ ○ ○

THE GRACE OF GOD SHINES THROUGH

Lamentations 1:1–2:22; Romans 15:8–21; Proverbs 30:1–33

I was once asked why the Bible is so brutal—why it depicts things like babies being killed and war. It's true, the Bible has many moments of darkness and violence. But these depictions of the rawness of humanity—in all its ungratefulness and depravity—demonstrate how much people need God. And more than that, through these moments, the Bible shows how much people need a savior.

The book of Lamentations is brimming with sorrow and gnashing of teeth. Little hope can be found in this book. The prophet weeps and moans over his fallen nation, over watching Jerusalem crumble. In this poetic work, we see people who don't follow the God who loves them dearly and so badly yearns to see them return to Him.

"How desolate the city sits that was full of people! She has become like a widow, once great among the nations! Like a woman of nobility in the provinces, she has become a forced laborer. She weeps bitterly in the night, her tears are on her cheeks; she has no comforter among all her lovers. All her friends have been unfaithful to her; they have become her enemies" (Lam 1:1–2). How can we process a passage like this? How can we handle this kind of depression?

The first time I read the book of Lamentations, I wept. I had grasped a bit of what the prophet felt, and weeping was the only natural response. But it wasn't just that. I saw myself as Jerusalem. I was her. I had walked away from God's desire for my life, and I deserved destruction.

Sometimes we must break before we can be rebuilt. Sometimes we must fall before we can rise to the greatness God has called us to. Are you Jerusalem? Call out to God like the prophet did. Tell God how you feel. Be honest with your mourning and your sadness. It may not make the fall easier, but it will surely make you more eager to accept the grace that God has offered. God wants you to experience His grace, including salvation in Christ. He wants you to live it. —JDB

Are you in need of a savior?
What are you requesting of God today?
What grace do you need to receive?

○ ○ ○ ○ ○

THE PROVERBS 31 WOMAN

Lamentations 3:1–66; Romans 15:22–33; **Proverbs 31:1–19**

A Proverbs 31 woman is hard to find, but it isn't for lack of effort. She's been the topic of more than a few Bible studies. She can be recognized by her many positive traits—strong, courageous, and trustworthy. She is hardworking, discerning, giving, dignified, business savvy, wise, and kind. If we're looking for a vice or an Achilles heel, we'll have to turn to another passage in the Old Testament (we're sure to find more failures than achievers within its pages).

As we look through the list of qualities, though, it's hard to check them all off, even for Type-A personalities. But the key to understanding the list of characteristics isn't found in what we can attain. It's found in the last verse—the crux of the poem. The crown of the woman's wisdom isn't her charm or her beauty or even her ability to "get things done." It is her fear of Yahweh. This relationship with God guides all of her actions.

If we're trying to earn favor with God by being "the best version of myself" or "being the best me," we'll fail miserably. If we live to define ourselves by a task, or even a role, we'll fall short every time. It's God's work in us—through Christ—that defines us.

As redeemed people, we can strive to be wise and discerning thanks to the work of the Spirit. We can strive to be stewards of the time He's given us. We can strive to live unselfishly in all of our relationships. When we fail, or when we fall short, we can trust that it's not on our own merit that we find favor with Him. His favor extends from His enduring faithfulness to us. —RVN

How do you rest in the "fear of the Lord"?
How do all of your actions proceed
from your relationship with Him?

December 31

∘ ∘ ◦ ∘ ∘

FROM BEGINNING TO END

Lamentations 4:1–5:22; Romans 16:1–27; Proverbs 31:20–31

Endings are always difficult. But when they're new beginnings, they're revitalizing.

At the end of Paul's letter to the Romans, we not only see Paul the apostle, but Paul the empathetic and concerned pastor. Paul knows that if dissension or temptation rules over the Roman church, they will fail in their ministry, so he warns them (Rom 16:17–19) and offers them a word of hope: "And in a short time the God of peace will crush Satan under your feet. The grace of our Lord Jesus Christ be with you" (Rom 16:20). Here, Paul is echoing God's words to Adam, Eve, and the serpent after the fall, when, instead of carrying out God's request to bring order to creation (as He had done in the beginning), humanity turned from Him, defacing His image (Gen 1:1–2, 27–28; 3:14–20). But while Genesis 3:15 merely depicts Satan biting the heel of humanity and being struck on the head in return (Gen 3:15), Paul depicts Satan as being *crushed* under the heel of the Church. Through Christ, people will be victorious over Satan. Christ did use, is using, and will continue to use people to restore order to the world.

Paul sees the end as a time when Satan will no longer have control and Christians will be victorious through Christ. Satan is fighting a losing battle. His ravaging of humanity is temporary; likewise, in the Old Testament, the prophet Jeremiah saw the other nations' ravaging of God's people as temporary. Jeremiah remarks: "You, O Yahweh, will sit forever on your throne for generation to generation. … Restore us to you, O Yahweh, that we will be restored; renew our days as of old" (Lam 5:19, 21). Yet Jeremiah must qualify his statement—he adds, "Unless you [Yahweh] have utterly rejected us, unless you are angry with us beyond measure" (Lam 5:22).

Today, there is no qualification. Christ loves us beyond all measure. Satan has lost this battle. The ravaging of God's people will come to an end when Jesus ultimately returns (Rev 22). The end is full of hope. The end is a new beginning. —JDB

How can hope restore and revitalize your life?

About the Authors

John D. Barry is the publisher of Lexham Press, general editor of Faithlife Study Bible and *Lexham Bible Dictionary*, and the previous editor-in-chief of *Bible Study Magazine*. He is the author of *The Resurrected Servant in Isaiah* and over 100 articles, as well as the coauthor of *Mary: Devoted to God's Plan*. John is also the author of Not Your Average Bible Study volumes on Malachi, Colossians, Hebrews, James, and 1 Peter, and the coauthor of a study on 2 Peter–Jude.

Rebecca Van Noord is editor-in-chief of *Bible Study Magazine*. She has developed content for several Bible reference products, including *Lexham Bible Dictionary* and Faithlife Study Bible.

Make Your Bible Study Even Better

Get 30% off Bible Study Magazine.

Subscribe today!

BibleStudyMagazine.com/Subscribe

1-800-875-6467 or +1-360-527-1700 (Int'l)